ORGANIZED CRIME, PRISON AND POST-SOVIET SOCIETIES

To my parents

Organized Crime, Prison and Post-Soviet Societies

ANTON N. OLEINIK
Moscow State University

with a Foreword by Alain Touraine

Translated from the French by
Sheryl Curtis

ASHGATE

© Anton Oleinik, Alain Touraine and Sheryl Curtis 2003

All rights reserved. No part of this publication may be reproduced, stored in a retrieval system or transmitted in any form or by any means, electronic, mechanical, photocopying, recording or otherwise without the prior permission of the publisher.

Anton Oleinik and Sheryl Curtis have asserted their right under the Copyright, Designs and Patents Act, 1988, to be identified as the author and translator of this work.

Published by
Ashgate Publishing Limited
Gower House
Croft Road
Aldershot
Hants GU11 3HR
England

Ashgate Publishing Company
Suite 420
101 Cherry Street
Burlington, VT 05401-4405
USA

Ashgate website: http://www.ashgate.com

Previous editions of this book appear in Italian, published by L'Harmattan Italia, Torino (2001) ISBN 88-87605-58-0; in French, published by L'Harmattan, Paris (2001) ISBN 2-7475-0949-4 and in Russian, published by Infra-M, Moscow (2001) ISBN 5-16-000765-2

British Library Cataloguing in Publication Data
Oleinik, Anton N.
　Organized Crime, prison and post-Soviet societies
　1. Prisons - Former Soviet republics - Sociological aspects
　2. Prisoners - Former Soviet republics - Social conditions
　3. Mafia - Former Soviet republics 4. Former Soviet republics
　- Social conditions
　I. Title
　365.9'47'09049

Library of Congress Cataloging-in-Publication Data
Oleinik, Anton N.
　Organized crime, prison, and post-Soviet societies / Anton N. Oleinik.
　　p.　cm.
　Includes bibliographical references and index.
　ISBN 0-7546-3251-2
　　1. Organized crime–Russia (Federation) 2. Russia (Federation)–Social conditions–1991- 3. Criminal justice, Administration of–Russia (Federation) I. Title.

HV6453.R8O44 2003
364.1'06'0947–dc21
　　　　　　　　　　　　　　　　　　　　　　　　　　　　　　2003050267

ISBN 0 7546 3251 2

Printed and bound in Great Britain by MPG Books Ltd, Bodmin, Cornwall

Contents

List of Figures	*vii*
List of Tables	*ix*
Foreword by Alain Touraine	*xiii*
Acknowledgments	*xvii*
Introduction	1
1 Understanding the 'Small' Society	7
2 Penal Society in Russia	45
3 Generalization Test: A Torn Society	151
4 Institutional Change: Two Cases Compared	197
Conclusion: About the Concept of the Mafia in the Post-Soviet Context	257
Postscript	267
Appendix	*271*
Bibliography	*289*
Index	*303*

List of Figures

0.1	Absent civil society	5
1.1	Research hypothesis	11
1.2	Types of authority	25
1.3	Imposed and total authority	27
1.4	Dynamics of the forms of the subject	33
2.1	Typology of prisons	47
2.2	Plan of a barrack	52
2.3	A typical dormitory	52
2.4	Plan of a typical facility	54
2.5	Ego development	55
2.6	Categories of the prisoners' society	65
2.7	Hierarchy of the illicit guards	74
2.8	Level of trust as a function of parameters of the transaction	113
3.1	*Coscà*'s structure	154
3.2	Vertical versus horizontal coordination	163
3.3	Family's universe	168
3.4	Plan of a typical room in a students' residence	178
3.5	Plan of a communal apartment	179
3.6	Plan of a standard apartment of the 1960s–1980s	180
4.1	Sequence of institutional changes	199
4.2	Sectors of the informal market	200
4.3	Monetary form of value	208
4.4	Process for appropriating new rules	213
4.5	Elements of rational decision-making	219
4.6	Sequence for institutional change	237
4.7	Mercantilist versus traditional behavior	248
5.1	An hourglass society	257
5.2	'Privatization' of the civil society	260
5.3	Market mediation between the State and the 'small' society	263

List of Tables

1.1	Comparative characteristics of habitus and set	31
1.2	A taxonomy of subjects	33
1.3	Rating of different socioeconomic systems	39
2.1	Number of prisoners in Russia	50
2.2	World prison population list	51
2.3	Usual psychological situation	57
2.4	Sources of social support	58
2.5	A system of encoding the information	61
2.6	Level of repeat offenders	61
2.7	Meanings of solidarity	62
2.8	The scope of the sense of responsibility	62
2.9	Rating of leaders in prison milieu	76
2.10	Sources of help and protection	77
2.11	Coincidence of private and collective interests	79
2.12	Informal norms (*ponjatia*)	80
2.13	Socially close persons	81
2.14	Attitudes toward homosexuality	84
2.15	Crime rate recorded in prison	86
2.16	Subordinates' game	91
2.17	Subordinates' game revisited	91
2.18	Level of institutional trust in prison	94
2.19	Parameters of institutional trust	95
2.20	Violation of norms: relative strength of sanctions	99
2.21	Level of personification in relationships	102
2.22	Reactions to uncivil behavior	103
2.23	Prisoner's dilemma	107
2.24	Level of interpersonal trust	108
2.25	Foundations of an ideal society	108
2.26	Trust game	113
2.27	Level of interpersonal and institutional trust in some Russian penitentiaries	114
2.28	A taxonomy of social climates	115
2.29	Collective protests	118
2.30	Willingness to protest	118
2.31	Scope of collective actions	119
2.32	Daily rations in Stalinist camps during 1930s	121
2.33	Families in prison	127
2.34	Structure of inmates' families	128

2.35	Frequency of changing families	129
2.36	Dynamics of violence	131
2.37	Methods of conflict resolution	131
2.38	Third parties in conflicts	132
2.39	Confidence in prisoners' leaders	133
2.40	Comparative characteristics of the illicit guard and a friend	136
2.41	Confidence in an assize court	137
2.42	Preferences about serving current sentence	139
2.43	A taxonomy of prison social climates: theoretical model	140
2.44	Recourse to violence by prison guards: at least one case during last 6 months	140
2.45	Levels of trust	142
2.46	A revised taxonomy of prison social climates	143
2.47	Types of social control in prison	146
2.48	Trustworthiness of staff as a function of inmates' expectations and judgments about the real actions of prison guards	148
2.49	Values and norms structuring inmates' everyday life	149
3.1	Russia's population	151
3.2	Associations with the word 'Law'	157
3.3	Opinion about the 'Law' in this country	158
3.4	Opinion about necessity to pay taxes	158
3.5	Opinion about a moral right to evade taxes	159
3.6	Conditions for considering taxes as a duty	159
3.7	Trust in the State	160
3.8	Hierarchy of the most important rights	161
3.9	State's ability to protect human rights	161
3.10	Priorities in government's expenditures	162
3.11	Impersonal trust	164
3.12	Normative basis of everyday life	165
3.13	Priorities in relationships with other people	166
3.14	Factors influencing relationships with other people	166
3.15	Constitution of family (1)	167
3.16	Constitution of family (2)	167
3.17	Decision-making in the family	169
3.18	Managing the family's budget	169
3.19	Sharing the domestic duties	169
3.20	Opinion about networks outside the family	169
3.21	Normative basis of the family	170
3.22	Households' portfolios	173
3.23	Justifying *blat*	173
3.24	Different degrees of social closeness	174
3.25	The least protected human rights	176
3.26	Size of the household compared with size of the flat	177

3.27	Spread of *mat*	182
3.28	Concept of order	183
3.29	Choosing between liberty and order	183
3.30	Relative significance of fears	185
3.31	Opinion about Chechens	186
3.32	Opinion about capital punishment	187
3.33	Trust in different social institutions	190
3.34	Evaluation of socioeconomic changes	192
3.35	Relevant features for men and women compared	193
3.36	Distribution of household chores	194
3.37	Trust in men and women compared	194
3.38	Characteristics of the female characters in a novel	195
4.1	Expectations about the material situation	197
4.2	Basic macroeconomic indicators	198
4.3	Share of household production	201
4.4	Attitude toward direct involvement of thieves-in-law in business	206
4.5	Scope of the informal market	206
4.6	Taxonomy of contracts	207
4.7	Popular support of different political regimes	212
4.8	Russian businessmen's normative basis of everyday life	217
4.9	Expectations about the results of the reforms	218
4.10	Conditions of success in Soviet and Russian societies compared	218
4.11	Hierarchy of values, conditions and resources	220
4.12	Trust game revisited	222
4.13	Modes of payment	222
4.14	Market principles perceived by inmates	223
4.15	Comparative characteristics of the legal, informal and criminal economies	228
4.16	Treatment of inmates under Soviet and post-Soviet rule	232
4.17	Assessments of personal situation in prison	233
4.18	Prisoners' expectations about improvements in the future	233
4.19	Russians' expectations about improvements in the future	233
4.20	Perception of the prison guards' attitudes towards inmates	234
4.21	Hierarchy of the most important prisoners' rights	235
4.22	Respect of the inmates' rights	236
4.23	Preferable time for serving the current sentence	239
4.24	Conditions for survival in the prison	245
4.25	Priorities after the release from prison	246
4.26	Means to attain the objectives	246
4.27	A model of market invasion in the penal city	248
4.28	Market constitutions compared	252
4.29	Usual feelings of the post-Soviet man	252

5.1	Two cycles in the history of Russia	259
5.2	Associations with the word 'Mafia'	260
5.3	Level of corruption	261
5.4	Attitudes towards V. Putin	263

Foreword by Alain Touraine

You are going to read this book. Note the author's name well: Anton Oleinik. You will be hearing more about him, first of all, because he brilliantly demonstrates that he is a true researcher. For example, he is the first to have studied prisons in Russia–as well as in France. Then, above all, because he developed an original and coherent analysis that adheres closely to the facts and the documents obtained from Russia, France and elsewhere, which he then used to construct his interpretation. Before we even crack open his book, let us clear up one possible misunderstanding. A. Oleinik makes no suggestion whatsoever that the Soviet regime functioned like a prison, forcing its citizens to bow under constraints as weighty as those borne by prisoners. Any such point of view would, in addition to being highly unoriginal, encounter very serious objections since the Soviet regime cannot be reduced to its most scandalous aspects, even if they have been terrible. In fact, this book is clearly positioned in the post-Soviet situation and the image it provides of prisons does not correspond to that of a generalized surveillance of the population. Moreover, A. Oleinik does not defend the Soviet system, much less through its prisons. Rather, he introduces a central opposition between two types of society, which he calls, with a well-calculated banality, the 'small' and the 'large' societies. This means the modern societies, with everything that makes them, and those societies that have been only partially modernized. This expression means– and herein lies the true originality of Oleinik's work–societies in which the world of daily practices, relationships and experiences remain separated from the official norms of modernization and efficiency. Between these two separate worlds, the one at the top and the other at the bottom, extends an immense void that can only be filled by a Mafia-type group. And this is the true object of Oleinik's study: the red Mafia. This study of prisons serves as a remarkable mirror of Russian society as a whole. At two levels, we find the same absence of the State as the organizer of social practices. As a result, it is the minor leaders who head groups that escape the State's control. The leaders impose a certain order and see that certain norms, which respond to personal choices, whether moral or other, are respected, rather than a strategy of influence or power. Just as a great distance separates the world of the Mafia and that of rationalization, so the public and private spaces in this world are confused. The relationships of power, in particular, are interpersonal relationships, as long as the imposition of general order is justified.

A. Oleinik notes here that power of the type exercised by the Mafia constructs a representation of social life that is dominated by the friend/enemy pair, as defined by Carl Schmitt. No negotiation or sorting of problems and conflicts. From the outset, the highest level of intervention, conflictual or otherwise, is attained. Everyday life is dramatic, punishment is brutal, and the power relationships are immediately visible. The 'small' societies are best defined by the absence of instances of mediation.

The originality and the strength of this analysis is revealed by comparing it to two others, long well known. Michel Foucault sees the prison as an extreme image, highly revealing of a society that is increasingly concerned with supervising and punishing itself. The prison is subjected to the same absolute power that eliminates any possibility of positive action throughout society. The inmates are considered solely as deviants who must be treated as excluded. Oleinik, on the contrary, defines the prison as a society that has been cut off from any relationship with the 'large' society, which cannot be completely absent from the national society. Goffman's vision, that of an institution closed in on itself, is not far from Foucault's and is open to the same criticism, since both Foucault and Goffman define prison as having an absolute control over itself, outside any relationship with an exterior world that would be, at least partially, different. Oleinik, on the contrary, sees in the prison, as in Russian society, a society that has been deprived of a portion of its modernity and is, as a result, incapable of establishing a relationship between that in it which is 'large' and that which is 'small'. As a result, he sees the prison not as a reduced reproduction of society, but rather an extreme degree of the separation of the 'small' society whose rationality is significantly reduced and which is dominated by operating criteria that could be referred to as primary, in the sense that they are independent of the rationalizing and organizing mind of the 'large' societies. An example demonstrates this: the inmates establish a hierarchy of crimes and culpability and those who commit the most serious crimes are isolated, rejected by the rest of the group. In particular, child rapists are subjected to a passive homosexuality that removes any possibility of choice and initiative from them. This type of analysis brings to mind the numerous descriptions of gangs of youths, as if the Mafia inside prisons were the same as the gangs who exert an unshared authority, punishing those members who do not respect the group's rules and, in particular, organizing gang rapes.

A. Oleinik quickly comes to realize that he can expand his analyses and use them to solve the most central problem of what is called development. This is not attained when abstract reasoning takes over from local customs but, on the contrary, when modernization incorporates traditional norms concerning actual life. His book was written before the Zapatista movement in Mexico saw the light of day, but it does facilitate the understanding of the analysis without which there is no solution for such a situation. A solution will only be possible when what was accepted by law in the State of Oaxaca is extended to the entire Indian population in Mexico. In that state, traditional customs take the place of the law. Yet, that could lead to a visible regression, in particular with respect to the status of women. The only way in which to eliminate this type of contradiction and this risk of regression is to ensure that, in the event of a conflict between old and new criteria, the authorities will have recourse to the most general human rights principles, as presented in the Universal Declaration of Human Rights in 1948. In this way, the individual can be integrated in the universal. It is this essential and difficult operation that defines development and not, as is all too frequently believed, the triumph of instrumental rationality that excludes customs as well as the defensive forms of organization that are imposed in prisons. Development is not the victory of the future over the past, but the capacity of the past to integrate the future, which so easily fails when strong, repressive pressure is exerted over a cultural heritage that is considered primitive and inferior, as was so often the case in the Mexico I have just referred to, in the struggle against the forces mobilized by the oligarchy and the Church.

Is this interpretation of the penal situation and its relationships with society entirely satisfactory? The only way in which we can answer this question is to put ourselves inside Oleinik's mind. Since, when it comes down to it, the idea of comparing the life of a society to that of a prison is not evident, particularly when the investigation in the prisons precedes the analysis of the post-Soviet Russian society. This means, I believe, that if an institutional order is not present at the bottom end of the society, it will not be found at its summit and, above all, that order will not descend from top to bottom. This view corresponds only to the countries that have been at the heart of Western modernity. It does not correspond to the French or American political tradition. It is much better suited for the political tradition in Great Britain and above all to that of Holland, a small province that has so often been ahead of all the other countries on the road to modernity. In such a country, education, morals and a spirit of freedom rise up against despotism. The respect for work is added to these fundamental principals. The search for profit has not played as generalized a role. It has defined capitalism, which is just one particular path towards modernity, which can be attained through other means.

This brings to light the extreme, and almost paradoxical character of Anton Oleinik's thesis: in order for development to occur, we would have to find the same control of the principals of public life over the passions and chaos of private life everywhere, even in prisons. Therefore, public life would have to be subordinate, within itself, to private virtues so that social sub-groups subordinated to force, fear and the arbitrary would no longer exist. It is for this reason that, in the countries where capitalist modernity developed most quickly, such a central position was maintained for the theme of trust. That is the most ambitious perception of freedom and modernity that it is possible to have. We even feel that A. Oleinik is prepared to say that it is the regime that wanted to be the most modern and the most 'socialized', that left the greatest space outside itself and even within itself for the forces of death. For a French citizen, this conclusion calls for reflection since the concept that has most strongly marked France is the separation of a public life governed by reason and the sense of national interest from a private life that is willingly left in the hands of inferiors: the clergy, tradition and women. A. Oleinik's book not only provides an overview of two excellent investigations into prisons and public life in Russia, it is also an appeal to the highest possible level of democracy in a country where democracy is so weak and the public interest and the Republic are void of meaning.

The reasons for which the 'large' Russian society remains a 'small' society are the same that applied in the 19th Century when Leopardi called France and England 'large' societies and Italy a 'small' one. With respect to Russia, Oleinik defines the 'small' society as one that is dominated by the *blat* and the *mat*. The *blat* refers to all of the relations through which an individual manages to attain rare resources: relations serve as the driving force, the piston. Yet, since this access is often impossible to achieve, most people withdraw into the *mat*, namely a language that is popular, vulgar and violent, particularly with respect to strangers. When Russian society eliminates the *blat* and no longer speaks the *mat*, when private life and public life have been reunited or at least put into communication, the 'small' Russian society will become 'large'. We may well ask ourselves, along with A. Oleinik, whether the former Soviet State, oversized and over-powerful, will ever allow Russian society to become autonomous and to allow rational behaviors into all its components. This is merely fantasy and illusion today. Instead of growing increasingly 'larger' Russian society appears to be becoming 'smaller' and 'smaller'.

Acknowledgments

This work would not have been achieved without the support of many people. First of all, I owe a deep debt of gratitude to Alain Touraine who encouraged my first steps in sociology at the French University College in Moscow ten years ago. His support, whether it took an obvious form or not, has helped me a great deal, especially when writing the final text. A. Touraine was the first to read the manuscript and his criticism and suggestions gave me some very important ideas.

Considering the fact that I initially obtained a degree in economics, my evolution towards sociology could have taken another forms if I had not worked with Laurent Thévenot. He is one of the founding fathers of the theory of conventions (*théorie des conventions*), which represents the French school in institutional analysis and serves to find a compromise between modern economic theory and sociology. Analytical frameworks of the 'conventionalist' approach structured my research, especially during the initial stages. Next, I would like to thank my research director at the École des Hautes Études en Sciences Sociales, Michel Wieviorka, for his confidence in me and for the freedom he granted me in my research.

The discussions with my Russian colleagues, Alexander Hlopin and Sergei Patrushev, contributed to a deeper understanding of the problems that post-Soviet society has been facing in recent decades. Our common work not only enriched the empirical data on which the research is based, it stimulates a non-negligible intellectual progress. The leading role played by Evgenia Gvozdeva, the other member of our research group, in the organization of a series of field studies should be especially emphasized. She demonstrated her organizational capacities on numerous occasions.

The field work in post-Soviet prisons was organized courtesy of Colonels Yuri Mukanov (Ministry of the Interior of the Russian Federation), Vitalij Polozjuk (Ministry of Justice of the Russian Federation) and Piotr Posmakov (Ministry of the Interior of the Republic of Kazakhstan). The kind assistance of my colleague Jean-Philippe Touffut and his patron the President of the Saint-Gobain group, Jean-Louis Beffa, were needed to obtain authorization to conduct the research in French prisons. A post-doctoral scholarship granted by the CICC, University of Montreal, allowed me to visit several Canadian prisons. The field work in Canadian prisons was done in cooperation with Sandy Lehalle.

Thanks to a scholarship from the French government, I was able to concentrate my attention on research and studies for several years. I am especially grateful to Alexis Berelowitch, the Cultural Attaché at the French Embassy in Moscow, 1996–1999.

The first draft of the text in French was kindly checked by my colleagues Sarah Carton de Grammont and Karine Clément. The joint work and discussions with Sheryl Curtis, who translated the book into English, were a real pleasure for me.

Introduction

Terre des dieux et des héros ! Pauvre Sicile !
Que sont devenues tes brillantes chimères ![1]

The political and scientific discourse of post-Soviet reforms is dominated by questions as to the nature of the obstacles that the democratic and market institutions encounter in the Eastern European countries, particularly those that belonged to the former USSR. The 'Red Mafia' is often evoked by Western observers, as well as by the national and international media, as one such obstacle. The Mafia shortcut appears to be very useful when it comes to discerning an invisible enemy of reform, which is also dangerous and violent. Moreover, by fitting into the logic of globalization, the Mafia loses its local and regional character, becoming a threat on an international scale. The series of scandals affecting Russian accounts in the Bank of New York, upsetting the international financial community in the second half of 1999, the Pavel Borodin affair (2001), in which eight Russian civil servants were suspected of transferring bribes to Swiss bank accounts, clearly illustrate the fear that the 'Red Mafia' will become an international phenomenon.

Media coverage of the image of the Mafia involves a vicious circle: as an image is broadcast repeatedly, the very conditions for reproducing that image are created, impeding an understanding of the true nature of the phenomenon. The role played by media image in the formation of the Sicilian and American Mafia is a good example of this. The very term 'Mafia' entered into common usage through a successful play, '*I Mafiusi della Vicaria*', performed in Palermo in 1863 (Gambetta, 1993, p. 137).[2] According to Diego Gambetta, certain elements in traditional Mafia dress, such as black sunglasses, first appeared in Mafia movies and then entered into everyday life (Gambetta, 1993, p. 135). Therefore, the image of a poorly studied and threatening phenomenon occasionally becomes a major factor in its development. By using an economic term, knowledge of the Mafia that is based on media images becomes self-fulfilling: if everyone believes in the reality of that state it becomes attainable and then reality. How can the political, economic and social actors whose very existence it calls into doubt, avoid this risk of involuntarily constructing the 'Red Mafia'?

---

[1] Tocqueville A. de, 'Voyage en Sicile', in Tocqueville A. de, *Œuvres*, Paris: Gallimard, 1991, t. 1, p. 18.
[2] Likewise, the term *Cosa Nostra* became popular in the 1950s after the American media reported on the testimony given by Valacchi on the scope of organized crime of Italian origin in the United States.

For several reasons, a direct analysis of the phenomenon we have become used to referring to as the 'Red Mafia' is impossible, first of all, because the meaning of this term is far from clear in the post-Soviet context. Is it a matter of a simple linguistic graft and a convenience of expression or does the term actually contribute to an understanding of the problems involved in the transformation? The functional definition of 'Red Mafia' brings the Italian Mafia to mind:

> 'The Mafia is a clandestine criminal organization, which belongs to the system of organized crime, is involved in corruption, and operates on a parallel market' (Ovchinskij, Ovchinskij, 1993, p. 8).

After noting the functional resemblance, we must then investigate the nature of the post-Soviet Mafia in greater depth. Research into the Italian Mafia presents that group as a phenomenon that is deeply rooted in the culture specific to Southern Italy. 'The Mafia could not be exported anywhere', concludes Giovanni Schiavo after his comparative analysis of the Italian Mafia and organized crime in the United States (Schiavo, 1962, p. 86). In order to verify this thesis, we must take a close look at the sociological structure of the 'Red Mafia'. It is precisely this aspect which has been less studied to date.

We believe that, before comparing the sociological structure of the two 'Mafias', it would be reasonable to use the term 'organized crime' to describe one of the obstacles to post-Soviet reform. 'Since it is a result of social life, organized crime becomes a factor which, in turn, starts to determine it' (Organizovannaja presupnost', 1993, p. 8). There are several ways in which to approach the matter of organized crime: criminology, economics, political science, sociology and anthropology. For example, economists can base their analysis on data concerning the role played by cash assets in the monetary flow within a country or a region: as the presence of organized crime increases, so does the role played by cash assets (Wiles, 1987, p. 30). Unfortunately, this type of approach concerns solely the manifestations of the phenomenon in question; it does not provide any ideas as to the principles of its internal functioning. Sociology, as one of the driving forces behind knowledge of organized crime, concerns itself with the normative organization, norms, values and the *suis generis* behaviors of organized crime. It goes even further, the focus on the normative aspects may constitute a basis for an interdisciplinary approach. This interest in norms does not appear strange to certain criminologists or economists.

> 'The distinctive trait of organized crime is the presence of specific behavioral norms' (Kulikov, 1994, p. 101). 'The parallel economy includes parallel legislation, parallel justice, a system of values and behavioral standards' (Kolesnikov, 1994, p. 82).

As soon as we take up a sociological reading of organized crime, the problem of accurate sources arises. The official sources (court documents) that often serve to support the study of organized crime are, first of all, virtually non-existent or, in any case, quasi inaccessible to independent researchers in today's Russia.³ Second, they are insufficient for making a complete evaluation of the normative criminal space. Attempts to organize interviews with criminals and ask them direct questions about organized crime cannot be considered trustworthy either since there is no guarantee that the interviewee is not involved in some manipulative game.⁴ As a result, an indirect analysis is required. We chose to study the prison situation as a track that would lead us to an understanding of organized crime and, through it, to an understanding of the problems inherent in post-Soviet transformations. The analytical position we adopted in this case differs from the critical sociology research program, which also views the prison as a major object of investigation. Michel Foucault, spokesman for critical sociology, was called on to treat the prison as a means of fighting against anomaly and deviation from the norm, starting from the norm to arrive at the prison.⁵ Yet, it is the opposite that is of interest to us: starting from prison and organized crime to arrive at the norm.

There is even some positive justification for our method, which could be presented as a second-best solution in situations where direct analysis is impossible. We often find indicators of the links that exist between the prison setting and organized crime. In particular, one of the hypotheses concerning the origin of the *camorra*, the Neapolitan equivalent of the Mafia implies that it 'it was created to serve the interests of the prisoners and defend them' (Cesoni, 1995, p. 41). In a similar manner, certain Russian criminologists regard the Soviet prison subculture of the 1930s as one of the sources of organized crime in modern-day Russia (Dolgova, Djakov, 1989, p. 109). But, it should be noted that these hypotheses have never been carefully verified.

This description of our research plan can be summed up as follows. The study of social relations in the prison guides our investigations into organized crime and

---

[3] Which is remarkably different from the situation in Italy. We will mention only two works based primarily on court documents: Arlacchi P., *Buscetta. La Mafia par l'un des siens*, Paris: Ed. du Félin, 1996; Cesoni M.-L., *Développement du Mezzogiorno et criminalités. La consolidation économique des réseaux camoristes*, Doctoral thesis in sociology: Ecole des Hautes Etudes en Sciences Sociales, 1995. A recently published book represents a first step in this direction in Russia: Skoblikov P., *Imuschestvennye spory i kriminal v sovremennoj Rossii*, Moskva: Delo, 2001 (it should be mentioned that the author works for the Ministry of the Interior and he has privileged access to court documents).

[4] Direct questions are effective in very limited conditions: in the case of a minor infraction, when the responses can be compared to police records, etc. (see Hirschi T., *Causes of delinquency*, Berkeley: University of California Press, 1969, pp. 59–64).

[5] Foucault M., *Discipline and Punish: The Birth of the Prison*, trans. by Alan Sheridan, Vintage Books, 1995, 2nd ed., p. 233: 'How could the prison not be immediately accepted when, by locking up, retraining and rendering docile, it merely reproduces, with a little more emphasis, all the mechanisms that are to be found in the social body'. Loïc Wacquant, continuing with this line of research, focussed on the links between the management of inter-racial problems in the United States and the prison policy of that country. His conclusion was very close to the principal idea of our work: 'Not a society with prisons..., but the first in the history society-prison' (Wacquant L., 'Deadly symbiosis. When ghetto and prison meet and mesh', *Punishment and Society*, 2001, vol. 3, n°4, p. 121).

the Soviet-type society as a whole. We plan to view these three constructions as equivalents from the point of view of their social structure. Instead of talking about the prison as a product of society, we would prefer to talk in terms of a reflection, a mirror. In everyday life, this equivalence is relatively obvious. For example, if we compare the criminal slang of the 1930s–1950s with daily language, we will see that one-third of the slang terms are used in contemporary linguistic constructions and, as a result, determine the perception of daily problems.[6] In turn, social psychologists refer to the presence of elements of a social type characteristic of prisoners in the daily behavior of Russians (Kim, 1999). In this context, there is nothing surprising about the title of a novel on Russian current economic events written by one of that country's business pioneers, '*Bol'shaja pajka*' (a large portion of daily bread distributed to inmates in Stalinist concentration camps).[7] Several rules of behavior governing the Russian market are the same as those that exist in the prison setting. Business slang (called rather pejoratively the slang of the 'new Russians') appears to be influenced to an ever greater extent by criminal slang than popular language. The criminal layers have given rise to several economic and political actors.

How can this similarity between the social organization of the post-Soviet world and the prison world be explained? One possible explanation could be found in taking into account the number of people with prison experience. These individuals may be viewed as carriers for prison values and norms. Nearly one-third of Soviets have been sentenced by court or have relatives who have been sentenced. Although the proportion of Soviets who have been sentenced to prison is significant (1/5 of the total population), those who have actually served time in prisons are much less numerous: 2 per cent (Levada, 1993, p. 67). Although some of these carriers of prison norms have access to key positions in the Russian economy and society, their relative number does not lend credibility to the scenario of an aggressive minority subjugating a poorly organized majority.

We are searching for an explanation for the omnipresence of the prison model in the institutional environment of Soviet and post-Soviet societies. First of all, it is a matter of the specificity of relations of authority, both in the prisons and in society as a whole. Although the role of the State is not as restrictive as that of prison guards, both types of authority exemplify the same relationship model with the social. In order to justify this point, it is hardly necessary to refer to the model of the totalitarian State. The totalitarian State of the Stalinist era provides a concrete image of the model produced by the social organization that we found in the prison. The *absentee* State, the State separated from society and responsible for its own problems which have nothing in common with the everyday lives of its citizens, encourages, by virtue of its very existence, the *reproduction* of the so-called prison social model. The State, deprived of its links with social life, deprived

---

[6] The author based his evaluation on 1,000 slang terms described in Rossi J., *Spavochnik po GULAGu*, Moskva: Prosvet, 1991. 33.6 per cent of the terms are included in both criminal and daily slang.

[7] Dubov Yu., *Bol'shaja pajka*, Moskva: Vagrius, 1999. For reference purposes: the daily bread ration varied between 300 and 850 grams, depending on the category of inmate.

of mechanisms for mediation and social representation, cannot allow the ordinary people to stray outside the reproduction of the prison model. In today's Russia, the place for institutions that mediate between the everyday lives of ordinary Russians and the State remains vacant (Figure 0.1).

Figure 0.1 Absent civil society

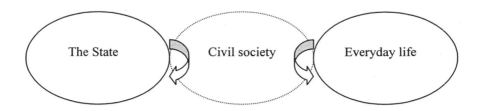

As a result, the resolute struggle against organized crime is not sufficient to ensure the success of the democratic and market transformations. Without the profound reform of the State itself, without the formation of civil society, this struggle may well turn into a war between one or two Mafias. It should be noted that this is exactly what happened in Sicily in the 1930s under the reign of the Prefect Cesare Mori. 'In order to fight against the Mafia, the state transformed itself into another Mafia' (Padovani, 1987, p. 148). Based on our analysis and the current situation in Russia, we cannot exclude this perspective.

Chapter 1

Understanding the 'Small' Society

Research problem: norms as 'frameworks' for action

Studying the penal world through the notion of norm appears natural in terms of sociological research. But sociologists and economists have long debated the nature of social action: is it rational or normative? In this way, the contradiction between the action that is guided by norms and the rational action could be described as follows:

> 'Rational action is concerned with outcomes... Action guided by social norms is not outcome-oriented... Even complex norms are simple to obey and follow, unlike the canons of rationality which often require us to make complex and uncertain calculations' (Elster, 1988, p. 357).

Consequently, let us discuss the role of the norm in social organization.

Institutional approach

Our first landmark on the road toward a better understanding of the norm is marked by the institutional approach, which currently lies at the border between economics, sociology, history and law. Although it is not yet a new theory based on its own methodology, the institutional approach is of interest to us when it comes to researching a composite vision of norm.[1] The strength and the weakness of this approach lie in its interdisciplinary character: it is the notion of institution that unites such very different disciplines.

> 'The institution [is] the set of norms and behaviors generally followed and spontaneously respected by the members of a group that acquire in this manner a character of stability independently of any explicitly stated legal obligation' (Lochak, 1993, p. 305).[2]

---

[1] We proposed an order for the various elements in the approach in Oleinik A., '*Institucional'naja ekonomika*', Moskva: Infra M, 2000 (second printing: 2002).
[2] The term institution (*instituto* = arrangement) was introduced in theoretical discourse in the 13th century by Sinibaldo de Fieschi, Pope Innocent IV.

Viewed in this manner, the institution distances itself from the behavioral model imposed on individuals to become, rather, a device for coordination. Although institutions are not imposed by a discretionary power, individuals respect them.

The focus on voluntary submission serves to develop an image of a compromise between the various social sciences: individuals respect the prescriptions of the institutions since this enables them to fulfill their own interests better. In situations of interdependence, the ability to complete an individual project involves taking the project of others into consideration and, as a result, considering actions.

> 'Even though other people's goals may not be incorporated in one's own goals, the recognition of interdependence may suggest following certain rules of behavior, which are not necessarily of intrinsic value, but which are of great instrumental importance in the enhancement of the respective goals of the members of that group' (Sen, 1987, p. 85).

In other words, the primary task of institutions involves facilitating the coordination of free agents whose actions are not subjected to an absolute determinant. Moreover, individuals have an interest in producing institutions in situations in which they are not provided *a priori*. Several experiments have demonstrated that individuals who are isolated from the influence of the usual institutions very quickly start building their own institutional space.

> 'This basic human need, which I choose to call law is related to what in other contexts is referred to as the product of socialization... People have a natural inclination to build laws governing their relationships' (Weyrauch, 1971, p. 58).

Penal subculture

The understanding of the dual nature of norm will guide our study of a particular institutional space–the norms that structure common life in detention. Two types of norms organize life in detention. The first includes the official norms and regulations, imposed by the Law and implemented by the penal administration and the corps of guards. These norms provide a perfect reflection of the understanding of norms developed by classical sociology. Although we will devote a portion of our study to these norms, we will not focus on them. The second type includes the norms that are spontaneously developed and applied by the inmates so as to make their life in detention more bearable, socially. Just as each closed group makes its own laws for social life, the prisoners draft their own 'constitution'. 'The law of a tribe or extended family... is really a program for living together supported by the basic logic of the system as a whole' (Weyrauch, 1971, p. 51). The 'law' of the inmates is distinct in that it cannot be based on the logic of the system as a whole.

> 'Prison subculture comprises norms, customs, rituals, language and mannerisms which depart from those required by penal law and prison rules' (Platek, 1990, p. 459).

The following analysis will focus primarily on the second type of norms essentially since these norms are constructed as devices for mutual coordination and interpretation, which classic sociology does not take into consideration. 'Here, people are entitled to do everything they want, within certain limits. No one imposes their will, no one violates the right to private space, no one forces another to do something that other person does not want to do. What is important is not stepping outside the borders, respecting the rules... rules which have been developed over dozens of years.'[3] From this perspective, the penal subculture may be viewed as the expression of the individuality of the inmates, the desire to create their own society, even under very harsh external constraints. As a result, the study of the penal subculture is part of the search for a response to a global challenge which sociology has been facing since its creation. The job of sociology is to 'give the right to speak to those who do not have it' (Touraine, 1993, p. 38).

After providing a functional definition of the subculture, we will proceed to sketch out its structure. The production of the subculture as a set of institutional frameworks for the everyday life of a small group is determined socially. The make-up of the group, its organization and its position with respect to the 'large' society characterize the subculture. 'Instead of using beliefs to explain the cohesion of the society, we have used the society to explain the beliefs' (Douglas, 1986, p. 40). In pursuing this line of research, we will attempt to trace the explanatory links between the special characteristics of the social organization of the penal world and the parameters of the penal subculture. For example, the social organization of the world of the guards does not allow them to develop a specific guard culture. As certain studies show, the guards develop cognitive markers individually and these markers vary from one guard to another (Chauvenet et al., 1994, pp. 192–193).[4]

When speaking of the penal subculture and its basic parameters, we will use a grid developed by Anthony Giddens. In particular, he makes a distinction between consciousness that is theoretical and practical (everything that individuals know tacitly, without knowing how to speak about it directly), extensive and intensive (frequently invoked during the course of everyday life), tacit and verbalized, formal and informal, weakly and strongly sanctioned (Giddens, 1984, p. 22). In this way, the penal subculture could be described as primarily practical, intensive, tacit and verbalized, informal and strongly sanctioned. As for its practical character, we encountered several problems when we asked our interviewees to theorize a little about their experience of life in detention. Although the rules of the penal subculture are carefully and clearly formulated, they still belong to the oral culture. The idea of drawing up a written 'code' of penal life has never been implemented,[5] despite the existence of a sophisticated, virtually democratic procedure (voting for 'representatives' by an assembly) for implementing a new norm. These characteristics must be taken into account by means of the

---

[3] Interview No. 7.

[4] On the other hand, James Marquart proposed several common practices for most guards known as 'career' guards: Marquart J., 'Prison Guards and the Use of Physical Coercion as a Mechanism of Prisoner Control', *Criminology*, 1986, Vol. 24, n°2.

[5] Police data confirms this observation (Skoblikov, 2001, pp. 118–119).

methodology chosen to research the penal subculture. We will detail this in greater depth later.

The search for a new societal model

The usual view of the penal world grants it a place 'outside' society. The alternative perspective proposed by Michel Foucault, in which the prison is merely a link in the chain of norm-setting authority, does not stand up to the criticism that stresses the complex character of the norm. We observe *voluntary submission* to the norm even in prison–the penal subculture is the invention of people who are *deliberately subjected* to a norm-setting authority that is virtually absolute. Simply mentioning the norm is not sufficient to account for the phenomenon of discipline in the prison and in the society that surrounds it. We need to question its social content, its sources and its social structure. If it is no longer the norm that makes the link between the 'small' penal society and the 'large' society, must we go back to the opposition between 'here' and 'there', which is so well-known as a result of anthropological research?[6]

Without claiming to be able to find a solution that can apply generally to other societies, we propose to make the following hypothesis in the post-Soviet context: *the study of the 'small' penal society gives us an understanding of the way in which post-Soviet society is organized since it can be broken down into several 'small' societies (not necessarily penal in nature) and does not exist in a normative, unified and homogenous space, namely a 'large' society.* In other words, post-Soviet society *in general* functions in a manner that is comparable to that specific to the 'small' penal society. The expression 'small' society, which we will refer to on several occasions during the course of our research, has several connotations that could hinder an accurate understanding of the opposition between the 'small' and 'large' societies. In fact, we use 'small' society to refer to a social organization that is not institutionalized, with no mediation between the State and the everyday lives of ordinary people, without any political representation of the interests of ordinary people. In short, it refers to an undemocratic society in which modernization has not been completed, which leads to the application of the modern analogue of the Latin term *pittittus* (young, not as old as the others).[7] In this way, when we speak of the 'small' society, we focus on the incomplete

---

[6] 'One of the principal foundations on which anthropological writings were based even recently, namely that their objects and their public were not only inseparable but morally distinct, that the objects had to be described without addressing them, and the public had to be informed without being involved, practically disintegrated' (Geertz, 1996, p.132).

[7] It should be noted that certain criminologists see the sources of delinquent subcultures in the specific characteristics of the social organization of the juvenile world, in the difficulties inherent in the transformation from adolescent into adult, from a boy to a man, etc. (Matza, 1990).

modernization, and the local, non-institutional and informal character of the social organization.[8]

Research hypotheses

When opting to research daily institutional frameworks,[9] we developed a series of hypotheses. While making no claim to produce a 'large schema', we can sketch them out as follows (Figure 1.1):

Figure 1.1 Research hypothesis

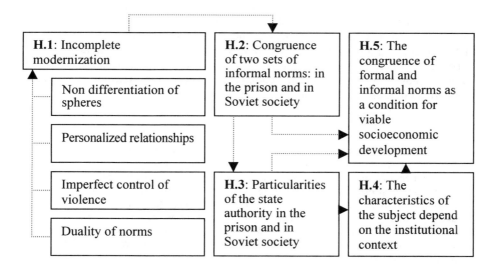

Incomplete modernization: the ideal type of 'small' society

Constructing an ideal type[10] of society that is characterized by the lack of differentiation of spheres, the personalization of relations, the imperfect mastery of

---

[8] Academic and university people are accustomed to call their world 'small' (cf. Lodge, 1985). This is not only a 'game of words': in fact, academic milieu has important elements of the 'small' society. Unfortunately, such an affinity does not usually attract the serious attention of researchers (Oleinik, 2002b; see also http://www.iforum.umontreal.ca/Forum/ArchivesForum/2001-2002/011001/514.htm).

[9] Harold Garfinkel expressed, albeit it in an exaggerated manner, the interest of studying the institutional frameworks of everyday life: 'In doing sociology every reference to the "real world" is a reference to the organized activities of everyday life' (Garfinkel, 1967, p. vii).

violence and the duality of norms, serves to qualify *the situation in which Russian society is found as a result of incomplete modernization* (**H.1**). In other words, the transformation of the 'small' society, which is both localized and personalized, into a 'large' society, has not been completed. This observation bears no value judgement; it merely reflects a particular structural and functional organization of society. As a result, we need to avoid using adjectives such as *primitive* or *less civilized* to describe it. As Alain Touraine correctly remarked with respect to Latin American societies, 'By what right can we consider the mixing of private and public life as more "primitive" than their separation?' (Touraine, 1988, p. 159). The other common differentiation, namely that between a non-industrialized society, an industrialized society and a post-industrialized society, does not seem pertinent to us within the context of our study since it focuses on the technical organization of the society. For example, it is possible to imagine an industrialized society that is not modern at the same time. In this way, we can define Poland's Solidarity, the first social movement in the Soviet-type societies, as 'the fight for modernization and economic growth in a society in the process of industrializing' (Touraine, 1992, p. 273). We prefer, as a result, to avoid shortcuts that have a value, judgment or technical connotation. For this reason, incomplete modernization seems justifiable.

---

[10] The ideal type (*Idealtypus*) serves the sociology of Max Weber as a means of knowing to describe the social reality. 'It is not in itself a hypothesis, but it does strive to guide the development of hypotheses. It is not an exposé of what is real, but attempts to give such an exposé univocal means of expression' (Weber, 1965, p. 180). This does not include any judgement as to the desirable or rather the undesirable character of a society that would be likely to be described using the same cognitive markers as the penal society. As Weber stressed, it is necessary to know how to differentiate the ideal types in a purely logical sense and the model or the 'ought to be' (Weber, 1965, p. 183). We will let the reader provide the normative evaluation.

Roughly, there are two ways in which to construct the ideal and ensure that it can be verified empirically. First, we start with the frequency of use of a given norm, measured statistically. Following that, we attempt to determine whether a statistically significant norm is viewed as the standard mode of behavior by the actors. Therefore, it is a matter of constructing the ideal type from the dominant social type. 'Values, points of view, for example, shared with the population can be dominant if they determine a value, a standard mode of social conduct, if they serve as a "universal" benchmark, a model that restricts "all"' (Levada, 1993, p. 26). Second, we address the types that individuals themselves construct during the course of their daily activities to organize their interactions. In this respect, the researcher uses, for his own purposes, the ideal types that already exist in everyday life. 'The objects of thought constructed by researchers in the social sciences are based on the objects of thought constructed by the everyday thinking of the man who lives his everyday life among his peers and refers to them... As the models of behavior become increasingly standardized and institutionalized, namely as their typicality is approved by laws, folklore, customs and habits, they become more of use for scientific thought than for daily thinking as a means for interpreting human behavior' (Schutz, 1987, p. 11, p. 82). We use these two sources in the construction of the ideal type of the 'small' society, basing our research on the results of investigations as well as on the results of interviews.

Non differentiation of spheres The structural definition of modernization implies the transformation of the simple society, without means for separating the various spheres of daily activity, into a complex society, including several normative sub-systems. Each sub-system has a degree of autonomy that is not negligible with respect to the others, and interference is reduced to nothing within the framework of the ideal type of modernization.

> 'The functional differentiation of sub-systems, particularly the separation of politics and religion or economics and politics, the formation of a universe devoted to science, art, private life, are all conditions of modernization' (Touraine, 1992, p. 237).

The economy of conventions speaks of the following spheres of activity (the cities): merchant, industrial, civic, domestic, opinion, inspiration. The ecological city and the city by projects were added to this list more recently (Boltanski, Thévenot, 1991; Thévenot, Lafaye, 1993; Boltanski, Chiapello, 1999). Let us take a closer look at the lines separating the daily fields of activity.

The first separating line sets out the border between the market and the other spheres. In order for a market to function properly it must be free of political, social and community influence. 'A self-regulating market requires nothing less than the institutional division of society into an economic sphere and a political sphere' (Polanyi, 1983, p. 105). If, as Karl Polanyi states, the installation of an 'iron curtain' between the market and the rest of society lay at the core of the Great Transformation experienced by the Western countries in the 19th century, the Soviet-type system required the almost total penetrability of the border between the economy and society in order to function. The symbiosis between the party and the State, a key point in the Soviet system, came about through the mixing of political, administrative, economic functions (Kornaï, 1992, p. 39). Furthermore, this accounts for the dominant form that economic science took during the Soviet period–political economy, which was as far from economics in the modern sense as from political science.

The other important distinction concerns private life and public life. Possessing a protected private space constitutes the starting point for subjective activity. This enables the individual to step outside the limits of a role and protect his individuality against the requirements imposed. The private space guarantees the individual 'the liberty to retain his individuality within any social structure' (Hlopin, 1994, p. 54). In this way, the individual remains himself in his private life and plays no role other than the freely chosen role. It is important to note that the private space must protect the individual not only against the roles imposed by the 'large' society but also against the occasionally indiscreet intervention of those close to him. When studying popular culture in England in the 1950s, Richard Hoggart noted that 'the family group does not preserve the intimacy of its members with respect to one another. Being alone, thinking alone, reading in peace and quiet is virtually impossible' (Hoggart, 1970, p. 69). As a result, the successful separation of private life and public life includes means for protecting the undesired intervention of those who are close, of those who are within 'arm's reach'. In other words, we can speak of 'the right of the individual to protect himself not only against the State but even against the primary groups to which he belongs' (Shlapentokh, 1989, p. 10).

The social construction of many societies excludes the separation of private and public life. The Latin American societies provide an example. These two spheres were never separated in the Soviet societies either. Totalitarian institutions, including prison, also serve to illustrate this lack of differentiation in the extreme since private life there is annihilated.

Personalized relationships One of the aspects of the inter-penetration of fields of activity lies in the fact that the choice of a partner during the course of social interaction is not free. This choice depends on the membership of the potential partner in a chain of personal relationships. All interactions take place within this chain and it is not possible to have one partner for commercial activity, another for civic activity and so on. The need to have a personal knowledge in order to organize any social activity makes each member in a local community the universal partner. As a result, the local community, regardless of its form–family, traditional community, friendships, 'friends of friends', the Mafia–closes in on itself. The family represents the ideal type of personalized relationships that are closed with respect to the outside world. In the case of lower-class English families, R. Hoggart illustrated the 'the irreplaceable value that [its members] grant to family life' and 'the fact that the domestic group closes in on intimacy' (Hoggart, 1970, p. 66). The primordial role of the family explains the use of the term *domestic* to describe personalized relationships. The analysis of the domestic city described by the 'traditionalists' illustrates the manner in which a 'large' society is built without taking leave of the 'small' society. In the domestic city, all social relations reproduce domestic relations. In this case, 'the grandeur of individuals depends on their hierarchical position in a chain of personal dependencies' (Boltanski, Thévenot, 1993, p. 116). In this way, the social organization of the domestic city includes three basic elements: the focus of the present on the past, the localization of transactions, and the chain of personal dependencies.

'The domestic order may be characterized by a triple gradient: temporal (by custom and precedent), spatial (by local proximity) and hierarchical (by authority)' (Thévenot, 1989, p. 185).

The domestic order allows for relationships of a different nature (merchant, civic, industrial, etc.) as long as they fit in with the logic of personalized relationships. Let us take a close look at the construction of merchant relationships within the domestic city. There are several examples of this anchoring in societies that are in the process of modernizing as well as in certain segments of modernized societies. An American anthropologist, Jane Ensminger, studied how the Orma, an African tribe, organized economic activity. It appeared that 'The Orma still place an exceedingly high premium on having at least one close relative of the family in the cattle camp', making it easier to control the conditions for handling herds and reducing the opportunism of shepherds (Ensminger, 1992, p. 116). Also, the development of commerce in the regions in which the trader has no family or relatives often involves the marriage of his daughter with someone residing in the region in question. Domestic rooting also serves as a trade device in certain Latin-American countries where 'the "extended family" has been transformed into a network of commercial or productive relationships' (Soto, 1994, p. 13). As in the case of the Orma, domestic anchoring helps to reduce transaction costs within a local community. In particular, the involvement of relatives in commercial activities reduces the costs incurred by the businessman to control and prevent the opportunistic behavior of his agents. Personal dependence transforms into a guarantee that the contract will be fulfilled (Soto, 1994, p. 131). This same logic accounts for the willingness of bankers, diamond brokers and stock brokers to form relatively closed societies that support them in their commercial activities. The New York Stock Exchange, the London bankers, the international network of diamond merchants can all be considered as examples of business that is built on the basis of personalized relationships (Coleman, 1990, pp. 109–110).

Despite the possible symbiosis between the domestic order and the merchant order on a local level, its internal limitations and contradictions become apparent as soon as the actors attempt to move out of the local setting and generalize their relationships. Even the possession of a very broad network of acquaintances does little to change the fact that the 'small' society does not truly transform into the 'large' society in domestic settings. The reference to the chain of personal dependencies continues to operate on a 'macro' social level. The famous principle of the Mafia, *Cosa Nostra*, 'he's one of us' is very pertinent in this context. The Mafia, a phenomenon that started out on a local and regional basis, transformed into a phenomenon that exists on both the national and international scales without losing its personalized character.

> 'To be introduced to the Mafia, you must be presented by another Mafiosi: it's the same thing–*Quisti è la stressa cosa–Cosa Nostra*' (Padovani, 1987, p. 45).[11]

Either one is *in*, inside the domestic world, or one is *out*, excluded from all social relationships.

Imperfect control of violence   The third marker on the path to modernization concerns the manner in which violence is controlled on a daily basis. There are several ways in which to manage the conflicts that arise in everyday life. Institutionalized violence, which implies a State monopoly of violence, is only one method among others. Moreover, institutionalized violence is the only means for managing conflicts that is accepted in a modernized society. In order to provide a brief overview of the entire range of means, we will refer to an anthropological study made by René Girard. He looked at the steps involved in controlling violence

---

[11] Market studies based on personified relationships demonstrate the existence of the same problem: 'The greatest of the non-financial barriers to entrance... concerns the difficulty of penetrating a network' (Lautier, 1994, p.56).

that preceded the institutionalization of violence. According to Girard, the first step involves the search for a *replacement victim*.

> 'Unappeased violence strives and always manages to find a spare victim. In place of the creature that excited its fury, it will suddenly substitute another that has no specific reason for attracting the lightning of violence, other than the fact that it is both vulnerable and within reach' (Girard, 1972, p. 15).

It should be noted that, as a general rule, the replacement victim does not belong to the local community within which the violence was born. It is individuals from outside the domestic world who are transformed into the targets of violent acts– strangers as well as the King–if their actions do not fit in with the logic of the other members of the community. As the border between the 'small' and the 'large' societies starts to erode, the nature of violence changes. If there is no longer any difference between those who are *in* and those who are *out* ('crisis of differences'), such differences must be recreated through the mythic development of a *scapegoat victim*. 'In place of widespread reciprocal violence, myth substitutes the formidable transgression of a unique individual' (Girard, 1972, p. 115). According to Girard, the Oedipus myth can be explained by the logic of creating a scapegoat victim rather than through psychoanalytical reasoning. The third step that precedes the institutionalization of violence supposes the construction of a *victim that can be sacrificed*. Unlike the scapegoat victim, whose strangeness was artificially constructed, the sacrificial victim is not found either inside or outside the community. The sacrificial victim takes the form of monstrous doubles that are potentially incarnated in each member of the 'small' society.

> 'The [monstrous] doubles provide, between difference and identity, the equivocal median that is essential for sacrificial substitution, for the polarization of violence focussed on a unique victim' (Girard, 1972, p. 224).

The community no longer needs to search for an external enemy or expel 'scapegoats' in order to channel violence, they simply need to progressively unveil the doubles hidden behind the appearances of people who are personally well-known.

Duality of norms The opposite behavior, on the one hand, with respect to the members of the community who really are *in* and with those, on the other hand, who are others, strangers who are really *out*, raises the idea of the duality of norms as criteria that encompass incomplete modernization. This duality of standards goes against the movement modernization and the major consequence of modernization is to erase the differences between individuals belonging to various communities. 'A certain dynamism draws first the West and then all of humanity towards a state of relative lack of differentiation never encountered previously' (Girard, 1972, p. 261). In the language of the theory of conventions, this is the principle of the human community. This principle implies that 'the same individuals could refer to all types of grandeur, unlike the hypothesis that attaches value systems or cultures to members of a single social group' (Boltanski, Thévenot, 1991, p. 188). In other words, the degree of the duality of norms can serve to measure the progress made by a given society towards modernization. The greater the duality, the greater the distance from modernization and vice versa. The idea of degree is important to us since it helps to avoid simplistic, black and white judgments as to the nature of the society in question. Instead of qualifying a society as modern or not modern, it would be preferable to evaluate the degree of its proximity to the ideal type of modern society.

We would like to stress the fact that the situation of dependence, the imposition of norms on a society, creates conditions that are particularly favorable to the duality of norms. The norms imposed are associated with an external enemy that provokes hostility, hate, violence whereas the native norms are associated with the community itself and promote voluntary submission, solidarity and non-violence. 'This is especially clear in the case of Goffman's "total institutions". These organizations manifest the principle of in-group solidarity and out-group hostility [as a consequence of generated ambivalence]' (Smeilser, 1998, pp. 8–9).[12] As the dependence becomes increasingly obvious, the norms are increasingly dual in nature. The Jewish ghettos created by the Nazis during WWII represent an extreme case of dual norms. As Bruno Bettelheim demonstrated, the ghetto mentality translates into a maximum ambivalence.

> 'They [the Jews in the European countries occupied by the Nazis] viewed themselves from the perspective of the ghetto; they saw themselves as a minority surrounded by an all powerful enemy' (Bettelheim, 1991, p. 300).

When speaking about the duality of norms in the penal world, there is no term that is unequivocally imposed. Let us briefly compare the advantages and disadvantages of each term. The selection will depend on their ability to portray the particularities of everyday life in detention. First, the biology of evolution deals with the problem of ambivalence starting with the hypothesis that all social beings are divided into two groups: altruists and egotists. Whenever an altruist and an egotist meet, the former is always placed in a position that is relatively disadvantaged compared to that of the latter: the standard of altruism cannot resist the egotistical aggression. However, the interactions between two altruists always give the two parties more than interactions between egotists give those two parties. In this situation, the altruists tend to form homogenous, closed groups (*clusters*) to reduce the risk of meeting egotists.

---

[12] 'A total institution–a link between residence and work, where a large number of individuals, placed in the same situation, cut off from the outside world for a relatively lengthy period of time, lead a cloistered life, for which the terms are explicitly and painstakingly regulated' (Goffman, 1968, p. 41).

'Group develops some mechanism to protect their own altruists in order for the group as a whole to compete effectively in the biological process of natural selection' (Monroe, 1994, pp. 870–871).[13]

The evolutionist logic explains the 'natural' subdivision of society into small, relatively autonomous and closed groups. But it gives each actor only a single role, transforming him into a sort of automaton. Moreover, the daily context is rarely taken into consideration.

Second, social anthropology interprets the duality of norms by means of the opposition between *Us* and *Them*. The organization of social relationships around two poles, Us and Them, is specific to traditional societies; it represents an important step in the transformation of the 'small' society into the 'large' one. For example, the opposition between Us and Them characterized the first steps in the founding of the worker movement. This opposition lies at the heart of the community conscience, a major source for the worker movements, which can be described as a 'defensive consciousness, turned in on itself rather than toward society, considered a hostile environment' (Touraine et al., 1984, p. 29). In terms of everyday life, the opposition between Us and Them takes the form of a total disregard with respect to Others, to the difference in the trust we place in Ours. 'When faced with "others", the first reaction is not fear but suspicion. We never trust them, even when they appear welcoming or well disposed' (Hoggart, 1970, p. 119). Also, in the collective consciousness constructed around the dual opposition, violence is associated with relationships with Others, whereas it has very little place in the relationships within the community.

'The matter of collective identities, the definition of a "them" and "us", appears in a central manner in the examination of the stigmatization of strangers as violent; it is associated with their expulsion from the city' (Roché, 1993, p. 142).

The uniquely traditional nature of the dual opposition between Us and Them limits the scope of its analytical application and excludes the slightest reference to the conscious and reasonable choice of the actors. This opposition applies at the very beginning of modernization and loses its validity as the society progresses towards modernization.

However, the third manner in which to deal with the duality of norms illustrates conscious and free action. This manner involves describing this duality in terms of sociology of action: the nature of the interaction of the *actors* changes as soon as one of them transforms into an *adversary*. This is illustrated by the explanatory chart developed by Alain Touraine to study collective actors: *I/O/T*, or Identity (actor) – Opposition (adversary) – Totality (stakes of the conflict). Involved in a conflict over the management of cultural resources, the actor builds his identity and his opposition to the adversary at the same time (Touraine, 1965, pp. 160–164). The set of 'identifying' norms does not coincide with the 'oppositional' norms. Moreover, the I/O/T logic requires a third set of norms,

---

[13] An application of evolutionary biology to economics was developed in Boyer R., Orléan A., 'How Do Conventions Evolve?', *Evolutionary Economics*, n°2, 1992.

respected by both the actor and the adversary (which Touraine refers to as Totality). For example, the 'total' norms take the form of the industrial culture in the case of the conflict between the worker movement and the bosses. The values of progress and economic development are common for the actor and his adversary. 'The actor as worker can only define himself in the worker movement through his opposition to the employer as actor and *through the fact that he belongs to the industrial culture*' (Touraine et al., 1984, p. 57).[14] If the collective actor does not recognize any common normative framework, he will transform into an *anti*-social movement. Violence starts to reign in the conflict following this disappearance of common normative frameworks. In other words, violence becomes the social norm as soon as the control over the duality of norms weakens.

> 'Violence makes its path through zones where the actors, who do not recognize one another, rub shoulders and bump into one another and can do without one another but whose eventual encounters are no longer structured by a fundamental conflict or regulated by norms, thereby running the risk of being reduced to interactions with unpredictable outcomes' (Wieviorka et al., 1999, p. 53).

Now, by definition, the relationships between inmates and their guards lack common frameworks, which means that the 'actor–adversary' model does not particularly apply to our analysis.

The collapse of the common framework gives rise to another model of dual relationships, one that differentiates *friends* from *enemies*. Political science gives this model a vast scope. According to a German political scientist at the start of the 20th century, Karl Schmitt, opposing relationships, on the one hand with friends and on the other with enemies, constitute the *differentia specifica* of all political relationships.

> 'The political enemy is the other, the stranger; it is enough to define his nature, in such a way that, ultimately conflicts with him are possible and cannot be resolved either by means of a set of general norms established in advance or by the decision of a third party, who is recognized as disinterested and impartial' (Schmitt, 1992, p. 65).

It is important to note the willingness of combatants to step outside the limits of everything that is acceptable, normal, human. In this case we witness 'a frightening pretension to deny the enemy status as a human being and to exclude him from the law and from humanity' (Schmitt, 1992, p. 97). The explicit reference to norms, therefore, characterizes only relationships between friends. This does not mean that the relations with enemies are void of any normative connotation. 'Rules of the game' exist in the case of enemies, but they are radically opposed to those for relations with friends. In particular, the 'rules' that apply to enemies include recourse to violence (each party to the conflict is aware of this possibility), the principle of 'might means right', the principle of 'someone who is not taken prisoner must be destroyed', etc. These principles are norms since they structure the interactions between the parties, making them applicable, although in a strange

---

[14] Our emphasis.

manner. We encounter certain elements of the 'friend–enemy' model in the penal world, particularly with respect to relationships between the inmates and the guards. But it would be impossible to describe the entire penal subculture in this manner: even the relations between the inmates and the guards imply a non-negligible degree of cooperation, negotiations, and reciprocal services.

Can we use the concept of *network* to account for this personalized reciprocity which is present in the penal setting? Social relationships that are organized in networks always include the aspect of personification and they are not necessarily differentiated by spheres of activity since the center of social life is found within them. This makes a discussion of networks pertinent, particularly in the case of the context studied. If we take various types of networks[15] into consideration–uniplex and multiplex (depending on the number of links joining the same actors, in the multiplex network the borders between fields of activity are more penetrable), active and latent, based on direct contact and based on 'friends of friends' relationships, egocentric and polycentric–a network organization covers a large specter of social activity. The concept of network has become popular recently, particularly in economic sociology, which can be explained by the obviously non-traditional character of this form of organization and its focus on one purpose, one project. The marketing success of organizational structures such as the Japanese firm, the industrial district including several small and medium business, is a result of their ability to use the economic potential of the network (Aoki, 1991, pp. 245, 260; Perrow, 1993). Does the network combining local relationships and the rational choice model allow us to understand the voluntary submission to the norms of the penal subculture? As a result of the necessarily open character of the network, we cannot respond positively: the social groups we are going to discover in prison are absolutely closed.

> 'Network–a structure that is only slightly, perhaps even not at all, hierarchical, flexible and not limited by limits in advance... The good network remains open and is continually extended for the benefit of all' (Boltanski, Chiapello, 1999, pp. 156, 181).

So, which term best illustrates the duality of personalized relations in prison? We still have to test the term *Mafia*. The Mafia fits in with the logic of the network as described above, with the exception of its openness to the outside world. We refer to a 'double definition of the camorrist phenomenon: both the camorrist *clans* and the *networks* in which they are integrated' (Cesoni, 1995, p. 366).[16] The Mafia structure, as a symbiosis of the clan, a traditional structure, and the network found in modern society, highlights the elements that constitute the ideal type of a 'small' society valid for our study: the non-differentiation of fields of activity, personalized relationships, non-institutionalized violence, the duality of norms. In practice, each operating principle of the Mafia has a double nature: traditional and

---

[15] See, for example Roché S., *Le sentiment d'insécurité*, Paris: P.U.F., 1993, pp. 174–180; Stephenson K., Hayden F., 'Comparison of the Corporate Decision Networks of Nebraska and the United States', *Journal of Economic Issues*, September 1995, Vol. XXIX, n°3, pp. 848, 855.

[16] Our emphasis.

modern at the same time. For example, relationships of friendship are given a new meaning in the Mafia organization.

> 'The friendship of the Mafioso is virtually deprived of the qualities usually associated with that term. It places a veil over what was simply a prosaic exchange' (Gambetta, 1993, p. 201).

It is not possible to either reduce the Mafia to the traditional society or associate it with modernization since it provides us with an image of *incomplete modernization* Therefore, the qualification of Mafia proposed by Pino Arlacchi appears to be the most pertinent to us: it is 'strange mixture of the traditional and the modern' (Arlacchi, 1986, p. 225).

In order to reduce the cultural connotations of the Mafia for the time being, we will attempt to expose its structure using the grammar of institutional economics. From this point of view, the Mafia organization presupposes an amalgamation between the domestic city and the city by projects. On the one hand, it is a world marked by a profound division between the interior and the exterior. 'Composed of a series of personal dependencies, the [domestic] world is ordered by the opposition of the interior and the exterior between which passages are either arranged or closed' (Boltanski, Thévenot, 1991, p. 218). On the other hand, personalized relationships are mobilized to attain a goal, a project chosen to bypass a traditional constraint. Mobilization by projects is positioned in the heart of the city by projects.

> 'The project temporarily brings very disparate individuals together and is presented as a very active segment of the network for a relatively short period of time, enabling the individuals to develop more lasting relationships that are then put on hold while remaining available' (Boltanski, Chiapello, 1999, p. 157).

In both cases, relationships are founded on a personal knowledge. In both cases, social interactions take place primarily within the chain of personal acquaintances. The only pertinent difference concerns the dynamic aspect of the personalized relationships. In the first case, the relationships are established in advance and not likely to change over time; in the second, they are 'elective' and likely to take on a new structure as often as necessary in order to attain an objective. The relative homology of these two cities led Luc Boltanski and Eve Chiapello to develop 'the hypothesis of a substitution or rather an absorption of the domestic logic by the connectionist logic' in order to trace the main lines of the evolution of Western societies (Boltanski, Chiapello, 1999, p. 205). As for the penal society, we would prefer to speak of an amalgamation of two cities: neither domestic logic nor logic 'by projects' enjoys absolute domination over the other. Furthermore, there is no compromise, no reconciliation of the two logics: each action excludes neither the domestic interpretation nor its interpretation 'by projects'.

Congruence of two sets of informal norms: in the prison and in Soviet society

We have defined the penal subculture as a set of informal norms that are developed and respected voluntarily and serve to organize everyday life in detention. According to E. Goffman, a subculture that is substantially identical to that of the penal subculture, unofficial life, exists in any society.

> 'In any social institution, we see members refuse the official schematics of what they must bring to the institution and what they can expect from it... Every time a society forms, clandestine life appears' (Goffman, 1968, pp. 233–235).

The greater the gap between the interests of the individual and those of the institution, the more chances there are that a subculture will form within the institution and that a clandestine life will flourish. Society adopts a dual structure, official and unofficial, if and only if three conditions are attainable: the individual enjoys some benefit; the individual finds a set of joint values in the organization where his own interests mingle with those of the institution; the individual's activities are rewarded, even negatively (Goffman, 1968, pp. 233–235). Many *real* societies do not satisfy one or more of these conditions. The Soviet society is one of those, which means that any study of daily social life is incomplete without a reference to its unofficial component that appeared despite the standards imposed from above.

Our hypothesis with respect to the institutional organization of penal life and daily Soviet life involves the supposition of their surprising homology. In goffmanian terms, this is a considerable value of the 'permeability coefficient'. This coefficient reflects 'the faculty under which the norms specific to the institution and the norms of the surroundings are likely to interfere to reduce the opposition between the two environments' (Goffman, 1968, p. 171). As a result of the large supposed value of the coefficient, we are able to borrow a rhetorical strategy, which is so apparent in the anthropological work of Benedict Ruth. This strategy implies

> 'the juxtaposition of the familiar and the exotic in such a manner that they change places. The immediately accessible culture is presented as bizarre and arbitrary whereas what is culturally distant is considered as something logical that cannot be bypassed' (Geertz, 1996, p. 107).

As we interpret it, this strategy presupposes that we view the Soviet-type society through the prism of the social organization of the penal environment. However, if the value of the coefficient tends towards zero, we observe a dissonance between the two sets of norms. The transition from an institutional environment to the other becomes problematic as a result of the total incompatibility of the rules for 'here' and those for 'there'. Several fragments of the social space do not interact with one another.

'Institutional dissonance refers to a disjuncture between institutional structures or rules that shape the ways people deal with one another or with the natural environment' (Thomas-Slayter, 1994, p. 1481).

Considering our desire to measure the degree of progress that has been made along the path towards modernization, let us consider the mathematical space of the conjuncture/disjuncture. Mathematicians speak of congruence in order to designate the comparable states produced by distinct processes. Let us take the example of the numbers 25, 7, 43, and 61. They are all congruent despite their apparent dissimilarity. The congruence is based on the likelihood that each number will undergo the same transformation: when they are divided by 6 (*modulo* 6), there is always a remainder of 1.[17] In this way, the congruence of social structures is achieved through the possible transformation of one set of norms into another through a sequence of intermediate states. As the number of intermediate states increases, the likelihood of the congruency of the sets of norms decreases. As a result, we can reformulate our initial hypothesis as follows: *in the Soviet case, the institutional structure of the penal environment is congruent with that of the society surrounding it because they share certain characteristics and are likely to be transformed* analytically *into one another* (**H.2**).

Gestalt psychology helps to clarify the mechanism for analytical transformation from a trait present in two sets of norms. Let us suppose that b is an attribute of a set and R designates the place (the function, the degree of importance, etc.) of b within the set (Duncker, 1964, p. 264). How can we describe the set if all we have is information about b and R: $?Rb$. The observer's previous experience includes an aRb relationship. Although it only corresponds partially to the relationship in question, Rb provokes aRb. In other words, the study of certain elements of the criminal subculture reminds the observer of the logic behind the organization of everyday life, with which we have practical experience. Therefore, the reflection concerning the possible connections between the hypotheses that an observer develops and his experience of everyday life provides for a better understanding of his approach, as well as the strengths and weaknesses of it. This aspect is all the more important since the social sciences prefer to hide the personality of the author behind the alleged objectivity of the analysis. Anthropology serves as a remarkable exception. In this case, the fact that the data obtained through field work cannot be re-examined (the societies studied are distant and often inaccessible to other observers) validates reasoning that is closely linked to the personality of the observer (Geertz, 1996, p. 14).

In summarizing the presentation of our second hypothesis, we want to stress the fact that in an ordinary situation, the permeability coefficient is high between the various institutions of everyday life, including both the formal and informal

---

[17] We borrowed the idea of applying the notion of congruence to socioeconomic analysis from Andreff W., 'Convergence or Congruence Between Eastern and Western Economic Systems', in Dallago B., Brezinski H., Andreff W. (eds.), *Convergence and System Change. The Convergence Hypothesis in the Light of Transition in Eastern Europe*, Aldershot: Dartmouth, 1992.

institutions, whereas the dissonance between the normative organization of the penal environment and that of everyday life outside the prison remains great. For example, the Mafioso consciously maintained the disjuncture between society inside the prison and that without. For them, it was 'a principle not to reproduce within the prison the divisions and hatreds of the external world of the Cosa Nostra' (Arlacchi, 1996, p. 185). Yet, we are presuming just the opposite in the case studied: the informal norms of the penal environment and the society that surrounds it are close whereas there is a major disjuncture between formal and informal norms in the prison *and* in the society that surrounds it.

Particularities of the state authority in the prison and in Soviet society

According to the third hypothesis of our study, the congruence of the penal subculture and the 'constitution' of daily Soviet life can be accounted for by the congruence of the relationships of authority in the prison and in Soviet-type society. Before going into further detail, we must, once again, highlight the fact that we are not claiming to make any universal generalizations that could apply to the studies of prisons in any society.

> 'There are no universal laws in the social sciences… The causal conditions involved in generalizations about human social conduct are inherently unstable in respect of the very knowledge that actors have about the circumstances of their own actions' (Giddens, 1984, p. xxxii).

On the contrary, it is the originality of the Soviet system that provides a link between the study of the penal system and the study of the society that surrounds it. And what does this originality entail, if we were to take a close look at the relationships of authority, a key element in any social construction?

In keeping with the usual definition, the authority of an individual (or an institution) over others translates into the possession of the right to control their actions. The concept of authority does not inevitably evoke the imposition of the will or the arbitrary power of the holder. Authority has a *voluntary* character 'only if the individual holds the right of control over a particular class of his own actions and holds the right to transfer that right to another' (Coleman, 1990, pp. 69–70). In other words, the individual voluntarily submits to the authority as long as he is not able to fulfil his interests better by maintaining control of that authority and as long as the scope of the authority is limited. James Coleman refers to this type of authority as *conjoint*, as opposed to *disjoint* for which the sole purpose is the extrinsic compensation that the individual receives for transferring the right to control his actions (Coleman, 1990, p. 72). To this latter, we can add the authority that is *imposed* through coercion that denies the individual compensation. In both cases the individuals who hold the authority, namely the Principals, do not coincide with those who are supposed to submit to the orders of the Principals, namely the Agents (Figure 1.2). Disjuncture causes unofficial life to flourish by giving rise to the so-called Principal and Agent problem, which recently held a significant place with respect to the institutional economics. The central problem lies in studying the means for ensuring that the Agents will submit to the orders of the Principal in a situation where, on the one hand, their interests do not coincide and, on the other hand, the Principal does not have all of the information pertaining to the actions of the Agents (information asymmetry) and the costs of control are high (Stiglitz, 1987, pp. 968–969). Imposed authority does not necessarily appear illegitimate. However, its legitimacy may be based on grounds other than rational considerations.[18]

Figure 1.2 Types of authority

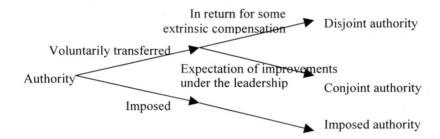

The eventual transformation of the voluntary authority in the relationships between the Principal and the Agent gives rise to a duality of norms and makes the border between the various fields of activity more penetrable. First, the non-coincidence of interests, even their opposition in the case of authority imposed through coercion, means that the actor becomes an Other, whose behavior is not governed by the same normative framework. For example, the maximization of utility concerns only the Principal, as does the standard of rationality. The actions of the Agent are described, instead, by the standard of rationality in value: he is free only to choose the means to attain the goals set by the Principal.[19] A system of equations that describes the relations between the Principal and the Agent illustrates this.

$$\begin{cases} \text{Max EU}_{\text{Principal}} = \text{EU}\,[\mu(Q), Q, A, S] \\ \text{EU}_{\text{Agent}} = \text{EU}\,(Y, A, S) > \bar{U} \end{cases}$$

---

[18] It should be noted that, according to Weber, the affirmation of legitimacy can be based on rational grounds, traditional grounds and charismatic grounds (Weber, 1968, p. 215).
[19] For a discussion of the duality of norms in relations between the Principal and the Agent, see Oleinik A., *Institucional'naja ekonomika*, Chapter 8, Reading 6.

Where EU = expected utility, Q = the output, μ(Q) = the system of remuneration, Y = the Agent's extrinsic compensation, A = the input, S = factors outside of Principal and Agent's control.

Second, the relations between the Principal and the Agent always contain a risk that the control will expand. The Principal tends to extend his control beyond the limits explicitly negotiated with the Agent.

> 'A fundamental problem for the agent: the very rights of control which have been transferred may facilitate the Principal's extension of control beyond the domain covered in the relation' (Coleman, 1990, p. 152).

This expansion of the control breaks down the borders between the fields of activity, including the border between the public and the private. In other words, the relations between the Principal and the Agent reproduce the model for non-modern social relations and constitute an obstacle to modernization. Thus, we can word our third hypothesis as follows: *relationships of authority in prison and in the Soviet-type society are congruent because they include the key elements of the Principal-Agent model. The omnipresence of this model makes the penal subculture and the 'constitution' of the everyday life of Soviets congruent as well* (**H.3**).

The unifying view of authority in both the prison and the society through the prism of the Principal-Agent model requires a correction with respect to the conventional approach used by studies on the penal world. This focuses on the determining influence that the 'large' society has with respect to the 'small' penal society. 'The role of the external society is over-determining in the understanding of the internal life of prisons' (Chauvenet et al., 1994, p. 10). For example, it is changes in French society of the 19th century that de Tocqueville used to justify his arguments for penal reform. His interest in the number of repeat offences as an integral indicator of the situation in prisons can also be explained by the concern for fitting the prison into the context of the 'large' society (Tocqueville, Beaumont, 1984, pp. 212–213). By simplifying, we can summarize the conventional approach as follows: the 'small' penal society tracks the evolution of the 'large' society and the organization of the 'small' society derives its functional place in the 'large' society. As for our approach to the prison study, we are trying to avoid placing the penal environment and the society that surrounds it into a causal relationship, regardless of its nature. For example, we do not want to postulate that the penal society is merely an elementary form of the 'large' society, which would lead us into the reasoning of the classical anthropology of Durkheim, Lévi-Strauss, and Malinowski (with respect to so-called primitive societies). *The two societies are congruent not because the first derives from the second but because they both derive from the same authority model.*

> 'The bond between recognition of the legitimacy of control and the sense of duty has been torn apart. The social system of the prison is very similar to a *Gebeitsverband*, a territorial group living under a regime imposed by a ruling few' (Sykes, 1958, p. 48).

This places the prison society and the Soviet-type society on the list of social systems governed by either a foreign authority or a native authority whose links with the population are virtually non-existent and/or broken.

> 'People [is] feeling like they are not represented in making the law [in] places where the forces of law come from outside and operate in the interests of outsiders' (Brigham, 1997, p. 365).

Citizenship, a key element in democracy, namely the 'the right to take part, either directly or indirectly, in the management of society' (Touraine, 1994, p. 102), has no place in such social systems.

The concept of imposed authority does not coincide with that of the total authority observed in total institutions. But there is a causal relationship between the two types of authority, the permanent tendency of the transformation of imposed authority into total authority. This tendency is explained by the Agent's interest in benefiting from the information asymmetry that exists between the Agent and the Principal and in behaving in an opportunistic manner (*shirking*–the Agent becomes a slacker). Considering the permanent danger of the opportunism of the Agents, the Principal tends to extend his sphere of control, making it total. The balance between the desire of the Agents to behave in an opportunistic manner and the efforts of the Principal to construct total authority is explained primarily by the degree of non-coincidence of their interests and the dynamics of the costs involved in controlling and collecting information (Figure 1.3). In other words, the imposed character of authority is necessary but not sufficient to make authority total.

Figure 1.3 Imposed and total authority

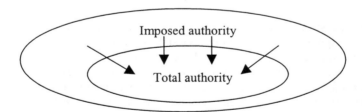

After summing up the broad lines of the idea of congruence, we will discuss the matter of its mechanisms, the means in which it is transmitted in the social system. Mathematical, geometric and chemical analogies are not sufficient to explain the fact that inmates and ordinary Soviet citizens use congruent normative markers in their everyday lives. The first solution would involve evoking the concept of habitus developed as part of critical sociology.

'The habitus is an infinite capacity to create, in perfect freedom, products–thoughts, perceptions, expressions, actions–which are always limited by the historically and socially located conditions of its production' (Bourdieu, 1980b, p. 92).

Critical sociology would, as a result, search Soviet society for conditions likely to reactivate the habitus produced first by the penal environment or by other total institutions. A study into the construction of the ordinary Soviet man fits in well with the concept of the production and the reactivation of the habitus, although this term is not specifically used. Yuri Levada and his colleagues focussed on the role that military service (namely the experience with a perfect totalitarian institution) played in Soviet socialization. In this case, a phenomenon specific to the Soviet army and, moreover, the Russian army, *dedovschina*, plays an important role. *Dedovschina* involves the construction of personal chains of dependency and the appropriation of informal authority within military groups by the most senior. 'The *dedovschina* is a system for re-socializing, transforming the individual' (Levada, 1993, p. 144).[20] If the individual is first socialized at the school, as Levada claims, causing young Soviet citizens to internalize modern values, the second socialization, through the *dedovschina* produces a more 'virile', cruel and roughly traditional morale. In this sense, the *dedovschina* is similar to 'pedagogical work' as a category of critical sociology.

'Pedagogical work–instilling work that must last long enough to produce lasting training, i.e. habitus as the product of the internalization of the principles of an arbitrary culture *capable of perpetuating itself after the pedagogical activity has ceased and in that manner to perpetuate the principles of the internalized arbitrariness in practice*' (Bourdieu, Passeron, 1970, p. 47).

The soldier who has completed his military service leaves the barracks with a habitus that continues on afterward and serves to organize his life within Soviet society.

One possible interpretation in psychological terms gives the concept of habitus a complementary viability. Gestalt psychology serves to develop a cognitive dimension of habitus. In the terminology of Gestalt psychology, the habitus reflects the specific organization of *traces* in the individual's memory. 'Traces produced by "similar" expectations do not remain independent of each other but form larger trace systems which influence newly formed traces' (Koffka, 1935, p. 473). The organization of traces in systems clarifies the means by which the habitus is transported from one social context to another. Once the trace system is formed by a Gestalt disposition, it starts to interfere with the new experiences.

'If a process communicates with a part of a trace system, the whole trace system will exert a force on the process in the direction of making it as complete as it was when it created this trace system' (Koffka, 1935, p. 567).

---

[20] According to the authors, young girls are socialized by young men who are slightly older and who have already acquired military experience.

The conditions needed to activate the trace system by new experiences include similarity, proximity, and good continuation, as well as the law of contrast. The *transposable* character, it should be noted, could account for the reactivation of a habitus produced, for example, by a totalitarian institution, in another social context, that is not necessarily congruent with the first context. 'Habits (personal forms of routinization) provide a structuring medium for the continuity of life across different contexts of action' (Giddens, 1996, p. 57).[21] In other words, it is a matter of a disposition that can be transposed *'to a large number of different fields'* (Bourdieu, Passeron, 1970, p. 49).

Social psychology explicitly established a link between the cognitive structures of the individual and the patterns of his daily behavior. In this case, the notion of archetype ensures psychological liaison in everyday life. The so-called social archetypes, acquired during individual socialization, determine the standards for perceiving socioeconomic reality as well as social and individual behavior (Diligenskij, 1996, p. 45). The organization of everyday life is reproduced by means of a series of archetypes specific to each socioeconomic system. In this way, the habitus can be transposed not only in the social space but also in social time.

The strength of the concept of habitus, its transposable character, is also a weakness that makes it impossible to apply this concept within the framework of our research. The universalism of this concept weakens its links with the social context, the context of everyday life. For example, the habitus of *dedovschina* would tend to reproduce itself in any society as long as young men did military service in a post-Soviet type army. The burlesque analogy of *dedovschina*, hazing, never played a comparable role in Western societies. Moreover, since the habitus is based on individual experience, it does not appear in a new social context unless there is a sufficiently large number of individuals with that habitus. Unlike the experience of military service, obligatory for all young men in the Soviet period, the experience of life in detention concerned only a marginal portion of the Soviet population (we already provided figures in the *'Introduction'* and will return to them in the section entitled *'The penal system in Russia'* in the second chapter). Now, the relative insignificance of the penal population did not reduce the scope of the prison subculture and its congruence with the normative structure of daily Soviet life, which means that we must continue to search for a more appropriate analytical concept, namely one that would meet the following requirements: the transposable character only in the congruent contexts, the durability in terms of the degree of congruence, as well as psychological and cognitive validity.

The investigation into the nature of the transmission of normative markers from one social context to another leads us to the theory of sets (*teorija ustanivki*) developed from the 1930s–1960s by Soviet psychologist Dmitrij Uznadze (1886–1950) and his disciples at the Psychology Institute in Tbilissi. The term *set* describes the processes that arise out of the sphere of the extra-conscience

---

[21] Let us provide a few other appropriate definitions: 'Habitus–a set of codes and dispositions acquired in a precocious manner that the individual implements in *a variety of circumstances'* (Dubet F., 1994, p.76). 'The habitus *re-activates* objectified sense in institutions' (Bourdieu P., 1980b, p.96). Our emphasis.

(*vnesoznatel'noe*). Unlike the Freudian concept of unconsciousness, the extra-conscience tracks conscious actions and serves as a reservoir for storing information about the actions that do not merit continuous attention. In other words, habitual, routine actions correspond to this level of consciousness. The set reflects 'an initial reaction to the situation in which the subject is encouraged to make a decision' (Uznadze, 1966, p. 150).[22] The repetition of the initial situation forms the set and makes it transposable to other contexts. The set concerns the perception of the material environment (volume, weight, color, etc.) as well as the organization of social interactions (routine,[23] mental model, etc.). Several experiments have demonstrated not only the presence of sets in various spheres of activity, but also their *inter-modal* quality, namely the proximity of their parameters in the diverse fields of activity of a particular individual, such as the reading of a text and the sensory perception of an object (Uznadze, 1966, p. 150). The profoundly contextual character differentiates the set from the trace and, as a result, from the habitus. 'The set can once again comply with the norm as soon as favorable conditions [which refer back to the initial situation] appear' (Uznadze, 1966, p. 181). If there is no context that is congruent with the initial situation, the set remains latent and progressively loses its ability to be reactivated.

First, let us discuss another advantage of the concept of set–this fits in with the discussion of the restrictive or, on the other hand, the liberating nature of the norm. Set as an element of the manner in which social space is organized on a daily basis helps the subject better control his cognitive resources. Set replaces attention in situations in which the activities do not require continuous control. For example, the initial actions that take place in the first few moments after waking are almost totally guided by sets. As a result, attention may be considered as an 'action by which the event or the object that is affected by the individual's activity is transformed into an object for controlling it' (Uznadze, 1966, p. 255). In other

---

[22] Uznadze D., *Psihologicheskie issledovanija*, Moskva: Nauka, 1966, c.150. English translation: Uznadze D., *The Psychology of Set*, New York : Consultants Bureau, 1966.

[23] The actor uses routine to optimize the use of his cognitive resources. The cognitive capacities of human beings are naturally limited (*bounded rationality*), everyday life forces humans to know how to 'close their eyes' or, in other words, how not to pay attention to its least important aspects. The transformation of a remarkable portion of daily activity into routine helps to concentrate cognitive resources on the more important aspects at any given point. 'Whatever their origin (imitation or conscious choice), repeated acts tend to congeal into habits, and become removed from the sphere of rational deliberation in the mind' (Hodgson, 1988, p.127). The thesis concerning the important role of routine is further justified in the penal environment. The various aspects of life in detention are so monotone and uniform that they quickly become routine. Predictability and stability, which are so desired outside the prison, take on an extreme and often unbearable form inside the prison. 'Here, time is very organized. We do exercises in the morning, then we make our beds, wash, get dressed.... A short break and then – college or trade school. There is almost no free time... We can only communicate with others on weekends' (Interview No. 32). In this way, submission to routine is spontaneous and voluntary outside the prison, yet in detention, the power of the routine takes on an imposed, tyrannical character.

words, set gives an individual with limited cognitive resources complementary liberty (cf. Herbert Simon's concept of limited, or bounded rationality[24]): instead of spreading his attention over several things, the individual focusses in on those that are essential for fulfilling his interests. A comparison of habitus and set is provided in the following table:

Table 1.1 Comparative characteristics of habitus and set

Characteristics of habitus	*Characteristics of* set
Durability in time – almost absolute	Durability in time – limited
Almost absolutely transposable	Transposable in congruent contexts
Exhaustivity: almost perfect reproduction	Limited stability (ability to reactivate itself)
	Very precise activation situation
	Inter-modality (proximity of parameters in various fields of activity) for a given individual

In short, authority in the prison and authority in Soviet society form congruent social contexts for which the conditions generate similar tendencies. As a result, in order to explain the significant scope of the penal subculture in a Soviet-type society, we do not need to suppose that the habits produced in the penal setting must be expanded. It is the perception of the authority on a daily level that produces a normative structure that is comparable to the penal subculture. As G. Schiavo remarked with respect to the context of the appearance of the Mafia, 'All people have reacted like the Sicilians *under the same circumstances* [it is a matter of the particular character of the State in Sicily]' (Schiavo, 1962, p. 68).[25]

The characteristics of the subject depend on the institutional context

The notion of set creates a link between the characteristics of the institutional organization of everyday life and the characteristics of the Subject.[26] Regardless of

---

[24] For a discussion of the current state of the theory of limited rationality, see Laville F., 'Modélisation de la rationalité limitée: de quel outils dispose-t-on?', *Revue Economique*, Vol. 49, n°2, March 1998.

[25] Our emphasis.

[26] 'The Subject is the will of an individual to act and be recognized as an actor' (Touraine, 1992, p. 241). The Subject exists in two forms: as a social movement (collective actor) and as an individual actor. In its first form, for which the worker movement serves as a classic example, the Subject contests and tries to change norms on a macro-social level. The purpose of the worker's struggle is 'influence, namely the ability to modify the rules of the game to one's advantage' (Touraine et al., 1984, p. 39). Thus, a refusal to submit to the norms that are imposed and to the production of norms within the framework of the 'large' society distinguishes the Subject from the socio-professional category or any other social aggregate. 'The Subject exists only as a social movement, as a protest against the logic of the order, regardless of whether it takes on a utilitarian form or is simply a search

the Subject, whether collective or individual, regardless of whether it is conscious, positive or negative, its formation and its actions are derived from the institutional context that is specific to it. Our fourth hypothesis is not a completely deterministic vision under which the Subject is not capable of stepping beyond the limits imposed by institutional environment. This vision does not take into consideration the dual nature of norms, which can be both constraining and liberating at the same time. *The Subject exchanges and constructs norms, but from elements that are available in the specific institutional context and based on sets produced by that context* (**H.4**). Let us attempt to use this hypothesis to interpret the taxonomy of subjects developed by sociology of action. Two classification criteria are pertinent: the character of the Subject (individual or collective) and the character of its conscience (positive, namely a carrier of a positive social or daily project, or negative, focussed on existing rules):

---

for social integration' (Touraine, 1992, p. 273). Yet, in order to form as a Subject, a social group needs to be based on norms that facilitate coordination and, as a result, collective action. For example, without the support of the norms of trust and cooperative behavior, the appearance of the social movement is brought into question as a result of the free-rider problem. Although all of the people concerned took a collective interest in the formation of a collective actor, they prefer to abstain individually. Robert Putnam calls the set of norms that promote collective action the social capital. He demonstrated that, in the absence of social capital, the actors cannot produce norms themselves (Putnam, 1993a; Putnam, 1993b). We studied the place of the traditions of solidarity in the formation of the miners' movement in the former USSR in Oleynik A., *La formation du mouvement des mineurs en ex-URSS. Une approche dans l'étude des mouvements sociaux*, post-master's thesis in sociology, under the direction of Wieviorka M., Paris: E.H.E.S.S., 1994 [for a report on this research, see also Oleinik A., 'Est' li perspektiva u social'nyh dvijenij v Rossii: primer shahterskogo dvijenija 1989–1995', *POLIS – Politicheskie issledovanija*, 1996, n°3].

With respect to the second form of the Subject, the individual actor, it also implies the ability to produce norms, this time at the micro-social level of everyday life. In this case, the ability to be the Subject involves leaving behind all of the roles that are socially imposed on one. From a psychoanalytical point of view, the construction of the individual Subject takes the form of a differentiation between the Id and the Self as a set of roles (Touraine, 1992, pp. 309–315). How can one play several roles while maintaining one's personal identity? It involves striving to reach a compromise between normative requirements that are often opposed, articulating distinct norms within the framework of the social experience that makes the actions of the individual Subject obvious. 'The actor is required to articulate different logics for action, and it is the dynamics engendered by this activity that constitutes the subjectivity of the actor and his reflexivity' (Dubet, 1994, p. 105). The search for a compromise translated into the production of local norms whose scope is limited in space and time. Each individual experiences the dispersion of the distinct logics in his own manner, and his normative response is original and daily by necessity.

Table 1.2 A taxonomy of subjects

		The Subject	
		Individual	Collective
Conscience	Positive	Ability to get out of socially imposed roles	Social movement
	Negative	Refusal to play a socially imposed role	Social anti-movement

The history of the workers' movement provides an example of the evolutive dynamics of the forms of the Subject. Alain Touraine and his colleagues view the sequence of these dynamics as follows (Figure 1.4) (Touraine et al., 1984, p. 41).

Figure 1.4 Dynamics of the forms of the subject

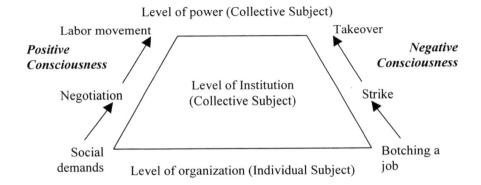

The diagram illustrates the fact that the passage from one form of action to another is dependent on the context: organizational, institutional or political (the level of power). Moreover, the non-rigid political system and the openness of management to negotiations facilitate the transition from a negative consciousness to a positive one.

> 'The worker movement is neither a negotiator nor a revolutionary by nature, it becomes one or the other in keeping with the characteristics of the political system' (Touraine et al., 1984, p. 394).

The formation of the first social movement in Soviet-type societies, *Solidarnösc* in Poland, provides an example of another sequence: 'top down', from the political level to the level of organization. Thus, the explanation of such an evolution does not lie in the characteristics of the social organization. 'Change in a society so close to the totalitarian model can only come from the center' (Touraine et al., 1982, p. 41). The other Polish characteristic, namely the Polish confidence in the

Roman Catholic Church, also facilitated the formation of a positive conscience. The sets, generated by the Roman Catholic Church, towards resisting the authority imposed by force were reactivated within the context of the protest movement that had no religious vocation.

> 'The church is a force of resistance to absolute power... Therefore, it plays an essentially democratic role' (Touraine et al., 1982, p. 79).

Placing the subject in context enables us to look at what goes on in the Soviet prison from another point of view. The eventual transformation of an inmate into an individual Subject trying to master the normative framework of his everyday life is at the very heart of our analysis. Individual attempts to master everyday life, regardless of their institutional framework, are always incomplete and limited, with their chances of success far from guaranteed. 'The [individual] Subject never triumphs', with the exception of geniuses (Touraine, 1992, pp. 245, 272). This case is very rare in ordinary life and all the more so in detention. We can only refer you to a few cases of individual resistance that have succeeded in a totalitarian institution, such as the experiences of two important writers in the Stalinist labor camps: Alexander Solzhenitsyn, who won the Nobel prize for literature in 1970 and wrote *Gulag Archipelago*, and Varlam Shalamov, who wrote *20th Century Kolyma Tales*. The transition to other levels of action, whether institutional or political, is seldom possible in prison as a result of the violent repression of any movement in that direction. As a result, the institutional context prohibits any explicit manifestation of the collective Subject. Nevertheless, the penal subculture as a set of norms and values that are respected by all inmates indicates the existence of a latent collective Subject. 'There is no class in itself, there can be no class without a class consciousness' (Touraine et al., 1984, p. 52). In the penal context, there is a consciousness without obvious collective action, which prevents the transformation of the negative consciousness into a positive one. The negative character of the consciousness is justified by the structure of most of the norms of the penal subculture. We will examine this in more depth in the section entitled '*Duality of norms*' in second chapter. Do not do something, do not act in such and such a manner, etc. The penal subculture includes few permissive norms and few norms that empower. Despite the fact that the penal subculture does not have much of a project for positive social organization, the manner in which it contests the disconnected authority imposed by force must not be under-valued. The elements of the resistance to absolute power found in the penal subculture appeared in the 1930s, historically well before the first obvious protests in socialist countries. This attempt to resist is particularly worth studying if we consider the virtual absence of any protestors in the former Soviet Union, as well as in post-Soviet Russia.

The congruence of formal and informal norms as a condition for viable socioeconomic development

The *differentia specifica* of the Soviet-type system implies that the 'constitution' of everyday life in prison and in the society that surrounds it are congruent, whereas the two 'constitutions' barely coincide with the norms imposed by the formal authority, and even contradict it. As a result, the actors find themselves in what Jean-Daniel Reynaud calls a 'conflict of regulations'.

> 'The parties can agree by means of recognizing a relative autonomy, either by admitting that each is taking part in the regulation (negotiation), or by sharing the territory' (Reynaud, 1989, p. 100).

Let us take a close look at these three variations. The joint participation in developing a compromise between formal regulation and informal regulation gives a most pertinent allure to the conflict. It is a matter of restoring the democratic participation of those governed by the regulation process. As a second alternative, the sharing of territory so as to ensure a territorial monopoly for each concurrent regulation. For example, 'there are neighborhoods [in Palermo] that have not seen a police car in ten years' (Padovani, 1987, p. 201), without the crime rate in that neighborhood being any higher. The final alternative, the relativization of regulations, brings to mind the social model which Richard Rose and his colleagues refer to as the hourglass society. The formal authority and the population agree on their virtually independent and autonomous lives.

> 'The narrow mid-point of the hour glass insulates individuals from the State; there is rich social life at the top and at the bottom. Ordinary people do not feel that they can influence government, but also government cannot interfere with their lives' (Rose, Mishler, Haerpfer, 1997, p. 9).

A conflict in regulations has numerous consequences, although we will only mention those of a social and economic nature here. On a social level, the conflict in regulations translates into a conflict of roles, both formal and informal, with the interpretation of the roles to be provided by the actor. This creates a 'situation in which one of the roles of the subject and the resulting obligations contradict the norms that pertain to the activities of that same subject within the framework of the other social role' (Yakovlev, 1988, p. 81). Each actor is doubled since each is obliged to play the role of the evil-doer and the role of the good genie at the same time. In order to preserve his integrity, the actor winds up selecting a single role, formal *or* informal, which he invests in. Generally, he chooses the role that corresponds to the norms that are developed or applied voluntarily, namely the informal role. As the conflict in regulations increases in intensity, the justification for belonging to the informal life also grows on a daily level. 'Informality occurs when the law imposes rules that surpass the socially accepted framework' (Soto, 1994, p. 20).

Seen through the prism of economics, the conflict of regulations ends in increased *transaction costs*. In particular, it is a matter of high bargaining costs and monitoring costs. The absence of benchmarks that are accepted by the parties to a contract complicates the negotiating process. It becomes more difficult to reach an agreement if the parties to the contract do not accept the same rules. For example, one party tries to apply the norms of the Law while the other follows the norms of the informal 'constitution'. As for the monitoring costs, the conflict in regulations promotes opportunistic behavior: what is acceptable from the point of view of the informal 'constitution' can transform into the 'pursuit of egotistical interest to the detriment of the collective interests (of the company, of the State)' from a legal point of view (for example, an employee who uses office supplies for his own needs). In short,

> 'when formal rules are in conflict with informal rules their respective incentives will tend to raise transaction costs of maintaining and enforcing the prevailing institutional arrangements, and to reduce the extent of economic activity in the community' (Pejovich, 1995, p. 7).[27]

It is important to note that the lack of congruence between the formal and informal norms in the Soviet case represents only one case among several others. Moreover, this lack of congruence accompanies not only the arbitrary authority whose activities are not limited by civic control and participation, but occasionally also the efforts of radically changing the formal frameworks, for example, in countries where the 'natural' evolution towards modernization takes too long and/or the results are not obvious. Without any guaranteed correspondence between the informal *'native'* norms and the 'progressive', 'modern', 'effective', but also *'foreign'* norms, the results of radical reform could well be contrary to expectations. In the best of cases, according to an expression that became popular in Russia in the 1990s, 'we strove for the best, but it came out as usual'. Before discussing a few examples, we will provide a complete formulation of our fifth, and final, hypothesis: *The capital condition for the continuous reproduction of a society and its sustainable socioeconomic development lies in the congruence of the informal norms developed through everyday life and the formal norms implemented by the State. Any democratic and market reform, no matter how progressive the initial idea was, is condemned to failure if this condition is not fulfilled* (**H.5**).

American legislators undertook an experiment in the 1930s, when the *Indian Reorganization Act* was enacted. According to that Act, the United States Constitution, apparently much more modern than Indian common law, was imposed on all reservations. Despite the expectations of accelerated development, the consequences of this constitutional reform appear very ambiguous. The tribes whose common law coincided with the United States constitution experienced a period of rapid modernization. However, the tribes whose common law was not congruent with the Constitution experienced crisis and profound stagnation. The conclusions of the authors of this study tie in with the logic of our final hypothesis: 'congruence between cultural norms and governmental form is part of a set of necessary conditions for creating economic growth' (Cornell, Kalt, 1995, p. 411). Since the Middle Ages, history has provided many examples of efforts, both

---

[27] On the contrary, 'the cost of enforcing exclusive rights is reduced when the public generally entertains social norms that coincide with the basic structure of rights that the State seeks to uphold' (Eggertsson, 1990, p.35).

successful and unsuccessful, to accelerate development through 'institutional imports'.

> 'In many regions [of medieval Europe], Roman Law, which was not in the least a part of the people's customs, encountered rigorous opposition' (Van Den, 1993, p. 515).

The adoption of the Napoleonic Civil Code in countries as diverse as Belgium, the Netherlands, Italy, Portugal, Egypt, Quebec, and Louisiana did not take place without more or less evident ruptures between the formal norms and the daily 'constitution'. Occasionally, the implementation of a set of norms can serve to obstruct the legal system. 'As long as the Federal Courts in Puerto Rico operate with the English Common Law, they will be foreign' (Brigham, 1997, p. 378) to the population of that country.

Importation involves not only norms of law, but also strategies for economic behavior, and organization and political structures. Regardless of the nature of the institutions imported, the congruence of the formal and informal norms remains the capital condition for ensuring that they function well. For example, marketing practices based on occidental manuals often appear inefficient in Third World countries, unlike native marketing means, despite the fact that they are too traditional and unsophisticated.

> 'The success of the informal merchants in Latin America results from the fact that that they have not been "contaminated" by management techniques imported from more developed countries... The informal merchants are much closer to the marketing philosophy than their competitors in the formal sector' (Arellando, 1994, pp. 335–336).

In the event that importing a commercial strategy results in a worst case scenario such as bankruptcy, the unsuccessful importation of political structures has much more serious consequences. Bertrand Badie demonstrated that the dissemination of the principle of territoriality specific to the Western concept of international law was behind several conflicts, particularly in regions where 'community cultures give the territory a significance that is fundamentally different from that found in Western cultures' (Badie, 1992, p. 93), such as Africa in the Middle East.

Likewise, the elements of institutional import and export are easily recognizable in Russian history since Christianity was imposed by the State at the end of the 9th century (*kreschenie Rusi*). The reforms of Peter the Great (the end of the 17th to the start of the 18th centuries) represent the most coherent and best planned case of institutional importation. The results are very significant. The counter-reforms allowed 'only those new elements which did not contradict the former order' (Morozov, 1992, t.3, p. 147). The conflict mentioned earlier between the *zapadniki* and the *slavianofily* in the 19th century started a debate on the perspective of Western theoretical models as a means for analyzing Russian problems. There is a hypothesis to the effect that materialism and Marxism, unlike other schools of Western thought, managed to take root in Russian soil as a result of the congruence between their structure and that of the national conscience

(Ahiezer, 1991, p. 11). Likewise, the economic reforms of the 80s decade in the 19th century (the reforms of N. Bunge) turned out to be unsuccessful because the underlying imported model of agriculture did not coincide with the traditional order. 'Peasants rejected "official" Russia and craved to be left alone; theirs was a culture of autonomy and independence' (Gatrell, 1995, p. 50). A grotesque situation, which also pertains to agricultural development, marked the 1960s. The key point of the agricultural program of Nikita Khruschev, who was the First Secretary of the Communist Party of the USSR at the time, involved reproducing the American agricultural system. In the end, the reform involved growing corn, whereas the 'the underlying value systems and organizational principles of American agriculture were completely ignored' (Ahiezer, 1991, p. 212).

Moreover, the history of the Soviet period provides more examples of institutional export than import. After becoming the second largest military and political power in the world, the Soviet empire started imposing its institutional model on other countries. 'There are no limits set in advance with respect to local regulations. It is when they come into contact with other spheres of influence' (Reynaud, 1989, pp. 136–137) that limits are set with respect to the scope of any given institutional model. The period after WWII was particularly marked by the expansion of the Soviet model. Countries in central and eastern Europe imported several political, economic and social institutions, so that we can now refer to the Soviet-type system. 'The Soviet example played an important part in all countries shaping specific elements of classic socialism (its official ideology, institutions, and norms of behavior)' (Kornaï, 1992, p. 374).[28] It is difficult to qualify this importation as successful. On the one hand, the so-called socialist countries experienced the same doubling of their social lives as we have supposed for the USSR. As several studies have demonstrated, the organization of everyday life in the socialist countries was almost uniform.

> 'The broad pattern of common responses emphasizes the pervasive influence of Sovietization in the experience of countries from the Black Sea to the Baltic' (Haerpfer, Rose, 1993, pp. 73–77).[29]

On the other hand, the Soviet institutions were almost always viewed as foreign, imposed by force or historical accident. The response given by the inhabitants of three socialist countries at the end of the 1980s with respect to the desirable origins of the institutional model to be imitated are significant (Rose, 1991, p. 13):

---

[28] Another testimonial, this time on the part of a Western observer, is also pertinent: 'As to the basic character of the social institutions developing over the years, the influence of Soviet example must undoubtedly have been immense' (Douglass, 1972, p.7).

[29] The authors used 14 different indicators for measuring economic behavior, attitudes and political opinions.

Table 1.3 Rating of different socioeconomic systems

Country serving as a model:	Czechoslovakia	Hungary	Poland
Germany	31	38	37
Sweden	32	34	21
The United States	14	10	30
Italy	9	9	0
France	5	2	7
USSR	0	1	0

In the list of examples of institutional imports, we will find very few successes. The case of China is one of the most notable. As a result of the success of the market reforms in the 1980s–1990s, observers can speak of the construction of a market in a country that had never experienced a strong market culture and where the culture is very different from that of the West. One explanation would highlight the congruence of the informal norms and market principles, despite their apparent similarities. 'Cultural traditions are compatible with a full-fledged marketization of the Chinese economy' (Hermann-Pillath, 1994, p. 237).[30] In particular, it is a matter of fit between tacit knowledge, on the one hand, and formal institutions and technological challenges on the other.

The Chinese experience enables us to make the hypothesis more precise in terms of the cognitive grounds for congruence. The apparent similarity is not a condition that is either necessary nor sufficient for the congruence of institutional contexts. It's *the possibility of building a chain of analogies* between formal norms and informal norms that makes contexts congruent. This argument is similar to that of Claude Lévi-Strauss with respect to tinkering in thinking. If the imported norms give rise to pertinent analogies, they are likely to be congruent with the informal norms. It is a matter of 'validation by analogy', a procedure that is necessary in order to make a social institution legitimate (Douglas, 1986, pp. 66, 76). In terms of Gestalt psychology, chains of analogies between two apparently dissimilar phenomena are built in keeping with the law of 'good continuation'.

> 'We could not perceive a melody if each new tone came to consciousness as an entirely new element. A person with no particular musical ability will forget a new melody rather quickly' (Koffka, 1935, p. 515).

In any case, successful imports are more the exception than the rule. The pertinent analogies do not arise in all contexts or at all times. Therefore, how can we explain the permanent and omnipresent recourse to institutional importation? Setting aside the imposition of a foreign institution through pure constraint, we will examine voluntary acts of importation. In terms of supply, the will to export an

---

[30] Another evaluation is similar: 'The social structures and cultural representations inherited from a history that is foreign to capitalism are not necessarily hostile to it... The capitalist transformation of the economy may take place through "traditional" modes of action, regardless of how "irrational" they may be' (Bayart, 1994, pp. 33–34).

institutional model, despite the absence of ownership rights in this field[31] can be explained by efforts to extend the influence of the exporting country and ensure a global aspect for the national authority. Moreover, the exportation of an institutional model helps to reduce transaction costs in international commerce and, as a result, to increase the sale of national products and services abroad. In terms of demand, importation also enables certain actors to achieve their interests. These stakeholders include 'a new elite whose survival depends on safeguarding, even reinforcing, the import process' and the intellectuals for whom 'recourse to Western thought [represents] the means for defending themselves against neo-patrimonial power as well as against traditionalism' (Badie, 1992, pp. 152, 158–159). Moreover, the importation strategy removes all responsibility from the actors who have the authority to make and change the Law, since they refer back to a model of international renown. Recourse to a foreign model hides the underlying interests of the reformers since, in this situation, they are not obliged to justify their policy (Offe, 1995, p. 55). In other words, the importation helps them to retain their rights within the framework of the Principal-Agent model and to cast off their obligations at the same time. No matter how good the initial reasons for the importation are at the start, this act is likely to serve to reproduce the Principal-Agent model and, as a result, create a lack of congruence between formal and informal norms.

Sources

In order to study daily behavioral norms, particularly informal norms, the researcher must have finely tuned tools for collecting information. Often, there is no discursive expression of informal norms, which limits the effectiveness of investigations, as well as that of interviews and sociological intervention.

> 'Practical consciousness consists of all the things which actors know tacitly about "how to go on" in the contexts of social life without being able to give them direct discursive expression' (Giddens, 1984, p. xxiii).

Participant observation will give the researcher all of the information needed to analyze the non-discursive dimension of the daily 'constitution'. Freed from anthropology, participant observation includes the following elements: the extended presence of the researcher at the site studied or within a specific group, the adoption a recognized functional role that is useful to or justified by the setting studied, familiarity with banal and routine situations, access to internal documentation, knowledge of internal codes and languages. As indicated by a researcher who took part in participant observation within a hospital, Jean Peneff,

---

[31] For a discussion on the perspectives of introducing ownership rights in the field of culture, see Brown M., 'Can Culture Be Copyrighted?', *Current Anthropology*, April 1998, Vol. 39, n°2.

'I was trying to determine not what the agents say they do but what they actually do' (Peneff, 1992, p. 10).

Unfortunately, we could not take part in participant observation within a penal institution. Although we were among the first external researchers of the Russian penal institution to conduct a sociological study with inmates, we did not obtain permission to adopt a functional role. There are as yet no social workers in Russian prisons whose role would enable a stranger to be both 'here' and 'there' at the same time. All those who work inside the prison walls are civil servants working in the penal administration, including the psychologists whose ranks have been growing since the start of the 1990s (1–2 psychologists per facility). This implies that they must go through a very lengthy admission procedure and make a commitment for the future. For these reasons, our work in the field took the form of stays lasting from a week to a month in 42 Russian prisons (over the period from the fall of 1996 to the summer of 2001).[32] The geographical area covered by our research, namely 10 regions (*oblast*) including Arkhangelsk, Ivanovo, Kostroma, Murmansk, Moscow, Perm, Sverdlovsk, Tula, Vladimir and Yaroslav, ensures that the results are sufficiently representative. Moreover, we were able to visit five types of prisons: a maximum security prison (*tur'ma*), a minimum security detention center (*kolonija obschego rejima*), a medium security detention center (*kolonija stogogo rejima*), a high security detention center (*kolonija osobogo rejima*) and a youth detention center (*vospitatel'naja kolonija*).[33] During the first few months of our field work, we accompanied a senior civil servant from the Russian penal administration, Colonel Yurij Mukanov, during his inspection trips. Following that, we were able to choose the facility we wanted to visit and the length of our stay.

The particular way in which our field work was organized accounts for the means for collecting information that were available to us:

- Structured interviews with unstructured elements, ethnological observation and sociological intervention;
- Investigation using a questionnaire; and
- Work with official documents and secondary sources.

We conducted 41 structured interviews (the list and the guide are appended). All in all, more than 50 interviews were conducted. However, since certain interviewees refused to allow us to record their interviews and as a result of certain technical difficulties, we retained only 41. The interview guide was not always rigorously respected, particularly if new elements arose during the course of the conversation.

---

[32] In 2000–2001 – as a result of a subsidy granted by the John D. and Catherine T. MacArthur Foundation (Chicago).

[33] Art. 74 of the Code for applying sentences for the Russian Federation defines a total of six penal establishments.

'Flexible interviewing led to superior accuracy when it was not obvious to respondents how the questions correspond to their circumstances' (Schober, Conrad, 1997, p. 588).

The flexible, less structured interviews were particularly pertinent during the first stages of the study. The other important aspect of the interviews involves linking them to the self-analysis of the actors. The self-analysis of the actors, according to Alain Touraine, constitutes the first element of the sociological intervention (Touraine et al., 1984, p. 93). For example, in our correspondence with Interviewee No. 3a (a total of about ten letters), we discussed the transcriptions of the interviews with him and with his fellow inmates. The interviewee was also invited to analyze an ordinary day in his life. We also asked Interviewees No. 35a and No. 35b to think about the preliminary results of the investigation after presenting the research hypotheses to them. Finally, the interviews served to support our ideal types on typologies developed by the actors themselves during the course of their daily activities. This helped us to identify 'the various modes of verbal classification used by the individuals to structure their vision of the world' (Piette, 1996, p. 51) and, in this way, to bring our research in line with the research program developed by Alfred Schutz that implies the construction of explanatory models using the elements that already exist in everyday life.

The quality of the information collected during the course of the interviews always depends on whether a relationship of trust is developed between the researcher and the interviewee. We tried not to ask direct questions or questions that could have been considered provocative. By constantly presenting ourselves as university researchers and, therefore, as someone outside the penal administration, we were able to enjoy a greater deal of trust than we would have otherwise. For example, even the prison psychologists are considered too close to the prison authority, which reduces the degree of trust they are given, particularly since they wear the same uniform as the other civil servants. 'I think that probably the psychologist should not wear the uniform. We can already start with that...'.[34] On the one hand, the inmates have an obvious need to have someone to talk to, someone who knows how to listen without judging. 'Here, I can't speak openly with anyone... We want some human communication, a willingness to understand'.[35] On the other hand, the psychologists are for the most part incapable of fulfilling this need, as a result of the lack of trust and the considerable volume of their daily work, which occasionally has nothing to do with their profession as psychologists (office work and even office maintenance). Under these circumstances, the sociological interview 'often takes on an intimate dimension, akin to a psychoanalytical relationship' (Rostang, 1994, p. 160).

The interviews were completed by means of an investigation conducted in the same penitentiaries, but using a larger sampling (for the questionnaire, see the Appendix). More than 1500 forms were distributed, of which 1310 were completed and processed. Most of the illicit categories of inmates, which we will describe in

---

[34] Interview No. 39.
[35] Letter from Interviewee No. 3a.

the section entitled '*Illicit categorization*' in the second chapter, are represented in the sample. As in the case of the interviews, all of the questionnaires were distributed personally by the author, on the condition of complete anonymity. Moreover, the quality of the statistical data was affected negatively by another factor. The statistical study of a 'small' society necessarily results in a dissonance between the average value and the norm. We calculate the average response based on local norms whose scope is limited to a segment of the social structure (an inmate, his subdivision, an illicit category of inmates). As a result, the average response does not coincide with the norm that exists throughout the penal world. Under these circumstances, the applied sociological research must be based on the construction of clusters or on the calculation of average values for each segment of the social structure taken separately. We should mention in parentheses that a similar problem also affects statistical studies of post-Soviet society in general, which indirectly justifies our second hypothesis. 'There is no unique solution with respect to the matter of what percentage of answers we can use to establish a norm' (Dubov, 1997, p. 144).

Of course, as a result of problems with organizing sociological research in French prisons, we were unable to conduct a study that was entirely similar to that in the Russian prisons, although spending three five-day stays each in the *Maison centrale d'Ensisheim* (Haut Rhin), the *Centre de détention de Melun* (Seine and Marne) and the *Centre de détention de Caen* (Calvados) has enabled us to make a few comparisons. Fifty-nine French inmates (14 in the *Maison centrale* and 45 in the *Centres de détention*) were invited to answer the same questions that we asked the Russian inmates. The choice of interviewees satisfied the requirements of representativity: we selected 10 per cent in each category of inmate, based on the nature of their crimes. Unlike our work in the Russian prisons, the questionnaires were completed by the interviewer based on the oral responses of the interviewees. In this way, we are able to clarify answers and adapt the questionnaire to the specifics of the situation in French prisons. This interview method increases the accuracy of the statistical results.

At the start of 2001, we spent a few weeks in penal institutes in the Republic of Kazakhstan (at the request of the penal institution of that country). Three hundred and ninety-six inmates in 12 facilities (one maximum security detention center, one minimum security detention center, seven reinforced security detention centers and three gaols) were interviewed. This work enabled us not only to complete the table of the post-Soviet penal world, but also to have an overview of the Soviet penal system. Unlike Russia, which initiated penal reform at the start of the 1990s, Kazakhstan is taking its first steps in this direction. Therefore, we saw a system that has remained virtually unchanged since the Soviet period. The time of the research was propitious since the penal administration in the Republic of Kazakhstan is currently trying to catch up. It has undertaken some very significant prison reforms that are, according to certain observers, even more radical than those undertaken in Russia.

Finally, in December 2001 we had got a chance to visit three penitentiaries (minimum, medium and maximum levels of security) in Quebec, Canada. This field work has been done in close cooperation with Prof. Pierre Landreville and

Sandy Lehalle (CICC, University of Montreal). One hundred and twenty inmates were randomly chosen to take part in the survey (10–20 per cent of their total number in the prisons visited). As a result, some tables in the book will include the data collected in the Canadian prisons.

In order to be able to verify our hypotheses concerning the congruence of the 'constitutions' in the penal world and Soviet society, we conducted a series of studies on the everyday lives of Russians. A team of researchers consisting of Eugenia Gvozdeva (of the Faculty of Sociology at the Lomonossov State University in Moscow), Alexander Hlopin, Sergei Patrushev (both from the Comparative Political Science Institution of the Academy of Sciences) and the author conducted three investigations, one in 1996 (a pilot investigation), another in March 1998, and a final one in June 1999 (namely after the crisis of August 1998[36]). The samples included 400 people from three regions (Moscow, Perm, St. Petersburg), 850 people from six regions (Moscow, Altaï, St. Petersburg, Ivanovo, Astrakhan, Perm) and 1351 people from 12 regions (Moscow, St. Petersburg, Altaï, Primorie, Tver, Cheliabinsk, Sverdlovsk, Novossibirsk, Lipetsk, Saratov, Astrakhan, and Briansk), respectively. The parameters for the final two, with the exception of the level of education,[37] enable us ensure the representativity of our results. Moreover, during the period from November 1998 to July 1999 and in November 2001, we conducted two surveys of Russian businessmen and a series of interviews with them.[38] The 1999 investigation sample included 174 businessmen in seven regions (Moscow, Novossibirsk, Tver, St. Petersburg, Primorie, Altaï, and Briansk) of whom 21 per cent headed small businesses, 57 per cent headed medium businesses and 22 per cent headed large businesses. In 2001, the sample consisted of 219 businessmen from six regions (Moscow, Kemerovo, Urals, Chita, Buriatia, Altaï). The ratio of small firms was larger than two years before, namely 44.5 per cent (large firms accounted for 15.5 per cent of the sample); thirty-one businessmen were interviewed, including nine from the banking sector.

Finally, we consulted the official documents of the Department of Internal Affairs (*MVD, Ministerstvo Vnutrennih Del*) and the Department of Justice (*Ministerstvo Yusticii*), as well as certain literary works that concern the penal subculture. Specifically, the works of Varlam Shalamov, who spent 20 years in the labor camps of Kolyma (Far East), served as major benchmarks for us.

---

[36] This investigation was conducted with a subsidy from the Osteuropa-Institut, Freie Universität – Berlin (in the framework of a project initiated by Prof. Klaus Segbers).

[37] The percentage of individuals who had completed higher education was almost 40 per cent, which is somewhat higher than the level reported by the State Statistics Committee (*GKS*).

[38] This work was done as part of a research project financed by the *Ufficio Italiano dei Cambi* (Rome). We are now continuing with this research with a subsidy from the *Institut des Hautes Etudes en Sécurité Intérieure* (Paris).

Chapter 2

Penal Society in Russia

After providing a general outline of our research, we will verify the hypotheses formulated in the section entitled *'Research hypotheses'* of the first chapter. Chapter 2 will focus on developing an ideal type of penal society in Russia; in Chapter 3, we will try to apply this ideal type to a reading of the typical Soviet society; and in Chapter 4, we will analyze the dynamic aspect of the interaction between formal and informal norms.

Historical markers

There is no ideal type of penal society. Its parameters depend on the institutional context in which the prison exists. Although the various prison models have common traits, including the imposed nature of authority, their details may vary considerably. Even the 'golden rule' of prison, which states that 'a prisoner's standard of living must be lower than that of the poorest worker in the society' (Perrot, 1997, p. 8), is applied differently in each country, based on the average standard of living, the crime rate, criminal and penal policy, and other socioeconomic and political factors. In terms of daily standard of living, details count: the organization of the penal space, imprisonment alone or with others, the officially recognized rights of inmates, etc. Therefore, we must consider the plurality of penal regimes known throughout history and position them with respect to the Soviet penal system.

Principal penal models

The logic of the evolution of the prison as a total institution is justified by its dual, even contradictory, nature. The prison has had two missions from the outset, namely from the time detention replaced corporal punishment and ordeal. First, the prison has a public security mission, which results in separating the criminal population from the rest of society, by placing the former under surveillance. This implies that the conditions of imprisonment are harsh enough that detention represents a true punishment for offenders.

> 'The sentencing system must be designed so that the groups mostly likely to become criminals prefer to vegetate in the most miserable conditions in freedom rather than being sentenced' (Rusche, Kirchheimer, 1994, p. 89).

In other words, the golden rule of prison is rooted in the security mission. Second, the prison's mission of social reintegration is just as important to the manner in which it functions: offenders must not only be separated and kept under surveillance, they must retain the hope of returning to normal life. The logic behind social reintegration requires a completely different approach with respect to organizing prison life.

> 'The length of the penalty must not be a measurement of the "exchange value" of the offence; it must be adjusted to the useful transformation of the inmate during his term of imprisonment' (Foucault, 1995, p. 244).

This mission gives rise to the so-called progressive system. This system exists to vary the length of the sentence and the harshness of sentencing conditions in keeping with inmates' behavior, their desire to submit to discipline, and their general docility. The first prison to operate in keeping with the progressive system was established in Australia (Norfolk Island) in the 18th Century. All of the inmates started their sentences in the harshest of conditions, and worked, in a variety of manners and at various paces, toward liberation (Tkachevskij, 1997, p. 16). The transition to a less harsh system of detention required discipline and conscientious work.

On a formal level, these two missions are equally important. Yet, in practice, the second imperative of penal policy often contradicts the first, making reconciliation difficult. The social reintegration mission questions the nature of the prison as a total institution. It presupposes the recognition of the not negligible degree of autonomy that the inmates enjoy in penal life. This autonomy is essential for learning or reactivating the norms for living in a 'large' society.

> 'When the prison is organized around the priority objective of social reintegration or treatment, it integrates, to varying degrees, the participation and representation of the inmates' (Chauvenet et al., 1994, p. 40).

The resolution of the conflict of these two missions concerning their equal importance *de jure* is left *de facto* to the discretion and the good will of the penal administrators. The results of social integration (which are distant in time) have no immediate impact for these administrators, whereas their view of the security mission is direct and prisons master this mission.

> 'If society is not sure of the priority to be attached to the tasks assigned the prison, the overriding importance of custody is perfectly clear to the officials... Rehabilitation tends to be seen as a by-product of successful performance at the tasks of custody and internal order' (Sykes, 1958, pp. 18, 38).

Although the internal operations of the prison result from its public security mission, there are several concrete models. Major prison models include convict prison, including galleys; the Auburn (Pennsylvania) system; the Philadelphia system; and the forced labor camp, including the concentration camp (Figure 2.1).

Let us take a closer look at each model, focussing on their impact on the organization of the inmates' everyday lives.

Figure 2.1 Typology of prisons

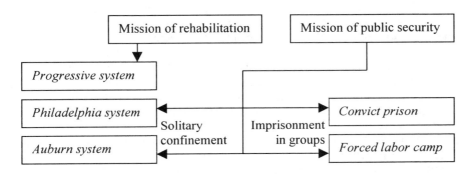

Historically, convict prisons preceded the other prison models. Convict prisons and galleys (a common practice in France from 1680 to 1810) involved imprisoning several, dozens, even hundreds of people who shared the same limited space and all moments of their everyday life. Large dormitories and large common beds (*taulas*) are also part of everyday life there. For example, in 1751 the Brest prison, which was planned to hold 2,000 inmates, housed more than 3,500 people who were placed on the *taulas* that served as beds for 20. The same brutal attack on private space was observed in the Rochefort prison, where two large rooms each held 500 people, also placed on *taulas* (Petit et al., 1991, pp. 220–221). In this respect, the situation on galleys was even worse. Two hundred to 300 galley prisoners lived on platforms measuring 45 meters long by less than 10 meters wide, chained to benches. On each bench, three to six convicts lived side by side (Petit et al., 1991, p. 100). Privacy was impossible. A more recent penal model from the 20th century is similar to the convict prison–the Stalinist forced labor camps and the Hitlerian concentration camps. Since this model will be examined in detail in the subsequent sub-sections, we will simply stress that it belongs to the model of imprisonment in groups. Large barracks of hundreds of individuals (200–400) with no internal separations became a symbol of this.[1] The first forced labor camps (*lagerja prinuditel'nyh rabot*) were created in 1918, shortly after the 1917 October Revolution, and then transformed into the Gulag (*Glavnoe Upravlenie LAGerej*) penal system, in 1934. It should be noted that there is a specific link between the Gulag model and the Hitlerian concentration camps. From 1939–1940, penal civil servants from both countries were in active contact (Rossi, 1991, pp. 182–183). This can be viewed as an example of an institutional import from one totalitarian state to another.

---

[1] See, for example, Durand Y., *La vie quotidienne des prisonniers de guerre dans les stalags, les oflags et les kommandos 1939–1945*, Paris: Hachette, 1987, p. 52.

Moreover, the magisterial path in the evolution of penal systems set aside imprisonment in groups for solitary confinement, as in the case of the Auburn and Philadelphia systems. Imprisonment in cells ensures separation and surveillance as means for maintaining order. The prisoner is separated from the least guilty–and the principle raised by Tocqueville was implemented. The Philadelphia system used solitary isolation in a cell day and night, without group work, whereas the Auburn system was characterized by solitary isolation at night and work with others in workshops during the day (Tocqueville, Beaumont, 1984, p. 68; Rusche, Kirchheimer, 1994, pp. 271–275). The absolute solitude of the Philadelphia system gave rise to various mental problems and illnesses: the only authorized activity was reading the Bible. Moreover, working in individual cells proved inefficient, unlike working in workshops: the obligation to work was often the only trace to be found of the prison's mandate concerning social reintegration. Under the Auburn system, efforts to leave the inmate nothing but his individual space were not limited to isolation in cells at night. Inmates were forced to maintain silence while working together. Despite these inconveniences, imprisoning inmates in cells has one important advantage for the inmates. It ensures minimal protection of the inmate's private space and constitutes a link with the principles for organizing everyday life outside the prison. Some comments from our interviewees concerning this matter are pertinent: 'Being imprisoned on a cell is always better [than barracks]... I felt all right in the maximum security facility, in the cells with three or four people... Why was life better there? – It's quieter there. You find your own people...'.[2] 'From my point of view, each inmate would enjoy more individuality [as long as the cell system is introduced]... It's easier to live when you choose the group... comfortable'.[3]

Despite its appeal for the penal administration and the inmates, access to the Auburn system, in its classical form, is reserved for rich societies that are prepared to allocate a portion of their resources to a sector that is generally not lucrative, the penal system. The history of cell imprisonment in France justifies this claim. In 1834, there were 11,000 cells for solitary imprisonment, with another 10,000 needed (Tocqueville, Beaumont, 1984, p. 90). In 1836, it was decided that any new prison built would provide for isolation in cells and, in 1841, *La Petite Roquette* became the first French prison to have cells. In 1853, isolation in cells was abandoned as a result of its cost. The Act of June 5, 1875 marked a return to isolation in cells as the basis for penal policy, but it could not be implemented as a result of budgetary constraints. One century later, in 1949, the penal administration implemented the cell system in seven gaols. This was increased to 25 out of 163 in 1955 (Petit et al., 1991, p. 301). Even today, it is not rare to see three inmates in a 9m² cell, although the Law requires isolation in individual cells (Observatoire international des prisons, 1996, p. 82).

---

[2] Interview No. 22. The author's questions are always <u>underlined</u>.
[3] Interview No. 23.

The penal system in Russia

Contrary to what is found in Western countries, imprisonment in cells has never played a major role in Russia. Prior to the October Revolution of 1917 (the penal administration appeared in 1879), the Philadelphia system was applied only in military prisons, whereas the barracks model (*katorga*) applied to the absolute majority of inmates. After the Revolution, the forced labor camp became the dominant model. Isolation in cells exists only in prisons (*tur'ma*), gaols (*SIZO*) and the disciplinary sectors of other types of penitentiaries (*PKT – Pomeschenie Kamernogo Tipa*, similar to the maximum security quarter; *ShIZO – Shtrafnoj IZOljator*, similar to the disciplinary quarter). Moreover, individual cells are not used. For example, the cells in *SIZO* hold from a dozen to 100–200 inmates. 'Let's look at the maximum security system. There–that's a cell system. Here, there were 14 cells in one barrack, each holding 14 people.'[4] Moreover, the cells are generally overcrowded; it's not rare to see thirty or so inmates kept in cells designed to hold 10–15. Although the new Code for Applying Sentences (CAS) includes standards governing the desirable character of cell detention, the situation has not changed much.[5] The budgetary crisis of the 1990s does not allow for much hope for radical change in the coming years. In other words, the Russia penal system is based on the principle of imprisonment in groups.

The other characteristic concerns the existence of certain elements of the progressive system. The classification of inmates had already been introduced by decrees issued by the Ministry of Justice (*NKYu, Narodnyj Commissariat Yusticii*) as early as in 1918. The first Code for Applying Sentences (CAS), enacted in 1924, defines three classes of inmates: beginner, medium and senior, with individuals shifting from one to another depending on the discipline of the inmates and their class membership: working, peasant, middle class, etc. The progressive system was abandoned in 1933 to reappear after Stalin's death in 1958 (Tkachevskij, 1997, pp. 29–35). For example, the CAS in effect classifies inmates according to their penal regime (minimum, reinforced, maximum security). Moreover, inside each penitentiary, the inmates are treated in three different manners (*uslovija soderjanija*): common, light, reinforced. Although the detention system for the inmate is determined by the Court sentence in keeping with the nature of the crime, the type of treatment depends solely on his discipline in prison.[6] Considering the two pillars of the Russian penal system described above, we would classify it as a *combination of the progressive system and the camp model* (the CAS in effect has removed the obligatory aspect of work in detention). Imprisonment in groups co-exists with the obvious differentiation of the inmates.

Imprisonment in groups and the classification of the inmates makes life in detention *social*. The cell system isolates the inmates from one another and does not allow them to develop social relationships. However, imprisonment in groups gives a social dimension to each of an inmate's actions. It is under these conditions

---

[4] Interview No. 21.
[5] *Ugolovno-ispolnitel'nyj kodeks Rossijskoj Federacii*, Moskva : Infra M, 1997, p. vi.
[6] Art. 74, 80, 121, 123, 125 of the Russian Federation CAS.

that we can speak of the penal *society*. 'The prison is a society within a society' (Sykes, 1958, p. xii). A language, a culture, social classes, and norms are all present in both cases. But there is nothing natural about the coincidence between the penal society and the society that surrounds it; it occurs under very specific conditions. Forced work in groups (first in barracks and then in the forced labor camps) accounts for the proximity of the penal society to the worker community, the artel (*rabotnaja artel*), that existed in Russia in the 15th–16th centuries. The 'constitution' of the artel included elements that we will associate with the ideal type of penal society in Russia in the following sections: an implicit contract between its members, exit barriers, egalitarianism, a sanction system, slang, a closing off from the outside, the rule that 'everyone must behave in a manner that others can understand' (Ovchinskij, Ovchinskij, 1991, p. 15; Morozov, 1991, vol. 2, p. 78).

The parameters of the Russian penal society imply the existence of a 'large' society. As at January 1, 1999, the Russian penal system included 731 facilities (all systems–minimum, reinforced and maximum security–combined), 191 gaols, 13 central facilities and 63 facilities for young people. Approximately 900,000 inmates, including 255,000 people who have been charged, are guarded by 300,000 penal administration employees. Women account for 4.4 per cent of the penal population and those under 18 years of age for 2.2 per cent. Today, this corresponds to a penal population rate equal to 730, namely 1.42 per cent of the active population–almost the same ratio as in the United States–despite the differences in the socioeconomic dynamics of both countries (Rossi, 1991, p. 449; Anisimkov, 1993, p. 25).

Table 2.1 Number of prisoners in Russia

Year	Number of prisoners
1912	183,000
1924	86,000
1927	200,000
1933	800,000
1936	839,406
1937	16,000,000
1942	18,000,000
1970	3,000,000
1980	4,000,000
2000	1,060,085

Russia and Kazakhstan, the other post-Soviet country to which we will refer, are among the most punitive countries. Although their penal population is what it was in the time of Stalin, the number of people incarcerated today (in absolute and relative figures) in both countries is greater than in most other countries in the

Table 2.2 World prison population list

Country	Prison Population	Prison Population Rate
Russia	1,060,085	730
The United States	1,860,520	680
Belarus	58,879	575
Kazakhstan	82,945	495
Bahamas	1,401	485
Belize	1,097	460
Bermuda	286	445
Kyrgyzstan	19,875	440
...	...	...
China	1,408,860	110
Canada	32,970	110
...	...	...
France	53,948	90
Italy	51,427	90
...	...	...
Indonesia	55,026	25

The 'small' society: incomplete modernization

Despite its quantitative significance, the penal society remains 'small' in terms of its structure and social organization. The transformation of the prison world into a 'large' society, namely a modern one, is far from complete. Four structural criteria–the degree of differentiation of the spheres of activity, the degree to which relationships are personalized, the degree to which norms are dual, and the institutionalization of violence–serve as markers in demonstrating this affirmation.

The absence of a public/private border

Imprisonment in groups affects the fundamental zones of autonomy, and this lack of respect could destroy the inmate's personality. With no private space in which the individual can leave behind the imposed roles and become his own master, the inmate loses control over his actions. In this way, the imposed authority is reproduced on a micro social level: the destruction of private space ruins the ability to act autonomously and, as a result, reduces the chances that the individual will start to master the transfer of control over his actions. The expansion of the public into the zones of fundamental autonomy takes place in three principal directions:

---

[7] Home Office Research, Development and Statistics Directorate, *Research Findings*, n.116, 'World Prison Population List. 2nd Edition', 2000.

- Spatial organization that excludes private space;
- Total surveillance; and
- Subjugation of actions to painstaking control.

Figure 2.2 Plan of a barrack

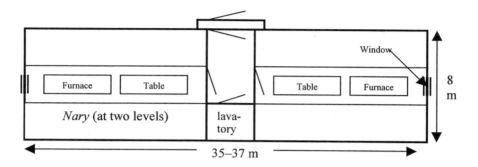

Life in a barrack (convict prison, forced labor camp, penal colony) involves sharing every moment of everyday life, even the most intimate, with other inmates. Until the 1960s, the Soviet inmate did not even have a personal place to sleep: he shared *nary*, large beds without partitions similar to the *taulas*, with dozens of inmates. That was the model of the forced labor camp in the Stalinist period (see Figure 2.2 for a scheme of a barrack for 200–300 inmates) (Rossi, 1991, p. 24).

Figure 2.3 A typical dormitory

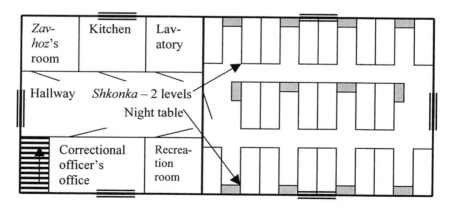

In other words, each individual in a barrack only had 0.8–1.5m² of living space. The *nary* still exist in certain overcrowded cells in gaols (*SIZO*). 'In overcrowded cells you have to sleep with someone beside you. Never alone'.[8] The CAS, implemented in 1961, replaced the *nary* with individual bunks, *shkonka* (1.8×0.5 m) (Abramkin, Chijov, 1992, p. 86). This type of bed is still used. Moreover, the spatial organization of the barrack is similar today to that described. Each subdivision in the penal colony (*otrjad*, 40–150 inmates) has a large dormitory with no internal partitions (see Figure 2.3 for a diagram of a typical dormitory). The beds, *shkonka*, are bunks–there is always one two-place bunk to the side and another above or below. The inmates are not generally allowed to select their neighbors–the officer in charge of the *otrjad* shows them their places.

This inability to master one's living space results in numerous conflicts. First, the person closest to the inmate in physical terms is not necessarily in his social space. 'I still have 12 years to spend here. They [the administration] put me beside a young guy. We look at the world in completely different ways... I can't do anything about it. He can't either'.[9] Even worse, overcrowding often deprives the bed of its individual character: two inmates share the bed, depending on their schedules. 'The guys, darn it (*blja*), come back from the shop–they share the same *shkonka*. When one inmate is in the shop, the other sleeps on the *shkonka*'[10] and *vice versa*. Second, the internal penal rules prohibit the inmates from dividing up the space in the dormitory in order to reduce the negative impact of unwanted neighbors. Moreover, the inmates are not allowed to personalize their living space with photos or postcards above their beds. 'Inmates are not allowed to place curtains over the bed, change the bed without permission from the administration, post photos, reproductions, postcards, newspaper clippings on the walls, night tables and beds'.[11] '[The administration] has not allowed us to set up areas for 4–6, 8 people. They made us break down the last partition. We come back from work, for example, and we want to rest. And the others want to listen to music. It's very upsetting... Every human being should have his own corner'.[12]

The natural reaction to conducting everyday life in public space involves searching for what Erving Goffman calls 'free places', 'the space that the individual demands for himself alone, where he tries to ensure... a certain degree of independence and tacitly recognized rights that he does not share with others' (Goffman, 1968, p. 298), namely through focussing on small material possessions as proof of autonomy. The model of the forced labor camp offers the inmate a few opportunities that help him find an almost private territory. First, the exercise of certain trades involves solitary work or work in small groups. One interviewee, a heating system mechanic, remains alone in a small shop that has become a sort of private space for him.[13] The librarians, carpenters, *zavhoz* (person responsible for

---

[8] Interview No. 28 (He refers to a cell with 150 inmates in the *Butyrka*, famous gaol in Moscow).
[9] Interview No. 36.
[10] Interview No. 38.
[11] *Pravila vnutrennego rasporjadka ispravitel'nyh uchrejdenij*, Moskva : 1997, p.5 (§3^3 of Regulations).
[12] Interview No. 1a.
[13] Interview No. 13.

maintaining the offices of the *otrjad*), *dneval'nye* (administrative building cleaning man) all enjoy the privilege of a personal 'office'. Most other inmates are forced to find private space on their beds. Occasionally, the only way to be alone is to 'live on one's bed and move as little as possible' (Rostang, 1994, p. 76). 'What do you do to get them to leave you alone, to be alone? – I lie down on the bed and cover my head'.[14]

Likewise, walks outside are another means for avoiding unwanted contact. The space in the facility is divided into several local zones (see Figure 2.4 for a plan of a typical facility). Since the 1970s, inmates have been allowed to walk about within the local zone of their *otrjad* without restrictions. A slang word that was very popular with young Russians in the 1990s, *tusovka*, originated in the inmates' walks there. Given the dimensions of the zones (approximately 150–400 m²), the inmate can only take a few steps back and forth without stopping, alone or accompanied (*tusovat'sja*). 'I go outside... I like to walk outdoors... I like to be alone. I really miss being alone'.[15] The inmates are very intolerant of restrictions on movements inside the facility but outside the local zones. Occasionally, an inmate's friends, therefore his 'reserved territory' (another Goffman expression meaning 'spaces reserved for a group') are not nearby but in another subdivision (*otrjad*). The willingness to negotiate the openness of the local zones, so obvious in many of the facilities visited, is just the opposite side of the coin in the fight for autonomy and the right to control social contacts in everyday life.

Figure 2.4 Plan of a typical facility

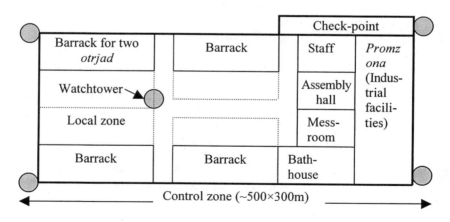

The absence of institutional devices for protecting private space gives value to owning small things. The ability to organize the material world *as he wants to*, control over it, serves the inmate as imperfect substitutes for social autonomy.

---

[14] Interview No. 19.
[15] Interview No. 9.

From this perspective, the contents of the night table become a symbol of the inmate's relative independence. There is even an expression concerning this way of life, 'me and my night table' (often used pejoratively). 'If someone lives like "me and my night table", he has created, as it is said, his own small form of communism, there are no problems'.[16] 'Since I've been here, I've never spoken to anyone, I've always managed on my own. I've never given anyone any pretext... I live like a snail... I have a night table, I have a *shkonka*. I come in, I lie down... What more...'.[17]

Moreover, even control over this very limited material world is never perfect. Restrictions about the possession of objects, and regular searches affect the material devices of autonomy. The list of objects inmates are allowed to own is *exhaustive*; it includes 19 items[18]. For example, toilet water, typewriters, cameras, video equipment, colored pencils are all prohibited in prison.

> 'Material possessions are so large a part of the individual's conception of himself that to be stripped of them is to be attacked at the deepest layers of personality' (Sykes, 1958, p. 69).

The transparency of the public/private border makes surveillance easy and omnipresent: both the penal authorities and all of the inmates are committed to it. Within the institutional context of the prison, people start to watch one another, whether voluntarily or not. Imprisonment in groups transforms this surveillance, a behavior that is viewed poorly in other contexts, into a natural strategy for everyday life. 'The camp system operates on denunciation... That's all there is. Everyone watches everyone else, denounces them, stares at them, indiscreetly'.[19] One of the higher levels in the informal hierarchy of the inmates, which we will refer to in the section entitled '*The illicit Guard: the figure of the smotrjashij*', is called *smotrjashij*, namely the one who watches. Obviously, it bears the mark of omnipresent surveillance.

Figure 2.5 Ego development

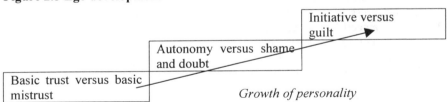

Growth of personality

Minute control of daily actions and the lack of space in which the individual can be his own master bring the psychological structure of the inmate in line with

---

[16] Interview No. 1b.
[17] Interview No. 36.
[18] *Pravila vnutrennego rasporjadka ispravitel'nyh uchrejdenij*, p.22–23 (Appendix nos. 1, 2 of Regulations).
[19] Interview No. 23.

that of the infant. According to Erik Erikson, transforming the infant into an adult capable of acting autonomously takes three steps (Figure 2.5). The situation of dependence raises doubt as to the completion of the last two steps. Step 1 will be discussed in the section entitled *'Norm of trust'* (Erikson, 1959, pp. 54–88).

Complete submission of control over authority suppresses the inmate's initiative. Moreover, the very fact of being placed in detention for an infraction fuels the sense of guilt (not necessarily with respect to the victim). Take, for example, the comments made by an inmate who had murdered his brother. 'It happened by accident. No, not by accident–I was performing my duty as a father. Well, so I committed an infraction. I don't regret anything that happened. He was filth, although you're not supposed to talk about the dead like that, although he was my brother... what's painful–is that my children are suffering for my lack of responsibility, my mistake... The children are suffering for my error... I couldn't stop myself, but it's my children who are suffering. Just after my arrest, my son went to prison too. They sent him to another facility'.[20] As for evidence of feelings of confusion, a total of 13 per cent of the inmates interviewed described their usual situation in these terms. As the penal psychologists we worked with confirmed, the profile of the inmates' answers to the standard MMPI inventory are very different from that for an adult and include several elements of that for a child. Therefore,

'The dependent status of the prisoner clearly represents a serious threat to the prisoner's self image as a fully accredited member of adult society' (Sykes, 1958, p. 76).

Personalized relationships

Detention places the individual in a situation not only of psychological stress (several of our interviewees experienced a psychological shock during the first days of their stay in the *KPZ (Kamera Predvaritel'nogo Zakluchenija)* which precedes the gaol), but also social stress. A study on the experience of the first few months spent living abroad shows that this change, which is less radical in a social context, does cause 'a statistically significant and clinically substantial increase in emotional distress in the course of acculturation' (Furukawa et al., 1998, p. 58). The social connections, which the individual is used to, including those that were most intense before, are destroyed, leaving him without social support. Not even family relations escape the crisis: 19.5 per cent of the Russian inmates in our sample are divorced and 50.2 per cent never married.[21] The inmate is obliged to

---

[20] Interview No. 16.

[21]Marital status:	Russia, N=1310	Kazakhstan, N=396	France, N=59	Canada, N=120
Married	20.9	26.8	28.8	34.2†
Divorced	19.5	21.2	25.4	12.5
Single	50.2	41.7	37.3	50
Widower/widow	2.7	2	6.8	×
No answer	6.7	8.3	1.7	3.3

† 5 per cent - lawful matrimony, 29.2 per cent - civil marriage.

rely only on himself to solve everyday problems and imprisonment results in a virtually complete atomization. The results of our investigation indicate the profound destruction of the usual social space. Despite imprisonment in groups, 25 per cent of the inmates describe their personal situation in terms of solitude:

Table 2.3 Usual psychological situation

What is your usual psychological situation?	Russia, %[22]	Kazakh-stan	France	Canada
N (number of responses)	1310	391	56	120
Expectation of changes for the better	43.2	53.5	×	×
Resolution to change the life	33.9	41.7	51.8	48.7
Fatigue	32.4	37.3	17.9	13.5
Solitude	25.9	25.3	19.6	17.7
Irritation	25.2	15.6	23.2	8.4
Compassion (*sostradanie*)	10.4	13.6	×	×
Anxiety	9.8	9.7	3.6	12.6
Confusion	3.2	3.3	8.9	4.2
Patience	×	49.9	64.3	32.8
Anxiety or *confusion* (see the characteristics of child's mentality)	13	13	12.5	16.8

Let us compare the parameters for social support in prison and in Russian society in general:

---

[22] Since it was possible to choose several responses to certain questions, the total number of answers may occasionally exceed 100 per cent.

Table 2.4 Sources of social support

Sources of anticipated (A) and real (R) help, %			N	Myself, nobody else	Close relatives	Friends	Other inmates / Colleagues	Government	Prisoners' leaders	Prison's ward and officers	Social workers
In Russian society		R[23] [99]	1351	63.1	25.7	6.9	5.1	5.6	×	×	×
		R [98]	850	42	41	18	4	4	×	×	×
		A [98]		49	44	27	6	5	×	×	×
In prison	Rus.	R	1310	19.8	61		19.3	1.1	5.4	4.6	×
		A		71.3	28.6		5.2	1.1	3.5	3.1	×
	Kaz.	R	391	15	44.9	20.4	21.7	0.5	6.7	5.2	×
		A		69.1	22.5	13	7.2	0.8	4.9	4.6	×
	Can.	R	120	58.6	57.8	21.6	11.2	0	×	5.2	7.8
		A		69.5	67.8	31.4	15.3	0.9	×	7.5	10.2
	Fr.	R	59	26.3	52.6	22.8	10.5	0	×	15.8	14
		A		47.4	57.6	17	8.5	1.7	×	27.1	17

The expectation of social support is visibly lower in prison than in the society that surrounds it, regardless of the parameter used. The prisoners rely on themselves and do not believe in social and institutional support. However, the need to feel support is felt more intensely in detention, as indicated by the answers to the question concerning the assistance actually received. On the one hand, the inmate's destroyed autonomy creates a very strong demand for assistance, for assistance in otherwise banal activities (such as purchasing consumer products); on the other hand, the destruction of social relations make such assistance unlikely and even exceptional.[24]

This dilemma between the destruction of old relationships and the need for social support implies a search for a new form of socialization, adapted to the conditions of imprisonment. This new form of socialization is built on personalized

---

[23] Question A: 'Where do you find support in a difficult situation?'. Question R: 'Who really helps you in a difficult situation?' Here, and in the rest of the text we use [98] to indicate the results of the survey made in March 1998 and [99] for the result of the June 1999 survey.

[24] Gresham Sykes noted that almost 40 per cent of inmates in a maximum security facility had received no visits from the outside in years (Sykes, 1958, p.65).

Have your close relatives visited you last month?	Russia, N=539	Kazakhstan, N=396	France, N=59	Canada, N=120
Yes	22.8	19.7	59.3	57.5
No	40.8	51.3	40.7	41.7
No answer	36.4	29	0	0.8

relations and seldom extends beyond their limits. For example, in the nazi concentration camps, the difference between the barrack, a 'mechanical' community produced by co-existence in the same limited space, and camaraderie, 'the relationships formed by each prisoner of war, not with the mass of men surrounding him but with a few, to whom he is particularly attached as a result of shared exceptional circumstances' (Durand, 1987, p. 156), was obvious. Our hypothesis involves demonstrating that *everything that is social in the penal world is local, personalized and rooted in face-to-face relationships*. The 'small' society includes only people who know one another personally, either directly, or through chains of personal acquaintances that are occasionally very long. Let us take a close look at certain pieces of evidence that enable us to define the social structure of the 'small' society both negatively and positively.

Let us start with a positive definition. The personalization of relationships helps inmates develop a complete portrait of the individual, which is not reduced to apparent traits, actualized in the concrete link. Face-to-face dealings provide information about *all* of the roles that make up the 'repertory' of the encounter. These details count in a face-to-face relationship.

> 'Detail is provided as a "surplus" that allows one to penetrate into "worlds" that are more or less actualized, more or less potentialized, within other worlds' (Piette, 1996, p. 170).

Unlike the ordinary man, the prisoner quickly learns to know a contact after a few minutes of conversation and even simple observation. Gestures, small words, posture, eyes, voice often say more about an individual than his words. 'In the time you spend here you learn how to pick people out after a half-hour, an hour'.[25] 'I can tell how honest someone is, without a doubt, as soon as he comes in the door'.[26] 'I know a guy, how would I put it, who spent a lot of time here. One glance and he could tell everything about a new guy. This one has just been incarcerated; that one already knows everything'.[27]

Personalizing the relationship highlights the link and, above all, the absence of a link between an individual's appearance and the hidden, invisible aspects of his behavior. 'Conversation is not just words, it includes emotions, feelings. It's a good thing to see who you're speaking to. Sometimes we write to an inmate in another cell. Everything is going fine, even fantastic. Unfortunately when you meet them, you find that people are completely different... And you get to thinking that it would be better to keep up the correspondence without seeing him [your contact]'.[28] Moreover, the impression that the inmate gives the other inmates when he arrives indicates the position he wants within the prison community (see the section entitled '*Illicit categorization*'). A character in the famous Soviet movie 'Gentlemen of Fortune' (*Djentelmeny udachi*), who looked like a very dangerous

---

[25] Interview No. 3a.
[26] Interview No. 23.
[27] Interview No. 28.
[28] Letter from Interviewee No. 3a. Several Internet users might agree with this observation.

criminal, who escaped from prison, plays that person in the prison community, at the request of the police. Although he has no in-depth knowledge of the criminal world, he tries to play, successfully, on appearances. One interviewee justified the conditions of the pertinence of such a strategy. 'What you don't talk about has no important role. The main thing is your behavior. The way in which you move, speak, behave. If you sit down and start to murmur... No one asks you too many questions. We talk a little and we watch. Where do you come from, what was your crime–these questions are not important... What type of information do you need to get an idea of what someone is like? – Information about the people who lived next to him'.[29] In other words, personal knowledge serves as almost the only guarantee as to the correct interpretation of the intentions and actions of others. In the penal world, where other means of interpretation are lacking (contractual or civic commitments, the institutional position), they are replaced by personal knowledge.

As the last sentence indicates, 'knowing how to create a good impression', is never enough, as a result of the underlying requirement to provide pertinent references, namely to justify one's reputation. Therefore, personalized relationships do not exclude their generalization, which is always incomplete since it is the result of a local chain of relationships. Moreover, this does not render reputation any less effective in providing each new contact of an inmate with information about the inmate's intentions and possible actions. 'Ten to fifteen years go by, I can confirm this personally, and you come across the same inmate. It [his previous behavior] becomes explicit even at the end of 10 years, he can't do anything about it. He will be treated as he deserves'.[30] 'There was one inmate who made a good impression when he arrived. But then we learned that 15 years ago he was... [a passive homosexual]. Did someone recognize him? – Yes, we recognized him, yes... You can't get away from that'.[31]

In order to explain the lasting character of reputation, we could refer, first, to the density of the chains of personalized relationships and the fact that they overlap. All you have to do is know an inmate in a facility and he will reactivate his knowledge and tell you everything you need to know about any inmate. The quest for information takes the form of *ksiva* or *maljava*, a small word used secretly with the convoys of prisoners from one facility to another, from one region to another. This system is referred to as the 'camp radio' (*lagernoe radio*). 'There are convoys every day, information is transmitted every day. Everything concerning the prison is disseminated instantly. So, how long does it take, for example, to send a message from Moscow to Arkhangelsk? – The length of an ordinary trip from Moscow to Arkhangelsk–one day, 24 hours. One day is enough to get the information you need? – Yes, easily'.[32] 'It's very simple. If he [the inmate from whom you want to get information] is in another facility, in one

---

[29] Interview No. 33
[30] Interview No. 3a.
[31] Interview No. 22.
[32] Interview No. 23. Arkhangelsk is approximately 1,500 km north of Moscow, along the shore of the White Sea.

month, in two months, when *maljava* has made a round-trip, we'll know everything'.[33] Inside the prison, information is disseminated even faster using 'Morse code': a series of taps on the cell wall corresponds to a given letter (Table 2.5) (Rossi, 1991, p. 222). The slang term *probit'* (literally, to knock) means that someone is asking for information with the 'Morse code' or any other aspect of the 'camp radio'.

Table 2.5 A system of encoding the information

		\multicolumn{5}{c}{Second knock (raw number)}
		1	2	3	4	5
First knock (line number)	I	A	B	V	G	D
	II	E	J	Z	I	...

Second, the high level of repeat offenders in Russia (see Table 2.6[34]) and the principle of the territorial application of the sentence (the convict usually remains in the region where he committed the crime) increase the likelihood that inmates will run across one another several times during their terms in detention. 'Do you already know everyone in your *otrjad* [one month after arriving] ? – Yes. All 70 people? – Of course. Some I met in the *SIZO*, some I knew before I came here. We're countrymen'.[35] 'Over there [in the *SIZO*] there were a lot of guys from my city, which made life easy–we had common interests, common acquaintances. It was easier to adapt there'.[36]

Table 2.6 Level of repeat offenders (per cent of repeated commitment of offence)

Year	%	Year	%	Year	%
1992	38.8	1995	33.5	1998	33.7
1993	37.1	1996	33		
1994	35.2	1997	33.3		

The strength of personalization as a major support in relationships becomes a weakness as soon as we take an interest in collective actions that extend beyond local relationships and the collective consciousness. There is an opposite side to personalization, its negative definition. Answers to the question 'What do you mean by solidarity?' reveal that the ability to act together decreases as the spatial distance between those who might take part in such action increases:

---

[33] Interview No. 33.
[34] Source: http://www.gks.ru *'Russia in figures – 1999'*.
[35] Interview No. 32.
[36] Interview No. 34.

Table 2.7 Meanings of solidarity

	Russia	France	Canada
N	719	57	120
Capacity to help the relatives	34.2%	68.4	48.2
Expectation of any reciprocal help	24.9	10.5	13.4
Support of any requirements which you consider as fair	17.3	15.8	19.6
Capacity to help the person who finds him or herself in the same situation	28.5	24.6	29.5

The concept of non-personalized solidarity, the support for just demands *regardless of their origin*, is accepted by less than one-quarter of the inmates. The sense of belonging to a collective, to a collective subject, can also appear in responses to the question on the scope of the sense of responsibility:

Table 2.8 The scope of the sense of responsibility

Do you feel responsibility for...	*per cent of answers*							
	Russia		Kazakhstan		France		Canada	
N	1310		396		59		120	
	Yes	No	Yes	No	Yes	No	Yes	No
Your own actions	86.6	2.6	88.4	2.3	91.5	6.8	94.2	0.8
Your children's actions	62.1	14.7	63.6	9.8	76.3	20.3	45.8	20
Actions of close relatives	45	32.1	42.7	26.8	45.8	49.2	14.2	52.5
Actions of your own people	37.5	38.9	38.4	31.3	39	50.8	11.7	54.2
Events in this prison	20	43.7	32.1	34.3	37.3	59.3	10.8	56.7
Actions of your ancestors	15.6	57.3	17.7	48.7	20.3	78	5	60
Actions of prisoners' leaders	12.2	60.5	12.9	50.5	×	×	×	×
Actions of other inmates	10.5	61.5	11.9	53	×	×	×	×
Actions of the government	6.6	65.6	7.6	57.3	18.6	78	5.8	59.2

In other words, there is a very strong correlation between the degree of the spatial and temporal proximity of an action and the willingness to take responsibility. Responsibility for everything that exceeds the local, the personal, is rejected.

Licit categorization

The tendency to personalize social relationships accounts for the characteristics of the progressive system that are specific to the Soviet prison. The progressive system supposes that the penal population is explicitly subdivided into several sub-categories, depending on the nature of the crime committed by the inmate and his discipline within the prison. For example, in the 1930s, inmates were classified in two categories: 'friends of the people' and 'enemies of the people' (Rossi, 1991, p. 105; Shalamov, 1998, p. 374). The first category included common-law prisoners, including repeat thieves. The reintegration mission applied only to this category:

the easiest positions and chores were reserved for these inmates. The se category included primarily political prisoners (article 58$^{1\text{-}11}$ of the 1926 P_ Code 'Counter-Revolutionary Crimes'), and reintegration was not considered.

Neither the crime nor the inmate's position within the licit hierarchy imposed by the administration completely and univocally determines his actual position within the prison community. Only exceptionally is the nature of the crime taken into account in the evaluation of the inmate. Even in such cases, the gravity of a crime, as perceived by the inmates, is very different from the manner in which it is qualified by the Penal Code. Rapists are an exception, particularly child rapists. 'We never respected rapists. We go after (*sprashivali*) child rapists... I've even done it myself. And I've seen it happen many times... even in the cell. We've broken people's arms in the cell. It was just a bit of meat that we would have thrown out of the cell if the guards hadn't stopped us in time... against those who rape children 12–13 years old. Children are children'.[37] 'We go after [rapists] of little children. We force them to become passive homosexuals (*opuskajut*). Have you ever met such an inmate? – Yes, I have. Are there inmates like that here? – No, I haven't met any. Hey, I did meet one. He raped a little girl, 6 or 8 years old... He was immediately placed in a separate cell'.[38]

Other types of crimes are not taken into consideration in everyday life. 'It's the person's characteristics that are really important. Where he comes from: whatever his crime is–Article 158 [of the Penal Code–banditry] or Article 162 [robbery]–it's not important'.[39] 'At the start, I thought that if you had killed someone, for example, a police officer, people would respect you... No. It doesn't matter whether you've stolen a wallet or killed someone. It's your basic characteristics, your true nature, that counts'.[40] The fact that licit categories are insignificant does not mean that the inmates have no interest in knowing them. Information about the nature of the crime sometimes serves to verify what the inmate says about other matters during his initial 'appearance'. In other words, verifying the information the inmate provides about his crime helps his fellow inmates ensure his minimal honesty. 'You go into the cell–and you're asked (*probivajut*) about your crime. No matter what you say. Usually your co-accused are aware of it. People find out right away. They read your charges'.[41] The transparency of the presumed crime goes against not only the presumption of innocence (in gaols) but also the need to protect the inmate's private space. For example, in France there is a rule that states that 'the guard cannot try to find out the crimes committed by the inmates' (Marchetti, 1997, p. 69) and cannot spread information about them either. In the Soviet facilities, the details of the crime were provided in the inmate's personal booklet, which was kept in the office of the person responsible for the *otrjad*. Not only the guards but also some of the inmates (such as those who clean the office), were familiar with the information. Common

---

[37] Interview No. 18.
[38] Interview No. 30.
[39] Interview No. 33.
[40] Interview No. 20.
[41] Interview No. 18.

knowledge of the details of everyone's crimes provides additional evidence that the private/public border is not respected in prison.

Illicit categorization

The inmate's personal reputation indicates to which category in the illicit hierarchy spontaneously developed by the inmates he belongs. Illicit categorization serves as an example as to how the individuals develop norms and their voluntary submission to them. Although the prison model does not exclude the formation of an inmate society, namely it is simply any variation of imprisonment in groups, the first proof of the autonomy of that society lies in the development of typologies that differ from those imposed by the formal authority. In his study of American prison society, Gresham Sykes speaks of thirteen categories used by American inmates to coordinate their interactions (Sykes, 1958, pp. 87–105). The inmates who give the guards information about the internal life of the prison community are called 'rats', which is very revealing. Rats are similar to another type of inmate, the 'center man', who internalizes the norms, values and behaviors imposed by the guards. The 'gorilla' does not hesitate to use physical force and violence to take what he wants. The 'hipsters' only use violence with weaker inmates, who cannot resist aggression, the 'weaklings'. The 'merchants' are peddlers who seek profit above all, even to the detriment of solidarity among inmates. The nickname 'fish' is used for a new arrival, an inmate who is not familiar with prison rules. The 'punks' are passive homosexuals and have been transformed into homosexuals by force whereas 'fags' are 'inborn' homosexuals. The 'ball busters' are known for their obvious disobedience of the guards' orders, totally refusing the licit system. The 'toughs' pick quarrels with other inmates rather than the guards. Finally, the 'real men', whose behavior is highly respected, try to maintain their integrity without submitting totally to the guards and without getting into an obvious conflict with them.

The cast system has a long history in Russian systems. Illicit categories existed in Russian prisons well before the October Revolution of 1917 (Gurov, 1995, pp. 91–94; Anisimkov, 1993, pp. 18–19). Audacity and cruelty set the *ivans* apart from the other categories of inmates and ensure them a role as a third party in conflicts among card players. The *hrapy* (contemporary Russian preserves a trace of this in the adverb *nahrapom* – right off, with no concern for means) preferred to have others act in their interests. The nickname *shuler* was used for the big card players and traces of this term are also present in contemporary Russian. The *asmadei* are the Russian equivalent of the 'merchants': they try to transform everything they get a hand on into merchandise. A position as a dependent with respect to the illicit centers of authority was described by the term *shpanka*. Small street gangs of youths aged primarily 8–16 kept the name *shpana* during the Soviet period. The *jigany* included inmates who had violated the norms and rules developed in prison. Finally, the most diverse group was the thieves (*vory*), which included more than 25 sub-categories, depending on specialization: house thieves, pickpockets, shoplifters, etc.

Although it is less diversified, the categorization is reinforced in the forced labor camps. The old categories disappeared, replaced by new ones. Farther on, we will speak only of those categories that still exist. Regardless of the type of inmate, or where he is located, the categories we will describe are omnipresent. In other words, these are general categories, specific to the 'small' prison society as a whole (Figure 2.6). 'I arrive in a facility, I go into a barrack, I go to a dormitory. The place occupied by an inmate tells me what he's like. Pederasts live here, "suits" live there... This place is for the "roosters", with "men" over there, and thieves there...'.[42]

Figure 2.6 Categories of the prisoners' society

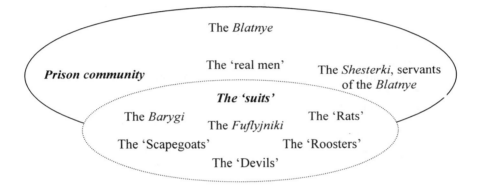

- The *blatnye* (*pripotelye*–in facilities for youths), carry the prison subculture as an alternative to the norms imposed by the penal authority. They respect illicit norms and values even when severely punished by the administration.
- The 'real men' (*mujiki, pacany*–in colonies for youths), who attempt to acquire autonomy by maintaining a distance with respect to the guards as well as the *blatnye*. 'The man, the real man, that was the second level after the *blatnye*'.[43] The *mujiki* view work as the solution to their problems in incarceration. Work in groups also gives them a sense of solidarity. 'The traditional norms consisted first... in humanity and aid to the "men", the workers (*rabotjagi*)'.[44]
- The marginal individuals in the penal world, the 'suits' (like in a card game; *masti, sherst', neputevye*), have no rights as citizens in the penal city. They are excluded from common social life and they interact only within their category. The 'suits' are always set aside, in a marginal position in the penal space. 'There was a special cell for the "suits". Was this an administrative decision? – Yes, the administration decided on that to avoid problems'.[45] The marginals

---

[42] Interview No. 21.
[43] Interview No. 21.
[44] Interview No. 25.
[45] Interview No. 32.

account for a small number (a few dozen) of the penal population. A recent tendency involves 'inflating' their number. 'Probably more than half of them rank lower than the *putevye*. I'd say 60 percent. The "rats" and the others'.[46] 'Not half. Maybe one-third... Not half of the lower guys'.[47] The marginals are divided into numerous sub-categories:

- The 'scapegoats' and the 'woodpeckers' (*kozly, djatly*), who collaborate openly with the guards. The 'scapegoats' count on the support of the administration in their everyday life; the other inmates often criticize them for their denunciations. 'They will denounce someone for a pack of cigarettes. Two "woodpeckers" meet and pick a fight. Both look for a guard. The second one denounces the first and gets a pack of cigarettes. The first denounces the second and gets a pack of cigarettes too. They're both happy. They walk about together'.[48] The case of the scapegoats clearly demonstrates the conflict between the principle of personalization and the general nature of the categories. On the one hand, 'being a "scapegoat" is painful'.[49] On the other, 'There are no bad positions, just bad people. The *zavhoz* [the person responsible for maintaining the premises, an official position involving ongoing contact with the administration] is the *zavhoz*. If he does his job right, no one will say anything to him. If he works with the administration, that's his problem'.[50]

- The inmates serving sentences for economic crimes (such as speculation, during the Soviet period) as well as those responsible for the trafficking that is omnipresent even in prison, are pejoratively called *baryga* or *baryjnik*. 'Before being imprisoned, he was a cooperator [a small businessperson in the Gorbachev period, when cooperatives were the only form of private enterprise recognized by the Law]. So, he's nothing. The pickpockets contribute [materially, see the section entitled '*Common funds*'] to our common cause, whereas these types never do. What about the speculators? – No. A *baryga* is a *baryga*. What do you mean by *baryga* ? – A guy who's been in business... A store employee is a *baryga*. He cheated everyone: me, you too... Cheated on the weight and the quality of the products, eh? Where was the *baryga* positioned in the illicit hierarchy? – Below the "men"'.[51]

- The sub-category of *fuflyjniki* includes card players who refuse to or cannot pay their gambling debts. The notion of debt is sacred in the penal world and a failure to recognize a debt forces the gambler outside the city. 'He didn't win enough to pay back the debt and he continues to play and lose. That's called *fuflo*. The *fuflyjnik* is worse than the pederast. He's got himself

---

[46] Interview No. 34.
[47] Interview No. 20.
[48] Interview No. 33.
[49] Interview No. 33.
[50] Interview No. 12.
[51] Interview No. 22. During the Soviet period, store employees enjoyed privileged access to products available in short supply and occasionally enjoyed them when the rest of the population could not.

in a painful position–he has to pay... He looks for money here and there. In short, he abases himself. He's already lost, capable of anything, any filth... A normal man is afraid of him'.[52]

- The inmates who do not know how to care for themselves and stay clean are called 'devils' (*cherti*). 'They're always dirty–they don't wash and they don't do the laundry'.[53]
- The 'rats' in Russia (*krysy*), unlike those in the United States, are punished for small thefts in prison: a pack of cigarettes from a night table, a pair of pants from the prison infirmary, etc.
- The 'roosters' (*petuhi*, the lowly–*opushennye*, the pederasts–*pederasty*) are converted by force into passive homosexuals. They are disciplined in this brutal manner for crimes that are considered capital crimes by the inmates: the rape of a young child, a denunciation that had serious consequences, recurrent petty theft, etc. The inmates positioned at the lowest level in the illicit hierarchy represent a non-negligible portion of the penal population. 'When I arrived in a facility for the first time, in 1970, there were three "roosters" out of a total of 1,200 people. Only three! Then their number grew to 23. In 1973, when I arrived in another facility, there was a special *otrjad* for "roosters". They lived apart; the administration kept them away from the others. And now? There are a lot in each *otrjad*'.[54] The stigma of passive homosexual alerts each new player to the potential of the 'rooster'. Crimes committed by the 'roosters' are viewed so poorly that not only social contact, but even physical contact can result in the 'contamination' of the unwary player, who then moves into a lower category. 'Yes, I'm not a good Christian; I'm not ready to eat with him [the degraded inmate]. I try to treat them all right, I let them smoke cigarettes... But I will never take a cigarette from one of them'.[55] This is why the 'roosters' are separated from the other inmates, physically as well as socially. 'The pederasts know their place. They sleep to the side, they eat to the side... Their *shkonka* are placed to the side, their mugs to the side. They were forbidden to enter a canteen. They were forbidden to sleep in a dorm. They slept in a hallway or elsewhere... they couldn't do anything, they had no rights... that's why it's called "disinfecting someone"; everyone knows he's a pederast–and will never speak to him'.[56] The norms that ensure social separation are particularly obvious and sophisticated in the case of young inmates. They pay attention to the small touches, regardless of how fortuitous they may be. 'How is one transformed into a *neputevye*? – Your fork, your spoon, your mug touched that of a *neputevyj* in the canteen. If you continue to eat, well...'.[57] 'You sit down, your mug touches that of a *neputevyj*. That

---

[52] Interview No. 21.
[53] Interview No. 33.
[54] Interview No. 21.
[55] Interview No. 13.
[56] Interview No. 21.
[57] Interview No. 30.

counts. However, if your plate touches that of a *neputevyj*, that doesn't count. There are six people at a table. It's not easy to avoid brief contacts. What do I do if I'm hungry? – That's normal. But you stay and you don't eat. Plus, it depends. Here's some soup, here's the dish for the day. If your soup mug touched that of a *neputevyj*, you can't eat the soup'.[58]

The hierarchical structure of the categories, its foundation in personalized chains of relationships, the rigidity of the norms that regulate interactions among their representatives illustrate the traditional nature of the prison city. Is the penal world completely reduced to the domestic world or is tradition one element among many in the social construction of that world? It appears that an initiation to the illicit rules closely resembles the initiation rites specific to traditional societies. An individual who arrives for the first time in a cell is ignorant of anything that is not obvious. The significance of a given behavior, action or a single word is not obvious and could appear contrary to the intentions of the neophyte. The new arrival

> 'must question almost everything that appears natural for the members of the new group. He is excluded from the experiences that make up the group's past. He is a man without a history' (Schutz, 1987, p. 224).[59]

In the traditional society, the uncertainty generated by the arrival of a neophyte is eliminated by having him go through all the steps in the evolution of the 'small' society in a symbolic manner (Girard, 1972, pp. 389–391).[60] The new arrival is obliged to learn the norms and the illicit categories by doing. Taking into consideration the high number of repeat offenders among Soviet delinquents, the initiation to the penal subculture occurs only once, during their initial incarceration, often when they are under 18 years of age. 'Today, there are few who have gone through that school (penal institution for young people) although it is necessary. It stays with you for life... what you learned on your own'.[61]

The study of a penal institution for young people demonstrates several variations on the treatment of new arrivals that could be interpreted as initiation rites. Penal institutions for young people, the *maloletka*, have a reputation as being painful places, as a result of both the omnipresent control of the prison administration and the multiple tests (*propiska*) that young inmates are obliged to go through. 'When I arrived in the cell, there were the "older guys" who had already spent a year or two in prison. It was a tradition. It was transmitted from one generation to the next. The various *propiski*... It was painful. Many couldn't stand

---

[58] Interview No. 33.

[59] An extreme case of the ignorance of the new rules in the case of people who have changed sex was studied by Harold Garfinkel (1967, pp. 123 et seq.).

[60] Moreover, rudiments of initiation rites are found in apparently more modern organizations. For example, there is 'a relative exploitation of the work done by interns to the benefit of the hospital system and the medical body as a whole which leaves the least prestigious duties to neophytes' (Peneff, 1992, p. 156).

[61] Interview No. 16.

it. There are even many adults who wouldn't be able to stand it'.⁶² It should be noted that this word is borrowed from official Russian: the *propiska* is a legitimate, very bureaucratic procedure that a person who is newly arrived in a city must go through to regularize his stay there. In the capital cities (Moscow, St. Petersburg), the procedure was so severe that it was almost impossible for someone from the provinces to obtain permission to stay there (a stamp in a Soviet passport). Here are a few examples of the initiation rites practiced in penal institutions for young people:

'A guy is placed on a bench. A jacket is placed over his head and he is allowed to look through a sleeve. Then, he's asked questions about the signs of the zodiac. As soon as the new guy says Sagittarius, a bottle of water is poured down the sleeve. But isn't it possible to guess the meaning of the test? – Virtually impossible... Here's an example. You're placed on a newspaper and asked to go crazy. Usually, the new guy starts to do crazy things, whereas all he has to do is place himself beside the newspaper. Here's another example. Your eyes are covered with a towel and you're asked to identify the objects you touch. The joke is that you're asked to touch two soapy elbows. You feel like you're touching someone's rear end, which means that you've become a pederast without wanting to. Then they take off the towel and you're given the impression that you actually touched someone's behind. It's only when this was all explained to me that I laughed, not before... It gives you some kind of inferiority complex'.⁶³ The purpose of the test is not to guess. Either you know or you do not. Either you are already initiated and can justify your right to citizenship in the penal city or you are still a stranger (Abramkin, Chijov, 1992, p. 91).

Moreover, the *propiska* procedure is only one way among others to enter the penal world. In other words, there is no insurmountable obligation to go through the initiation rite. Adult inmates prefer to explain the rules instead of imposing them through force or humiliation. Occasionally, adult inmates even try to distance themselves from the rules that exist in the institutions for young people by stressing the rigid, cruel nature of those rules. 'The people, who come [from the institutions for young people], abide by the rules, their own rules. They have very particular rules. They're not like ours – they're stricter, harder'.⁶⁴ This does not mean that a new arrival will automatically be admitted to the illicit society. The initiation exists, but it takes on a more human, less restrictive form. 'When a new inmate arrives in a colony, even if he has already experienced detention–the inmates who respect the criminal norms [*blatnye*] observe his behavior. How does he behave in a given situation, what are his movements, his actions, his contacts, etc. If they see that the new inmate behaves as he should, they accept him into their environment'.⁶⁵

Paradoxically, the inmate is frequently initiated before he first arrives in prison, which serves as an argument to support our hypothesis concerning the high

---

⁶² Interview No. 3a.
⁶³ Interview No. 34.
⁶⁴ Interview No. 25.
⁶⁵ Interview No. 21.

degree of permeability of the penal society and the Soviet society. 'Who explained the rules to you? – They were explained to me when I was outside. I already knew a lot of things before I arrived here. I knew someone I met here. That made life easy for me'.[66] The other source of information about the hidden life of the prison consists in an image created by artistic and popular works on the criminal world. We will return to the analysis of the phenomenon of the *blatnaja* culture in Soviet society on the section entitled '*On the congruence of norms*'. Now, we will merely mention the efforts to refer to the sphere of the imaginary in order to build real relationships. 'What are you reading now? – Books. About the criminal world. About the rules that are respected now... Do you try to reproduce the things you learn in this manner? – Not really. But, if I read a book that contains advice, I'll keep it in mind. Here, you have to avoid failing to respect the rules (*bespredel*); in order to acquire authority, you have to be backed by intelligence... What music do you listen to? – Mostly, I listen to *blatnye* songs... "*Lesopoval*", Krug...'.[67] We were really surprised that our young interviewees referred to a book of stories about prison life that we used as a source of information for our work (the book by Valerij Abramkin and Yuri Chijov)[68]. This reference is all the more surprising since the book was published in an outlying area, far from Moscow, in a very limited edition. Therefore, Diego Gambetta's observations with respect to the role of media image in the construction of the Mafia remain pertinent in the case studied.

Nevertheless, if the neophyte needs help to find markers for his behavior, he will receive it. It is important to note the efforts made to make things that are obvious to the initiated explicit for the new arrival. 'The first step [after arriving in a cell] is: don't go there, you can sit here... As soon as the person arrives, we have to explain everything to him. Here's the place for the *blatnoj*, there...'.[69] The focus on explanation and, as a result, on understanding encourages the inmate to choose a strategy for penal life. Using the grammar of the theory of conventions, each inmate develops his own 'project'. 'Each new arrival first learned about life here. We didn't ask him to decide right away, we initiated him. "So, do you understand? – Yes, I understand." This is authorized, that is forbidden. We explained all of the details. "Do you want to live like this? – Live like this. Do you want to live like a man? – Live like a man. Do you want to live otherwise? Are you strong enough for this? – Live like this. How do you want to live? – I want to live like this... – Go ahead"'.[70] Summing up our sketch of the illicit categories, we can confirm our initial hypothesis concerning the amalgamation of the two cities: domestic and by projects. The differentiation spontaneously developed by the inmates does not exclude either its domestic interpretation or its interpretation within the context of

---

[66] Interview No. 30. We find the same type of reasoning in the discourse of Interviewee No. 32.
[67] Interview No. 30. The pop group '*Lesopoval*' and singer Mikhail Krug (killed in summer 2002) are known for their songs about life in the forced labor camps.
[68] Collective Interview No. 33. All of our interviewees read this book!
[69] Interview No. 29.
[70] Interview No. 18.

project. Yet, a compromise between the two logical systems is not achieved within the 'small' penal society.

The illicit Guard: the figure of the smotrjashij

Imprisonment in groups and the illicit differentiation imply a need for a figure in the social structure whose functions include the organization of community life in the broad sense. The order of things (cleaning has always been done by the inmates) and the public order (categorization has made conflicts between the groups inevitable) must be carefully ensured in everyday life. The control exercised by the guards in group imprisonment has never been sufficiently omnipresent to exclude all other sources of organization. Russian prisons prior to the October Revolution of 1917 had a cell leader (*kamernyj starosta*). He was elected by all of the inmates in a prison and his primary function was to represent their interests in relations with the administration. Although the Soviet prisons initially kept this institution, at the start of the 1930s, the administration introduced its right of veto with respect to the inmates' candidates. In 1938, such elections were eliminated and the administration started to appoint the cell leader unilaterally (Rossi, 1991, p. 391; Shalamov, 1998, p. 267).

Although the institution of leader existed primarily in the military prisons and the gaols, when the system was implemented in the forced labor camps in the 1930s, a new institution was developed, that of the thief-in-law (*vor v zakone*). This bizarre and contradictory term is explained both by the origin of this institution–thieves-in-law were recruited in a category of thieves, *urki* (important and audacious thieves)–and by the function of maintaining order based on illicit norms–their body is also called the 'law'. Another explanation focusses on the desire of the thieves-in-law not to violate the official Law personally; if necessary, they prefer to have others violate the Law. 'I respect the Penal Code,' says a famous character in Soviet literature in the 1930s, a crook, Ostap Bender. Finally, there is an hypothesis, which has never been proved or disproved, to the effect that the thieves-in-law were occasionally supported in their actions by the State security committee (*OGPU–Ob'edinennoe Glavnoe Politicheskoe Upravlenie*, which was organized on November 15, 1923 and preceded the *KGB–Komitet Gosudarstvennoj Bezopasnosti*) which used them to influence daily prison life. For example, observers noted a 'striking resemblance between the recommendations of the *OGPU* concerning work in the criminal world and the illicit norms of the thieves-in-law' (Podlesskih, Tereshonok, 1995, p. 162), including the rejection of any political commitment. Moreover, the oath sworn by the thieves-in-law started with a phrase similar to the oath sworn by a member of the Communist Party: 'I, as a true man (*pacan*), I have entered into a criminal life...'.

In any case, the relations of the thieves-in-law with the penal administration, the interaction of the two branches of power, licit and illicit, clarify the internal dynamics of this institution. On the one hand, the thieves-in-law support the norms and values of the penal subculture as an alternative to the official rules. Their lifestyle is characterized by the total rejection of anything that is formal, licit, official. The following norms established the code of behavior for the thief-in-law: life outside the interests of the licit society; a refusal to serve the State, regardless of the political regime; a refusal to work with their hands; an ability to adapt to any circumstances; cruelty with respect to traitors; honesty towards other thieves-in-law and mutual support; a disregard for ownership; an effort to remain well connected at all times and maintain relationships within their circles (Podlesskih, Tereshonok, 1995, pp. 233–235). 'The thief had nothing. He was forced to depend on the other inmates (*arestantov*). He was even forbidden to marry since, otherwise, he would think more of his family than the inmates'[71]. The prohibition against any social roots other than those established within penal society generated a lot of tension among the thieves-in-law. For example, the 1960–1980s were marked by a conflict between the thieves-in-law of Russian origin and those of Georgian origin. The Russians held to traditional norms whereas the Georgians accepted the family and ownership as a support for their activities as thieves-in-law (Podlesskih, Tereshonok, 1995, p. 87, p. 207).

On the other hand, the administrative resources in a total institution are so rich that there is always a desire to use them, at least partially, in organizing everyday life. The period following WWII made the conflict between the rejection of licit authority and the willingness to collaborate with it obvious. The institutional context was as follows: at the start of the war, the thieves-in-law were given a choice. They could either agree to go to the front, namely to serve the State, or they could run the risk of being executed as deserters. Certain thieves-in-law took up arms and even enjoyed remarkable military careers. In 1948, after the thieves-in-law were returned to prison, with even harsher sentences for theft[72], a new thieves law, *suchij zakon*, was implemented in the Vanino transit prison (Far East). The most innovative element of this law involved the authorization of collaboration with the administration (Anisimkov, 1993, p. 30; Shalamov, 1998, pp. 60–63). The converted thieves-in-law, *suki*, had access to dominate positions in the *licit* hierarchy of the camps: *zavhoz*, foremen, team leaders, etc. The rite of passage of the thieves-in-law to the new faith, developed by the *suki* leader, the Korol' (the 'King'), reproduced several of the elements described by René Girard: the 'orthodox' thieves-in-law had to go through all the steps the *suki* had had to go through.

> 'The rite of passage: kiss a knife or death. The Korol' put all of his former comrades in the same situation–life or death–in which the Korol' demonstrated his weakness with respect to the "orthodox" types. They had to prove their courage too! The test is the same' (Shalamov, 1998, p. 65).

A series of guerrillas followed the implementation of the new law: the defense of the 'orthodox' types never allowed the new law to be transformed into the 'cement' of the penal society.

---

[71] Interview No. 18.

[72] The increase in sentences was so severe that even the judges hesitated to apply the Law. For example, the sentence for an unqualified theft of private property increased 20-fold (from 3 months to 5–6 years in prison) (Solomon, 1996, pp. 405–413).

Moreover, the duality in the relationships that the thieves-in-law maintained with the licit authority in the prison had little effect on their organizational functions within the penal city. Within the context of prison society, there is a *functional* need for this position. 'What was the key function of the thief-in-law in the colony? – To maintain order, for everyone to live correctly, to ensure material aid (*gret'*), to prevent painful incidents'.[73] Moreover, numerous accounts, which occasionally take on the form of tales, demonstrate that the scope of the authority of the thieves-in-law was not confined within prison walls. This authority remained pertinent throughout the entire criminal world. 'In the past, if an old lady had been robbed in a flea market–if her pension had been lifted from her pocket–she could not call the police. All she had to do was contact a thief-in-law. Her purse would have been returned promptly, in keeping with our law'.[74] In other words, the primary concern of the thieves-in-law was to maintain order in the penal and criminal city. This order was based on the norms of the penal subculture, which they were responsible for reproducing. The complete list of the functions of the thief-in-law includes: developing new norms in joint local, regional or national meetings (*shodka*), in keeping with a changing licit context or precedent; the organization of joint meetings; the exercise of justice (see the section entitled '*Illicit justice*'); propaganda about the criminal lifestyle; the organization of a joint fund (see the section entitled '*Common funds*'); material aid to inmates; the organization of the racket of the players in the illicit economy; the organization of information services; responsibility for contacts with the outside world (Gurov, 1995, pp. 160–163; Abramkin, Chijov, 1992, p. 97).

As a result of the very complicated and sophisticated 'crowning' procedure (*koronovanie*) the number of thieves-in-law in all of the Soviet Union never exceeded a few thousand. A *blatnoj* could only become a legally 'crowned' thief-in-law by:

- successfully completing 'tests';
- being recommended by at least two thieves-in-law, who would remain responsible for their protégé throughout his criminal career; and
- by being approved at the meeting of thieves-in-law (*shodka*).

For this reason, there were approximately 3,500 thieves-in-law at the start of the 1950s, approximately 600 at the start of the 1980s, approximately 300 at the start of the 1990s (after the dissolution of the USSR) (Gurov, 1995, p. 112; Podlesskih, Tereshonok, 1995, pp. 238–252).[75] The 'rarity' of thieves-in-law has made it impossible to assess their presence in terms of the everyday life of inmates. 'There were thieves, but they played no important role. They were placed in the cells, there were so few of them… they played no role in the facilities, particularly in the Ukraine. Even in the maximum security facilities, no one saw them.

---

[73] Interview No. 24. The verb *gret'* comes from mutual help, 'sticking together'.
[74] Interview No. 25.
[75] See Podlesskih, Tereshonok, 1995, pp. 238–252 for a complete list of these thieves.

Basically, I didn't see them. From 1967 to the 1990s, I didn't see a thief-in-law'.[76] 'Did you live in a facility where there was a thief? – No. A thief was on his way through once, but he didn't leave his cell'.[77] Only four or five of those we interviewed had personally met one or more thieves-in-law. Under these conditions, management of everyday life remained unassured.

The void was filled by the *avtoritety* (literally, renowned people, the 'authorities'), whose functions were virtually identical to those of the thieves-in-law, although they were not required to go through the 'crowning' procedure, and in particular by the illicit guards, *smotrjashie*. Although the *avtoritety* are much more numerous than the thieves-in-law (numbering 10,000–20,000 for a prison population of 1–2 million (Gurov, 1995, p. 165), it is their lieutenants (*namestniki*), *smotrjashie*, who actually organize everyday life. Each cell in the gaol (6–150 inmates), subdivision (*otrjad* – 40–120 inmates), barracks (80–400 inmates), prison (800–2,000 inmates), important sphere of activity (canteen, card playing, etc.), city and occasionally each relatively important towns has its own *smotrjashij* (Figure 2.7).

Figure 2.7 Hierarchy of the illicit guards

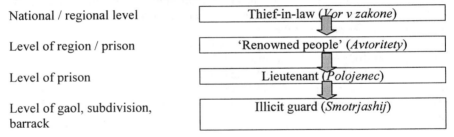

Let us start with a brief sketch of the figure of the *smotrjashij* through a semantic analysis of this term. As observed, the verb *smotret'* means to look at, to observe, to watch. In other words, the *smotrjashij* is someone who watches over maintaining order in everyday life. The inmates also have relationships with guards, particularly those inmates who have spent many years in prison. 'I remember, in 1997, I met a *smotrjashij*, staring, watching…'.[78] 'Take the *smotrjashie*. I think it's funny. The guy in charge of the *otrjad* watches me, the guards watch me, the administration watches me. Guards and watchers are everywhere. But, when there's more than one guard here…'.[79]

As demonstrated by the first quote, the illicit guard only appeared recently. Although it is difficult to provide an exact date, particularly since it varies from one region to another, our interviewees did not encounter any *smotrjashij* before 1985. The presence of illicit guards became obvious as of 1991–1994. 'It started

---

[76] Interview No. 18.
[77] Interview No. 36.
[78] Interview No. 18. Similar associations are found in Interviews No. 22 and No. 23.
[79] Interviewee No. 3a.

recently. I was here for the first time–it started in the 80s. 1985, maybe'.[80] 'I met a *smotrjashij* in 1994. Where? – I went to a maximum security facility in Revda [Sverdlovsk region]... There was already somebody watching the canteen... There were guards for everything. It made me think of a nursery. I told them not to touch me'.[81] The skepticism of the long-term inmates with respect to the illicit guards can be partially accounted for by the fact that, unlike the thieves-in-law and *avtoritety*, the *smotrjashie* are recruited not only from among the *blatnye*, but also other layers of the penal population. 'Men' and occasionally 'suits' can become illicit guards. 'He [the *smotrjashij*] is not necessarily a *blatnoj*. Not necessarily. I wouldn't say he was a thief. He's just an inmate'.[82]

As for the procedure for nominating an illicit guard, it is neither rigid nor uniform. In general, there are two methods. The first, which is widespread throughout the facilities, involves having the *avtoritet* or the thief-in-law responsible for the region in which the prison is located nominate each illicit guard. The *avtoritet* appoints someone he trusts to the position of *smotrjashij* for the facility who, in turn selects the *smotrjashie* at the lower levels. 'The illicit guard is appointed by the person familiar with the situation... by the *avtoritet*'.[83] The illicit guard, backed by the renown of the *avtoritet* is called the *polojenec* (literally, lieutenant). 'The lieutenant watches over the colony, whereas the thief-in-law watches over an entire region. The thief's scope of activity is broader. The lieutenant's responsibility is local'.[84] The individual who appointed his lieutenant is responsible for his actions and tries to control how order is maintained. This control takes the form of inspections by the thieves-in-law and the *avtoritetov*. 'They [the thieves-in-law] are appointed by someone to watch over the facility. Then that person appoints the illicit guards in the subdivisions, etc. Once, the thief-in-law arrived and started to speak with the men: what's going on and how. They told him everything. So he called the illicit guards and hit them. Order was re-established'.[85] In turn, the lieutenant is responsible for the actions of the *smotrjashie* he appoints. As a general rule, the illicit guard must keep the lieutenant informed about any major decision. 'If it's serious, the lieutenant is contacted. According to our rules, the illicit guard must inform the lieutenant that he has made a decision in a given situation. "Jora [name of the lieutenant], we've decided such and such in X..." The lieutenant must be informed'.[86] A serious error committed by the *smotrjashij* is called a *kosjak*; normally it results in his resignation. Several of those we interviewed insisted that being an illicit guard is a major responsibility.

---

[80] Interview No. 21.
[81] Interview No. 22.
[82] Interview No. 18.
[83] Interview No. 16.
[84] Interview No. 24.
[85] Interview No. 22.
[86] Interview No. 21. The comments of an illicit guard (Interviewee No. 24) confirm this procedure.

'If you take on that responsibility, you have to really watch. Guarding means suffering'.[87]

As a second, less widespread means of deliberation, the inmates elect the illicit guard ('suits', particularly 'roosters', are not entitled to vote). 'This [*smotrjashij*] is no imbecile, if he was elected by the entire *otrjad*. If people chose him, then he deserved it, he could be trusted'.[88] In any case, the appointment of the illicit guard 'from above' does not exclude his validation 'from below': the lieutenant generally selects an inmate with a good reputation for his candidate.

After describing the social origins of the illicit guard, we can discuss his functions. As noted, the illicit guard personalizes the order maintained by the inmates themselves. The answers to the question 'Do you think the management of a colony can be entrusted to the inmates' representatives?' provide a concrete illustration (N=581 in Russia):

Table 2.9 Rating of leaders in prison milieu

No	32.5%
Yes, *avtoritety* could be entrusted with this mission	27.4
Yes, elected representatives of prisoners could be entrusted with this mission	15.3
Yes, prisoners having official duties (*zavhoz*, etc.) could be entrusted with this mission	5.7
Yes, *smotrjashie* could be entrusted with this mission	7.6
No answer	11.5

The representatives of the illicit authority received most of the votes, namely 35 per cent. 'The administration is there now, but it will leave in 15 minutes. The inmates stay alone, who will control the situation? That's why there are people, who are respected by the others, who can stop someone if needed'.[89] The illicit authority protects and supports the inmates in their everyday lives. Illicit authority, unlike licit authority, is similar to the joint type of authority, as shown by the responses to the question 'If you need help and protection, can you contact':

---

[87] Interview No. 24.
[88] Interview No. 1.
[89] Interview No. 12.

Table 2.10 Sources of help and protection

	Russia	Kazakhstan	France	Canada
N	1310	375	55	120
Yes, the prisoners' leader (*avtoritet*)	35.9	20.3[90]	29.1[91]	30.2
Yes, the *smotrjashij*	18.6	26.9		
Yes, the prisoners having official duties (*zavhoz*, etc.)	7.1	6.9		
No, I can not contact any of these institutions	25.2	33.3	×	×
Yes, the administration of the penitentiary	17.4	16	81.8	41.5
Yes, the public prosecutor or the magistrate	3.3	2.7	25.5	3.8
Yes, my lawyer	×	×	43.6	70.8
Yes, the judge responsible for application of sentences	×	×	49.1	×

Let us attempt to prepare a functional description of the position of illicit guard. This 'guard's manual' will include the following obligations:

- Maintaining the social situation within acceptable limits in keeping with the norms and values of the penal subculture. The non-intervention of the illicit authority or his absence is often described in terms of *bespredel* (without limits, literally, a fight without rules). 'Imagine what would happen with *bespredel* and fights everywhere? I can imagine. So, who keeps the situation within the limits? – The *smotrjashie*, for example. Everything is settled peacefully'.[92]
- Exercising justice. The illicit guard serves as a third party or arbitrator in conflicts and differences among the inmates. 'Two inmates fight over nothing. The reason for the conflict is not important. You can never give in because each one has his dignity. We have to have a third person to say, "Stop it. You're fighting over nothing. Leave each other alone"'.[93] 'You resolve all the problems in a cell. For example, if there's a conflict, I ask the parties about it: "What's happening? Why are you fighting?" I study the matter and punish the guy who started the fight. The *smotrjashij* plays a positive role. When too many people are kept together, someone has to see to order. There has to be an arbitrator'.[94] 'Take an example from everyday life. There are two beds, side by side. One night, one inmate hits the other in his sleep. How do we handle this

---

[90] Even during the Soviet period, there were no Kazakh thieves-in-law or *avtoritet* (they were primarily Russian, Georgian and Armenian). However, illicit guards are present in each former Soviet republic.
[91] 'Another inmate'.
[92] Interview No. 39.
[93] Interview No. 27b.
[94] Interview No. 18.

situation? Discuss it with the head of the facility? No. With the head of the *otrjad*? No'.[95]
- Organizing a common fund to help the unfortunate inmates.
- Organizing the secret service. 'You know, I have to be informed about everything. I don't collect information to punish people, to accuse them. I collect it to know if I can trust what someone says. Nothing more'.[96]

If we compare this list with the responsibilities of the thief-in-law, the similarities are obvious, with the exception of the legislative functions that are exclusive to the thieves. Therefore, everyday life in the prison is organized around the *smotrjashij*.

Duality of norms

Order in the everyday life of the inmates does not imply an equality and symmetry in their obligations. On the contrary, the capital condition for its stability lies in non-reciprocity, the radical asymmetry of rights and obligations. Each category of inmate has its own rights and obligations, and their equilibrium is only ever provisional. Therefore, the illicit norms (*ponjatia*) vary from one layer of the prison population to another. It is the respect for their asymmetry that supports order and ensures stability. 'Everyone has his one level of living here. For example, I judge by one criteria, someone else judges by another. Could it be said that people refer to different illicit norms? – Yes'.[97] 'The illicit category, the position in the illicit hierarchy, are decisive. The inmate bases his conversation on these factors. They affect all discourse, conflict resolution'.[98] 'Life is morally easier in maximum security facilities. Maximum security? – Yes, no doubt about it. First, people there have a lot of experience with life. *Everyone knows his place*... People understand what they can and cannot do'.[99] As a result, 'knowing his place' is the first thing an inmate must learn in the penal city. Otherwise, correct interpretation during an interaction is not guaranteed.

In this context, it would be preferable to speak of the bod*ies* of illicit norms, rather than the bod*y*. There are norms specific to the men, the norms of the thieves-in-law, as well as the norms that structure the interactions between the representatives of the distinct categories: thief / man, man / 'rooster', etc. First, let us take a look at a few norms that structure relationships among the thieves-in-law, taking into consideration the fact that the lieutenants (*polojenec*) and the illicit guards (*smotrjashij*) also refer to them in their interactions. Above all, let us stress the duality of the norms that are valid inside and outside this community. First, there is absolute honesty in relations within the community. 'The traditional laws

---

[95] Interview No. 29.
[96] Interview No. 27b.
[97] Interview No. 1.
[98] Interview No. 3b.
[99] Interview No. 18. Comparable ideas are found in Interviews Nos. 16, 19 and 28.

of the thieves focus first on honesty and justice towards their comrades'.[100] On the other hand, 'they are permitted to do anything with respect to others that solidifies the authority of the thieves' (Gurov, 1995, p. 109). The traditional philosophy of the *blatnye* supposes that all of the inmates are divided into two basic groups. The title of 'human being' applies only to those whose lives are organized around the norms of the *blatnye*. The others are pejoratively referred to as *fraer*. 'Lies, deceit are the rule in relationships with the *fraer*. That group was created to be cheated' (Shalamov, 1998, p. 17). Another observer who took part in the internal life of the Stalinist forced labor camps, Jacques Rossi, expressed the point of view of the *blatnye* even more brutally: 'The *fraer* is game to be hunted' (Rossi, 1991, p. 434). During the 1930s–1950s, there was nothing exceptional about stealing, even murdering if necessary, the *fraer*. Possibly the distance that separated the *blatnye* from the rest of the penal population accounts for the completely confused assessment our interviewees made of their ability to affect life in the penal world. For example, half of those interviewed (43 per cent, N=504) think they can affect the decisions made in there are, whereas the other half (43.5 per cent) do not. Here are the responses to the question 'Do the decisions made in your area meet with your interests':

Table 2.11 Coincidence of private and collective interests

	Russia	France
N	504	59
These decisions do not depend on my interests	28.6%	×
These decisions do not contradict my interests	22.6	30.5
These decisions sometimes infringe upon my interests	15.9	40.7
These decisions contradict my interests	8.7	
These decisions meet my wishes	7.7	15.3
No answer	16.5	13.6

As these results seem to imply, the right to speak is reserved primarily for the inmates who enjoy illicit authority. 'What does that mean – not to lose honor? – In our life (*po nashej jizni*)? – Yes. – It means that you acquire a certain authority, how would I put it, that you are entitled to speak'.[101] The possession of authority ensures a fairly broad margin of liberty and autonomy, which supports self-respect.

As for the 'real men', duality is not absent from their everyday lives either. A superficial study might give the observer the impression that this is not contradictory. For example, there is the degree to which our interviewees agree with the norms that are usually considered key elements of the constitution of the 'real men'[102] (Table 2.12; the question asked – 'Do you agree with the following norms?'). In Kazakhstan, where the penal work, as we already stated, is closer to the Soviet models, the inmates give more support to the informal norms than in

---

[100] Letter from Interviewee No. 3a. See also: Rossi, 1991, p. 60.
[101] Interview No. 30.
[102] For a more complete list, see Anisimkov V.,1993, p. 13.

...ussia (the particularly high score of the norm that ensures the integrity of the prison community, 'Do not do anything that could harm us all', should be noted).

Table 2.12 Informal norms (*ponjatia*)

	Russia		Kazakhstan	
N	1120		396	
	Yes	No	Yes	No
Do not cheat your neighbor	83.9	3.3	83.8	1.8
Know how to defend yourself	81.7	2.3	83.1	0.8
Do not denounce others	78.8	6	79.3	4.3
Do not stare at others	76.2	5.8	75.5	4.3
Do not do anything that could harm all of us	76.1	6.1	85.9	2.3
Do not settle differences after drinking	72	5.6	74	4.8
Do not ask too many questions	70.1	10.7	72.7	7.3
Do not lose too much while playing cards	67.5	7.7	66.7	8.1
Deny bad rumors about yourself. Otherwise they are true	66.9	10.7	73.5	5.8
Do not ask the administration to settle conflicts	63.4	16.7	64.9	15.2
Do not take knives. Everyone is entitled to personal inviolability	60.4	16.6	65.9	8.6
Do not have contact with the 'roosters' (N=539 in Russia)	51.9	23.7	56.6	18.9
Do not ask for more food at the canteen	38.5	37.6	42.4	31.6

Let us focus on the reticence to completely refuse recourse to the administration in everyday life. 'For the man, going to the administration or not is all the same thing. But a *blatnoj* would never go to the administration, it's painful for him'.[103] The progressive system reinforces the inmate's dependence on the administration whose position remains preponderant in any decision concerning parole (*UDO – Uslovno-Dosrochnoe Osvobojdenie*). In this context, the duality in the relations between the inmates and the administration, which lies in the total dependence and the just as total refusal, transforms into a duality of norms. Contacts with the administration, as well as the desire for parole, are only tolerated on the part of the men. 'For the men, parole has never been painful. A man is a man. He has a family, children. However, if he considered himself a *blatnoj*, a bearer of the thieves' subculture, parole would be disastrous for him. Generally, enjoying any good provided by the administration or the Soviet authorities was painful. It was forbidden'.[104] The duality of the norms that structure relations with the administration occasionally places the inmate in a situation where he has to choose between two necessary actions. Either he goes to the administration, or he cannot defend himself. Thus, the inmate develops a hierarchy for the norms, adapting them to his needs. He seeks an individual compromise, since the duality

---

[103] Interview No. 38.
[104] Interview No. 18.

of the illicit norms does not allow him to generalize it. 'Even the Penal Code does not exclude the situation in which respecting a norm causes you to violate another. It's the same here. You respect one illicit norm and violate another. Which illicit norms would you never violate? – Don't cheat your own, don't denounce, don't ask for extra food'.[105]

The attribute[106] 'your neighbor' and its variation 'your own' in the norm 'Don't cheat your neighbor' should be noted as complementary evidence of the duality of norms. Cheating is not prohibited, cheating *your neighbor, your own* is. 'Don't take things from others–we can go after someone who does that. When you're free, you can borrow a car from your neighbor, Ivan Ivanovitch. He won't complain to the Court. Whereas, here... Well, if you get out of prison and run into Ivanov, who is also an ex-con, you won't cheat him. However, if Ivanov was part of the illicit authority in the prison, he can cheat you. But you can't'.[107] 'Before, even the burglars weren't respected [in prison]... A burglar doesn't ask the victim you're burgling who he is. It might be someone who has just got out of prison, who spent his entire life in detention. I would never let myself do that...'.[108] In other words, you have to know how to chose the victim for your crime. Order does not imply the total elimination of delinquency, it implies channeling it, *directing it towards others*. The victim is chosen because he does not belong to those close to you, to yours. 'Before, thieves and hoodlums were not respected. Why? – Because. Who's a hoodlum? The hoodlum. He has no principles and he hits men'.[109] Personal knowledge, the experience of prison life ('An inmate will quickly understand another inmate'[110]) and membership in the same illicit category are all needed for an inmate to transform into one of yours. The responses to the question 'Who can become one of yours (*svoj*)?' justify this supposition:

Table 2.13 Socially close persons

		Rus.	Kaz.	Fr.	Can.
N		1310	367	54	120
I do not differentiate the people in this way		36.2	40.9	5.6	13.9
A close relative		30.3	26.4	77.8	80.9
A person with the same vision of world	The characteristics of the same illicit category	22.9	19.6	16.7	19.1
A person who does the same things		9.1	11.4	3.7	1.7
A compatriot (native of my region)		8.1	4.6	7.4	7.8
A person I became acquainted with in prison		5.7	3.5	11.1	2.6
Somebody introduced by the person I know		0.4	1.1	×	×

---

[105] Interview No. 33.
[106] According to a structuralist approach, the attribute determines the group affected by the norm (Crawford, Ostrom, 1995, p. 584).
[107] Interview No. 2.
[108] Interview No. 3a.
[109] Interview No. 18.
[110] Interview No. 27b.

The relatively high number of interviewees who chose the first response should not be deceptive. We have already referred to the semantic difficulty that prevents us from finding a univocal term. The term pairs Us / Them, Yours / Others, Friend / Enemy have their advantages and disadvantages. They are found in scientific and daily discourse. Therefore, the term 'Yours' does not define the duality of norms in an exhaustive manner. 'Were hostel relationships painful? – Not necessarily. There was no cruelty with respect to class comrades. We tried to live together peacefully, to help one another. However, the administration, the older guys, were cruel'.[111]

Finally, relations between the men and the 'suits', particularly the 'roosters' illustrate the extreme duality of the norms. For the inmates, the 'roosters' personify the others, those who are foreign to the prison city. Although the men do not enjoy the right to speak throughout the penal city, they do enjoy it in their relations with all the 'suits'. Those who represent the 'suits' can only impose themselves within their community. 'The man (*pacan*) can't really live in peace, he doesn't have enough authority. He can only impose his will on inferiors [in the illicit hierarchy], such as the "suits", but not on their superiors'.[112] What the men are authorized to do in their relations with the 'roosters', does not give rise to reciprocal rights. The asymmetry of norms and rights is firmly rooted in everyday life. 'Giving them [the "roosters"] something–no problem. Taking something from them–never... A "rooster" insults a man? God protect him! The real man who respects himself must beat him up immediately. Even if the "rooster" merely raised his voice...'.[113] 'If one is a "suit", all of his acquaintances are there... How can I stand him up, see that his words are respected? A "rooster" who speaks up?!'[114] The conflict in norms is so obvious that it makes compromise impossible, even on an individual level. Personal sympathy does not change the relationship between two inmates who belong to separate categories. 'For me, it's enough not to eat with his spoon, not to descend to his level. Yet, we're quite good friends [with a "rooster"]. I don't smoke after him. He smokes after me. Generally, he eats and smokes after me. I can eat and smoke after a man. That's acceptable. I'd prefer to go hungry than to eat after a "rooster"... Maybe, if we were free, it would be acceptable for me to eat after him. I don't know. I don't know how to behave with a "rooster" outside prison'.[115]

Summing up our brief analysis of the duality of norms, enables us to put the penal society into perspective. It is divided into several layers, categories, and groups and does not form a homogenous whole. 'Here, people do not live in a single heap. They live in several small piles... Everyone has his illicit norms, in addition to the things we all try to respect'.[116] Although the penal society is a

---

[111] Interview No. 25. In this case, the duality takes the form of an opposition between the older and younger guys.
[112] Interview No. 33.
[113] Interview No. 21.
[114] Interview No. 30.
[115] Interview No. 20.
[116] Interview No. 27a.

'small' society, it breaks down into several even smaller societies. It is not the scale of a society that defines its nature, but its internal working. The 'large' society, city, comes into being only if there is a unified body of norms that applies to all of its citizens.

Image of relations between the sexes: homosexuality in prison

The use of passive homosexuality as a means of differentiation, as a stigmata for pariahs in the penal world, invites us to reflect on the specifics of the image of sexuality in the prison context. One of the modern concepts of love relationships involves the equal status of the participants. Moreover, if the equality and liberty of the participants is not assured *ex ante*, they become the raison d'être of the love relationship. 'Love is one place where the subject appears' (Touraine, 1993, p. 329). Therefore, love relationships are not reduced to sexuality, although it plays an essential role. Another ideal type of sexuality, specific to traditional societies, is typified by the radically unequal status of the participants, their non-reciprocal behavior, even the submission of the woman to the man's sexual desire. '"Naked", "pure" sexuality is on a continuum with violence' (Girard, 1972, p. 169). Is the image of sexuality held by Soviet inmates closer to the first or second ideal type?

The participating observers of prison life highlight the radical opposition between the image of the man and that of the women in penal subculture. The role of the man is to impose his will on the woman, to make her obey, *to subject her to his power*.

> 'This inferior being, the woman, exists solely to satisfy the animal desires of the thief, to serve as a target for his brutal jokes and as an object for his blows when the thief kicks up a row. A living being that the thief temporarily possesses' (Shalamov, 1998, p. 43).

The will of the man to impose his power over the woman also marks the image of sexual relations.

> 'For most inmates, making love means imposing their desire. We think that the woman should resist. Otherwise, she's considered a prostitute' (Rossi, 1991, p. 107).

Criminal slang makes the duality of this behavior–imposition vs. resistance– obvious. One synonym for woman is prostitute. Therefore, we can propose a macho view of the prison subculture where this duality takes on a new dimension: the separation of the two sexes. The border that separates the masculine and feminine worlds is not transparent, unlike that which separates the public and the private in prison. The total rejection of the feminine role and the will to associate it with a sanction are particularly obvious in Kazakhstan.

Table 2.14 Attitudes toward homosexuality

What do you think about homosexual contacts between inmates?	Russia, N=539	Kazakhstan, N=396	Canada, N=120
I completely reject them	37.5%	40.4	25.8
It's quite normal if these relations are voluntary	26	15.4	55.8
I don't know	19.1	19.9	14.2
It's a kind of sanction for those who do not respect the norms of our milieu	7.2	20.2	2.5
No answer	10.2	4	1.7

The dual image of sexuality in a context of involuntarily sexual abstinence (the prison population includes members only from the same sex) results in a series of taboos. The slightest movement likely to give rise to associations with the feminine role can lead to the reclassification of the inmate downwards, to his transfer to the 'suits' category. 'Recently, there was a conflict here. While sleeping, one inmate inadvertently placed his hand on his neighbor. That person interpreted this gesture incorrectly...'[117] 'There's a movement among the young people–the homosexuals (*golubye*), I don't know what to call them. They have oral sex, you know. With them, being a homosexual inspires respect. If you don't have sex here, you're not a man. I listen to them and I start thinking that I'm the idiot. The world is upside down'.[118]

Among the young inmates, there is an even more bizarre taboo. Someone who is found masturbating is downgraded–he becomes a 'rooster'. 'The "roosters" include those who have oral sex, anal sex. Even if someone merely masturbates, he's treated like a "rooster"'.[119] The only sexual pleasure for young inmates (visits with young girls outside a visiting room are forbidden) appears to be prohibited by the taboo. The separation of the masculine and feminine worlds is so profound that playing a double role (the masculine and the feminine roles simultaneously) is excluded. Either sexuality exists in prison in a pure and brutal form or it does not exist at all. This former applies only to relations between thieves and 'roosters', men and 'roosters'. This was indicated by a guard, who even witnessed efforts (albeit unsuccessful) to transform the areas inhabited by the 'roosters' into a sort of house of prostitution for the 'respectable' inmates.[120] In the penal subculture, the 'rooster' is as undesirable and foreign as the prostitute. Both attract and channel violence.

---

[117] Interview No. 10.
[118] Interview No. 21.
[119] Interview No. 34.
[120] Interview No. 40.

On violence in prison

In modern societies, the principal justification for the existence of the prison lies in institutionalizing violence. The State monopolizes violence and the prison serves to materialize this monopoly. Thus, we need to re-touch the image of the prison as a device for institutionalized violence as soon as we look at the Soviet model of society. On the one hand, the penal administration does not always act within the framework established by the law and enjoys significant latitude in terms of its daily operations. The discretion of the licit authority in the prison reinforces its perception by the inmates as an authority that is imposed and purely restrictive, even hostile. On the other hand, imprisonment in groups generates violence within the prison.[121] 'Prison. A permanent pressure. Everything places the man in an abnormal position. Of course, his psychic situation is far from balanced. There is a permanent moral pressure. Like the weight of a rock. Sometimes, it's overwhelming. It accumulates all the times. We always try to find some way to reduce it. Otherwise, there's a psychological crisis. You understand? The man is nervous. And there are daily conflicts. You didn't put your slippers away, you put your blanket on my bed as you make yours, you take something without asking, etc. In a usual situation, these conflicts aren't serious. However, here, they can push people to the limits. You might smash in someone's head, cut his throat... sometimes you lose your patience and a crisis erupts. *It seems like someone else is responsible*'.[122] As for the violence generated within the prison, mastering it sometimes means finding a substitute victim, a sacrificial victim, which contradicts the imperative of institutionalization. In other words, neither licit violence nor illicit violence is completely institutionalized in the Soviet type prison.

Conceptions of violence

Instead of providing a common point of view, for both the external observer and a participant observer, the prison does not appear particularly violent. 'This place is not more violent than the outside world' (Chauvenet et al., 1994, p. 118). This means that violence is not obvious in the prison, including the Soviet prison. At the start of the 1930s, the Soviet penal administration offered a group of artists, headed by Maxim Gorkij, an opportunity to visit the Belomor-Baltic canal construction site, where the work was done by prisoners. The artists were so impressed that they boasted about the forced labor camp system and its merits for reintegration in several works (Rossi, 1991, p. 27). It would be too simplistic to view this as a

---

[121] Although several criminologists are against the idea of the 'accumulation' of violence, they do agree that certain places like prison are more violent that others. 'It is not that aggressiveness accumulates like water behind a dam, it is simply that the organism lacks stimulation. This need for action naturally manifests itself in an aggressive manner... in individuals who have learned to behave aggressively' (Cusson, 1981, p. 149). Regardless of the nature of the accumulation of aggressiveness, the prison serves as a reservoir for it.
[122] Interview No. 18.

result of constraint or an illusion created consciously by the penal administration. Ignorance of several aspects of violence must be taken into consideration in any discourse concerning prison. Even the statistics appear to justify the non-violence of the penal world: the crime rate recorded in prison was 3.67 for 1,000 inmates in 1995, compared to 29.92 for 1,000 active citizens in Russian society, namely eight times higher (see Table 2.15 for an overview of the total number of crimes recorded by type of penal facility) (Tkachevskij, 1997, p. 83).[123] How can we account for this blindness, conscious or unconscious, statistical or discursive, with respect to violence, considering the fact that the penal world could serve as an encyclopedia of violence since all forms are present there?

Table 2.15 Crime rate recorded in prison

Year	In medium and minimum security prisons	In maximum security prisons	In prisons for young delinquents
1992	2588	24	157
1993	3012	15	139
1994	2785	12	91
1995	2280	0	93

First, we must exclude the hypothesis of symbolic violence according to which the 'transition from brutal techniques to more subtle techniques' can account for the impression of non-violence. From the viewpoint of critical sociology, ignorance of the violent side of the prison can only occur if the external observers internalize the judgment markers that exist in the prison. The less interest society shows in the problem of penal violence, licit or illicit, the smaller the distance is that separates it from prison society. This reasoning could serve to demonstrate our hypothesis on the congruence of Soviet society and the 'small' prison society, if we did not discover similar faulty perceptions in many other social contexts. By obscuring the discretion of the licit authority in American prisons, de Tocqueville and de Beaumont gave it the following excuse. 'How can absolute silence be maintained among the criminals if we do not dominate them ceaselessly with the terror of prompt and rigorous punishment' (Tocqueville, Beaumont, 1991, p. 192)? By extension, the imaginary transformation of the prison into a non-violent setting implies an almost absolute capacity on the part of the licit authority to impose its rules since, according to critical sociology, 'physical repression sanctions the failure to internalize a cultural arbitrariness' (Bourdieu, 1980, p. 51). Otherwise the penal subculture would not exist.

An alternative explanation would involve placing the ignorance of penal violence within a specific institutional context. For example, an act may be considered violent outside the prison, whereas it draws no attention inside as a result of its habitual and expected character. 'Violence can never be reduced to the image of pure objectivity simply because what is designed or perceived as

---

[123] See also http://www.gks.ru *'Russia in figures – 1999'*.

"violent" varies in time and space' (Wieviorka et al., 1999, p. 19). Several studies on the feeling of insecurity justify the hypothesis that there is no strict relationship between an act and whether it is perceived as violent or not.

> 'The victim of an act of violence will experience the consequences of that act in keeping with how the act is classified within a pre-existing perceptual structure' (Roché, 1993, p. 204).

The lack of congruence between the penal world and the 'large' society implies that the inmate does not perceive penal violence in the same matter as he reacts to violence outside the prison. In this world, which is violent by definition, one consciously raises the tolerance level for violence, as one stops reacting to the suffering of others in a war. 'Can we talk in terms of a decrease in violence, including words, actions, looks? – Here, when you think of violence, all that comes to mind is fights'.[124] However, the discourse of our interviewees provides certain evidence as to the failure to perceive violence in both the penal world and the post-Soviet society. 'If you pay attention to everything... Here everything happens the same way as outside. For example, someone pushes you in the subway or the bus. I'm always tolerant towards those things, I don't pay attention to such trivial things. You only react when it's serious'.[125] We would like to stress that imprisonment in groups causes more conflicts in everyday life than imprisonment in cells. Thus, fights are *physically* inevitable when 100 people are kept in a very reduced living space (a few hundred square meters), that is poorly arranged when it comes to respecting the public/private border.[126]

An institutional solution for micro-conflicts in a prison is not always possible for two reasons. First, as a result of the focus on its security mission, the penal administration does not want to intervene in smaller conflicts among inmates. The administration intervenes only if the conflict could result in a serious crime that would bring the efficiency of its work into question. The possibility that a conflict will become more serious is often under-estimated.

> 'Disputes occur over anything. Quarrels immediately reach a point where it seems that the only possible solution is to take up knives' (Shalamov, 1998, p. 50).

The case of Victor Mantulin, an interviewee who committed a murder in prison after a guard failed to intervene serves as an illustration. 'There are various conflicts, like on the outside. Sometimes, a quiet talk settles the dispute. Sometimes a fight is inevitable. I remember a conflict in a maximum security facility. With the *zavhoz*, from my country. He had put me in solitary several times. He'd make a statement for any trivial failing, such as if I wore slippers in a local zone. The administration punished me with 15 days in solitary. During that time, I

---

[124] Interview No. 13.
[125] Interview No. 26.
[126] A study of violence among college students demonstrated that narrow, poorly lit and poorly arranged hallways are a major source of micro-conflicts in the everyday life of a college (Peralva, 1996, p.17).

was given food every other day. I shut up. The second time exactly the same thing happened. A report on the pretext that my jacket wasn't buttoned properly. I was put in solitary again. I was fed up. I didn't cut his throat right away. First, I showed him the knife. "Once more and I'll cut your throat." He smiled and said I wouldn't dare. The head of our *otrjad* heard the conversation. He sent for me and asked, "What did you threaten him with?" I explained and said that if the *zavhoz* continued to report me, I'd cut his throat. I said that right to the guy in charge. "Get lost," he replied. I continued to keep quiet and I waited for the next time. The *zavhoz* put me in solitary a third time. When I got out, I couldn't stand it'.[127] There is no lack of evidence of the administration's absence in the discourse of the other interviewees either. 'One inmate [who had lost a large sum playing cards] asked the administration to protect him against the other players. "Get lost, scapegoat," they said. "You lost, get to work, take the worst work, but pay up." Would the administration hide him or protect him? Never. "Did you ask us for permission to play and lose? Get lost. Go pay"'.[128]

Second, the existence of multiple categories of inmates prevents the institutionalization of conflicts since that would involve the equal treatment of the parties concerned, regardless of licit or illicit social rank. On the contrary, certain illicit categories serve as targets to channel the violence generated in everyday life. The destiny of the 'roosters' is particularly pertinent in this context since they attract the violence of the upper layers of the prison population. 'Before, he [the "rooster"] could not raise his eyes, he always let you past'.[129] 'We know who we can insult here. I remember a situation where your category wasn't important. Whoever you are, your insults will never be unanswered. There is even a rule in the maximum security facilities: whoever insults you, you hit right away. That rule no longer exists'.[130] Insults are reserved primarily for the 'roosters' and other pariahs in the prison world. In other words, the logic of searching for a substitute victim, a sacrificial victim, dominates the logic of institutionalizing violence. Therefore, the micro-conflicts are transformed into a source of non-institutionalized violence, which is not controlled in keeping with the ideal type of modernity.

The logic of forced tolerance serves to provide a link between the presence of violence, licit and illicit, in prison and the ignorance of violence in the discourse of the inmates as in the case of conflicts in everyday life. The situation of imprisonment in groups implies that daily conflicts will be inflated. Neither the social structure nor the particular authority model provide for an institutional solution. Therefore, violence in all its forms becomes inevitable.

> 'Violence is an action, [...], a translation of a conflict that does not find other means for expression, other means for dealing with the aspirations it raises and which take on the form of frustrated subjectivity or a prohibition of expression' (Wieviorka et al., 1999, p. 19).

---

[127] Interview No. 3a.
[128] Interview No. 21.
[129] Interview No. 16.
[130] Interview No. 13.

Yet, the omnipresence of violence prevents its adequate perception: we pay attention only to the most violent acts, setting aside violence in words or gestures and even actions that would be criminalized on the outside. According to our hypothesis, which we will return to in the sections entitled '*Does the public/private border exist?*' and '*Constructing the enemy: then and now*' in the next chapter, the order to master and perceive the violence that we have just described is also characteristic of post-Soviet society in general. The congruence between the prison society and the post-Soviet society is explained less by the symbolic violence of the penal subculture than by the comparability of the social organization in both societies.

Characteristics of relations with the licit authority

The purely restrictive and imposed, even hostile, character of licit authority is one of the essential obstacles to the modern control of violence. Let us take a closer look at the role of the licit authority in the organization of everyday life in incarceration. From this point of view, we must focus on the three elements that characterize the functioning of the penal administration. First, let us stress its intra-muros omnipotence: the licit authority can intervene in any aspect of the inmates' everyday life. 'They [the administration] do what they want. It was that way before. It's that way today. It will be that way in the future. The administration (*nachal'stvo*) controls the ball. No one, not the inmates, no penal subculture can upset the balance of power. Understand? Everything depends on the administration'.[131] The illicit title of the ward, the master (*hozjain*), reflects the capacity of the members of the administration to impose their will on the inmates without limits. Our interviewees stressed this aspect several times. 'I don't feel at all protected here. If someone [from the administration] wanted to do something to me, he would do it'.[132] The licit authority can create unbearable conditions for an inmate or greatly facilitate his life in prison. 'The administration decides everything'.[133] Everything, from simple matters such as assigning a bed to each inmate to decisions concerning his parole or transfer to another prison/subdivision, comes under the exclusive jurisdiction of the administration. A sociological study made in 317 prisons in the United States provides statistical evidence of the capital role played by the administration in the everyday lives of inmates. Its results support the 'administrative-control theory [which] posits that collective violence is a product of unstable, divided, or otherwise weak management' (Useem, Reising, 1999, p. 735).

Second, the legal frameworks are not limited to the omnipotence of the penal administration, which enjoys a significant degree of latitude even in the modern construction of society where there are several external measures for controlling the actions of the licit authority, including the checks and balances that transform

---

[131] Interview No. 18.
[132] Interview No. 27a.
[133] Interview No. 38.

the principle of the differentiation of spheres of activity into a tool of the institutional organization.

> 'Not only are all of the professional rules and means implemented by the guards to control the penal population not covered by a recognized, formal framework, but often they are included falsely against the texts or violate them' (Chauvenet et al., 1994, p. 123).

The only way in which to eliminate arbitrariness in the way in which the prison manages everyday life would be to place it under the control of another total power. The situation in the Stalinist forced labor camp proves this hypothesis. Despite the appearance of the Gulag as a 'State within a State', the discretion of its administration was clearly limited. The inhuman treatment of the inmates is explained less by the arbitrariness of the prison administration than by characteristics of the policy of the central power and the laws in effect. 'It wasn't all arbitrary. There was always an order. In the very important cases, all [of the inmates] were required to sign documents' (Shalamov, 1998, p. 88).[134] Therefore, in order to fight against a total authority, one needs another total authority, even more omnipotent and all-powerful than the first.

The other institutional contexts do not exclude the opportunism of the penal administration. Moreover, a centralized model of power, but not total, involves a certain degree of arbitrariness in the actions of the subordinates, including in the relations between the central power and its lieutenants in the various spheres, including the prison administration. The costs of control and the complexity of the means of control, make a strategy of 'closing one's eyes' to the opportunistic behavior of the subordinates essential. We will illustrate this point in terms of game theory. We have given a close interpretation of our subject to the model developed by Elinor Ostrom (Ostrom, 1990, p. 11). Let us take two subordinates who are under the care of the State and they have the choice of two strategies: to concentrate on completing the tasks assigned by the authority or to behave in an opportunistic manner and take advantage of the opportunity to reduce their efforts. The respective gains of the two players are represented in the following chart. The game has two Nash equilibria, (11, -1) and (-1, 11), that do not coincide with the Pareto equilibrium (10, 10).[135]

---

[134] The passage in the official telegram dated 10.01.1939 and signed by Stalin confirms this point: 'The application of physical force in the practice of the NKVD [Ministry of the Interior], permitted since 1937 by the Central Committee [of the CPSU] has spent up the exposure of enemies of the people. The Central Committee thinks that this method must be applied from now on, as an exception, to clear and still dangerous enemies as correct and expedient one' (quoted in Solomon, 1996, p.258).

[135] Nash equilibrium refers to an issue in which no player can increase his gains unilaterally. Pareto equilibrium refers to an issue in which no player can increase his gains without reducing the gains of the other player.

Table 2.16 Subordinates' game

		Second subject	
		To concentrate on tasks given by the government	To behave opportunistically (to shrink)
First subject	To concentrate on tasks given by the government	10, 10 [P]	-1, 11 [N_2]
	To behave opportunistically (to shrink)	11, -1 [N_1]	-2, -2

Let us now suppose that the custodial organization attempts to control the subordinates and punish opportunistic behavior with two units of utility. Thus, the probability (y) of sanctioning and the probability (x) of unjust sanctioning must be taken into consideration since the custodial organization never has all of the information concerning the actions of the subordinates. If $x>25$ per cent and $y<75$ per cent, State intervention will only aggravate the situation: the only Nash equilibrium coincides with the least optimal outcome (-2, -2). Therefore, in certain situations, the State would be wise to abstain from intervening in the actions of its lieutenants, just as the lieutenants abstain from intervening in the business of the rank and file.

Table 2.17 Subordinates' game revisited

		Second subject	
		To concentrate on tasks given by the government	To behave opportunistically (to shrink)
First subject	To concentrate on tasks given by the government	10-2x, 10-2x [P]	-1-2x, 11-2y
	To behave opportunistically (to shrink)	11-2y, -1-2x	-2y, -2y [N]

It should be noted that the fact that the prison is closed to the outside world increases the value of x when the State tries to impose the legal frameworks of the penal administration. 'I think it is very difficult to define all this [the administration's actions] in the law. That would make the administration's work much more complicated'.[136] In turn, the administration tries to retain the image of the 'black box' associated with prison, which enables it to continue to enjoy a significant amount of autonomy. In a private, unrecorded conversation, the acting

---

[136] Interview No. 27a.

head of a maximum security facility in northern Russia nostalgically recalled the period when no State organization (except for the custodial ministry, namely the Ministry of the Interior) was entitled to intervene in the affairs of the prison administration: not the traffic police (*Gosudarstvennaja Avtodorojnaja Inspekcija – GAI*), the sanitary authorities or the fire department.

Third, the daily actions of the guards and the representatives of the penal administration are often constructed around the imperative of the extreme duality of norms, which we attributed to the penal subculture. The ineffectiveness of legal constraints does not mean that the administration acts without any reference to the normative frameworks. The norms of the 'small' society replace the legal rules and the duality of the norms replaces the imperative to respect the basic rights of each human being. The price to be paid for not respecting the legal frameworks entails the reproduction of the model of the 'small' society. As paradoxical as this may seem, the administration's actions respect the logic of the penal subculture, which it is supposed to fight.

Since we do not have the information we need to apply all of the criteria of the 'small' society to the penal administration, we will limit ourselves to a study of the duality of the norms that serve to organize its daily actions. As the 'suits' are deprived of citizenship in the penal city, the administration refuses to recognize the inmates' membership in the human community and assigns them the status of pariahs. Generally, from the administration's point of view, there are two classes of people–'normal' people and inmates. 'There's a civil servant and an inmate. A fence and a step the height of three ordinary men separates them. If you are an ordinary citizen, you can try to talk [with the administration] as equals, whereas here...'.[137] It should be noted that this illicit classification, 'human beings versus inmates', does not contradict the licit classification: the Soviet penal system bypassed the Law that set out the rights of inmates (we will discuss this matter in more depth in the sub-section entitled '*Brief history of the Code for Applying Sentences*'). Is there any better evidence of State recognition of the autonomy of the penal institution in matters that concern the treatment of inmates?

Expelling the inmates outside the human community seems to give a degree of latitude to civil servants whose behavior towards the inmates exceeds all acceptable limits. For them, theft, humiliation and insults are accepted as soon as they concern relations with the 'others', namely the inmates. 'They [certain members of the penal administration], steal food from our canteen. There is canned pork (*tushenka*) – they carry the cans home in large bags. They see a truck park and start unloading it immediately. That's why you never see semolina, rice or buckwheat here'.[138] Clandestine production in prison is another example of an administration racket. In each facility, small objects and souvenirs are produced under the table (pens, cutting boards, etc.), as well as knives, wooden panels, even firearms (Makarov pistols, *PM*). The inmates use these objects to trade with the guards and foremen, and even, through them, with the outside world. This type of production is prohibited in prison, but the administration generally tolerates it

---

[137] Interview No. 1b.
[138] Interview No. 38.

because it constitutes a serious source of revenue, in the form of the illicit 'taxation' of the inmates work. 'They take the consumer goods (*shirpotreb*), well, they take everything... How do they use these products? – I don't know what they do with them, re-sell them maybe... Imagine, you find this normal? Plus, in one way, it's good for us... You hide a knife, you sharpen a blade, no one says anything... they're used to confiscating things. What would you say: you're given an order, either you bring me a knife or.... It's normal? If you don't bring it, you'll go to solitary!'[139]

Moreover, when viewed through the prism of dual relations, violence loses its exceptional character and is transformed into the rule for daily behavior. Unilateral violence is often used for the perfectly licit objective of ensuring inmate discipline and docility. Thus, the arbitrariness of the penal administration creates the conditions necessary for its abuse of power, whereas the duality of norms forms sufficient conditions. 'There is painful administration, which tries to humiliate the individual, his human dignity. They torture people physically. You're taken to solitary, you're locked up, put in shackles. For nothing, you just didn't please them. They hit you until you let go of your bowels, you piss yourself. I was struck with a rubber hose. You've seen it, the rubber hose with a metal screw? I was young. They start to hit you. They want to know how long you can hold on. They wait until you start to beg them. In an hour, two... If you pass out, they throw water on you, they leave you... Real Gestapo torture... There was maximum security. And the administration kept a close eye on the law and *even went beyond the law*. In other words, they only torture those who committed infractions? – Yes, they tortured for infractions. There were no purely arbitrary tortures? – No, there weren't'.[140] The discourse of certain members of the administration proves their resolve to go beyond legitimate violence, if needed. One young officer, the head of the *otrjad*, told us in a private conversation that he wanted to put the inmates 'in their place' using any means available. It is interesting to note the use of one expression in his discourse: 'to beat up in the john' (*mochit' v sortire*), which he used to speak about a fight with no rules and no pity for the adversary.[141]

Speaking about the 1970s–1980s, and particularly the start of the 1990s, our interviewees often used the word *bespredel* (without limits) to describe the actions of the administration. 'If the guards, the young soldiers, were cold, or bored, they would warm up by hitting you. I remember it well'.[142] 'There was a great deal of *bespredel* at the start of the 1990s. What did that involve? – They got used to living without responsibility: to humiliating someone, to hitting someone, to enjoying

---

[139] Interview No. 18. It should be noted that as a result of the delicate character of the subject, several interviewees could not talk freely.

[140] Interview No. 18.

[141] As bizarre as this seems, the acting President of the Russian Federation also used the same expression in his public discourse to refer to the war in Chechnya.

[142] Interview No. 13. Until the start of the 1990s, the guard positions in the facilities were given to young people doing their required military service in the internal army (*VV– Vnutrennie Vojska*).

their privileged position. They view us as slaves'.[143] The maximum security facilities created specifically to house the most sensitive inmates, who refuse to submit to the discipline imposed by the administration, the 'white swans' in prison slang (*belyj lebed'*), have a reputation as places where the administration can go beyond the law in order to 're-educate' the inmates, most of whom belong to the *blatnye* category. 'When a "swan" was opened in Ercevo [Arkhangelsk region] in 1990, we were placed there. There you were told how to do things in a very arbitrary manner. We were placed in a hallway and we had to pass between two lines of guards who hit us with paddles'.[144]

The failure to respect the human dignity of the inmates, their treatment as 'others', as non-humans, causes the prisoners to act in a similar manner. They question the need to refer to the licit authority to organize their everyday lives, which they associate with a pure constraint that must be bypassed at the slightest opportunity. 'From the inmate's point of view, all these leaders (*nachal'niki*) symbolized oppression and constraint' (Shalamov, 1998, p. 141). The administration considers the inmates as others, and the inmates view it likewise. In this situation, the only reasonable strategy pre-supposes a distrust of strangers (*chujie*), personified by the representatives of the administration. Here are the responses of the interviewees to the question 'Do you trust the penal administration?' (Table 2.18). It should be noted that it is the trust in the facility that determines all aspects of everyday life in prison!

Table 2.18 Level of institutional trust in prison

	Russia, N=1120	Kazakhstan, N=396	France, N=59	Canada, N=120
Yes	19.9	25.3[145]	59.3	23.3
No	73.1	69.9	37.3	68.3
No answer	7	4.8	3.4	8.3

That is where we find the origin of the norm, 'Don't go to the administration to settle conflicts', which constitutes one element of the prison subculture. 'If I went to the administration, the other inmates would consider me as a stool pigeon, and treat me with suspicion'.[146] When contact with the administration is absolutely inevitable, there is a series of precautions and control devices. The prisoners, particularly those in the *blatnye* category, are obliged to warn their fellow inmates and/or be accompanied during their visit to the administration. 'In the case of a joint cause, why not [contact the administration]? But, of course, I would keep

---

[143] Interview No. 24.
[144] Interview No. 38.
[145] Without a doubt, the fact that the level of confidence is higher in Kazakhstan than in Russia is the result of the harsher control exercised in the Soviet model by the custodial Ministry (the Ministry of the Interior until 2001 in Kazakhstan), which reduced the discretion of the administration (see Oleinik, 2002a).
[146] Interview No. 20.

those with [illicit] authority informed'.[147] 'Before, if the administration brought someone to its offices (*shtab*), he could not go there alone. If he wasn't going to denounce someone, he wouldn't go alone. He would ask any other inmate to accompany him. "We have to talk together"'.[148] 'Before, no one talked to the administration alone. You'd need to be accompanied. You never know what someone says to the administration! You can be converted into a passive homosexual (*opustit'*) for that. If the inmate is a *blatnoj*, he could be downgraded for an unaccompanied visit. They'd say, "Listen, you go into the office [of the administration] and we don't know what you talk about". People were very strict on this point'.[149]

The gap that separates the inmates from the penal administration excludes any compromise with their interests. 'There is always room for a compromise. If you can't feed us, at least give us the opportunity to cook. Hot plates are forbidden...They removed all the hot plates. We never reach a compromise'.[150] The inmates criticize the administration particularly for this refusal to look for a compromise. When they responded to the question, 'What would re-establish your confidence in the penal administration?', half of the inmates mentioned the willingness of the administration to consider their interests:

Table 2.19 Parameters of institutional trust

	Russia	Kazakhstan
N	1310	396
Willingness of the administration to take into consideration our interests	42.5	41.9
Respect of the Law by the administration	21.5	21.7
Personal qualities and trustworthiness	14.1	14.4
Nothing could make me trust them	12.5	16.4
No answer	9.3	5.6

It should be noted that only one-fifth of the interviewees mentioned legal guarantees to respect their interests. Paradoxically, but one element of the 'small' society, personalized relations, opposes another, the duality of norms, in the inmates' minds. Is it a matter of transforming the administration into 'one of yours' by personalizing relations with it? Therefore, the 'small' society is reproduced in the inmate's minds, which makes it harder to abandon. We found evidence of this hypothesis in a discussion of the results of our investigation with an illicit guard. 'I'd choose the option "Personal qualities and trustworthiness". <u>What do you mean by that</u>? – First, their ability to treat us appropriately (*normal'no*), keep their word. <u>To what they promise? Is that rare here</u>? – Very. Take the canteen for example. They promised to correct the situation. Nothing happened... <u>You say that the key</u>

---

[147] Interview No. 1a.
[148] Interview No. 21.
[149] Interview No. 18.
[150] Interview No. 14.

condition for respect is keeping one's word. Yes, if he [a member of the administration] behaves like a man (*po mujski*). What does that mean–like a man? – I don't know... When you talk to him, he doesn't view you in the framework of the "administration–inmate" (*zek*) model. I can say it like that... They don't behave like humans, like men. Another example–with solitary. The head of the *otrjad* doesn't tell the director the truth, he'll criticize you for imaginary things'.[151]

In summing up our study of licit authority, we must focus on the profound duality of the inmates' perception of it. On the one hand, the omnipotence of the administration and its close control over all aspects of everyday life in incarceration explains the inmates' total dependence on it.

> 'If the individual does not make himself a subject, the centers of power that define and sanction his roles will constitute him in itself' (Touraine, 1993, p. 270).

On the other hand, the abuse of power and the treatment of inmates as inferior beings, reflected in the guards' slang by the pejorative term *zek, zechara* (from the official acronym *Z/K, Zakljuchennyj Kanalarmeec* used to designate the inmates in the forced labor camps created to build the Belomor-Baltic canal, in common use in the 1930s–1960s) (Rossi, 1991, pp. 130–131) results in a rejection of the licit authority. The total dependence on the licit authority and its total rejection lie at the core of penal society and, as we will see later, the Soviet model of society.

Illicit control of violence

The vector of violence generated by the licit authority is co-linear with another vector of violence, which reflects the violence produced within the penal society. The organization of penal space and time result in everyday conflicts. Let us take a close look at two sources of violence: the first pertains to the transparency of the public/private border, the second to the difficulty involved in organizing time, which is very limited in keeping with the official use of time.[152] The transparency of the public/private border places the notion of personal property in perspective. The night table serves to protect it. Obviously the norm 'Don't cheat your neighbor' at the very core of the penal subculture is explained by the willingness to develop a norm to protect personal property. Therefore, the prison situation facilitates petty theft and supposes that it will be punished in time. It should be noted that the punishment of thieves inside the penal facility is the harshest. Regardless of the damage caused by the theft, occasionally just a few cigarettes, the inmates consider theft a capital crime. From the outset, 'the primary, major sanction is exclusion' (Reynaud, 1989, p. 39) of the thief from the penal city, his downgrading, and consequent marginalization.

---

[151] Interview No. 35a. The ward is responsible for deciding to use solitary confinement for punishment.
[152] According to standard regulations, free time must not exceed one hour per day (*Pravila vnutrennego rasporjadka ispravitel'nyh uchrejdenij*, p.25).

The flagrant crime of a thief provides an opportunity to cause violence and direct it towards the 'rat' (*krysa*). 'If someone stole from me, I would have smashed a stool over his head, without asking anyone for permission... Without judgment? – What for? I caught him, that's enough. It's an obvious truth. We go to the *blatnoj* for the complicated cases. We strike the hands of the thief mercilessly; it's an obvious truth'.[153] 'Maybe I've run into violence once or twice. A guy was beat up because he stole something. We hit him, as usual'.[154] It should be noted that the thieves' pleas are often accepted by public opinion in the penal city. 'We shouldn't hesitate to use force more often. Before there was less fraud (*krysjatnichestvo*). Before? – Yes, now we punish them ['rats'] less harshly'.[155] Violence must find its 'lightning rod'.

The punishment of the thief is not limited to merciless blows, particularly in the case of a recurrence. The other inmates may decide to convert the 'rat' into a passive homosexual (*opustit'*). The conversion often occurs in the gaols, where the shortage of living space and the permanent rotation of the inmates makes punishment crueler. 'When a man arrives from a gaol (*SIZO*), he knows that if he did something dishonest, stealing or denouncing, he would be punished very harshly, for example, by being converted by force into a passive homosexual'.[156] 'Now, the thief knows that he will be hit about head, at the worst, whether he's a first offender or a repeat one. Before, he was afraid that that if he had been tortured for a first offence, he would inevitably be converted into a passive homosexual for the second'.[157] Even worse, the conversion by force into a passive homosexual means that the thief would become the target of daily violence for the rest of his life in prison. We have already noted that passive homosexuals bear the stigma of pariahs, which encourages daily violence against them. For this reason, inmates view murder as less cruel than conversion into a passive homosexual. Inmates who have spent several years in prison refuse to apply this sanction even though the guilty one deserves it. They view *bespredel* (without limits), as a lack of respect for human dignity, this time admitted by the inmates themselves. 'We don't use the prick to punish, they say. Before, it was rare. Before, if someone was converted into a passive homosexual, it was *bespredel*'.[158] 'If someone converted the other, even someone guilty of theft, into a passive homosexual, his hands would be broken. Even if he did it for punishment. Human beings don't accept that punishment... It's *bespredel*. If he's guilty, I can kill him. It's more humane to kill the guilty guy than to convert him into a passive homosexual. If I converted him into a passive homosexual, the others would wipe their feet on him for the rest of his life. That's worse. It's better to kill him. Otherwise his life is ruined, he's condemned to hell'.[159]

---

[153] Interview No. 38.
[154] Interview No. 39.
[155] Interview No. 36.
[156] Interview No. 29.
[157] Interview No. 16.
[158] Interview No. 1a.
[159] Interview No. 3a.

The other crime that incurs punishment that is just as violent, namely the conversion into a passive homosexual, is the refusal to pay gambling debts. Card games, which are officially prohibited in prison, are an important element of clandestine life. Each regular search uncovers several decks made in hiding. There is an entire technology for making cards from the materials available in prison: old books, newspapers, pieces of paper, etc. The inmates' interest in cards is a result of the lack of other leisure activities. Athletic fields are rare in prison (we did not see one in the prisons visited!), not to mention sports rooms. The libraries are poorly equipped. There is often no time to take advantage of movies or interesting TV shows. As an illicit guard who is responsible for the card games in a maximum security facility in northern Russian explained, there is a rule that limits gambling in keeping with the player's monthly revenue and his rank in the illicit hierarchy.[160] When cards are temporarily unavailable, anything, even matches, is used.

The importance of playing cards is reflected in the existence of numerous painstaking rules. 'The card games of the *blatnye* have a unusual number of rules' (Shalamov, 1998, p. 35). Failure to respect the rules and a refusal or inability to pay debts results in the attribution of the status of *fuflyjnik* and occasionally the conversion by force into a passive homosexual. 'Before, if you did something serious, you could be converted into a homosexual. Do you remember that time? – Yes, it was at the start of the 1990s. That could happen for a loss. Now the loser walks around freely, as if nothing happened. Before, we would have bashed his head in or converted him into a homosexual. It was shameful! Why not pay the debt? The debt must be paid. Period. If you have to pay today, after midnight they could do anything to you. After midnight, you're no longer a human being'.[161] The risk of rape increases if the loser tries to obtain shelter from the administration. When explaining the recent inflation in the number of 'roosters', one interviewee focussed on the willingness to punish those who seek refuge from the administration after committing a crime against the penal community. 'They try to find refuge in the maximum security quarters. They hide there. In any case, those who refuse to pay their gambling debts must be punished. We punish them like this, even though it's inhuman'.[162]

The severity of the punishment, as well as its inevitable character, are two key factors in the norms of the penal subculture. Most inmates think that the respect for informal norms is more important than respect for the Law, even in a total institution! Any violation of the informal norms, *kosjak* (Abramkin, Chijov, 1992, p. 109),[163] appears more dangerous than violating the Law. Here are the answers to the question, 'Which norms do you consider it more dangerous to violate?':

---

[160] Interview No. 41.
[161] Interview No. 18.
[162] Interview No. 21. We find the same reasoning in the discourse of Interviewee No. 41.
[163] For example, the expression '*zaporot' kosjak*' means 'to violate an informal norm (*ponjatie*)'.

Table 2.20 Violation of norms: relative strength of sanctions

	Russia	Kazakh.	France	Canada
N	1310	396	59	120
The norms imposed by the administration	31.6%	29.6	33.9	52.3
Law	22.4	16.5	22.4	35.5
The norms I've accustomed to respect since my childhood	19.1	20	×	×
The informal norms structuring the relations with the prison guards	×	×	28.6	15
The norms set up by the prisoners' leaders (*avtoritety*)	15.1 (35.2)	15.2 (43.2)	×	×
The norms of our milieu	15.2	18.9	16.1	21.5
The norms set up by the *smotrjashie*	4.9	9.1	×	×

In other words, the characteristics of the control of violence within the framework of the 'small' society helps to minimize the number of infractions and ensure that the 'constitution' of everyday life is respected. It is the absence of the public/private border and the personalization of relations that serve as major guarantees of the inevitable character of the punishment. This manner of fighting criminality applies only to the 'small' society. Delinquents are expelled outside the penal city, which reduces the crime rate within. The existence of an infinite regression should be noted: society expels the criminals into the prison and the prison society expels its own delinquents outside the penal city, etc. Crime is not suppressed in this manner, it is expelled by creating 'reservations' for violence.

Let us demonstrate the hypothesis that the effectiveness of the illicit control of violence decreases spectacularly as we move away from the model of the 'small' society. The transparency of the border between the distinct spheres of activity facilities the capture of the delinquent: his actions and possessions are in view. 'Outside the prison, it is difficult to find a thief. If someone is robbed, only God knows who did it. However, here everything is in view. There are 100 people. You know them and they know you. You communicate often. If someone steals something, people will know. Sooner or later, everything is found out. Impunity pushes people towards crime outside the prison. There, only a small percentage of thieves are caught'.[164] The personalization of relations makes it easier to predict the possible actions of a given inmate, including infractions. Moreover, the transparency of the public/private border means that stolen objects cannot be hidden, their possession is public. 'I placed a pack of cigarettes on my night table. Then it disappeared. You start to ask questions about those who were in the dorm then. Did you find the thief? – Of course. Let's say no one has cigarettes in the *otrjad*. You smoke *Prima* [inexpensive cigarettes]. You see someone smoking *Prima*, while you pack has disappeared. You ask him for a cigarette to make sure. In this way, you can always find a grass. Something happened, then someone went

---

[164] Interview No. 27b.

out, then the administration called someone else'.[165] One interviewee described a rather caricatural case to us. 'An inmate went to the hospital. There were receipts for clothing. Another inmate saw the receipts for the first: good clothing, jeans, shirts... the second inmate stole the receipts for the first. When he left the hospital he took the first inmate's belongings. Before, he was poorly dressed. But when he left the hospital he put on black pants, good shoes. We thought he had won at cards. No one was interested. But, after the first inmate discovered his loss, he sent a messenger. To find out. So, the situation was explained to him. The prison mail system works well. The illicit guard called the thief and beat him. It was all over for him. He could have been converted into a passive homosexual'.[166]

The effectiveness of illicit proceedings against delinquents forms a lasting link in the minds of the inmates between the stimulus (the violation of an informal norm) and the reaction (punishment). The norms of the prison subculture *must* always be applied. 'We always go after someone who has committed an infraction,' say the prisoners. 'Before, we could go after someone for each bad word'[167] regardless of whether reprobation is unjust or interpreted too freely. 'Before, every word like that said in public could be punished severely. I think any affront could be punished by physical force. If someone is vexed, the person who vexed him must be put in his place. That's what I think'.[168] It should be noted that the informal norm requires the inmate to refute any rumors that concern him.

Violence does not disappear from the penal city, but the social structure there channels it toward the 'suits', who have become the sacrificial victims after committing infractions. Once again, the extreme violence of the punishments should be noted. The Soviet prison model even places the value of human life in perspective. For a particular infraction, the illicit 'penal code' often provides for harsher punishment than the Soviet Penal Code, which has often been criticized for its inhumane character. 'Here, in the maximum security system, nothing disappears from the kitchen. The slightest doubt would entail the capital punishment of the cooks. If we learn that the cooks are trafficking, we kill them without asking for explanations'.[169] The execution procedure deserves discussion in more detail, taking into consideration its complexity and sophistication. 'For punishing a *kosjak*, there were [during the Soviet period] executioners, convicts sentenced to 25 years in prison. They execute the delinquent, while their official sentence only increases 2–3 years. People respected the rules because they were afraid of having their throats cut'.[170]

Although the inmates are subjected to the violence of the State and the penal administration, they do not hesitate to apply it further. Violence is well accepted and often even welcomed, as long as it targets a victim that can be justified from

---

[165] Interview No. 33.
[166] Interview No. 37.
[167] Interview No. 16.
[168] Interview No. 25.
[169] Interview No. 21.
[170] Interview No. 21. Under the rule concerning serving of sentences, the inmate's sentence increases only slightly.

the point of view of the penal subculture. 'Only a small percentage of inmates are subjected to violence and executed. There are people who bother others, either as a result of particular consequences, or as a result of personal characteristics such as haughtiness, insolence... Generally, the recourse to violence is always justified. Someone who has done nothing serious will never be subjected to violence. If he is, it's because of his character, or some error he committed. For example, you're never forced to play cards. But if you do play, you need to know the consequences. You don't think of that when playing cards'.[171] Generally the inmates excuse the recourse to violence because they see it as the only way to maintain order. Is the value of order greater than the value of human life in the 'small' society? 'Before, prison taught inmates to live. Don't insult anyone, don't sit on anyone's bed... *Prison taught people order.* If you take things that belong to others, you will be punished. The punishment is worse than the deeds'.[172] A discussion on the place of religious faith in the prison focuses on the sacrifice of human values for the value of order. Conversion results in the following paradox: according to our interviewee, the ten commandments have the most force in prison. 'Do the commandments apply more in prison? – Yes. In order to make someone respect a norm, you must impose it. We fulfill the obligations because we can go after those who don't respect them. As for sanctions, I'd rank physical force first'.[173]

Moreover, as a result of recent changes in penal society, the origins of which will be analyzed in the section entitled '*Illicit justice*', we can talk of a movement towards a more modern control of violence. Since the appearance of the illicit guards (*smotrjashie*) at the start of the 1990s, penal society has started to move away from the model of the 'small' society, in terms of controlling violence. It is up to them to determine the recourse to violence, to define the punishment for a given infraction. 'Generally, the illicit guard decides whether the guilty inmate is to be beaten or not. Creating a precedent in order to the give the punishment a public resonance..... It makes things easier'.[174] Begging loses its essential importance as the base for order in the penal city. The penal administration has also noted a decrease in violence in the prison setting, following its partial institutionalization. 'For five or six years now, corporal punishment has been declining in importance. The inmates are starting to resolve conflicts in other ways'.[175] A comparison of the responses given to two questions, 'Do you continue to deal with a person who is unpleasant yet useful?' [A] and 'Can you respect someone whose actions more or less correspond to the ideal for the illicit guard, yet who is essentially unpleasant?' [B], confirms the hypothesis of the partial institutionalization of violence.

---

[171] Interview No. 7.
[172] Interview No. 13.
[173] Interview No. 2.
[174] Interview No. 10.
[175] Interview No. 3b.

Table 2.21 Level of personification in relationships

	Russia, N=1310		Kazakhstan, N=396		France, N=59
	A	B	A	B	A
Yes	48.5%	47.3%	52	53.3	23.7
No	46	43.7	44.9	40.2	72.9
No answer	5.5	9.1	3	6.6	3.4

Bespredel: the lack of normative markers as a source of violence

Violence, whether institutionalized or not, is never completely controlled in prison. Regardless of the source of the uncontrolled violence–the actions of the administration or daily conflicts between inmates–it is referred to by the popular slang expression *bespredel* (without limits) in prison. 'What do you mean by *bespredel*? – When everything goes against my wishes. Yes, against my interests'.[176] Therefore, it is the inability of the inmates to effect their situation, the rules, that defines the negative content of the term *bespredel*. The inability to find appropriate frameworks for the conflicts, including their daily repetition, as we have seen, remains inevitable in prison, leaving them only one way out, pure and uncontrolled violence.

> 'A social conflict means that the adversaries share certain cultural values and even certain forms for the institutional resolution of their conflict' (Touraine, 1993, p. 331).

However, in *bespredel* situations 'there is no set rule for relieving tension or for getting out of a violent situation' (Peralva, 1996, p. 35).

Unlike violence that serves to maintain order, violence resulting from a failure to respect the rules is a serious threat to order. The slightest conflict for which there is no means to channel violence, whether institutional or not, could disrupt the general order. Uncivil actions, 'infractions to the designed order encountered in everyday life, [...] are experienced as threats to order. [...] By perceived order, we mean the social order (and not legal order) as it should be in the minds of individuals' (Roché, 1993, p. 142). In prison, uncivil actions include shoving, verbal insults, a refusal to keep clean, a refusal to stop smoking in the TV room, etc. For example, shoving, even when not intentional, quickly progresses, in *bespredel* conditions, to fights. The lack of means for managing conflict forces the inmate either to engage in the spiral of violence or 'close his eyes' to provocative situations, even at the cost of marginalization. 'I try not to pay attention to the others. To avoid situations when someone shoves another, one says "Hey, take care." And the other reacts with "Shut up, don't give orders" and so on. All the small conflicts start like that'.[177] Perhaps the desire to 'close one's eyes' to the others says a lot about the comfort of social life in 'small' society than many other criteria.

---

[176] Interview No. 20.
[177] Interview No. 20.

If escalation of the conflict becomes inevitable, the absence of a unique exit strategy is apparent in the response to the question, 'How do you react to uncivil behavior?':

Table 2.22 Reactions to uncivil behavior

	Russia	Kazakhstan	France
N	925	396	55
I will fight for my safety (cf. the norm 'Know how to defend yourself')	60.9	59.8	×
I will make use of my connections	8.2	9.8	×
I will contact the prisoners' leader (*avtoritet*) or the *smotrjashij*	9.4	12.1	×
We'll try to find a compromise	8.9	7.1	12.7
I will join my efforts with those who are confronted by the same problem	3.4	3.3	×
I will contact the administration	4.5	5.6	67.3
I will resign myself	1.7	0.8	×
I will contact the public prosecutor or the magistrate	0.3	0	40
No answer	2.7	1.5	

In other words, there are at least four strategies that the inmates choose with a more or less equal probability of relieving tension. 'How do you resolve any conflicts? – We fight, we may reconcile, we may have some tea together and discuss the situation. It's preferable to talk quietly'.[178] 'I resolve conflicts on my own. How? – It depends. With some, we fight. There aren't many of them. With others we try to talk'.[179]

Situations of *bespredel* highlight the value of physical force, virtually unimportant in most other cases. 'Physical force attracts respect, regardless of intellectual ability. The weak are expelled. It's the law of the jungle. I didn't agree with the fact that you have to fight each time. Order is only established through physical force'.[180] The only rule that is absolutely respected in *bespredel* implies that 'might means right'. The roots of this rule are found in pre-modern society. *Trial by battle* was broadly applied in medieval times when 'a claim to land upon a writ of rights was settled by physical combat between the parties or their hired champions, and the verdict was left to the God of Battles' (James, 1989, pp. 62–63). It is interesting to note the expression 'might means right' in the discourse of some of our interviewees. For example, one young inmate (Interviewee No. 30) spontaneously formulated this rule to describe his experience in a gaol (*SIZO*).

There is nothing accidental about the reference to preventive detention as one of the most obvious examples of *bespredel*. The gaols are places where the penal

---

[178] Interview No. 32.
[179] Interview No. 20.
[180] Interview No. 9.

subculture comes up short. Also, 'the transit prisons stand out for the marked degree of *bespredel*' (Abramkin, Chijov, 1992, p. 122). Among inmates, one transit prison in Moscow, *Krasnaja Presnja*, is notorious for the lack of respect for the rules. We are interested in the characteristics of the social structure that causes *bespredel* to flourish. First, the populations are unstable and the high turnover rate means that personal relationships do not last. The inmates spend from a few months to a year or two in the gaol and during their preventive detention they often change cells and do not have the time to set down social roots. Moreover, the high percentage of new arrivals who are familiar with the penal subculture (*pervoprohodchiki*) also makes it hard to resolve conflicts arising out of uncivil behavior. 'Sometimes, we see such stupid people... "This is black", he says while I can see that it is white. We'll never change him. He acts like a wild beast, and jostles me. "Be careful. Can't you see?" I say. For him everything looks the same. He keeps on walking'.[181]

Paradoxically, the same argument concerning the instability of the population remains valid for describing the situation in another total institution, the Soviet army. Military service lasts two years and, during that time, soldiers often move from one group to another. The rule, 'might means right' unifies the phenomenon of *dedovschina* specific to the Soviet army and that of *bespredel*. One interviewee who had recently completed his military service described his experience in terms of *bespredel* (although he was a parachutist, considered the military elite): 'Everything is based on physical force. I was at Kursk, Briansk, Tver, etc. *It's easier to live here.* There, there was *dedovschina*... Pure physical force, humiliation... physical and moral pressure'.[182]

Second, the fight of the penal administration against the penal subculture often has unexpected results: the inmates are deprived of the illicit mechanisms for resolving conflicts while the licit mechanisms remain confusing and ineffective. What a brilliant example of the 'unintended social repercussions of intentional human actions', according to the famous expression used by Friedrich August von Hayek.[183] For example, the administration gives its full support to the capos (*bugry*), the inmates responsible for heading the other inmates. The practice that involves the transfer of discretionary power to the inmates' representatives is widespread in facilities for young people. But, instead of respect for formal norms, *bespredel* flourishes. 'There [in the youth facility], there were *bugry*, capos. They sowed *bespredel*. We had to fight for survival each day. It was worse there than here'.[184] The *bugry* enjoy discretionary power since the administration both lacks the means to control them closely and protects them against the social control assured by the penal subculture.

---

[181] Interview No. 1a.

[182] Interview No. 8.

[183] Quoted in Langlois R, 'Rationality, Institutions, and Explanation', in Langlois R. (ed.), *Economics as a Process. Essays in the New Institutional Economics*, Cambridge: Cambridge University Press, 1986, p. 236.

[184] Interview No. 3a. This observation is also justified by the testimony of Interviewee No. 31.

Third, the probability of *bespredel* increases in the large institution as the increase in the number of participants in interactions renders the 'small' society model ineffective for controlling violence. The forced labor camps of the Stalinist period serve as an example. Moreover, the fear of 'large numbers' is decisive for the prison conscience – the illicit devices for organizing everyday life appear drastically inadequate as soon as one has to deal with the *large number* of actors. 'There are five people here [the cell], two, three. There, in one facility, there are 1,000 people. Either I jostle someone or someone jostles me. I'm afraid of that. Even if I don't jostle anyone, someone will jostle me. By chance, deliberately or not... Conflicts arise everywhere. Here I can avoid them'.[185] In other words, *bespredel* reflects the price that the 'small' society pays for its inability to become a 'large' society.

Norm of trust

The penal situation implies a transparency of intentions and actions that is essential for building relationships based on trust.[186] The absence of the public/private

---

[185] Interview No. 3a.

[186] Its institutional status remains vague: is trust a frame of mind, a value, an affect or a norm? Needless to say, the four definitions are entitled to exist and are correlated. For example, trust is often an obvious emotional expression. 'With many students the assumption that the other person was to be distrusted was the same as the attribution that the other person was angry with them and hated them' (Garfinkel, 1967, p. 51). On the other hand, trust as a frame of mind affects the development of the interaction plan. Trust is 'the expectation of one person about the actions of others that affects the first person's choice, when an action must be taken before the actions of others are known' (Ostrom, 1998, p. 12). Trust may also be considered a traditional value. 'Tradition provided an anchorage for that "basic trust" so central to continuity of identity' (Giddens, 1996, p. 35). Moreover, trust loses its character as imposed and supported by tradition as our society becomes increasingly modernized.

Without wanting to reduce trust to a single dimension, we will concentrate on trust as a norm that is applied voluntarily and enables the players to organize their daily interventions. Several sophisticated interactions involve the existence of trust between the parties. For example, any transaction using money for payment is based on trust: trust in the bank that issues the means for payment and trust that the partner will respect the payment terms. 'With the exception of barter transactions, virtually all economic transactions leave open the possibility of cheating' (Milgrom et al., 1990, p. 6). It is the trust institution that makes the major role played by trust explicit. 'The trust and confidence imposed in the trustee by the creator of the trust is the core and essence of the matter [the institution of trust]' (James, 1989, p. 499). It is not by chance that the word trust in English describes both relationships of trust and a trustee. Therefore, an understanding of trust as a norm must focus on the correspondence between the appearances of the players, including their promises, and their actual behavior. From this point of view, the definition of trust in terms of an 'undeniable correspondence' proposed by H. Garfinkel appears most appropriate. 'For the conduct of his everyday affairs the person assumes, assumes the other person assumes as well, and assumes that as he assumes it of the other person, the other person assumes it of him, that a relationship of

border as well as the personalization of relationships increases the volume of information available to the social partners and facilitates the mutual interpretation of their intentions. Now, the paradox that we describe below in further detail involves the virtually total absence of the norm of trust in the 'small' penal society. How can this be explained on a theoretical level before proceeding to an empirical analysis? The more or less complete differentiation of the spheres of activity 'splinters' the general norm of trust into several sub-norms: trust in business, trust in private life, trust in public institutions, etc. As a result, as the spheres of activity are less differentiated, the norm of trust is less splintered. In the prison, an extreme case of non-differentiation, either trust exists in a total form or its does not exist at all. In this case, it is not enough for the actions in a sphere of activity to be transparent. Transcendental transparency, non-opacity, is required.

In response to our question concerning the understanding of trust, only one of the interviewees progressed to 'splintering': 'I'd define it as follows. If I have a very large amount of money, I would not be afraid to leave it with someone I trust'.[187] Most of the others mentioned the need to share all aspects of one's life, even the most personal, with the trustworthy person. 'It [trust] involves sharing without reservation. Doing something jointly. Some common cause...'[188] 'I can share [with the trustworthy person] everything I have in my soul. There are people I discuss more neutral, impersonal matters with... I must not be afraid that the trustworthy person will treat me badly'.[189] 'It's one thing to confide about a business matter, it's another to confide your soul. I think I need very intimate relations in order to be able to trust... I need for [the trustworthy person] to know and understand this without reservations'.[190] Therefore, our hypothesis supposes the existence of a contradiction in the framework of the model of the 'small' prison society. On the one hand, this model facilitates trust by breaking the barriers between distinct spheres of activity. On the other hand, it makes trust transcendental and increases the requirements with respect to the conditions for

---

undoubted correspondence is the sanctioned relationship between the actual appearances of an object and the intended object that appears in a particular way' (Garfinkel, 1967, p.50).

The anticipation of the undeniable correspondence between the appearance and the actual actions of others is clearly present in the discourse of the actors when we ask about their understanding of trust. Trust is 'the possibility of believing what the other tells me and not controlling his actions' (Interview No. 9*). The * is used to indicate interviews conducted with Russian businessmen from November 1998 to July 1999, for more details, see the section entitled '*Sources*'. Trust appears when 'the interviewee says what he thinks and does' (Interview No. 21*). 'By trust, I mean cooperation with the partner, when is open enough in financial, economic and technical terms' (Interview No. 3*). In other words, in order to build relationships based on trust, the actors need to make their plans transparent and keep their promises. Transparency of intentions and actions constitutes, as we have already stressed, the very reason for trust as such.

[187] Interview No. 16.
[188] Interview No. 20. Cf. the Italian term *Cosa Nostra*.
[189] Interview No. 27a.
[190] Interview No. 26.

trust. Apparently, the penal institutional context does not satisfy these requirements.

Trust in the prison

Several observers have noted the norm of mistrust that reigns in the prison world. In fact, this world is particularly hostile to friendly, solid relations. There, there are 'no friends, at the best allies and temporary mutual assistance' (Marchetti, 1997, p. 123). Moreover, the obviously distrustful character of the prison environment was at the source of the basic model in game theory, the 'Prisoner's Dilemma', whose very name reflects the questioning of trust in prison. The difficult choice faced by an inmate who is suspected of the same infraction as another inmate involves either trusting that other inmate and refusing any acknowledgement of guilt or not trusting him and acknowledging his guilt. If one single inmate confesses, he is freed at the price of adding to the sentence of the second whereas if both confess together, they minimize their sentences. Let us use a tale recounted by one interviewee to illustrate this. 'Two 18-year-old men, from Moscow, were questioned. One was placed in prevention detention whereas the other was on parole. It was the first judicial experience for both. They had stolen a car cassette machine, through an open window. The first fled, the second was caught. He confessed their guilt...' Let us use a matrix to interpret the prisoner's dilemma in terms of game theory. R, what each player has to win if both refuse to confess, equals three units of utility. T, what is gained by the player who confesses while the other refuses, is equal to five units. Therefore, the player who refuses to confess obtains S=0. K, while each player gains one unit when both confess:

Table 2.23 Prisoner's dilemma

		Second player	
		To refuse	To confess
First player	To refuse (=cooperate)	R=3, R=3 [P]	S=0, T=5
	To confess (=not cooperate)	T=5, S=0	K=1, K=1 [N]

The sole Nash equilibrium (1, 1) does not coincide with the Pareto equilibrium (3, 3), which justifies the impossibility of trust in prison. As a major analytical tool the Prisoner's Dilemma is not restricted to studies of prison. 'In fact, many of the best-developed models of important political, social and economic processes have the Prisoner's Dilemma as their foundation' (Axelrod, 1990, p. 28).

The results of our survey confirm the hypothesis that the prison institutional context is hostile to trust. Between two judgments, 'You can trust people' and 'You must be wary of people', 14.6 per cent of our interviewees selected the first, with 80.2 per cent selecting the second, namely they are wary of people they do not know personally. A direct question, 'Do you trust other inmates in this penitentiary?", gives rise to very similar figures:

Table 2.24 Level of interpersonal trust

	Do you think the people around could be trusted?		Do you trust other inmates in this penitentiary?		
	Yes	No	Yes	No	Don't know
Russia, N=1310	14.6	80.2	13.7	43.2	41
Kazakhstan, N=396	17.7	74.7	14.4	55.6	27.3
Canada, N=120	37.5	60.8	15	77.5	-
France, N=59	45.8	54.2	20.3	79.7	-

The lack of trust does not mean that the inmates consider this norm superfluous. On the contrary, they view it as the basis for any social construction. The norm of trust heads the list of responses to the question concerning the ideal foundations of Russian society ('On what foundations should Russian [Kazakh, French, Quebec] society be built?'). At the same time, it is only sixth in France where the level of trust expressed by people *in general* is three times higher than in Russia (the level of trust expressed by inmates in all three countries is almost the same!).

Table 2.25 Foundations of an ideal society

	Russia	Kazakhstan	France	Canada
N	769	374	55	120
Freedom	38.7%	45.5	72.7	73.5
Trust	36.5	37.7	45.5	55.9
Equality	32.3	38.8	60	64.7
Family	28.2	31.8	61.8	68.6
Labor	24.8	26.7	41.8	66.7
Empathy	22.9	18.5	20	22.6
Law	20.6	18.7	52.7	38.2
Tradition	14.7	13.4	23.6	22.6
Moral	13.9	14.2	50.9	24.5
Property	8.8	9.1	3.6	18.6
Profit	4.2	3.5	5.5	15.7

The lack of trust is experienced clearly in everyday life. It deprives the inmate of any social support. In a difficult situation inmates rely on themselves. 'I trust only myself. I don't trust anyone else'.[191] 'The only thing that is truly important is trusting only in yourself'.[192] This posture explains the 'inmate's commandments' formulated for the first time in the 1930s. They include three imperatives: 'Don't

---

[191] Interview No. 6.
[192] Interview No. 19.

believe', 'Don't be afraid', 'Don't ask' (Shalamov, 1998, p. 21; Rossi, 1991, p. 50). The three commandments form a coherent unit. The distrust of others make any expectation of assistance pointless. There is no point asking for it. The desired self-sufficiency means that the inmate is always prepared for the worst. Therefore, he is not afraid. Whatever happens, the ideal inmate must be ready to overcome all obstacles on his own. Therefore, prison would create supermen, if it were not so hard to respect the commandments in everyday life.

An individual learns distrust as soon as he is placed in prison or another total institution. It is part of the initiation to penal life. 'The time I spent here taught me to doubt everyone, to be distrustful'.[193] 'You can't trust anyone. So, what does trust mean to you? – When I'm sure that someone I confide in here will not tell others what I've said. That's why you're warned that in the gaols (*SIZO*) you should not say too much. Everything you say about yourself can be passed on to a trial judge and used against you. You have to keep quiet'.[194] As interviewee No. 25, whose experience is not limited to prison (he spent several years as a child and teen in a residential school), distrust towards others is the result of the social structure formed by the total institution. No matter how dense personalized relationships may be, the 'small' society is not protected against the spread of distrust. Thus, Mary Douglas was right when she commented that 'smallness of scale does not account for the origin of cooperative communities' (Douglas, 1986, p. 31).

Let us now look at the characteristics of the social construction of the 'small' society that prohibit the referral to the norm of trust. First, the 'small' society cannot ensure the minimum respect for others that takes the form of tact, etiquette, good distance in everyday life. The transparency of the public/private border deprives interpersonal relationships of the markers needed to maintain a good distance. The lack of tact is the inevitable consequence. Now,

> 'tact–a latent conceptual agreement among participants in interaction contexts–seems to be the main mechanism that sustains trust or ontological security' (Giddens, 1984, p. 75).

Clumsiness destroys confidence even with respect to the closest people, not to mention people that are placed together against their will.

Second, the efforts of the licit authority to ensure the omnipresent and minute control of the everyday life of prisoners encourage denunciations. Dependence on the omnipotent power encourages certain inmates to win favor to the detriment of others. The policy of support and the protection of grasses enable the administration to reduce the risk of collective action to zero, to fight the penal subculture. 'Denunciations (*stukachestvo*) are the surest way to destroy the resistance of the oppressed and the exploited' (Rossi, 1991, p. 371). The fear of being denounced by another inmate eliminates any efforts to protest, whether, as in the terms introduced by Albert Hirschman in his book, *Exit, Voice and Loyalty*, this means exit efforts, namely efforts to escape, or voice efforts, which involve

---

[193] Letter from Interviewee No. 3a.
[194] Interview No. 28.

formulating demands and forcing the administration to respect them. The history of the Soviet prison has known very few examples of collective escapes, although surveillance in the forced labor camps was never comparable to that in the prisons.

> 'The main danger [of escape] has nothing to do with the convoy, the guards. It concerns the actions of the other inmates. Escapes in groups or more than two or three is unthinkable' (Shalamov, 1998, p. 563–564).

The inmates have a clear understanding of the risk of denunciation. 'There are seventy people [in the *otrjad*], thirty of whom denounce the others'.[195] By considering this risk, the inmates attempt to minimize the number of people involved in a given illicit matter. Social life, already fragmented as a result of the existence of illicit categories, is now broken down into even smaller segments. 'If I did something now in the barracks, the administration wouldn't worry. It knows that I'd be denounced immediately... We always have to get away from indiscreet glances'.[196]

Third, a vicious circle appears following the contradiction between the need to close in on oneself as a reasonable strategy for life in detention, and the need to share all aspects of life as a key condition for trust. On the one hand, the rule 'each man for himself' minimizes the risk of action on the part of the administration. On the other hand, it excludes the return to the norm of trust. The transparency of the border between the spheres of activity authorizes only one single form of trust–total trust. But turning in on oneself makes this impossible. One of our interviewees highlighted this perspective. 'From the point of view of criminal traditions, the most important thing in prison is personal trust. No matter what he says, maybe even demands, whether he only describes fantasies–trust comes first. Because we don't know enough people here. You cannot look at his soul, know everything about his life before detention. That's why we need to be able to trust... If you have no positive proof, you can't complain about anything. *Here trust is forced.* If you think he will denounce you, you must have grounds for your accusation. In other words, how can you distrust him? There is no trust here. Not in anyone. There is only an appearance of trust, an illusion...'.[197] In summary, the context of the total institution gives rise to a demand for trust at the same time, it excludes the production and reproduction of trust. The desire to trust and the impossibility of trusting are the two sides of the coin in the 'small' society.

Common funds

Objective and statistically observable proof of the problems pertaining to the norm of trust is found in the dynamics of the common funds (*obshak*) created illicitly by the inmates to help those in material difficulty (placed in solitary, in the hospital, transferred recently to another institution, etc.). The common funds existed prior to

---

[195] Interview No. 33.
[196] Interview No. 21.
[197] Interview No. 25.

the October Revolution of 1917. Those convicted of political crimes, regardless of their ideological convictions, voluntarily donated 10 per cent of their food packets to a common fund (Rossi, 1991, p. 162). Moreover, this practice did not concern common-law inmates. The practice of mutual assistance was taken up again in the 1930s under the form of *kombedy*. The inmates voluntarily transferred 10 per cent of their food product packets and 10 per cent of the sum paid into their accounts by relatives to the poor in the penal world, who were deprived of outside assistance (Shalamov, 1998, p. 269). During the 1930s–1940s, the common funds existed only in the gaols. The similarity between the prison slang and the official acronym used at the start of collectivization, *KOMitety BEDnoty* (the 'poverty committees' created in the country to defend the interests of poor peasants), should be noted, serving as an additional argument in our discussion of the degree of permeability between the penal world and Soviet society. The term *obshak* (literally, a common thing) appeared at the end of the 1940s or the start of the 1950s to designate an illicit tax imposed by the *blatnye,* varying between 1/3 and 2/3 of the monthly salaries of the 'men' (Anisimkov, 1993, p. 35). According to criminal ideology, the *obshak* was set up in part to provide material support to the common cause, the defense of common interests and to help underprivileged inmates.

The duality of trust in the penal setting is translated by the duality in the functioning of the common funds. As demonstrated during our brief historical overview, the common funds did not exist in all times and in all places (in all regions, in all types of facilities). For example, the testimony of some of our interviewees indicates that there was no *obshak* in several regions of the USSR in the 1970s. 'There was no *obshak* in the 1970s. I was in detention and I didn't see it. Now those who work and receive a regular salary contribute to it. I give what I consider necessary'.[198] 'Before, there was no *obshak*. I was in detention in the Ukraine in the 1970s and I didn't see it. I was in a maximum security facility. I spent five years in maximum security facilities and there was no *obshak*. But we helped those placed in solitary directly. We supported them... The *obshak* disappeared apparently in 1959, when they started to separate the regimes [in keeping with the new Code for Applying Sentences]'.[199] In other words, the common funds do not have their own dynamics and they evolve in keeping with the policy changes of the licit authority.

Then, there is tension between two principles, voluntary and obligatory, for contributing to the common fund. Voluntary contribution is only possible with a high level of trust. As a general rule, the donors, the 'men' know nothing about the daily management of the common fund, although everyone knows which night table the fund is stored in (portions of tea, pieces of soap, toothpaste, other small objects, coins). The *blatnye* and the illicit guards manage the common funds. As in the case of a trust, the inmates assign their representatives to manage a portion of their resources for the benefit of a group of beneficiaries. These relationships are based on trust. 'If I can, I contribute. For example, we make repairs to the *otrjad*'s rooms. That's a common cause. If someone cannot make a financial contribution,

---

[198] Interview No. 13.
[199] Interview No. 18.

he can contribute work. No one is forced to contribute. Everything depends on the will of the individual'.[200] 'The *obshak* is sacred. It's voluntary. No one who is honest will say "Give to the *obshak*"'.[201] However, a lack of trust quickly results in a refusal to contribute to the *obshak* voluntarily. 'Before, there was no mutual assistance. If there was a portion of tea, we used it together. Now, the guy who has it takes the tea alone, the others are left out'.[202] The common funds we saw give the impression of a deep crisis: several portions of tea, several pens for about 100 potential beneficiaries. The inmates cannot (given the lack of work resulting from the economic crisis) and, what is more important, will not give to the common cause. The level of impersonal trust in the prison accounts for this refusal.

Level of trust as a sociological indicator

The fact that trust is essential for a society to function properly and the fact that it varies in various institutional contexts facilitates the transformation of the level of trust into a key indicator of the social situation. In order for the level of trust to serve as a social 'thermometer', we need to make this indicator more operational. In particular, we must question the manner in which questions concerning trust are asked, as well as the scale for evaluating the level of trust and the interdependence of the various forms of trust (personalized, impersonal, institutional, observed in a given sphere of activity, etc.).

The conventional method for measuring the level of trust involves asking this question: 'Do you think you can trust those around you?'.

> 'Trust measured by "How far would you say that people around can be trusted?" – one cannot easily separate out the extent to which these variations in trust reflect either a) variations in the effectiveness of the relevant institutional arrangements, b) cultural norms or values that are independent of the effectiveness of these institutional arrangements' (Moore, 1999, p. 78).

In other words, tact can be assured in daily relationships either spontaneously by the players themselves (as in the case of trust as a social norm) or by formal institutions that lead the players to respect the appropriate distance and fulfill their obligations (as in the case of trust resulting from the institutional context). In order to differentiate these two paths for generating trust, we must complement the question on the level of impersonal trust (formulated above) by that of the level of institutional trust: 'Do you trust the State/administration, etc.?'

Then it is necessary to develop an approach that enables us to determine, based on empirical data, whether it is a matter of total trust, specific to traditional and pre-modern societies, or modern trust. The latter means that the trust is generated separately in each sphere of activity (business, civic, domestic, etc.) and its level depends on distinct factors each time. Therefore, a society is closer to the

---

[200] Interview No. 1b.
[201] Interview No. 12.
[202] Interview No. 35. A portion of tea (~50 g) is sufficient to prepare a very strong tea, which the inmates call *chefir*.

traditional model if there is a strong degree of correlation between the levels of trust in the various spheres of activity. On the other hand, a society is closer to the modern model if there is no correlation.

As for the scale for evaluating the level of trust, there are two alternatives. First, we can develop it in keeping with a theoretical model. This is the approach of James Coleman, who refers to the following game theory model:

Table 2.26 Trust game

		Second player	
		To honor with the trust [P]	To deceive [1-P]
First player	To trust	G	L
	Don't trust	0	0

Namely L (*loss*, L<0) is the loss of the first player if the second betrays his trust, while G (*gain*, G>0) is what the first player gains if the second honors his trust (the matrix reflects only the utilities for the first player). The first player knows the probability P that his social partner will honor his trust and the probability (1-P) that he will betray his trust. Let us calculate the expected utility associated with the two possible strategies for the first player: $EU_{to\ trust} = G \times P + L \times (1-P)$; $EU_{not\ to\ trust} = 0 \times P + 0 \times (1-P) = 0$.

Figure 2.8 Level of trust as a function of parameters of the transaction

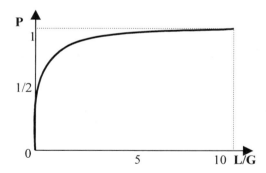

Therefore, for the first player to trust, $EU_{to\ trust} > EU_{not\ to\ trust}$, namely $P/1-P > L/G$. The minimum level of trust (probability P evaluated subjectively) depends on the values L and G as follows (Figure 2.8) (Coleman, 1990, pp. 99–100).

Although this model applies only to the case of impersonal trust, a family of analogous models could be developed to cover other cases. On the other hand, the scale for evaluating the level of trust can be constructed empirically, based on comparisons between societies, regions, organizations, etc. The *ordinal* approach (we have borrowed this term from economic theory) supposes, therefore, the study of a deviation compared to the average level for a sample, unlike the *cardinal* approach, which requires the knowledge of a transcendental level of trust as a marker.

For our research, we have used three indicators to measure trust. First, we asked the question on impersonal trust in its usual form. Second, we asked about institutional trust, namely the trust in the administration. Third, in a portion of the surveys, we introduced a question about the trust in the illicit guards and the degree to which it is personalized.

Table 2.27 Level of interpersonal (A, per cent) and institutional (B, per cent) trust in some Russian penitentiaries (legend of Graph 1)

Penitentiary	N	A	B
Minimum security penitentiary camp (region of Ivanovo) [1]	17	33.3	5.6
Minimum security penitentiary camp (region of Moscow) [2]	29	27.6	3.4
Medium security penitentiary camp (region of Ivanovo) [3]	23	21.7	13
Gaol (region of Ivanovo) [4]	20	20	0
Minimum security penitentiary women's camp (region of Ivanovo)[5]	31	19.4	41.9
Medium security penitentiary camp (region of Ivanovo) [6]	21	19	19
Maximum security penitentiary camp (region of Murmansk) [7]	32	18.8	18.8
Medium security penitentiary camp (region of Tula) [8]	38	18.4	39.5
Medium security penitentiary camp (region of Arkhangelsk) [9]	34	17.6	11.8
Minimum security penitentiary camp (region of Ivanovo) [10]	18	16.7	5.6
Minimum security penitentiary camp (region of Moscow) [11]	37	16.2	18.9
Medium security penitentiary camp (region of Arkhangelsk) [12]	85	13.9	10.6
Medium security penitentiary camp (region of Tula) [13]	42	14.3	11.9
Mean (Russia)		**13.7**	**19.9**
Minimum security penitentiary camp (region of Tula) [14]	36	11.1	44.4
Penitentiary camp for young delinquents (region of Tula) [15]	79	8.9	31.6
Minimum security penitentiary camp (region of Murmansk) [16]	23	8.7	21.7
Penitentiary camp for young delinquents (region of Moscow) [17]	36	8.3	13.9
Medium security penitentiary camp (region of Arkhangelsk) [18]	37	8.1	16.2
Medium security penitentiary camp (region of Murmansk) [19]	25	8	32
Gaol (region of Murmansk) [20]	13	7.7	30.8
Minimum security penitentiary women's camp (region of Moscow) [21]	35	2.9	34.3

A few observations are required as soon as we proceed to a comparison. First, it should be noted that there is a positive correlation (0.06 in Russia, N=1000 and 0.06 in Kazakhstan, N=396, at $p<0.05$) between interpersonal trust and trust in the administration. Although the correlation is not narrow, it proves our hypothesis concerning the proximity of penal society to the traditional model of society. Moreover, we can compare the relative importance of two sources of trust, social and institutional. When two sources reinforce one another, trust in the administration and interpersonal trust are both above average. On the contrary, the low level of interpersonal trust and institutional trust means that no mechanism assures the respect of mutual interests and obligations in everyday life. Finally, the intermediate cases, the high level of interpersonal trust and the low level of institutional trust and *vice versa*, are set apart by the substitution between two sources of trust. In prison slang, institutions with a high level of institutional trust and a low level of interpersonal trust are referred to as 'red' (*krasnye*). The adjective 'black' (*chernye*) is attributed to facilities with a high level of interpersonal trust and a low level of institutional trust. Everyday life in the red facilities is subjected to the minute and omnipresent control of the administration, whereas the inmates have a greater margin of freedom in their everyday lives in the black facilities. It is interesting to note that the inmates themselves often use level of trust as a criteria for differentiating between the 'black' and 'red' facilities: 'If people come up to you [when you arrive in a facility], are interested in you, ask questions–where are you from, what is your sentence, who arrived with you–basically if they pay attention to you, that already tells you a lot [about the situation in the facility]'.[203]

Table 2.28 A taxonomy of social climates

		Level of interpersonal trust	
		High	Low
Level of institutional trust (confidence in administration)	High	Low level of social tensions, the administration does control the situation (for example, prison [8])	So called 'red' prisons, they lie close to the ideal type of total institutions (for example, prisons [14, 15])
	Low	So called 'black' prisons, the clandestine life is flourishing there, social control is done by the prisoners' leaders (for example, prison [2])	High level of social tensions, there exists a risk of *bespredel* (for example, prison [17])

Although this table is schematic (see also Graph 1 for the distribution of 21 penal facilities in Russia by type[204]), it has passed one test of validity. The results of our survey confirmed, in most cases, the reputation of the penal facilities. Moreover, we were able to point out critical situations in two facilities in the

---

[203] Interview No. 24.
[204] The situation in 10.3 per cent of the facilities visited may be described in terms of a social optimum, whereas the majority, 37.9 per cent, more or less, correspond to the ideal 'black' facility (27.6 per cent – the 'red' facility).

Arkhangelsk region without having *ex ante* access to privileged information. In summary, the empirical study confirms that trust plays the role of an integral indicator of the social situation. The correspondence between intention and action, found at the core of any norm, is highlighted in trust relationships. All of the trust indicators provide information about the degree of 'social comfort' assured by a given institutional context, as well as that concerning the possible evolution of the social model in question. For example, from the point of view of social comfort, the high level of impersonal trust and institutional trust appear preferable: tact in everyday life is supported as much from above (through the intervention of the licit authority) as from below (by norms and values that are spontaneously respected). Merchant communities with strong traditions of mutual trust serve as an example (Caillé, 1994; Orléan, 1994).

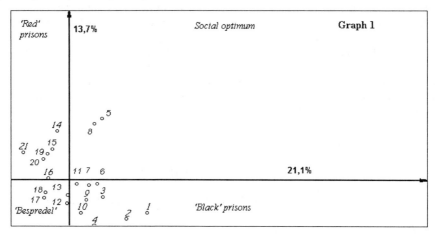

Graph 1

Is it possible to remain a Subject in prison?

The study of trust also constitutes the crucial element in placing the Subject in context. The lack of trust makes solidarity fragile and without viable solidarity the transformation of the individual subject into the collective subject becomes impossible. Therefore, the overt repression of the collective protests of inmates is merely one obstacle among many others, which are not necessarily as obvious, to the construction of the collective subject. And the construction of the individual Subject cannot be taken for granted either in the total institution. As we have already observed, the distrustful environment and the impossibility of support from the licit authority in the organization of everyday life imply a degree of autonomy that is comparable to that usually attributed to the ideal type of superman. For example, the 'real man', the most respected inmate in American prisons,

> 'is urged to "play cool", to control all affect in a hard, silent stoicism which finds its apotheosis in the legendary figure of the cowboy or the gangster. The society of captives

Penal Society in Russia

has institutionalized the virtue of dignity–the ability to maintain the self–in a series of norms and reinforced these norms with a variety of informal social controls' (Sykes, 1958, p. 101).

Now, the price for this autonomy is very high in prison and most inmates are not prepared to pay it. 'It's painful to bear this entire nightmare alone. I've been transformed into a true wildman. I don't want to depend on anyone. I'd rather eat the prison soup (*balanda*) and settle for what I have'.[205] Therefore, what happens to the subject in the total institution?

Being free or enjoying freedom

The history of the Soviet prison has not been marked by large protest movements. Apart from the series of strikes that followed Stalin's death in 1953, the Soviet prisons did not experience revolts comparable to those that took place at the start of the 1970s in France. A fragmentary list of collective protests includes, in particular, the revolts in Vorkuta (1936), Leningrad (1941), Vorkuta and Magadan (1947), and Vorkuta (1948). The demands basically concerned easing the system: providing protection against the discretionary fire of the guards, limiting the work day to nine hours (during the 1930s–1940s, this exceeded 12–14 hours), eliminating restrictions on mail, eliminating the obligation to wear numbers, opening the barracks at night, 'respect for the human dignity of the inmates' (Rossi, 1991, pp. 117–118). A more recent revolt, which took place in the Vladimir minimum security prison (July 1993), also questioned the system and restrictions placed on visits from relatives (Tkachevskij, 1997, p. 82).[206] Moreover, revolt represents only the most extreme case of collective protest. Taking hostages, refusing to work, going on hunger strikes, refusing to go to the canteen, to the showers, are less violent forms of protest. 'Before, if the showers were like this [no hot water in summer, no cold water in winter], no one would have gone. They [the administration] would have repaired them'.[207]

Regardless of their form, collective protests remain isolated. Statistics concerning the application of two articles of the Russian Federal Penal Code, Article 77^1 (disruption in the operations of the penal facility) and Article 77 (riots, Article 321 in a new redaction of the Penal Code), prove the absence of a well-constituted collective player (Tkachevskij, 1997, p. 82) (Table 2.29).

---

[205] Letter from Interviewee No. 3a.
[206] Other cases of collective protests include hunger-strakes in gaols of Yujno-Sakhalinsk (800 participants in April 1992), Ekaterinburgh (4,500 participants in August 1994 and 100 participants in February 1998), Moscow (4,000 participants in September 1994; 1,500 participants in February 2000 and 400 participants in August 2001), Smolensk (700 participants in April 2001) and Astrakhan (300 participants in September 2002), riot in a Moscow gaol (1,500 participants in May 1992) and capture of hostages in a Ekaterinburgh gaol (July 1994) (see *Kommersant*, n°170, September 20, 2002, p. 6).
[207] Interview No. 22.

Table 2.29 Collective protests

	1992	1993	1994	1995
Total number of infractions (art. 77[1])	32	23	19	6

While it should be taken into consideration, the relatively strong desire to take part in collective protests measured in our survey through the direct question, 'Do you support the other inmates in collective protest?', should not be deceptive:

Table 2.30 Willingness to protest

	Russia, N=1310	Kazakhstan, N=396	Canada, N=120
Yes, but it will depend on requirements	45.8	55.1	40.8
Don't know	15.4	11.6	11.7
Yes, without any doubts	12.8	13.6	20.8
No	12.8	8.6	19.2
Yes, but it will depend on personalities of other participants	9.5	9.6	5.8
No answer	3.6	1.5	1.7

As our discussion of these results with the inmates revealed, the fear of violent repression determines any discourse on collective protest in prison. 'People who organize [protests] develop a strategy, they consider all possibilities... If the specialized police forces (*OMON*) are called in, there are victims, the number has to be minimized... that's why we usually look for more loyal means: we go to the administration, we try to speak quietly. If the administration does not react, we warn them about the possibility of protests, about a complaint to the solicitor...'[208] In any event, taking violent repression into consideration does not appear to account for the rarity of collective action such as protests. For example, we discovered that the inmates almost never organize collective celebrations, including the holiday most respected by Russians, New Year's Day. Regular surveys by the Russian public opinion center (*VCIOM – Vserossijskij Centr Izuchenija Obschestvennogo Mnenija*) demonstrate that an absolute majority of Russians (94 per cent) celebrate New Year's Day.[209] Preparations for this holiday begin one-two months in advance. But the inmates cannot collect enough resources to arrange for even a drinks party in their basic group, the *otrjad*. Answers to the question, 'Do you remember any collective action to improve conditions in detention?' confirm the rarity of collective actions in everyday life, including the most benign (Table 2.31). There is no doubt that the general atmosphere of distrust adds to the impact of the licit authority and also complicates social mobilization.

---

[208] Interview No. 35a. For example, the Vladimir riot resulted in 52 victims (five killed).
[209] VCOM investigation conducted December 17–20, 1999. Source: http://www.polit.ru, December 27, 1999.

Table 2.31 Scope of collective actions

	Russia	Kazakhstan	Canada
N	1025	372	120
Yes, renovation of residential units	48.6	42.2	7.9
No, I don't remember any	26.6	14	52.5
Yes, public discussions of the common problems	21.8	36.3	6.9
Yes, common leisure activities	17	12.9	25.7
Yes, contributions to public funds (*obshak*)	8.8	12.4	×
Yes, helping the inmates who were abused	×	×	12.9
Yes, putting forward collective requirements	7.1	15.1	6.9

The explicit constitution of the collective Subject is not possible in prison for reasons both within and without the prison community, which means that any rejection of the total institution takes on more individual forms. Can we consider freedom of action, even individual actions, in a total institution? Moreover, this question has a more general scope since the contradiction between the social determinants and the will to act freely exist in all institutional contexts.

> 'The Subject is the effort to transform a given situation in a situation of free choice, he introduces freedom in what initially appears as social determinants' (Touraine, 1993, pp. 23–24).

The prison context accentuates only the dialectic of freedom and the institutional determinants, without being its major source. Testimony by Varlam Shalamov is pertinent from this point of view.

> 'Being free and enjoying freedom is not the same thing. I never enjoyed freedom, but I was free my entire life' (Shalamov, 1998, p. 231).

But, how does one remain free within prison?

Although the question is formulated in a paradoxical manner, the answer to it is not. The imperative of freedom in detention involves maintaining personal integrity, trying not to change under the pressure of unfavorable and painful conditions. 'In detention, as well as outside, I remain myself. I don't change, if I may say so'.[210] 'Basically, I want to remain a normal man. So what if people don't respect me. But I can remain a man in my own eyes. I don't need anything else'.[211] Personal integrity as a final goal allows for a plurality of means for attaining it. Without drawing up an exhaustive list, let us look at some of them: maintaining one's dignity and having it respected by the other inmates, controlling one's

---

[210] Interview No. 21.
[211] Interview No. 3a.

emotions and desires, mastering different, frequently contradictory logic systems by transforming them into personal experience, not yielding to the routine imposed by the licit authority and trying to personalize penal time and space. In short,

> 'The ability of the officials to physically coerce their captives into the paths of compliance is something of illusion as far as the day-to-day activities of the prison are concerned' (Sykes, 1958, p. 49).

The penal subculture institutionalizes the virtue of dignity: the imperative 'Know how to defend yourself' ranks first among the illicit norms. It requires the inmate to know how to defend himself physically and morally. 'The inmates have a great deal of respect for the notion of dignity. The man who has his dignity is always ready to defend himself against any attack, in any situation'.[212] It would be too simplistic to view physical force solely as a support for dignity. It only starts to play a primary role in situations of *bespredel*. On the one hand, the inmate has several ways in which to defend himself, apart from physical force. 'Here, physical force has no role. Would he be like Sylvester Stallone. If I can't fight him face-to-face, I'll get around him. In the end, the man occasionally sleeps. As weak as I am, you can always kill someone morally, with words'.[213] On the other hand, it's the will to defend oneself that counts. The inmate who gets into a fight with a visibly stronger adversary will earn the respect of the other inmates. Whereas once an inmate refuses to defend himself, he is gradually transformed into a permanent victim of daily violence. He will be insulted, jostled and subjected to other forms of daily violence. 'If someone hits you, for no reason, you have to respond. If you are weaker than he is, you still have to respond. Then... you must never admit that you've been humiliated. If you don't admit it once, they won't offend you the next time'.[214]

Controlling one's emotions and desires is the other pillar of the concept of dignity. Detention makes it impossible to satisfy various needs, including basic needs occasionally. The quantity and particularly the quality of prison food have never been sufficient for an adult man. For example, the daily rations of the various licit categories of inmates during the 1930s–1950s follow (Rossi, 1991, pp. 472–473):[215]

---

[212] Interview No. 7.
[213] Interview No. 3a.
[214] Interview No. 27b.
[215] The punishment ratio was for inmates who had not reached the daily rate of output; the hunger ratio for inmates who did not work.

Table 2.32 Daily rations in Stalinist camps during 1930s

Type of ration, g	Bread	Sugar	Mush	Fish	Meat	Vegetables	Fat	Oil	Flour
Basic ration	450	7	80	132	21	500		9	6
Penal ration	400		35	80		420		5	5
Starvation ration	300		35	73		400		5	
Ration of those who are under investigation	400	9	35	73	18	400		5	5
Prison's ration	600	14	60	80	18	420		5	5
Convicts in transit's ration	700	15		167					
Activists' ration	600	25	138	173	48	913		20	10
Engineers' ration	800	32	170	223	69	1080		27	13
Juvenile ration	450	25	100	170	50	500	66	20	200

Popular slang has a pejorative shortcut for any poorly cooked, insubstantial food, *turemnaja balanda* (prison soup). The lack of food is a painful trial for the inmates. Are they able to control their needs to avoid, on the one hand, dependence on the administration, which 'buys' denunciations through additional rations, even packs of cigarettes, and, on the other hand, begging other inmates, with the loss of face that incurs? 'Some are ready to turn coat on any occasion. They work for the administration, sell it to the inmates, sell them to the administration... These guys have two personalities. They'd do anything to satisfy their hunger'.[216] Begging in prison is also poorly viewed. 'Someone will sit down in front of you and watch you eat. They'll humiliate themselves so that you will leave them something to eat. Here, people sometimes lose all of the human dignity. It's unbearable'.[217]

The next element in prisoner dignity involves 'normative tinkering', specifically the reconciliation of contradictory logic systems in everyday life in detention. First, it is a matter of knowing how to resist the complete reduction of one's life, either to the licit logic imposed by the administration or to the illicit logic, whose values are transmitted by the *blatnye*. Now,

> 'the player constructs an experience that belongs to him, based on the logic of action that does not belong to him and which is given to him by the various dimensions of the system' (Dubet, 1994, p. 136).

The actions of the *blatnye* are completely determined by the penal subculture, whereas the actions of the 'scapegoats' are reduced to the reproduction of official norms. It is the men, the largest category of inmates, who benefit from leeway in their everyday life: they try to pass from Scylla into Charybdis, between the two authorities, without approaching either. 'A man lives in his own manner. He lives

---

[216] Interview No. 18.
[217] Interview No. 20.

by the illicit norms (*ponjatija*) while refusing to apply the laws of the administration. He lives, he works for himself, for no one else'.[218] Moreover, there is a sort of pact that is never explicitly stated among the men, the administration and the *blatnye*. The administration grants a relative amount of autonomy to the men in exchange for the zealous work. In turn, the *blatnye* also respect the autonomy of the men in exchange for their contributions to the common fund. The price for the relative autonomy of the men takes, therefore, the form of a double tax: on the part of both the State whose interests are represented by its lieutenant, the penal administration, and the illicit authorities. In other words, the prison deprives the expression 'freedom is costly' of its metaphorical character.

The incomplete submission to the licit authority also translated into a refusal to accept routine as the unique basis for the organization of everyday life. The penal ideal implies the total internalization of the formal norms, their transformation into routine. Regardless of the value of the formal norms, they can only be substituted by routine if the people involved are also transformed into automata. In the end, the metamorphosis of routine into the Alfa and Omega of everyday life refutes the idea of using it in the teaching of discipline as a means of reintegration. The education of the good citizen is not reduced to the internalization of norms because this deprives the citizen of autonomy and a sense of responsibility. In keeping with this reasoning, Bruno Bettelheim criticizes certain Nazi victims for their 'as usual' (*comme d'habitude*) philosophy, an extreme form of reducing everyday life to routine.

> 'The "as usual" philosophy (to not leave, to not escape, to not leave one's home, one's work...) led millions of Jews to live in ghettos where not only did they work for the Nazis, but they also provided contingents of their brother Jews, selected by themselves and destined for the gas chambers. Those who stuck with routine doomed themselves to their own destruction' (Bettelheim, 1991, p. 315).

Are the inmates aware of this danger?

In order to find an answer to this question, we have decided to reproduce a large extract from our correspondence with one inmate. We asked him to describe a usual day in the maximum security prison. We have quoted him, without improving or cutting his words.

'It may seem as if my day always starts in the same way. That's not true. I wake up 15 minutes before the wake-up alarm sounds. When I hear the noise of large pots with breakfast. First, I look out the window at the sun. If the sky is clear and the sun is shining, I'm happy, despite the bars and the closed door. I wash up, brush my teeth and start the tea (*chefir*). I can't be bothered exercising, even though I ought to. At 6:00 the alarm sounds and they start distributing the bread and broth. I light up a cigarette and I start to destroy (sic) the tea. I destroy it and it starts to destroy me in turn. Cigarettes and tea have made a pact against me. I'm afraid they'll win. I drink the tea and swear at myself. After tea, I clean up. Now, it's time for the broth. This is where my good mood leaves me a bit. How can I

---

[218] Interview No. 33.

look at it without tears? The crisis in the country is reflected in our food. It was never good, but now... Very quickly, to avoid the taste, I finish the broth. I figure it's worse for my health than the cigarettes and the *chefir*. It's good that the bread has a taste, I take another slice, I sprinkle salt on it and eat it with hot water. After finishing breakfast, I light a cigarette and stretch out on a bed (*shkonka*), I listen to the radio and wait for the inspection tour. As I wait, I may drowse for an hour. But I can't miss the inspection tour, or I'll be in trouble. Sleeping in the morning is marvelous. I'm in a good mood again. I close my eyes and I don't see the bars or the door. The sun is shining, I'm seated at the edge of a lake... I hear a motor boat... but it's not the usual sound. Yeah, the door is opening with the clanking of metal. They're making sure I'm present. Now, I can spend two or three hours pacing (*tysovat'sja*) in the cell. There's nothing else to do. I've read all the books available. A newspaper is distributed before breakfast. It might have a crossword puzzle. That will interest me. As I pace, I listen to the radio and learn what's going on in our country. All the news seems extremely pessimistic. Why don't people want to see good in the world? Even I can see it through my bars. Strange. A noise in the hallway districts me from these sad thoughts. I walk to the door and listen. A search has started. The door opens and the guards enter my cell. I'm taken out into the corridor and seated near a wall. After fifteen minutes, I return to my cell. I start to put things away. That will keep me busy until lunch. The photos are lose. I glance at them and memories move me. I try not to look at them often so I can remain calm. Here, I can't describe my emotions... So, I can already hear lunch in the corridor. I'm given prison soup (*tjuremnaja balanda*). For ordinary people, lunch is a pleasure. Not here and not for me. I eat because it's necessary. After lunch, I have two hours to lie down and dream, then I'll be taken for a walk. I haven't gone in a long time, I have to go. To look at the snow. I haven't walked on the snow this year. I don't often go out for a walk in the winter. I hate the cold. I got enough of that in solitary. It's a wonder that my soul hasn't been transformed into a piece of ice. Well, maybe it's only an impression... After the walk, I'm cold. Today, I'll go to the shower. I love that. Meanwhile, I make a tea (*chefir*) and I try to warm up. I don't have any more cigarettes. I'll have to make my own with butts. I never throw the butts out, I keep them in a box. I don't work, so I don't go to the canteen either. Now, I'm all alone. My cell mate went to another facility. Solitude calms me. I rarely manage to stay all alone. That terrible peephole in the door! That's what I hate the most about prison! I can't get used to it, despite my years in prison. It seems that I'll never have a peephole in my door when I get out. I also hate the howling. My good mood vanishes as soon as I hear the dogs howl. I don't know why, maybe my mind associates the howling with the Nazis and the concentration camps. We go to the showers. When you're in the showers alone, it's fantastic. No one jostles you. There's just that hated peephole in the door... Nothing else is scheduled for today. Only dinner. But that's not worth talking about...'.[219]

In this discourse we find the traces of two strategies for fighting the omnipresent routine: retreat into the imagination and the non-routine interpretation

---

[219] Letter from Interviewee No. 3a, written on November 23, 1998.

of apparently routine events (the search, for example). The inmate learns to look for small pleasures where they appear to be absent by definition. The attention to details–to the newspaper, the photos, tea–provides some leeway in the organization of everyday life. This helps the inmate remain within the 'framework' while doing the opposite. 'We no longer see a "unique man" identifiable with the others whose behaviors are strictly determined in advance' (Piette, 1996, p. 163). As for the withdrawal into the imagination, some of our interviewees also expressed a very obvious desire to find faith in God. Recently, chapels were built in three of the facilities visited. '<u>How many true believers do you think there are</u>? – About a dozen come to the services. The weekly service draws about 50. Plus, there are about 100 who come to light a candle or simple to spend a moment there'.[220] While the number of believers is not impressive, religious faith gives them a shelter against their hostile and routine reality. Occasionally, the inmates even try to take refuge in the chapels, to withdraw into their own imaginary world, which does not always coincide with that of the Church.

Devices for protecting private space

The model for the 'small' society provides another very powerful tool for controlling social space and allowing the inmate to remain himself. This involves personalizing penal time and space, transforming his area, no matter how small it is, into a welcoming environment. The context of the total institution and the distrustful environment means that the inmate considers not only the representatives of the administration but also the other inmates as Others. Therefore, he must make a portion of the others' world 'his'. The 'appropriation' of daily space takes the form of building small groups: the group of countrymen (*zemljachestvo*) and the inmate family (*kentovka*). They serve as social devices for protecting private space where other devices are lacking.

The group of fellow countrymen includes those who come from the same region, the same neighborhood in a large city. 'Suppose they come from the Kursk region, for example, and there are thirty. First, in a foreign facility, they know one another better. They support and help one another'.[221] The groups of countrymen flourished particularly well during the Soviet period when there was no rule that the sentence had to be executed in the region where the crime was committed. During that time, the Russians, Ukrainians, Georgians, etc. formed groups of countrymen, regardless of their places of residence in the corresponding republics. Occasionally, the Russians, the Ukrainians and the Belorussians formed a single group of Slavs, whereas those from the Caucasian and the central Asian republics formed their own groups. The dissolution of the USSR and the implementation of the policy concerning the regionalism of the execution of sentences in the 1990s reduce the importance of geographic belonging: the principal of residing in the same district, the same city, the same town, the same neighborhood replaced the principal of macro-regional belonging.

---

[220] Interview No. 29. This facility holds approximately 1,200 inmates.
[221] Interview No. 36.

The reason for *zemljachestvo* is mutual support, the joint organization of leisure activities. The group of countrymen serves as a means of communication, a device for associative life. 'The *zemljachestvo* was privileged before [among other means for associative life]. We met often. There was a common movement, communication... We even went to the movies together. About thirty countrymen got together: "Let's go to the movies?"'[222] The groups of countrymen often have their own material basis–a common fund. Not only do the inmates from a given region contribute to it, they also benefit from the material and financial support from the criminal world in their region. 'For example, the inmates from Apatity [a city in the Murmansk region] were assisted (*ih greli*) by the people of Apatity. Was there a single common fund in the facility? – Yes, there was. But the inmates from Apatity received more help than the others and they felt that their contribution to the common fund was greater... They supported one another. Whatever happens, they meet and find a solution together'.[223]

The broad scope of the more or less open hostility towards Muscovites, those who come from Moscow, should be noted. As a result of a shortage of penal facilities in Moscow, those who are sentenced for crimes committed in Moscow are dispersed among the other regions in the Russian federation. 'Here, it's another region, another area, said one Muscovite. I wouldn't say that we were humiliated, but...'[224] As a general rule, those from the provinces consider the Muscovites foreigners, others. As a result, opportunistic behavior is accepted with respect to them. 'If, for example, you come from the Tula, your participation in a common cause will be treated with more loyalty. As for the Muscovites, we try to trick them, to cheat them'.[225] The last quote highlights the principal idea of the group of countrymen: yours are in, others are out.

The explanation of the hostility towards the Muscovites takes us outside the penal world. This hostility is rooted in the characteristics of the Soviet model of society: the simple fact of living in the capital ensured privileged access to economic resources (shortages affected stores in Moscow less than those in the provinces), cultural resources (all the most prestigious higher education institutions are located in Moscow) and administrative resources (we have already discussed the control system [very sophisticated and painful to bear] for access to Moscow, the *propiska*). Therefore, the inmates try, when organizing their illicit life in prison, to re-establish a justice that does not exist, from their point of view, in the licit lives outside prison.

Although the scope of the groups of countrymen varies in time and space, the other means for protecting private space, the inmate family, is omnipresent. Several studies on total institutions have focussed on the efforts of inmates to create small groups of 2–3 people. In particular, Erving Goffman speaks of the existence of small groups of inmates with 'a tendency to support one another under

---

[222] Interview No. 1a.
[223] Interview No. 22.
[224] Interview No. 25. Moreover, the interview was conducted in the Tula region, close to Moscow!
[225] Interview No. 10.

ircumstances and to provide reciprocal emotional support' (Goffman, 1968, 4). Prisoners of war have also attempted to create a social space smaller than the barrack. A household analogy, cooking, appeared as a means for managing the everyday lives of prisoners of war in the Nazi concentration camps. '"Meals" taken together [were] a true social rite, a simple and profound source of sociability' (Durand, 1987, p. 128). It should be noted that socialization in these small groups occurs in keeping with the logic of the 'small' society, namely the gap between yours and strangers serves as the basis for forming small groups.

> 'The meals sometimes took on the appearance of closed small groups, jealously guarding everything they could pull together for their members' (Durand, 1987, p. 150).

Small groups only appear within the total institution if the social space is already fragmented by other means. For this reason, there are no families of inmates in prisons using the cell system. Corinne Rostang, author of a study on women's prisons in France, states: 'I found no signs that families were formed–the existence of cells in France does not facilitate the forming of groups' (Rostang, 1994, p. 126). This observation supports our hypothesis that it is the lack of other means for protecting private space that gives rise to the social means, including inmate families.

Post-Soviet inmates are no exception to the rule. The forced labor camps of the 1930s–1950s had an analogy to the 'meal', the *kolkhoz*. The term, borrowed from official Soviet language, designated the group of inmates who usually ate together (Rossi, 1991, p. 161). In the 1960s, prison slang abandoned the borrowed term. Today, prisoners use the term *kentovka*, *kenta* (members are called *kenty*), namely the common term for 'family' (*sem'ja*, with members called *semejniki*). 'What were the *semejniki* called before? – The *kenta*. There are two, three, five family members. They share everything, except their underwear, of course. Food, the night table, everything was shared. We ate together. I recall it fondly'.[226] Most inmates live in families with 2–3 members.[227] 'In your *otrjad* there are 127 people. How many of them live in families? – I don't know. Sometimes people live together for a week and then separate. There are about 20 families that have lasted. Good, stable families. There are also the solitary guys'.[228] In the gaols, larger families are not uncommon, with 6 to 20, even 30 people. All of the inmates placed together in a cell (except for the large cells for about 100 people) generally form a single family. One interviewee described his everyday life in a gaol as follows:

---

[226] Interview No. 13.

[227] *How big is your 'family' (mess)?*	Russia, N=153	Kazakhstan, N=242	Canada, N=50
Two persons	48.4	20.2	28
Three	25.5	18.2	12
Four or more	13.1	29.8	0
It's very variable	10.5	28.1	56
No answer	2.6	3.1	4

(The question was addressed to those with a family.)

[228] Interview No. 1a.

'We were a single family there. Both in the residence and the prison... I tried to see that everyone depended on everyone else. If someone is suffering, we suffer together; if someone is happy, we're all happy'.[229] Our survey confirms the omnipresence of the family: an absolute majority of our interviewees live in a family (see Table 2.33 for the answers to the question 'Do you live in a family?'):

Table 2.33 Families in prison

	Russia, N=1120	Kazakhstan, N=396	Canada, N=120
Yes	53.3	61.1	41.7
No	41	33.8	56.7
No answer	5.7	5.1	1.7

As we have already mentioned, the inmate family is formed primarily to manage the material aspects of everyday life in detention. 'What is the basis for building a family? – The simplest: I work and earn money here, the others are supported by their relatives who provide food for them. We share the food and I ensure that relations within the administration are good'.[230] Moreover, the possession of 'comparative advantages' is necessary, but not sufficient to give rise to a family. Eating together, even drinking tea together, implies a considerable degree of mutual trust. 'If I don't know someone, I won't have tea with him'.[231] In prison slang, the expression 'eating bread with someone' (*lomat' vmeste hleb*) has a meaning very close to that of the verb 'to trust someone'. 'People who eat together are considered sure friends, ready to defend one another. Often, there are two' (Rossi, 1991, p. 178). On the one hand, sharing food, a rare and very important resource in prison, implies that an inmate agrees that his own well-being will depend on the actions of other members of the family. For example, sharing bread made by an inmate who specializes in that job, *hleborez*, is never objectively perfect, and using one's ration is important. The inmates are particularly fond of croutons, because they contain less moisture. Without trust, each distribution of food could become violent. 'This system focuses on several human qualities. Without meaning to. You don't want to pay attention to it, you know you shouldn't pay attention to it. I wake up once in the morning, they distribute the rations (*pajki*). A poor inmate tries to take a larger ration. I don't think he should be criticized. But the others blame him for his behavior. He takes a larger ration a second time... He wants to eat. I understand. I'd simply step aside. I'd take my ration at the end. The second or third time, he'll be beaten. Before, he would have been beaten violently'.[232]

On the other hand, the explanation of the close link between trust and family lies in the fact that a 'meal' taken together encourages people to open up to one another, particularly in the case of the prisoners' tea, *chefir*, which the inmates use

---

[229] Interview No. 25.
[230] Interview No. 29.
[231] Interview No. 22.
[232] Interview No. 3a.

to replace alcohol (for that reason, *chefir* is forbidden in facilities for young people). Communication within the family, either consciously or unconsciously, becomes more open and more intense, which requires trust. The inmate wants to make sure that all of the information transmitted to his listeners during the 'meal' does not leave the confines of the small group, of his circle. 'There is more communication within the family: daily communication, but also conversations to pass the time, with no specific topic. It's always like that: people sit down at the table, they drink alcohol, and they don't watch their words. Here, too, we have some *chefir*, or some tea with chocolate. It's almost like a drug that frees your tongue'.[233] In other words, within the family, the inmates can be themselves, without having to watch their words or actions. They are among their own. 'Are there many in your family? – We're three. You found them soon after your arrival? – Yes, I did. I looked around me; it's easy to see who does what, *who will be yours*. Is talking with them interesting? – At least they're not mean. Some people here smile at you but are mean behind your back. It's hard living alone here… Everyone has to communicate with someone'.[234] The key role of trust in intra-family relations is confirmed by the analysis of family make-up. When answering the question 'Who is in your family?' (addressed to those with a family), most interviewees spoke about trustworthy people:

Table 2.34 Structure of inmates' families

	Russia	Kazakhstan	Canada
N	584	239	50
Trustworthy people	56.3	56.5	34
People with the same vision of the world	33.9	33.1	×
A close friend	×	×	32
Compatriots (*zemljaki*)	21.4	17.2	4
Close relatives	6	8.4	×
People committed the same crime	1.2	0.8	×

Despite the apparent similarity between the inmate family and the usual family, we would like to point out a few differences in the social structures of the two phenomena. First, the inmate family generally excludes any sexual connotations. The sexual taboo in the inmate family is a result of the obvious gap between the image of femininity and masculinity in the penal subculture. Only inmate families of female inmates, according to the testimony of female guards, do not totally exclude the sexual aspect.[235] Also, the inmate family must not serve to

---

[233] Interview No. 29.
[234] Interview No. 39.
[235] The families formed in detention by women require a particular analysis: in their environment, sexual relations are not excluded. On the contrary, they are largely the rule. As an hypothesis, we could suppose that the perception of the duality of the masculine/feminine roles is less obvious among Russian women than men.

transmit social status in the penal city. One tradition, although it is not respected rigorously everywhere, prohibits the guards from living in families. 'According to the old tradition, they [the illicit guards] must not continue to live in families'.[236] This enables them to avoid favoritism in their conflicts with the other inmates. As for the family in the usual sense, 'The principal objective of the family is not simply mutual affection, it is also *a strategy for defense and transmitting status*' (Reynaud, 1989, p. 141).

Finally, the inmate family is often far from the traditional model for domestic relations which implies a chain of personal dependencies and an obvious hierarchy.

> 'The family embodies the archetypal protection contract in its elementary form, whereby men are expected to protect weaker members, who in exchange accept the high price of submitting to the will of their protectors' (Gambetta, 1993, p. 57).

This brings us back to our initial hypothesis that the penal city is not reduced to the domestic city, it also includes certain elements of the city by projects. We are particularly interested in the division between the principal of the priority of family interests over the individual interests of its members and the principal of the priority of individual interests over the family interests. Certain prison observers have focussed on the principle of collective responsibility:

> 'The members of the family bear a collective responsibility (*krugovaja poruka*) for the actions of each family member. Departure from the family is considered a violation of the illicit norms (*kosjak*)' (Abramkin, Chijov, 1992, p. 125).

However, we found certain evidence to the contrary in our research. The inmates are relatively free to leave their families when they want to. Here are the answers to the 'Did you change families one or more times when in the facility' (addressed to those with a family):

Table 2.35 Frequency of changing families

	Russia, N=597	Kazakhstan, N=242
Yes	48.6	35.5
No	46.9	60.3
No answer	4.5	4.1

The making of family decisions does not exclude the imposition of one individual's will on the other members of the family. 'Does the family have a leader? – No. We share everything equally. As for joint decisions… For example, we're three in the family. If I have to make a decision–I make it and I inform the two others. No one will blame me. It's a sort of mutual support. To have someone to talk to in a difficult situation'.[237] Moreover, the members of the family are protected against undesirable intervention in their private affairs or, at least, this

---

[236] Interview No. 1a.
[237] Interview No. 1a.

type of intervention is poorly viewed in prison. 'No matter what, the man lives in each family independently. Each person has his own life. I try not to intervene. But if he needs my help, I give it'.[238] In other words, inmate families include some of the principles formulated by Walter Weyrauch in his study of small groups.

> 'Everybody is left to his own devices and may do as he pleases as long as the level of utmost toleration is not exceeded. A desire for privacy has a higher priority than a desire to socialize... Any inquiry into personal matters should permit equivocation in the response' (Weyrauch, 1971, pp. 59–62).

The analysis of the inmate family highlights the following paradox. The 'small' society tends to break down into smaller and smaller elements. Social life fragments infinitely; fragmentation reflects the price to pay for the efforts to make everyday life more comfortable in the 'small' society. The illicit categories, groups of countrymen, inmate families are components of the fragmentation vector. Yet, no matter how small these elements are, they are always based on the radical opposition between yours and others, strangers. Therefore, the term 'society' barely applies to the social construction of the penal world that we conveniently call the 'small' society. It is, rather, a *socium*, an amalgamation of heterogeneous elements that are autonomous and closed to the outside. Moreover, this is the only way to allow a 'hell' to coexist on a macro social level with a 'paradise' on a micro social level, thereby ensuring the relative stability of the 'small' society and its capacity to reproduce.

Illicit justice

Our sketch of the Soviet penal world would be incomplete without the indication of a few recent trends concerning the role of the illicit guards in the organization of illicit justice. These trends are of interest not only in the context of the more modern control of violence, but also as an example of the institutionalization of personalized relations. Moreover, the illicit justice system, a means for protecting the rights of the inmates in their interactions, is part of the logic of the construction of the individual Subject. The case of the transformation of the private mediators of the medieval fairs into the judges of the *Lex Mercatoria* serves as a marker.

> 'The role of judges in the system, far from being substitutes for the reputation mechanism is to make the reputation system more effective as a means of promoting honest trade' (Milgrom et al., 1990, p. 3).

Therefore, does the 'small' society include the bases for its transformation into the 'large' society?
Since the start of the 1990s, we have observed a significant decrease in violence in its more obvious forms in the post-Soviet prisons. The official statistics, although they also indicate a decline in the number of violations

---

[238] Interview No. 27a.

committed in detention, do not tell us much about the dynamics of daily violence. In order to evaluate it, we asked the question 'Do you think the level of violence has declined recently in your facility?'. The answers indicate that one-third of inmates think it has:

Table 2.36 Dynamics of violence

	Russia, N=1120	Kazakhstan, N=396
Level of violence has reduced	29.3	33.8
No changes	10.3	10.4
Level of violence has risen	10	10.4
Don't know	44.2	42.9
No answer	6.2	2.5

The analysis of the preferences of the inmates with respect to the principles of conflict resolution provides additional evidence of the decrease of internal violence in the prison. The hierarchy of the *declared* principles observed in prison does not seem to differ much from that observed in the outside world:[239]

Table 2.37 Methods of conflict resolution

Prisoners	Rus.	Kaz.	Fr.	Can.	*Russians [98]*	
Dialogue and search for a balance of interests	31.2	27.7	55.4	47	Treat others as you would like them to treat you	68
The best solutions are usually found by wise people	21.4	30.1	53.6	46.1	Pig who breaks his promises (*dogovor doroje deneg*)	23
Might makes right	19.9	12.5	14.3	16.5	You do not choose your family (*svoj svoemu ponevole drug*)	11
A bad arrangement is better than a conflict	14.2	13.6	0	8.7	Might makes right	8
If the adversary does not capitulate, he deserves to be destroyed	8.5	6.4	×	×	Ill-gotten gains benefit no one (*chto siloj vzjato, to ne svjato*)	8
First come, first served	10	15.7	0	1.7	What is unfortunate for some is good for others	5
Conquerors are never judged	3.9	4.3	×	×		
An eye for an eye	×	×	12.5	13		

---

[239] The table includes the inmates' responses to the question 'Which principal of conflict resolution do you prefer?' and the responses of the Russians to the question 'Which principles do you prefer for resolving conflicts between your family and others?' The variations in the responses were not identical.

The fact that the timing of the decrease in violence coincides with the large increase in the number of illicit guards is not haphazard. The frequency with which the inmates chose the response 'The best solutions are usually found by wise people' (particularly in Kazakhstan) should be noted. Our hypotheses suppose that the illicit guards play a very positive role in the mediation of daily conflicts and that there is a tendency for this role to be institutionalized. The inmates willingly accept the intervention of the illicit guards in managing their conflicts. They view it as a crucial guarantee that the parties to the conflict will remain within acceptable limits, that the situation will not deteriorate into *bespredel*. 'When was it easier to resolve conflicts, now or before? – Now. Before we did everything with force. Skulls were cracked, jaws were cracked. Now everything is easier. Because of the illicit guards? – Yes, that too. If the illicit guard is good (*putevyj*), I explain the situation to him. Before, I would have needed a stool'.[240] The intervention of the illicit guard is suggested even in obvious cases such as catching a thief. 'If someone stole something from me and I catch him, I have to justify my accusations for them to authorize me to settle our accounts (*razobrat'sja*). What does that mean, "authorize you to settle your accounts"? – If I beat him, it would not be considered *bespredel* if I had explained the situation first to the illicit guard. If I'm not sure I can beat him [*krysa*], I will ask for help'.[241] 'Before, the entire *otrjad* would have beaten a thief that was caught (*krysa*), whereas now we start to explain, the illicit guard intervenes... Without the permission of the illicit guard, you can't beat anyone. Before, at least 10 per cent of the inmates had a black eye or a split lip. That was so the person wouldn't do what he wasn't supposed to do. Now, we try to get a judgment first. Before beating someone, we determine the degree of guilt with the illicit guard. Whether he deserves to be punished, so...'.[242]

Table 2.38 Third parties in conflicts

	Russia, N=1310	Kazakhstan, N=396	France, N=58	Canada, N=120
Intervention of prisoners' leaders / mediators	33.4	39.4	17.9	66 1
No external intervention	33.3	26	23.8	24.4
Intervention of the prison guards	20	25.8	48.7	13.9
Call for the official justice	1.6	2.8	9.5	3.5

As shown in Table 2.38 above (answers to the question 'What type of intervention do you prefer for conflicts in your facility?'), the intervention of the illicit guards is highly appreciated. Moreover, the level of trust in the illicit guards is visibly greater than that of impersonal trust and the level of trust in the penal administration. Thirty-eight percent (41.4 per cent in Kazakhstan) of our

---

[240] Interview No. 13.
[241] Interview No. 20.
[242] Interview No. 16.

interviewees trust the illicit guards (Table 2.39). In other words, the inmates believe that the intervention of the illicit guards in daily conflicts will be in their interests.

Table 2.39 Confidence in prisoners' leaders

Do you trust the prisoners' leaders (smotrjashie)?	Russia, N=925	Kazakhstan, N=396	Canada, N=120
Yes	37.5	41.4	33.3
No	48.2	49.5	57.5
No answer	14.3	9.1	9.2

How can this obvious desire to accept mediation by the illicit guards be explained? First, it is mediation without any claim on the part of the third party to impose his view of matters. Let us look at the list of procedures possible for resolving conflicts. It includes (Bonafé-Schmitt, 1993, p. 15; Le Roy, 1993, p. 89):

- mini trial – the presentation of the arguments to a third, impartial party;
- reconciliation – a third party is called on to intervene in a difference to propose an acceptable solution that applies voluntarily to the parties and includes a certain minimal authority so that consequences can be drawn from the right to apply or not apply the reconciliation; and
- arbitration – the decision of an arbitrator binds the parties.

The actions of the illicit guards fall between reconciliation and arbitration: they have the power to apply their decisions, but this power is not absolute. In fact, it is their ability to propose a solution that is acceptable to the parties to the conflict that counts, even for the party that is presumed guilty. 'Here, we try to explain the problem first. We don't judge [as the court does], we explain'.[243] The decision-making procedure limits the discretionary authority of the illicit guard. The party judged guilty can exercise recourse to a 'higher jurisdiction' (namely a *polojenec*, an *avtoritet*, or even a thief-in-law) in order to have the judgement reviewed. In difficult cases, the illicit guards hesitate to render a judgement and prefer to ask for additional investigations. 'After considering the explanations of both parties, I decided not to make a decision. I trust the words of the first guy, but I have no reason to doubt the arguments of the other. Why should I trust only one party? So, you didn't make a decision? – Yes, I sent them to the *polojenec*. He had to get more information, to contact other people…'.[244] Therefore, we could say that the principal task of the illicit guard is to explain the illicit norms, to see that they are respected on the basis of their understanding. The fear of punishment loses its importance following the mediation of the *smotrjashie*. The logic of their actions proves Alfred Schutz' statement that 'understanding is above all not a method used by the researcher in the social sciences, but the particular experiential form by

---

[243] Interview No. 1b.
[244] Interview No. 24.

which current thinking appropriates the socio-cultural world through knowledge' (Schutz, 1987, p. 75). It was not by accident that Schutz used the discussion of a jury during a trial as an example for focussing on the value of understanding in everyday life.

Second, the focus on understanding and explanation make the informal norms less rigid, ensuring their flexibility and the ability to be adapted to the circumstances of a concrete situation. A crucial division between the image of the Law as a rigid, static construct and the image of the informal norms as flexible and dynamic, appeared spontaneously during our discussions with the illicit guards. 'If we referred rigorously to the illicit norms, we'd wind up spilling blood. We wouldn't see any nuances. On the other hand, we can treat each individual in a human manner. We have to warn him three times, four times...'[245] The flexibility of the illicit norms is not guaranteed by definition, its source lies in a set of decision-making procedures. Without the support of these procedures, the illicit norms would transform into a copy of the formal laws, which are so rigid they incite violence when applied. 'We look at the papers, we find an article [of the Penal Code–he is referring to a court] that corresponds – three to ten years. This guy's not bad, so we'll give him three years. This guy's a repeat offender, we'll give him the maximum, a good ten years. No, I don't agree with this type of justice. I have to judge based on my actions, what I've actually done. Concrete actions...'[246] The inmates criticized the licit justice system several times for its summary nature, which does not allow for the specific conditions of a given act to be taken into consideration.

As for illicit justice, the 'judges', illicit guards, have a significant amount of leeway with respect to the interpretation of the norms of the penal subculture. 'Are you free to interpret the illicit norms? – Yes, to a certain extent. What's important for me is to avoid fights, theft, murders in my *otrjad*. The means for that are not important. I want everyone to live properly, to live well. So, I exaggerate a little. Not too much, but they live more freely. I treat each individual differently. It's important to know the reasons for an act, not the act as such. Like a day-care nanny – here's a noisy gang of kids, but she manages to scold someone, to hit someone, always based on personal knowledge. There's a factor of personal antipathy or sympathy. Understand? Is it good for justice? – From the point of view of justice, it's not normal, but you have to take many factors into consideration. Suppose that I know someone better than the others. If he did something, it wasn't to hurt the other. I know why he did it. The other may do something unjust to hurt someone... I'd prefer to be judged along these lines. Unfortunately, I was judged in keeping with the Penal Code. The article, the corresponding sentence... They judged me without knowing why and how'.[247]

The illicit guards use a term that is difficult to translate into English, *ludskoe* (literally, everything that is human, that is part of human nature). They view it as a guarantee of the principle of flexibility in illicit norms: they must always be

---

[245] Interview No. 1a.
[246] Interview No. 16.
[247] Interview No. 27b.

interpreted in a human manner. 'We base ourselves on everything that is human, everything that is natural for man. There are no rigid rules: this is permitted, that is prohibited. For the Penal Code, the results of your actions are important, not the situation, the reasons... Here, it's the contrary, the situation counts, not the action... You said *ludskoe*. What does that mean? – People... An association with "crowd" comes to mind. So, what are the other associations? – People who respect the illicit norms (*ponjatija*)... No, I'd like to put that another way. Did you kill cats as a child? No. – Well, that's *ludskoe*. Did you beat a guy weaker than you? No. – Everyone has his own code of honor. You can't afford to anger the weak, to rape a girl or hit her. That's *ludskoe*. Washing up in the morning, brushing your teeth – that's also *ludskoe*. It's a correct way of living... Could we say that *ludskoe* means the same as another term, good sense? – Yes, they overlap, but not perfectly. Good sense, well people outside prison don't understand the people here'.[248] Perhaps *ludskoe* means good sense within the prison context. Therefore, each illicit norm must be placed in context, must be interpreted on the basis of good sense as understood by the inmates. The interpretation is the responsibility of the illicit guards, those who comment on the sacred texts, *ponjatija*, of the penal world.

The third, final characteristic of the illicit mediation of conflicts lies in development of a concept of what is just specific to it. In the case of the 'small' society, 'the search for justice focuses on the personal relations between people' (Boltanski, Thévenot, 1991, p. 206). Efforts to construct an abstract definition of what is just are not very successful. The criteria for justice have a very concrete, situational and personalized connotation. Questions about the criteria for just actions and decisions resulted in a wealth of answers from our interviewees. 'In order for a decision to be just, must it correspond to the illicit norms? – There must always be a correspondence. So, respect for the illicit norms ensures justice? – It depends on who makes the decision. Yes, the decision must be based on the *ponjatija*, but it must also be just'.[249] A reference to the norms is not sufficient, therefore, to support illicit justice. The search for a just solution means that the norms have to be adapted to the situation and the individuals involved in the conflict. 'The decision must first be human. No, I said that badly. It must correspond to the illicit norms, that's essential. But it must also include a compromise, so that it does not harm anyone. You understand, we have to look for a compromise. So there is less tension, so people get less upset'.[250]

The characteristics of the justice dispensed by the illicit guards are highlighted in the ideal type of illicit guard developed by the inmates. The comparison of the ideal guard with an ideal friend serves to differentiate the attributes of a good illicit guard. We find the respect for others' opinions, good sense, and a sense of justice at the top of the list of attributes. In other words, the good illicit guard is first a good mediator, a good judge, in the penal city.

---

[248] Interview No. 27b.
[249] Interview No. 30.
[250] Interview No. 27b.

Table 2.40 Comparative characteristics of the illicit guard and a friend

Prisoners' leader, *avtoritet*			Qualities	Friend			
Russia	Kazakh.	Canada		Rus.	Kaz.	Fr.	Can.
1224	381	116	N	1280	388	55	117
69.5 (+11.4)	71.7 (+12.2)	53.5 (+9.9)	Common sense	58.1	59.5	10.9	43.6
55.8 (+15.9)	55.6 (+20.8)	59.5 (+25.3)	Sense of justice	39.9	34.8	30.9	34.2
49.1	49.1	56	Honesty	50.1	52.6	63.6	70.1
50.2	50.1	35.3	Responsibility for his / her own actions	43.8	45.4	27.3	32.5
38.6 (+18.2)	42.3 (+24.5)	58.6	Respect for other people	20.4	17.8	67.3	59.8
29.5	24.9	36.2	Intelligence	23.7	19.3	36.4	33.3
22.3	16.5	32.8 (+22.5)	Will-power	32.3	34.5	x	10.3

As a result of their freedom to interpret the illicit norms and the principles of equity in keeping with the context of the disputed action, the illicit guards are more like the Common Law judge. In the context of Common Law, the judge is considered a major source of the Law.

> 'The judge explains and develops the Law through arguments and counter-arguments, in keeping with a subjective and discursive style' (Arnaud-Duc, 1993, p. 353).

Also,

> 'equity is an almost intuitive notion that the [Common Law] judge draws from his individual conscience to develop a personal and distinct conviction' (Manaï, 1993, p. 235).

In this respect, it should be noted that the explanatory role also unites the Common Law judges and the illicit guards. 'Every tribunal should make known to the parties the reasons for its decisions' (James, 1989, p. 149). The link between the understanding of the reasons for an act and the interpretation of the general norm in keeping with these reasons is particularly evident in the assize court. As demonstrated by Harold Garfinkel, juries try to make a connection between the general principles of the Law and the context of a particular act, based on common sense: 'Jurors are engaged in deciding "reasonable causes and remedies"' (Garfinkel, 1967, p. 105). For this reason, the inmates interviewed support the idea of introducing the assize court into Russian judicial practice, although it has never been developed in keeping with Common Law. When asked 'What do you think of setting up an assize court?', more than half of the inmates were in favor of it:

Table 2.41 Confidence in an assize court

	Russia, N=902	Kazakhstan, N=396
This will probably increase the confidence in the system of justice	50.2	51.5
This won't change anything	26.7	29.5
This will make the situation worse	11.5	10.1
No answer	11.5	8.8

Moreover, our interviewees proposed several judicial innovations, never found, unlike the idea of the assize court, in the current discourse on the reform of the Russian justice system, although they fit in with the logic of the illicit justice system. First, they proposed the institution of the family solicitor. 'Starting at the instruction stage, he will defend the accused. A family solicitor. He will defend the same family for five, ten, twenty years. He will defend the parents, the children, the grandchildren. He will know the family. He will know its positive sides. When the judge listens to the opinion of the solicitors, it will change everything'.[251] Then the inmates referred to the lack of a personal reputation on the part of the judges as an explanation for their lack of responsibility. The personal reputations of the illicit guards, as well as control from above, provide better guarantees as to their impartiality. 'If I live with someone, I can't treat him unjustly. I can't. I'd feel bad about it. The judge doesn't live with the inmate, doesn't eat with him. So, he doesn't care'.[252] Returning to the example of the private mediators at medieval fairs, we note the role that personal reputation played in the process of their institutionalization. One interviewee summarized these arguments as follows: 'It's a particular justice system. It concerns only our world. If this type of justice system existed in your world, the situation would be better than now, I'm sure'.[253]

Moreover, we have no intention of advocating the justice of the illicit guards. The inmates often criticize them for being unable to find a compromise between the need for flexibility and the need for equitable treatment. We noted a tendency to judge people based on their belonging to a specific illicit category. 'Your category (*mast'*) should not be considered. If I'm right, then even if the guilty one is *blatnoj* and belongs to a higher category, he must be punished'.[254] Yet, the illicit categorization lies at the heart of the prison organization and ignorance of it does not depend on the good will of the illicit guards. The alternate solution, a focus on the need for equitable treatment, receives the same criticism as the licit justice system. 'If the illicit guard sees that order is respected, asks about what is done, and not about who did it, I support him'.[255] In other words, the institutionalization of illicit justice, although it is attractive when compared to *bespredel*, does not serve to dispose of the inconveniences of the 'small' society. The elements of the

---

[251] Interview No. 2.
[252] Interview No. 27b.
[253] Letter from Interviewee No. 3a.
[254] Interview No. 20.
[255] Interview No. 4.

justice system that coincide with the Common Law institutions can only form a stable whole and demonstrate their effectiveness in another institutional context, namely that of the 'large' society. On the contrary, in the context of the 'small' society, either in prison or outside, illicit justice is closer to the justice of the Mafia, namely effective and quick for yours and arbitrary and violent for others. It should not be forgotten that 'the mediation of conflicts within the local society, the mediation of relations between it and the outside world' (Arlacchi, 1986, p. 45) gave rise to the Mafia phenomenon.

A plurality of total institutions: towards a comparative penology

If one compares prison with other social institutions, it is always close to an ideal type of total institution (Goffman, 1968). A 'golden rule' for the penal system, that the prisoners' living standard should not exceed that of the worst paid unqualified worker, limits the willingness to go to prison. A very approximate analysis of the Federal Budget of the Russian Federation (Zakon o federal'nom budgete 2002 goda) shows that the government expends an equivalent of about US $40–50 monthly per inmate. This figure corresponds to the above-mentioned rule (without taking into account issues of efficiency of the budget expenditures). It should be noted that penitentiary system costs represent 1.7 per cent of the federal budget, which is ten times more than, for example, those of the justice institutions (0.17 per cent).

Despite this reasoning, empirical evidence suggests a more complex picture. A non negligible number of Russian inmates, 31.2 per cent of a poll including 1120 prisoners, think that their life in prison is simpler than life outside prison walls. Cross-tabulating these answers with responses to the question 'During which period of time would you prefer to serve your current sentence?' provides us with additional information (Table 2.42). The percentage of those who have a positive view of prison is maximal in the group of prisoners preferring to serve their current sentence in today's Russia. By contrast, their number is less than the average in the group composed of those who are ready to go to prison of any other country except today's Russia. In other words, the idea of comparing prison with other institutions in national and international perspectives is not purely speculative. Inmates are able to make such comparisons, despite their rather artificial character (there are many cooperation and exchange programs between national penitentiary administrations, but they concern correctional officers, not prisoners). How do they compare different institutions, if living standard is not a unique criterion? In the framework of the present analysis, we will try to introduce into scientific discussion arguments developed by prisoners themselves. In A. Schutz's words,

> 'the objects of thought constructed by researchers in the social sciences are based on the objects of thought constructed by the everyday thinking of the man who lives his everyday life among his peers and refers to them' (Schutz, 1987, p. 11).

Analytically speaking, international comparisons are necessary to better understand the situation in each of the compared countries: they serve to find points of reference. Country-specific data can be assessed only in relation with analogous figures in a number of other countries. For example, we could not judge the Russian data without likening it with responses of inmates in other post-Soviet and Western prisons. So, the principal task of our study here consists in a practical and theoretical evaluation of different approaches to comparing penitentiary institutions.

Table 2.42 Preferences about serving current sentence

			Do you think the prisoner's life is simpler than life outside of prison walls?	
			Yes	No
During which period would you prefer to serve your current sentence?	N=960	100%	31.2	68.8
	Anywhere and anytime except in today's Russia	45.2	27.9	72.1
	Today	21.2	40.4	59.6
	1991–1997	14.8	35.2	64.8
	Brezhnev's rule (1970–80s)	12.5	25.8	74.2
	1985–1990	3.9	29.7	70.3
	Before 1917 revolution	1.6	26.7	73.3

Probably the simplest and the most popular way to compare penitentiary institutions consists in referring to statistical data at a macro level. The Prison Population Rate (PPR), a ratio of the number of prisoners for 100,000 in total population, represents one such basic indicator. The values of the PPR in the four countries studied are quite different: Russia – 730, Kazakhstan – 495, Canada – 110 and France – 90 (Table 2.2). Both post-Soviet countries appear to be more punitive than the two Western countries in our sample. But these figures say nothing about the everyday life of the two principal actors, inmates and prison guards. In the list of countries ranked by their PPRs Russia's closest neighbor is the United States (680), while communist China has the same PPR as Canada. Obviously, this does not mean that Chinese inmates are as happy as their counterparts in Canada, a country known for its investments in penitentiary facilities and educational programs for inmates.

While looking for a better criterion of comparison, one could consider statistical data at a micro level. The US Federal Bureau of Prisons (FBP) operates with the notion of prison social climate. Social climate is perceived as a function of admissions and discharges, average daily population, inmate demographics, security designation, custody classification, urine surveillance, assaults, escapes, disciplinary hearings, inmate grievances, education program enrolments and completions, staff demographics, staff and inmate perceptions of the intensity of social tensions, and financial management (Saylor, 1989). It is important to note that social climates are assessed neither on the basis of an established normative profile (a 'cardinal' scale) nor by means of a simple comparison (an 'ordinal' scale).

'Organizational administrators appear to be more interested in comparing an assessment of an institution's climates to some common sense understanding... of what a particular type of institution ought to look like' (Saylor, 1984, p. 4).

The focus here is on prison guards' common sense.

Table 2.43 A taxonomy of prison social climates: theoretical models

The level of control exercised by guards	The level of cooperation and solidarity among inmates	
	High	Low
High	Model 1	Model 3
Low	Model 2	Model 4

Practically speaking, since the late 1980s, the FBP has been conducting surveys of prison social climates on a regular basis on a sample of correctional officers directly involved in interactions with inmates. Their results are processed through a computerized system of Key Indicators/Strategic Support System (KI/SSS) which is available at each level of decision-making. The system user decides how to configure the data, which indicators will be analyzed and for what purpose. Thus, the system is operated exclusively by the commonsense of its users. Theoretically speaking, there exists a taxonomy of prison social climates. While discussing case studies of prison social climates known in criminological literature, P. Tremblay develops a taxonomy based on two criteria, the level of control exercised by guards and the level of cooperation and solidarity between inmates (Tremblay, 1991, see Table 2.43). For example, the case of a maximum-security prison studied by G. Sykes (1958) corresponds to Model 1. A high level of social control, especially in maximum-security prisons, often results from recourse to physical coercion and verbal violence practiced by the staff (Marquart, 1986). Our data confirms this observation. Violent behavior on the part of the staff in all its forms (except intimidation) is more common in the maximum-security prisons of our Canadian and Russian samples than in the medium- and minimum-security prisons (Table 2.44).

Table 2.44 Recourse to violence by prison guards: at least one case during last 6 months (prisoners' evaluations)

Forms of violence	Security level						Ca-nada 2001	Rus-sia 2001
	Minimum		Medium		Maximum			
	Can.	Russia	Can.	Russia	Can.	Russia		
N	38	294	44	91	38	23	120	408
Physical violence	5.3	34	0	28.6	19.4	65.1	7.8	33.5
Verbal violence	7.9	×	11.9	×	30.6	×	16.4	×
Intimidation	36.8	×	33.3	×	33.3	×	34.5	×
Exclusion	5.3	×	4.8	×	22.2	×	10.3	×
No one case	55.3	43.5	59.5	46.2	50	17.4	55.2	42.6

Here we propose a different perspective. Instead of analyzing assessments of the institutional climate by staff, one could look at those made on the basis of inmates' commonsense. Seen from this new perspective, the taxonomy of prison social climates becomes more operational. A key indicator here is the level of confidence. Total institutions in general and prisons in particular differ from other institutions by their extremely low level of interpersonal trust. A famous Prisoner's Dilemma clearly illustrates the atmosphere of distrust generated by penitentiary institutions (Axelrod, 1990). It is not surprising that the 'three commandments' of the Russian (previously Soviet) prisoner include such a norm as 'don't trust anybody' ('Don't believe, don't be afraid, don't ask'). Our interviewees stress the fact that everyone in prison learns to be distrustful, whatever his or her initial convictions are. 'I trust only myself... I can't trust anybody else'.[256] 'The time I'd passed here persuaded me that I must consider everybody with suspicion and distrust'.[257]

In all the countries of our sample except France, the most frequently mentioned response to the question 'Where do you find support in a difficult situation?' is 'myself, nobody else' (Table 2.4). Relatively low expectations about the help of close relatives in post-Soviet countries could probably be explained by the fact that their visits are less frequent than in France and Canada. Although about two-thirds of inmates in France and Canada have had visits from their close relatives during the last month (59.3 per cent and 57.5 per cent respectively), only 22.8 per cent of Russian inmates and 19.7 per cent of Kazakhstan inmates are so happy. Organizing the visits appears to be more complicated and difficult in post-Soviet countries (distant locations of prisons, transportation problems, poor facilities and so on). Inmates rarely count on prison staff as a source of help. France differs from the other three countries in this respect. The low expectations about staff helpfulness in Canada contrasts with a positive image of psychologists and lawyers, whereas post-Soviet inmates lack such alternative sources of institutionalized help (as we mentioned before, psychologists arrived in Russian prisons only recently, in the second half of the 1990s). Figures of really received help analyzed through the question 'Who really helps you in a difficult situation?' (Table 2.4, sources of real help) show that, in Western countries, the expectations about help are more intense than the support actually received. The opposite is true in post-Soviet countries where inmates do not expect much help from others and they are pleasantly surprised when help finally comes.

The answers to direct questions about trust in different forms show convergent as well as divergent figures (Table 2.45). Divergences in the level of impersonal trust basically result from differences in mechanisms of primary socialization: in general, Western people have more confidence in others than post-Soviet people do (Inglehart 1990, Levada 1993). The results of a survey conducted in two control groups composed of students in Law at three major Moscow universities and students in criminology at a major Canadian French-language university confirms this assertion. In other words, one should look for an explanation of differences in the level of impersonal trust outside prison. By

---

[256] Interview No. 6.
[257] Interview No. 3a.

contrast, the level of confidence in other inmates of the same penitentiary does not vary greatly in the countries of our sample. Even the difference of five percentage points between France and Russia lies within the limits of the standard error (5.3 per cent in France, 1.9 per cent in Russia). While deciding whether to trust fellow inmates, prisoners assess the situation in their penitentiary according to their understanding of what a prison milieu ought to look like. For example, the level of trust in other inmates varies from 0 percent to 33.3 percent in the 43 prisons visited in Russia. The low variability of the national averages suggests that the Prisoner's Dilemma is not a country-specific phenomenon. The control groups show completely divergent figures which confirm the explanatory value of our variables.

Table 2.45 Levels of trust (per cent of those who can trust...)

Country		Impersonal trust	Personal trust		Institutional trust	
		Trust in the other people	Trust in the other inmates	Trust in the prisoners' leaders	Trust in the prison staff	Trust in the government
France, N=59		45.8 (6.5[258])	20.3 (5.3)	×	59.3 (6.5)	×
Canada, N=120		37.5 (4.5)	15 (3.5)	33.3 (4.6)	23.3 (4.2)	15.8 (3.7)
Kazakhstan, N=396		17.7 (2)	14.4 (2)	41.4 (2.6)	25.3 (2.3)	15.9 (2)
Russia		14.6 (1.9) N=1310	13.7 (1.9) N=1310	37.5 (1.3) N=925	19.9 (1.8) N=1120	9.9 (1.2) N=769
Control groups: students in Law	Canada, N=195	76.4 (3)	92.8[259] (1.9)	×	88.2[260] (2.3)	30.2 (3.4)
	Russia, N=117	32.5 (4.4)	×	×	51.3 (4.6)	7.7 (2.5)

If the prison milieu cannot generate an atmosphere favorable to trust, one could think about its external sources. In Canada as well as in post-Soviet countries prison guards recognize (in Canada – *de jure*, in post-Soviet countries – *de facto*) the role of prisoner leaders in organizing the everyday life of inmates. As our data shows, official support does not count for much because the level of confidence in prisoner leaders is lower in Canada than in both post-Soviet countries. In any case, in all three countries, the level of trust in prisoner leaders exceeds the level of trust in the administration, another possible player in the trust game. A relatively high rating of the administration in French prisons should be assessed by taking into consideration its willingness to reduce the number of middlemen in relationships with inmates. Finally, trust in the government could be viewed as a substitute for (or a complement to) general trust in other people. Once again, the differences in the national averages result from processes outside prison. An explanation of the

---

[258] Standard error.
[259] Trust in the people you see frequently at the university.
[260] Trust in the administration of your department at the university.

low level of trust in the government in Canada probably consists in the fact that the survey was conducted in Quebec, a province known for its permanent conflicts with federal authorities. Even university students there do not trust the government much.

The level of trust assessed on the basis of the inmates' commonsense allows for the development of a new version of the taxonomy of prison social climates. Trust in other inmates influences the level of solidarity and cooperation among inmates. On the other hand, the level of real control exercised by guards is determined by the confidence that prisoners have in the warden and his colleagues. In contrast with Tremblay's approach, these key indicators first and foremost exist in the prisoners' minds and the researcher makes use of them instead of inviting differentiating criteria in a purely analytical way. Empirically driven indicators can, nevertheless, lead to a theoretical interpretation. Relations of authority lie at the core of any total institution. Generally, the authority within total institutions lies close to a pure exercise of power. According to Max Weber,

> 'power is the probability that one actor within a social relationship will be in a position to carry out his own will despite resistance, regardless of the basis on which this probability rests' (Weber, 1968, p.53).

Table 2.46 A revised taxonomy of prison social climates

		Level of personal trust	
		High	Low
Level of institutional trust (confidence in administration)	High	Model 1. Conjoint authority. Democracy applied to prison. Prison as a means of rehabilitation.	Model 3. Disjoint authority. Prison as a means to pay back the offender. So called 'red' prisons.
	Low	Model 2. Lack of authority. A 'self-managed' prison. Prisoners' leaders play an important role in organization of everyday activities. So called 'black' prisons.	Model 4. Imposed authority transforming into pure power. Prison as a method of discouraging the actual or potential criminal. So called *'bespredel'* prisons.

Cross-tabulating the levels of personal and institutional trust helps us to see a whole range of authority relationships within total institutions and to relativize in that way the transformation of authority into power (Table 2.46). J. Coleman's classification of authority relationships seems to be fruitful from this perspective. He speaks about three types of authority: conjoint, disjoint (both types derive from a voluntary transfer of the right of control) and involuntary, or imposed. In the case of conjoint authority, 'the actor believes that he will be better off by following the other's leadership' (Coleman, 1990, p. 72). Disjoint authority implies that 'the actor transfers rights of control without holding this belief, but in return for some extrinsic compensation' (Ibid.). Imposed authority supposes neither the coincidence of interests nor extrinsic compensation. The coincidence of interests of prison guards and inmates might result from a priority attached to the task of rehabilitating and reintegrating delinquents. For this reason, prisoners do trust the staff whereas the prison guards create conditions favorable for an increase in the level of personal trust in the inmates' milieu without which an autonomy of social behavior could not be re-established (Giddens, 1984, p.50–53). Literally speaking, it is the case of democracy applied to prison. The constitution of disjoint authority necessitates only a high level of institutional trust. Disjoint authority appears as a result of a priority attributed to the task of paying back the offender. Expectation of compensation for obedience (for example, parole) means that prisoners do trust the ability and willingness of staff to reward their efforts fairly. Any relationship between Principal and Agent, another expression of the disjoint authority, involves the Agent's trust in the Principal (Kreps, 1990). Imposed authority is associated with the perception of prison as a method of discouraging the actual or potential criminal; it excludes both personal and institutional trust.

An additional argument in favor of the proposed taxonomy consists in the fact that a very similar typology exists in minds of both inmates and prison staff. The penitentiaries with a Model 3 social climate are called 'red' in Russian prison slang. In fact, 'red' prisons have many features in common with the ideal type of total institution, first and foremost a detailed control of all aspects of the inmates' everyday life exercised by prison guards. The prisons where distrust governs relations both between inmates and between inmates and staff lack mechanisms of social control. The authority of prison guards is not limited by any bond and it naturally transforms into a pure exercise of power. But the distrusted authority is never able to impose efficient control due to the opportunistic behavior of its subjects. Efficient control could only be total, whereas such a control becomes prohibitively costly. So, the term *'bespredel'* (literally 'without limits') fits the resulting anomie well. Model 2 has not been described so far. A weakness of the administration is balanced here by high capacities of inmates for self-organizing. They organize everyday life themselves. In this case, the lack of authority gives rise to 'self-managed', or 'black' prisons, according to a slang expression.

Empirical tests confirm that personal and institutional trust allows for differentiating a sample of prisons on a national scale. For example, most of the 29 Russian prisons visited in 2000–2001, 38 per cent, are close to Model 2. Twenty-eight percent were classified as 'red' (Model 3) and 24 per cent have many Model 4 features. Finally, the authority in only 10 per cent of prisons of our sample could be considered conjoint. Unfortunately, the size of our international sample makes it impossible to test the taxonomy on an international scale. Despite this fact, the following paradox could not be ignored. The social climate in Canadian prisons appears to be very similar to that in post-Soviet countries, especially in Kazakhstan. The result is especially surprising if one remembers that penitentiary reform in the latter country started relatively recently and standards of living in Canada and Kazakhstan (and, hence, the inmates' living standards) differ radically. In other words, the Soviet-type prison has a somewhat better performance than the post-Soviet prison (represented by Russian penitentiaries) and even approaches the North American prison (in its Canadian version). Before trying to explain this paradox, some control variables should be used to confirm the closeness of the two national models. A comparison of behavior in situations of conflict with the other inmates reveals that inmates in the three countries, Russia, Kazakhstan and Canada, have common strategies (Table 2.38). Firstly, they prefer to ask the prisoners' leaders for help. Secondly, they settle conflicts among themselves. Thirdly, they wait for the intervention of the prison guards. The preferences of French prisoners are different: they like the prison guards to get involved in conflicts. A low rating of the alternative 'Call for the official justice' in all four countries should be noted. The prisoners do not believe that they can be protected by the official justice system (this pessimism is slightly less obvious in France).

The next control variable is the intensity of hidden protest. The answers to the question about whether inmates are ready to join in mass protests (this was not asked in France) convince us that the prisons in Russia, Kazakhstan and Canada have a very similar potential for riots (Table 2.30). The differences concern rather insignificant issues. For example, Kazakhstan is characterized by a high level of protest under certain conditions, whereas Canadian inmates are divided between unconditional protest and an absolute refusal to demonstrate their disagreements collectively.

Another control variable was introduced to compare the situation concerning the protection of prisoners' rights. The idea that prisoners may have rights is relatively new even in Western countries. A movement to recognize prisoners' rights started only after World War II. For example, in Germany this movement led to important changes in law only in the early 70s (Feest, Weber, 1996). While a concept of prisoners' rights was not totally foreign to the Soviet prisons, inmates only learned about their rights following the penitentiary reforms of the 1990s. Although the State was solely responsible for protecting prisoners' rights previously, the recent reforms gave an initiative to the inmates themselves and shaped the protection as basically a bottom-up process. Prisoners know about their rights much better in Russia, where the reforms are more advanced, than in Kazakhstan. In fact, according to this criterion, Russia is positioned close to Canada (see Table put in the note n°31, p. 235).

A less optimistic picture arises from comparing national practices for implementing legislation concerning prisoners' rights. In all the countries of our sample, the most valuable rights from inmates' point of view are at the same time the least protected. An average level of satisfaction with real respect for the prisoners' rights is higher in the two Western countries than in the two post-Soviet countries (Table 4.22). At the same time, the most important rights (e.g., the right to correct treatment is ranked first on the prisoners' list of priorities in all the countries except Canada where it is ranked second, after the right to have visits) are far from being fully respected by staff even in the Western countries. The rank of the right to correct treatment on a list of the most respected rights appears to be very low in every country, which explains the huge difference in its rank in the two lists. It should be noted that the right to correct treatment is less protected in Canada than in France. A more detailed analysis shows that the respect for this right determines the level of trust in staff. A correlation of the two variables is positive and statistically significant (0.5, N=304 in Kazakhstan; 0.38, N=874 in Russia; 0.28, N=98 in Canada; 0.22, N=56 in France, at p<0.05).

Most of the control variables confirm a convergence of prison social climates in Russia, Kazakhstan and Canada. We could not concentrate our attention here on the gap between these three countries and France. It is possible that our sample in France is too small to generalize the results. By contrast, the similarity of the three countries needs explaining. A set of preliminary hypotheses could be put forward. The first one concerns issues of organization of social control in prison. The control of the interactions between inmates and prison guards, two principal actors in the 'prison game', can be organized in the three following ways (Table 2.47). A bottom-up social control implies the ability of prisoners to control staff and enforce their rights. Administrative hierarchy represents another way to control social interactions and ensure that rights and obligations of both parties are respected. Hierarchical control is carried out by the superiors of the warden and his colleagues: regional and national penitentiary officials and the Ministry of Justice (the Ministry of the Interior in the Soviet case). Mechanisms for external control include the intervention of civil institutions such as associations focussed on protecting human and prisoner rights.

Table 2.47 Types of social control in prison

Models	*Social control*		
	Internal		*External*
	Bottom-up	*Hierarchical*	
Soviet type (Kazakhstan)	-	+++	-
Post-Soviet type (Russia)	-/+	+/-	-/+
Western (Canada)	+	+	+
Western (France)	+	++	+

The Soviet model of social control in prison (the situation in Kazakhstan of the late 1990s could be viewed as a rough approximation) is built upon a very strong hierarchical control exercised by the all-powerful Ministry of the Interior. An idea of either bottom-up control (prisoners were ignorant about their rights, they even had no access to the Penal Code and the CAP), or external control was not acknowledged. Treatment of inmates was regulated by a series of internal orders issues by the Ministry. A strong internal hierarchy ensured that all the orders were carried out; another mechanism of vertical control was represented by the institution of Procuracy, a key element of the centralized juridical authority (Solomon, 1996). A witness confirms that the authority of prison guards over inmates in Soviet prisons was cruel, but not arbitrary (p. 106, Interview No. 18).

Post-Soviet transformations weakened hierarchical control. Paradoxically, attempts to democratize prisons, a central element of the penitentiary reforms of the 1990s in Russia, can lead in the short- and probably mid-term to unintended consequences (Oleinik, 2002a). The principle of the division of power implies that prison should be placed under the administrative supervision of the Ministry of Justice, as in most Western countries. But the Ministry of Justice (including the penitentiary administration) in Russia has a budget three times smaller than that of the Ministry of the Interior, according to the Law on Federal Budget 2002 (Zakon o federal'nom budgete 2002 goda) and the penitentiary administration's share of the Federal budget is ten times greater than that of the Ministry of Justice. In other words, the Ministry of Justice does not possesses the human and financial resources necessary to control its quasi-autonomous 'department'. Bottom-up control is far from being efficient too: prisoners now know their rights, but they still lack the legal mechanisms for protecting them.

All three mechanisms of social control function in the two Western countries of our sample. For instance, decision-making about parole in Canada involves a multi-stage process and no single actor, prison staff, judges or communal institutions, has full control over it (Vacheret, Dozois, Lemire, 1998). Obviously, a detailed comparison of the systems of social control in France and Canada would require a special study. But the collected data does provide certain insights. The ranking of the most approachable persons and institutions (Table 2.10) shows that the principal differences between the two Western countries concern the role of the prison guards in carrying out social control. Appeals to the administration are two times more frequent in France than in Canada. Bottom-up control seems to be efficient in both cases, but this procedure is rather different. In Canada, the call for justice is mediated by lawyers, whereas in France direct contacts with the representatives of justice are more frequent and, consequently, easier. In short, hierarchical control appears to be more efficient in France, which could explain the divergence observed between France and Canada and the relative closeness of the prison social climate in Canada to that in Russia, where the weakness of the administrative hierarchy leads to opportunistic behavior on the part of the staff.

Since the data collected did not definitely confirm or refute the hypothesis concerning the key role of administrative control in differentiating prison social climates (it was partially tested on a sample of American state prisons: Useem, Reising, 1999), we should turn our attention to an alternative hypothesis. It stresses a moral dimension in human activities, including the everyday actions of the prisoner.

'Normative-affective factors shape to a significant extent the information that is gathered, the ways it is processed, the inferences that are drawn, the options that are being considered, and the options that are finally chosen' (Etzioni 1988, p. 94).

This approach is justified if the task of rehabilitation is ranked at the top of a list of different, sometimes contradictory, duties assigned to prison. The delinquent is conventionally perceived as an individual lacking moral and normative constraints (Merton 1938). A prison focussed on rehabilitation 'teaches' inmates to pay attention to the moral and legal frameworks of everyday activities. Thus, the evaluations that they have made of different aspects of the prison social climate result from a moral judgment. Inmates not only compare benefits and losses conditioned by the stick-and-carrot tactics of the staff, they judge prison guards on the basis of moral values and norms. Hence, the same level of trust in staff could correspond to different social situations, because the judgment might have been made on the basis of divergent sets of norms and values.

An administration which does little could nevertheless be trusted if inmates do not expect a lot. By contrast, an administration playing an active regulatory role in the inmates' everyday life could be distrusted if their expectations about such a role are higher still. A degree of correspondence between value-determined expectations and real actions of partners in social interactions really does matter (Table 2.48). The following definition of trust illustrates this aspect: it is 'the expectation of one person about the actions of others that affects the first person's choice, when an action must be taken before the actions of others are known' (Ostrom, 1998, p. 12). The underlying idea here resembles those on which a concept of multiplicity of social equilibria is founded (Azariadis, Guesnerie 1986; Dasgupta, 2000). Analytically speaking, we propose to view the level of trust as a variable dependent on various sets of values and moral expectations.

Table 2.48 Trustworthiness of staff as a function of inmates' expectations and judgments about the real actions of prison guards

Expectations about staff's involvement in inmates' everyday life		Judgment about the real involvement of staff in inmates' everyday life	
		High	Low
	High	Staff is trustworthy (1st social equilibrium)	Staff merits to be distrusted
	Low	Staff merits to be distrusted	Staff is trustworthy (2nd social equilibrium)

Table 2.49 provides us with an approximate picture of values and norms structuring inmates' everyday life in the four countries (the four most frequent alternatives are provided on a gray background). Two contrasting figures should be noted. Firstly, trust in general plays a relatively less important role in Canada than in the three other countries. Trust is perceived only as a resource for everyday activities by the Canadian inmates, whereas French prisoners see in it a resource and a condition. Secondly, moral considerations play a visibly more important role in the two Western countries than in the two post-Soviet ones. This could mean that French and Canadian prisons are more focussed on the task of rehabilitation than their post-Soviet counterparts. By contrast, profit is ranked high in Russia and Kazakhstan, which gives us a picture of anomie: profit-maximizing behavior is not constrained by moral or legal bonds. These observations allow us to suppose that the low level of trust in staff in Canada could be due to a divergence between high expectations and a relatively low staff' involvement in the inmates' everyday life. Meanwhile, two additional remarks should be taken into consideration. On the one hand, the staff is not the only social partner of inmates in Canada: social workers, professors, educators, and others complement the prison guards' involvement. On the other hand, trust is less suited to be the key indicator of prison social climate in Canada than even in France. Finally, the broken expectations about the staff's role

in inmates' everyday life do not seem to be too dramatic in the case of Canadian prisons.

Table 2.49 Values and norms structuring inmates' everyday life

	Russia, N=769			Kazakhstan, N=396			France, N=59			Canada, N=120		
	V.[261]	C.	R.	V.	C.	R.	V.	C.	R.	V.	C.	R.
Trust	2	2	2	3	2	1	6	1	2	5	10	1
Family	4	1	8	4	1	9	2	2	3/4	2	5	2
Work	5	9	1	5	7	2	7	7	5/6	3	11	8
Property	10	10	6	10	10	8	11	11	11	10	7	10
Empathy	6	3	5	7	5	5	9	5	5/6	8/9	3	4
Moral	9	6	9	8	9	10	5	3	3/4	7	2	5/6
Freedom	1	5	4	1	4	4	1	4	7	1	1	3
Law	7	8	7	6	6	6	4	6	1	6	4	5/6
Equality	3	7	10	2	8	7	3	8/9	8	4	8/9	7
Tradition	8	11	11	9	11	11	8	10	9/10	8/9	8/9	11
Profit	11	4	3	11	3	3	10	8/9	9/10	11	6	9

Our comparative study of the prison social climates adds new arguments to an old debate about the relationship between, on the one hand, feelings of social comfort and happiness, and, on the other hand, income and material wellbeing (Easterlin, 1974, Oswald, 1997). Previous studies have shown that there is no significant correlation between the growth of the GNP and happiness. A conventional explanation consists in referring to a complex role that reference groups play in determining the level of satisfaction with the current situation. We stress another reason explaining the lack of correlation and propose a kind of 'Easterlin paradox revisited'. A given standard of living or a given prison social climate can be evaluated on the basis of different sets of norms and values. The same action of a correctional officer could be judged as 'good' from one normative perspective and 'bad' from another. Thus, in order to understand the social atmosphere, we need to know the basic values and norms of the social actors. This knowledge helps the observer guess whether the social climate does correspond to an equilibrium and whether this equilibrium is stable. The Soviet and French penal models appear to represent two different types of social equilibrium: non-democratic and democratic. Two other country-specific models, post-Soviet (Russian) and Canadian, have many features of unstable, non-equilibrium situations. The instability in Canada results from the process of opening up the prison, whereas in

---

[261] V. – terminal values (ranged on the basis of frequencies of responses to the question 'On what foundations should Russian [Kazakh, French, Quebec] society be built?', Table 2.25), C. – conditions (ranged on the basis of frequencies of responses to the question 'What do you think about while resolving an important problem?'), R. – resources, means (ranged on the basis of frequencies of responses to the question 'What can you make use of to resolve an important problem?').

Russia it is determined by the lack of mechanisms for social control. The characteristics of the administrative control become a major explanatory variable in case of the prisons which are less focussed on the task of rehabilitation than the task of paying back the offender or of discouraging the actual or potential criminal. Obviously, these conclusions are more preliminary than definitive and they need to be tested on a more representative sample (on a national as well as on an international scale). Our main purpose here consists in initiating debates and attracting the attention of researchers and policy makers to the issues discussed instead of proposing ready conclusions and solutions.

Chapter 3

Generalization Test: A Torn Society

From a quantitative point of view, how can the border of the 'small' society be defined: a location, a region, an institution, a dozen, thousand or million people? Any quantitative scale excludes a country such as the USSR or Russia from consideration as 'small' societies. The total population of the USSR was approximately 290.1 million in 1990, making it the third largest country in the world after China and India, based on population (see Table 3.1 for a breakdown).[1] Even after the break-up of the USSR, the Russian Federation had approximately 150 million inhabitants.

Table 3.1 Russia's population

Year	Population (millions)
1940 (USSR)	195
1950	180
1960	214
1970	242
1980	265.5
1990	290
1999 (Russian Federation)	146.3
2000	145.6

As a result, how can the model of the 'small' society be applied to the study of such a large country? We do not propose to question the quantitative value of the post-Soviet society. However, we do want to stress a paradoxical situation: a society of that size can be based on the logic behind the 'small' society, without changing it greatly. Although the Soviet society has changed significantly since the Stalinist period, setting it apart from the totalitarian model, the type of relations between the licit authority and the everyday lives of ordinary people has not changed greatly to date. This hypothesis will enable us to 'surf' rather freely over the time and space of the Soviet model.

The imposed and restrictive character of the licit authority creates a link between the organization of the penal society and that of the Soviet society. Wherever this type of society exists, in prison, in certain regions in Southern Italy,

---

[1] UN data and national statistics: *Britannica. Book of the Year. 1991*, Chicago: Encyclopaedia Britannica, 1991, pp. 750–751 ; http://www.gks.ru '*Russia – 2000*'.

or in a society including several million inhabitants, it promotes the reproduction of the 'small' society model that we have just described. Let us start this brief, fragmentary overview of the 'small' societies that exist outside the penal world with a sketch of the Italian example.

Example of Southern Italy

Regardless of which term comes to mind as soon as the historical development of Southern Italy is mentioned, the Mafia, the *camorra*, the *'ndrangheta* or even amoral familism, it is associated with the image of the local society, hostile to the outside world. Setting aside the purely criminal associations of the Mafia reveals a particular social organization. The vision of the Mafia as a social model is of particular relevance for our research. The impact of the Mafia on the organization of everyday life is more important to us than its internal functioning, particularly since 'the Mafia is a behavior and a power, not a formal organization' (Arlacchi, 1986, p. 16).[2]

The Mafia originates in a form of state absenteeism specific to Southern Italy in the 18th century. On the one hand, the democratization of property rights in Sicily multiplied the number of large owners tenfold around 1860 (from 2,000 to 20,000), creating a demand for the protection of property rights (Gambetta, 1993, pp. 79–91). On the other hand, the State had never been viewed there as supportive in the resolution of daily conflicts. First, in the 17th and 18th centuries, Spain had treated Sicily as a vassal whose interests were not to be considered. Then, the transition to Italian jurisdiction did not change the will of the State to take without giving anything in return. 'The Mafia developed in the absence of public justice… the State had forgotten that Sicily existed' (Arlacchi, 1986, pp. 29, 31). Moreover, the economic policy of the Italian state was based, up to the second half of the 20th century, on the exploitation of the poor regions (the *Mezzogiorno*, the South) by the industrially developed regions (the North). 'A national economic policy reinforced the economies of the strong regions to the detriment of the weak regions' (Cesoni, 1995, p. 159). This policy caused a number of economic, social and political conflicts, rather than resolving them.

Since the local society could not refer to the licit authority as a resource in the organization of everyday life, it closed in on itself, developing its own procedures for resolving conflicts, more effective than the official procedures. Therefore, the Mafia was created to manage conflicts and serve as a mediator.

> 'The honorable man resolved differences in a few weeks and not several years, *because he had accurate information*' (Arlacchi, 1986, p. 120).[3]

The final portion of this sentence is revealing. The local and personalized character of relations makes it easy to obtain accurate information. In other words, the price

---

[2] Giovanni Schiavo expressed this thesis in other words: 'The Mafia expresses an idea rather than a definitely organized institution' (Schiavo, 1962, p. 21).

[3] Our stress.

for the autonomy and efficiency of the illicit institutions is the refusal to transform the 'small' society into a large one. In order to prove the membership of the traditional society of Southern Italy in the family of 'small' societies, we will attempt to describe it using the four parameters developed in our analysis of prison society: the non-differentiation of spheres of activities, the personalization of relations, an imperfect control of violence and the duality of norms.

The modern concept of private space that is separate from public space is foreign to the traditional Sicilian society. Possibly, the exaggerated sensitivity with respect to feminine honor, which is one of the most common causes of conflicts, can be explained by the failure of means other than physical force or recourse to Mafia norms to ensure that private space is respected. 'In Mafia zones, feminine honor is the most typical example of family integrity' (Arlacchi, 1986, p. 19). In terms of the illicit means for protecting family space, there is a Mafia behavioral norm that 'one knows very little about other families' (Gambetta, 1993, pp. 118–126). Therefore, the informational space is fragmented. No important information is transmitted outside the family. Moreover, the family space is separated from the public space in the best cases. Protecting the individual against unwanted interventions on the part of those close to him is not considered necessary. According to the testimony of Tommaso Buscetta, a reformed Mafioso, 'in Sicily, the "individual" did not exist' (Arlacchi, 1996, p. 158).

The Mafia transposes the principle of the non differentiation of rules to any sphere of daily activity. For example, the presence of the Mafia in a market means that the market cannot function autonomously. The manner in which a company organizes its work and its strategy for competition is subject to the traditional imperatives of the Mafia. Paternalism is not compatible with the representation of wage interests by unions, vassalage and protectionism make free competition impossible, etc. (Arlacchi, 1986, pp. 105–123). It is no longer a market in the modern sense, but an amalgamation of traditional values and practices for maximizing profits.

Life in a hostile institutional environment with no licit devices for protecting private space accounts for the need to find asylum in family and personalized relations.

> 'The Mafia can be understood as a response to the lack of trust specifically affecting Southern Italy. All that remained was *la fede privata*, that private realm populated only by kin and close friends in which people take refuge from high levels of social unpredictability, aggression, and injustice' (Gambetta, 1993, p. 77).

The basic Mafia unit, the *coscà*, reproduces the family structure. Generally, it includes 15–20 Mafioso (7–80 individuals at most) with a first-degree biological relationship. Moreover, the external environment of the *coscà*, its protective belt, includes only those known personally to the family members. They are organized in networks of friends and clients (see Figure 3.1). In other words, there are at least two levels of protection against the disastrous influence of the outside world. This serves to maintain a fairly comfortable climate in the center of this figure paid for by the almost total ignorance of what is going on along the periphery. Edward

Banfield referred to this organization of social space as 'amoral familism' which can be reduced to the following imperative:

> 'Maximizing the short-term material advantages of the nuclear family means that all other act in the same manner' (Banfield, 1958, p. 85).

Figure 3.1 *Coscà*'s structure

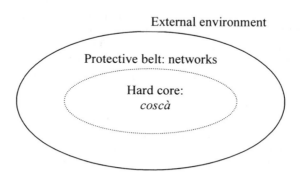

The separation between the center and the periphery of the social space makes it easy to channel the violence generated in everyday life to the outside. The spatial organization of the Calabrai village of the 1930s is remarkably similar to that of the penal world, described in the section entitled '*Illicit categorization*'. The sacrificial victims of the local community, its pariahs, are always set to the side, along the periphery of the village (cf. the periphery of the areas occupied by the *otrjad*). 'The truly dishonored categories were even physically separated from the rest of the community' (Arlacchi, 1986, p. 19). This dual organization accounts for the strange coexistence of the freedom to kill outside the Mafia organization and the extreme control of violence in relations between members. In the latter case, an entire series of procedures is implemented to prevent recourse to violence.

> 'Conflicts that occurred within the complex coalitions of relatives and friends were resolved through informal meetings, dominated by the ostentation of loyalty and traditional familiarity' (Arlacchi, 1986, p. 94).

The absence of inter-family rules and the danger of unending wars gave rise, in the 1950s–1960s, to provincial and inter-provincial commissions, *coupole*, whose primary duty was to develop procedures for non-violent conflict resolution between the *coscà*.

Moreover, these commissions added only a third level of protection, a common space for all Mafia families, without changing the principle of duality. The limits of the 'small' society were extended (the members of other families become members of your family), but it was not transformed into a 'large' society. Let us take a close look at some of the key elements of the unwritten Mafia constitution as a normative space common to all *coscà*. Most of these norms have a profoundly dual nature. On the one hand, there is the norm that 'honorable men must tell the truth' (Arlacchi, 1986, p. 203). On the other hand, this norm only concerned relations between Mafioso. Relationships with outsiders were based on the *omertà*, namely the refusal to 'tell anyone about the deeds and misdeeds of the Mafia' (Arlacchi, 1986, p. 58). Since the State is a stranger, contacts with its representatives are particularly discouraged. One should 'avoid passing information to the police' (Gambetta, 1993, p. 147). This brings to mind the norm of the penal subculture 'Don't ask the administration to resolve conflicts'. These norms seem to have the same roots. At the same time, relations within the Mafia are based on trust. There, a word of honor has the same value as a contractual obligation. Moreover,

> 'Mafiosi operate in those economic transactions where it is either inefficiently supplied or cannot be supplied at all by the State (illegal transactions in otherwise legal goods, or in all transactions in illegal goods)' (Gambetta, 1988, p. 128).

On the other hand, the level of impersonal trust in Southern Italy, 50–60 per cent, represents the absolute minimum for Western European countries (Inglehart, 1990, p. 35). Then, there are the norms that prohibit people from stealing from their own (namely other Mafioso), seducing the wives of their own, fighting with their own, etc. (Gambetta, 1993, p. 147). In short, traditional society in Southern Italy is organized exactly as the ideal 'small' society.

Incomplete modernization: about the Soviet society

Before applying the same analytical markers to the study of the Soviet society, we need to examine the nature of State authority in that society given, according to our initial hypothesis, the imposed, restrictive, even hostile, character of both the post-Soviet State and the licit authority in prisons. The history of relations between the State and society merits close examination. We will settle, at this time, for sketching out the main lines.

Role of the Soviet state

The model for relations between the State and society observed today is not an invention of the Soviet period. The authority of the Russian sovereigns, *tsars*, was very different from that of most Western sovereigns. The model of the domestic city, in keeping with the term introduced by Luc Boltanski and Laurent Thévenot, focusses on the reciprocity of the rights and obligations of Western sovereigns. The king 'compensates for his privileges by sacrificing his person to others: "He is not born for himself and forgets himself"' (Boltanski, Thévenot, 1991, p. 123). In comparison, the *tsar* 'has no obligations, determining all the rules on his own' (Morozov, 1991, t. 2, p. 113). The image of the *tsar* as God's lieutenant on Russian soil, gives him absolute discretionary authority. The laws he enacts reflect his will, excluding any reference to the context to which it is applied. For a Russian peasant, the law is always associated with something sinister, 'its meaning is obscure, but its force is irresistible' (Ahiezer, 1991, p. 240). The optional character of the reactions of the subjects to the tsarist authority condemns each new initiative to failure, however good and progressive it is at the outset. The correct interpretation of the intentions and actions of the authority is never assured. For example, the results of the abolition of serfdom in 1860 were a negative surprise for those who initiated it.

> 'The failure of the reform is less a result of the insufficiency of the rights given to the peasants than the fact that they did not understand the rights they were given' (Ahiezer, 1991, p. 244).

The Soviet model did not fill the void that separated the State and the everyday lives of its subjects. On the contrary, the reciprocal isolation of the State and its subjects was aggravated following the subsequent suppressions of the elements that could give rise to a civil society. Therefore, we can speak of the efforts to build Soviet society in keeping with the total institution model. Under the total system 'social organization is based on atomization, on the suppression of all elements of society that are independent of the State' (Ahiezer, 1991, p. 178). The results of 'atomization as a vector of State policy' (Timofeev, 1993, p. 121) justify the analogy between the totalitarian State and the prison that breaks social structures foreign to it. A VCIOM survey of a representative sample conducted at the end of the 1980s demonstrates that a non-negligible portion of Soviet society describes its usual situation in terms of solitude. More than 40 per cent of those questioned acknowledge that they are alone. Therefore, 'the Soviet system creates a solitary man and uses his demonstrative a-sociability' (Levada, 1993, p. 68).

Moreover, given the high cost of having the State organize everyday life, it has never been possible to construct society in keeping with the totalitarian institution, even during the Stalinist period. Rather, it is a negative compromise based on the reciprocal ignorance of the State and Soviets. The State refuses to control all aspects of everyday life and Soviets refuse to question the discretionary authority of the State.

> 'The population learned to keep the State at a distance, to bypass it, to make do, by giving it a monopoly over public space and political discourse, and protecting its private life, without forming a true civil society, and without presenting itself as a society that has been massified or completely absorbed by the Party-State' (Berelowitch, Wieviorka, 1996, p. 22).

This negative compromise makes the voluntary submission to the Law optional without, however, legitimizing the total rejection of the Law. A recent survey indicates that a majority of Russians (58.5 per cent) think that when the Law collides with commonsense, priority must be given to commonsense.[4] The same attitude with respect to the Law determines the behavior not only of ordinary

---

[4] *Monitoring obschestvennogo mnenija : ekonomicheskie i social'nye problemy*, March–April 1999, n°2 (40), p. 75

people but also Soviet company managers. The managers prefer to use commonsense as a result of the enormous number of regulations which the supervisory organizations use to control them. Each department has an average of 10,000–30,000 normative acts in effect. Moreover, the number is increasing as a result of a vicious circle specific to any bureaucratic and centralized regulation. 'The effort to deal with problems through centralized regulation is not effective since it increases the distance between the autonomous regulation and the control regulation. The fact that the control regulation is ineffective means that it is sought more ardently. This excess centralization accentuates the ineffectiveness of the regulation' and so on (Reynaud, 1989, p. 201). Under these conditions, 'even loyal managers use usual practices and commonsense' (Dolgova, Djakov, 1989, pp. 216–217) rather than submit to the Law.

A more recent investigation we conducted in 1999 and 2001 (on samples consisting of 174 and 219 businessmen, respectively) indicated that Russian businessmen often associate the Law with a restriction that they must get around at the first opportunity. The frequency with which this association is made by both the businessmen interviewed and the inmates is illustrated in Table 3.2. It is obvious that post-Soviet inmates occasionally view the Law more positively than the businessmen do, despite the fact that the inmates were deprived of their freedom under the Law! Therefore, it should be no surprise that only one-third of those interviewed are convinced of the need to respect the Law (see Table 3.3 for the answers to the question 'Do you think that...').

Table 3.2 Associations with the word 'Law'

	Businessmen, Russia		Prisoners		
	[99*]	[01*]	Russia	Kazakh.	Canada
N	174	219	769	396	120
Coercion	34%	40.7	6	4.1	7.1
Prohibition	28	31.5	8.3	3.5	23.2
A tool used by some people	28	43.4	45	49.1	29.5
Citizens' duty	21	53	6	5.7	53.6
Guarantee	12	43.8	×	×	×
Voluntary obligation	10	19.9	2.4	2.7	32.1
Justice	4	×	22.8	23.1	48.2
Rule which corresponds to interests of the majority of citizens	1	×	16.1	18.2	41.1
Common good	0	×	4.6	6	16.1

Table 3.3 Opinion about the 'Law' in this country

Do you think that...	[99*]	[01*]
There are some Laws which should be respected whereas some others are not worthy of respect	43%	53.4
Laws must always be respected	35	22.4
Good Laws are absent, they are even impossible in this country	16	22.4
No answer	7	1.8

The negative compromise does not exclude a high degree of dependency on the part of Soviets with respect to the State and *vice versa* as long as that dependency is also negative. First, the prosperity of the State is not assured unless its subjects work zealously in the legal sector of the economy. Now, ignorance of the everyday interests of Soviets has re-directed a portion of their economic activity towards the black market, the illegal economy (we will analyze the basic parameters of the illegal Soviet economy in the section entitled '*Parallel market as a starting point*'). The illegal economy appears because 'the organizational and normative structure of the [legal] economy does not satisfy the objective needs for organizing and coordinating economic activity' (Yakovlev, 1988, p. 43).

Moreover, the market reforms of the 1990s caused the State to be dependent on the will of its economic subjects to pay income tax: it was much easier to ensure fiscal discipline under a command economy. The accumulated volume of outstanding income tax amounted to 31 per cent of the annual GNP in 1996 and 41 per cent in 1997.[5] In order to verify the hypothesis that the State's refusal to take its subjects' interests into consideration results in tax evasion, we asked a series of questions concerning fiscal discipline, in 1998 and 1999. The contradictory responses to two questions (see Tables 3.4 and 3.5) indicate that Russians do not view income tax as a basis for contractual and reciprocal obligations between the State and its citizens. For them, it is a forced obligation and there is no reasonable justification for respecting it.

Table 3.4 Opinion about necessity to pay taxes

What do you think about the need to pay taxes in this country?	[98]	[99]
Taxes need paying	62	50
If there are opportunities for evading taxes, they should be seized	33	24
No answer	5	26[6]

---

[5] *Ekonomika perehodnogo perioda*, Moskva : Institut Ekonomiki Perehodnogo Perioda, 1998, p. 347.
[6] In 1999 the responses to the two questions considered had an optional character.

Table 3.5 Opinion about a moral right to evade taxes

Do you believe the citizen has a moral right to evade taxes?	[98]	[99]
Yes	55	32
No	40	40
No answer	5	28

The contractual relations between the State and the taxpayers imply a positive dependency: the citizens pay for services that the State agrees to provide. This purely market model can only function if the taxpayers trust the State. The taxpayers must believe that the State does not opportunistically waste the resources they entrust to it. This is precisely the question posed by our interviewees: more than half of them are convinced that as long as the State does not have to account to the taxpayers for its expenses they will continue to evade income tax (see Table 3.6). In other words, the post-Soviet lack of trust in the State transforms income tax into a tribute and authorizes them to use any means possible to minimize it.

Table 3.6 Conditions for considering taxes as a duty

What should be changed in the government to make citizens consider taxes as their duty?	[98]	[99]
Fiscal system which actually incites the people to evade taxes	57%	52.4%
Government must render an account to citizens of its expenditures	47	51.1
Governmental policy has to be more consistent and predictable	33	44.3
Taxes should encourage the productive activities	36	43.5
Government should educate the respect of Law	33	37.9
Investment climate: it should be more favorable	27	29.5
Control over business has to be more severe	17	16.4

It should be noted that the serious economic crisis of August 1998 had shaken up the economy when these two investigations were conducted. Therefore, this event influenced the dynamics of our short-term indicators. The post-Soviet lack of trust in the State, which was already intense prior to the crisis, became extreme at that time. Only 9 per cent of those interviewed thought in 1998 that the State could be trusted. This decreased to 3.4 per cent in 1999 (Table 3.7, 'Do you trust the State?').

Although trust in the prison administration is rather insignificant (19.9 per cent), it still surpasses the level of trust in the State![7]

> 'All previous efforts to reform within the Soviet Union were viewed as a "big lie" by the citizens of the former Soviet Union... The only way out of this policy impasse is to establish a binding and credible commitment to economic reform' (Boettke, 1995, p. 25).

Unfortunately, the current situation has convinced us that the post-Soviets continue to see the State's actions as a big lie. The State remains ignorant of the interests of its citizens and depends on them solely for its fiscal needs.

Table 3.7 Trust in the State

Do you trust the State?	*Ordinary citizens*		*Businessmen*	*Prisoners*		
	Russia, [98]	Russia, [99]	Russia, [01*]	Russia, 2000–01	Kazakhstan, 2001	Canada, 2001
N	850	1390	219	769	396	120
Yes	9	3.4	8.2	9.9	15.9	15.8
No	89	94.1	89.5	82.4	77.3	74.2
No answer	2	2.5	2.3	7.7	6.8	10

Second, with respect to the negative dependency of post-Soviets on the State, they must deal with the following dilemma. On the one hand, they need legal means to ensure that their interests are respected. On the other hand, their lack of trust in the State eliminates their hope of finding legal support for the organization of everyday life. Let us look at the hierarchy of the priorities of the ordinary Russian family (Table 3.8). The expectation of legal protection ranks second–third place in the list of priorities meaning that our interviewees *want* to count on the State in their everyday lives.

---

[7] Associations with the word 'State' are significant:

	Businessmen	*Prisoners*		
	Russia [01*], N=219	Russia, N=508	Kazakhstan, N=396	Canada, N=120
Corruption	65.8%	58.4	59.1	47.6
Prison	19.2	55.1	48.8	28.2
Mafia	37	46	48.5	23.3
Violence	26.5	39.3	34.4	11.6
Stable rules of the game	25.1	26.9	23	16.5
Human rights	35.6	25.9	29.3	45.6
Justice	35.6	19.3	22	51.5
Security	25.6	17.6	22	36.9

Table 3.8 Hierarchy of the most important rights

What is actually the most important for your family?	[98]	[99][8]
A correct living standard	92	93%
Personal security	34	71.4
Legal protection	57	68
Right to work	37	66
Protection of private property	36	65
Protection of private life	35	61
Right to choose freely the job	34	54
Right to education	48	52
Right to social security	38	51
Right to choose freely the residency	×	30

With respect to *actual* support, Russians are skeptical concerning the State's ability to give them support (see Table 3.9 of the answers to the 'Do you think your family can count on legal protection?'):

Table 3.9 State's ability to protect human rights

Type of relations	Yes, %		No, %		No answer, %	
	[98]	[99]	[98]	[99]	[98]	[99]
Inside the family	54	37	40	53	6	10
In relations with other people	40	28.4	56	63.9	4	7.7
In relations with the government	22	10.1	73	84.4	4	5.5

Russians feel they enjoy the least legal protection in their relations with the State! This does not appear paradoxical if one considers the negative character of the compromise between the citizens and the State, the Devil's pact on which Soviet society was based. The State allowed ordinary people to manage on their own, which excludes any assistance on its part, but does not prevent conflicts of interest, as in the case of fiscal matters. In the case of a conflict between an individual (or even a private organization) and the State, the former loses. The post-Soviets' lack of trust in State justice is so strong that they do not see any reason for financing the legal justice system, despite their obvious need for legal protection (see the answers to the question 'What would your priorities be if you were responsible for preparing the State budget?').

---

[8] In 1999, the interviewees had three options: 'Very important', 'Relatively important' and 'Not important'. We have reproduced the frequency of the first alternative.

Table 3.10 Priorities in government's expenditures

Items in the State budget	Rank of priorities [98], %		
	First	Second	Third
Social security (medical care)	77	15	4
Public security	71	21	3
Public education	65	23	8
Industrial policy	61	26	9
Social protection (welfare, pensions, etc.)	57	32	7
Agrarian policy	54	29	12
Science, culture	43	39	12
National defense	28	41	26
Justice	12	33	48
Government's employees	5	13	76

The lack of legal justice results in a high level of latent criminality. The violence generated in everyday life is controlled by means other than institutionalization (we will return to this problem in the section entitled 'Constructing the enemy: then and now'). According to a survey of 2,068 individuals in six regions in the former USSR, conducted at the start of the 1990s, latent criminality was estimated at 70 per cent. Forty percent of the victims of crimes covered by the Penal Code decided not to inform the police, 39 per cent of them because they did not believe in the ability of the public forces to protect their rights and 45 per cent because they defend their interests on their own, with no recourse to State justice (Gorjainov, 1993, pp. 24–25). Another study conducted at the end of 1998 of a representative sample confirms that post-Soviets do not take the legal procedure for defending their rights seriously, particularly in their relations with the State. Only 4.5 per cent of Russians had submitted a dispute to the court in the past 12 months in order to defend their rights in their relations with the State while 6.8 per cent had filed a complaint against State representatives for an abuse of power and 1.7 per cent and 2.8 per cent of Russians, respectively had taken such steps on several occasions during the past 12 months (Mansurov, 1999, p. 18). Therefore, the post-Soviets do not view themselves as true subjects of the Law. 'In order to file a complaint, one must first consider himself an individual, a subject of the Law' (Timofeev, 1993, p. 55). Yet, how can one ensure that his individuality is respected without the support of the rights and obligations defended by the Law?

A mistrustful society

The task of protecting interests is complicated by the lack of trust specific to Soviet society. Bureaucratic coordination, the basis of the Soviet model, extends the Principal-Agent model to all levels of the social organization. Starting at primary school, young Soviets learn to submit to their superiors. At school, next to the teacher hierarchy, there is an internal hierarchy among students, materialized by the young sons of October (*oktjabrjata*), the pioneers (*pionery*), and the young communists (*komsomol*, *VLKSM – Vsesojuznyj Leninskij Kommunisticheskij Sojuz Molodeji*). Each group of five to ten students has its own leader, who serves as the Principal in the organization of public activities. Next, there is the school 'capo', the neighborhood 'capo', etc.

We have already mentioned the profound duality of the norms that govern relations between the Principal and the Agent. One of the divisions concerns the duality of the trust/mistrust norm. On the one hand, the Agent must trust the Principal because the Agent appoints the Principal to organize and control part of his everyday activities. If it is not a case of authority imposed by pure constraint, the Agent believes that, in conditions of risk and uncertainty, it would be better to submit to the decisions of the Principal (Kreps, 1990, pp. 113, 119). The Agent controls risk and uncertainty in such a way that he refuses the right to determine his own actions, delegating this right to the Principal in exchange for an indemnity which will be paid, no matter what happens. On the other hand, as a result of the asymmetry of information and the eventuality that the Agent will behave in an opportunistic manner, the Principal never trusts the Agent. The Principal's main task is to control the Agent's actions as closely as possible. 'No superior has full confidence in his subordinates' (Kornaï, 1992, p. 98).

Figure 3.2 Vertical versus horizontal coordination

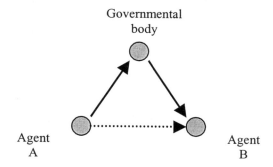

Bureaucratic coordination renders impersonal trust, namely the trust Agents have in one another in horizontal relations, superfluous. Since all horizontal contacts in a totalitarian system are established through vertical relations, trusting in one's direct superior is sufficient (Figure 3.2). Moreover, the officially recognized solution to the Principal–Agent problem, namely competition among Agents (*socialisticheskoe sorevnovanie*, 'socialist competition'), creates a climate of mistrust affecting their interactions. The special reward for Agents who worked more zealously than others to complete the tasks assigned by the Principal implies rivalry in the Agents' interests (Rosen, 1998, pp. 82–85; Schlicht, 1988). Rivalry destroys the basis of cooperation: Soviets view their compatriots as competitors rather than potential partners. Certain characteristics of the social promotion system constitute the other factor in the destruction of impersonal trust. Bureaucratic coordination allows only one form of social promotion: the consecutive movement from one level of hierarchy (*komsomol*, State, Party) to the next one up. The number of places in the levels of power is always limited. It should be noted that the contradiction between bureaucratic promotion and the climate of trust finds a solution in the Japanese firm (Aoki, 1990, pp. 10–13). First, the promotion does not depend on the relative performances of the Agents but on the duration of professional experience. Then, the firm focuses its activities on expanding the market share, even to the detriment of maximizing profits. This helps to ensure the increase in the number of levels in the internal hierarchy and exclude a conflict in interests.

A grotesque comment by a Soviet satirist, Dmitrij Knyshev, clearly illustrates the spirit of rivalry and its place in everyday life: 'Ivan felt very bad. But as soon as he learned that Petr was suffering more, his mood improved.' One of our interviewees expressed this hatred for others more brutally. 'I studied during the Soviet period. We learned to hate others from the first grades at school. If you're taught to hate your mother and father from your first years in school, what about the others? The first thing you learn in the residential school is hatred. You're taught to hate; you're told that your mother is nothing, your father is nothing, they've abandoned you... We, the State, we're good'.[9] Several surveys confirm the existence of a causal link between the Soviet model and the climate of mistrust. The level of impersonal trust, namely the percentage of post-Soviets who agree with the statement 'We can trust people' is lower than in any Western country (see Table 3.11[10]). As a comparison, the level of impersonal trust is 94 per cent in Denmark, 90 per cent in Germany, 88 per cent in Great Britain, 84 per cent in France, 72 per cent in northern Italy and 65 per cent in Southern Italy (Inglehart, 1995, p. 35).

Table 3.11 Impersonal trust

Year	*Level of confidence in the people around, %*
1989	54
1991	36
1992	33
1995	31.5
1998	32.1

The high level of lack of impersonal trust contrasts strongly with the need for trust experienced by post-Soviets. In 1998 and 1999 we asked a series of questions concerning the role of trust in the organization of everyday life. Specifically, we

---

[9] Interview No. 25.
[10] Sources: Levada Yu., *Op. cit.*, p.112 – for 1989 and 1991 ; Rose R., Mishler W., 'Mass Reaction to Regime Change in Eastern Europe: Polarization or Leaders and Laggards?' // *British Journal of Political Science*, 1994, Vol. 24, p.208 – for 1992 ; our investigations of 1996, 1998 and 1999.

compared the frequency of the responses (the list of their variations was identical) to the six following questions:[11]

(a) What is most important for your family?
(b) What is important for the well-being of the family in Russia today?
(c) What is the basis for Russian society today?
(d) What is the basis for an ideal society in Russia?
(e) What do you consider when making an important decision?
(f) What can you use to resolve an important problem?

The hierarchy of the responses is provided in the following table [99]:

Table 3.12 Normative basis of everyday life

Alternatives	(a)	(b)	(c)	(d)	(e)	(f)
Trust	1	4	8	4	4	11
Family	2	1	3	3	1	9
Work	3	3	5	2	5	1
Property	4	2	2	8	2	5
Empathy	5	7	10	7	8	6
Moral	6	8	11	5	7	10
Freedom	7	6	4	6	9	4
Law	8	9	6	1	6	3
Equality	9	10	9	9	11	7
Tradition	10	11	7	10	10	8
Profit	11	5	1	11	3	2

Questions (a) and (d) enabled us to judge the hierarchy of the terminal *values* on which everyday life is based; Questions (b), (c) and (e) – on the relative importance of the *conditions*, Question (f) – on the relative importance of the *resources* available for attaining various goals. As a result, Russians view trust as a value and a condition, and refuse to see it as a resource. In the hierarchy of values, trust shares the first three places with family and work, whereas in the hierarchy of resources, it ranks last! People greatly appreciate trust and need it but do not rely on it in everyday life.

The answers to two other questions reinforce our hypothesis concerning a profoundly contradictory sentiment related to the trust norm:

---

[11] The methodology is presented in greater detail in Oleinik A., 'Changes in the Organization of Everyday Life in the Wake of Financial Crisis', in Segbers K. (ed.). *Explaining Post-Soviet Patchworks*, Aldershot: Ashgate, vol. 2, 2001.

Table 3.13 Priorities in relationships with other people

What do you consider important in relationships with other people? [98]	%
Trust	77
Respect of other people	67
Moral principles	35
Love	33
My own interest	20
Utility	17
Mood	9

Table 3.14 Factors influencing relationships with other people

What influences your relationships with other people? [99]	Yes, %	No, %	No answer, %
Trust	85	8.3	6.8
Love	71.5	14	14.5
Moral obligations	71.5	15	13.5
My own interest	55.4	26.4	18.2
Utility	48.1	32.8	19.1
Habit	46.1	38	15.9
Tradition	43.9	41.7	14.4
Law	22.4	62	15.6
Constraint	14.3	69.2	16.5

In other words, post-Soviets want to trust others but cannot, wanting and fearing to do so at the same time. Is there a solution to this contradiction within the Soviet model? There is a solution and it is not greatly different from the solution inmates have found for the problem of trust: relationships must be personalized. 'The communist system left a dual heritage: people trust the members of their close network and are extremely distrustful with respect to formal State institutions' (Rose, Mishler, Haerpfer, 1997, p. 10). Therefore, the ideal for relationships based on trust, so greatly desired by post-Soviets, is materialized within the network of those close to them. The center of this small social universe lies in the family, the terminal value of post-Soviet society. The responses to our questions prove that trust serves as a basis for the family:

Table 3.15 Constitution of family (1)

Between parents and children, %	What governs the relations in your family...? [98]	Between adults, % (rank)
57.7	Love	50.7 (#4)
54.4	Trust	56.7 (#2)
48.8	Control exerted by the mother (wife)	10.8 (#9)
47.1	Mutual aid	55.1 (#3)
42.5	Mutual comprehension	66.8 (#1)
38.3	Control exerted by the father (husband)	3.8 (#13)
28.2	Discipline	10.7 (#10)
26.6	Moral principles	32.6 (#6)
25.5	Family traditions	35.2 (#5)
11.3	Habit	23.6 (#7)
11.3	Utility	14.6 (#9)
9.3	External pressures	21.7 (#8)
8.4	Tradition	8 (#11)
7.9	Constraint	4.6 (#12)
2.4	Law	2.1 (#14)
2.3	Religious norms	2.1 (#15)

Table 3.16 Constitution of family (2)

What governs the relations in your family? [99]	Yes, %	No, %	No answer
Trust	86	6.7	7.3
Love	77.5	10.6	11.9
Moral principles	70.7	18.6	10.7
Utility	49.3	31.7	19
External pressures	47.3	37.4	15.3
Habit	45.3	39.9	14.8
Private interest	40.6	41.6	17.8
Tradition	37.3	46.5	16.2
Control exerted by the wife	13.7	58.6	27.7
Control exerted by the husband	13.7	60.3	26
Constraint	13.7	70.1	16.2
Law	13.7	71.9	15.5

The family as the core of trust is found outside a protective belt, the network of friends and acquaintances (*znakomye*). It should be noted that there is an internal hierarchy within the network: friends are close to the family whereas mere acquaintances remain at the edge of its local universe.

'Because friendship is based on trust, Soviets prefer to have friends they have known for a very long time: childhood friends or at least friends from school or university' (Shlapentokh, 1998, p. 177).

Figure 3.3 Family's universe

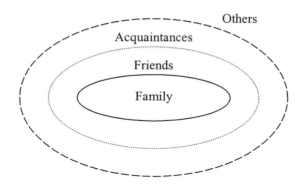

Generally, work colleagues are relegated to orbits distant from the family and are, at best, transformed into acquaintances.

The system with several orbits reproduces the distrust in the 'cosmic space', namely in the environment outside the family (Figure 3.3). As trust is increasingly focussed within the 'solar system', there are fewer reasons to trust others, people outside the system.

> 'People who have few friends are usually ready to trust and develop new contacts faster than people who have many alternate friends' (Coleman, 1990, p. 105).

The family universe, this 'small' society, tends to be self-sufficient. The lack of impersonal trust is reproduced in the Soviet system, namely from the top as well as the bottom. Therefore, Soviets can provide a completely new interpretation to the currency of the Sun King: 'Society is our family.'

Role of the family and personalized relationships

The durability and internal stability of the family universe does not prevent it from expanding into the surrounding social space. The family develops, *appropriates* the hostile environment, transforming part of it into the family universe. Why does it need to expand rather than close in on itself? It must be admitted that the post-Soviet family does not correspond to the ideal of the traditional family, which is static and subject to centripetal force. Neither the structure of the family nor the motivation for its daily activities is purely traditional in character. To start verifying our initial hypothesis that the post-Soviet family is based on a compromise between the domestic world and the world by projects, let us look at it from the perspective of traditional family relations.

We have already noted the minor influence that tradition has over daily family life: it ranks second among the factors that govern family relations. Although the answers to our questions indicate only known and declared norms, which provide no indication as to their actual application, they are nevertheless significant. The image of the ideal family developed from our interviews includes more elements from the modern family than from the traditional family. According to post-Soviets, decisions should be based on a joint procedure. They do not accept the traditional distribution of household chores either, namely with the woman taking care of the household and the husband assuring the material well-being of the family. Almost two-thirds of those interviewed say that responsibilities should be shared equally by spouses. Moreover, the same two-thirds support the freedom of spouses to choose their friends and acquaintances. According to them, the fact that the social networks of the husband and the wife do not overlap does not hamper family relations, but supports them (see the following series of tables).

Table 3.17 Decision-making in the family

How are decisions in the everyday life of your family made?	[98], %	[99], %
Every important decision is made jointly	60	76.4
There are situations when the spouse makes the decision unilaterally	22	×
At home, there is the boss who makes important decisions	12	20.3

Table 3.18 Managing the family's budget

Who is responsible for managing the family's budget?	[98], %
Usually, the decisions are made jointly	62
Usually, the wife	21
Each spouse makes his or her own decision	10
Usually, the husband	5

Table 3.19 Sharing the domestic duties

Which one of the following statements is closer to your opinion?	[99], %
Today the wife and the husband should share the domestic duties equally: care of children, housekeeping, etc.	58.1
The husband has to take care of material comfort, the wife – housekeeping and children	40.6
No answer	1.3

Table 3.20 Opinion about networks outside the family

If each spouse has his or her own network of friends and acquaintances...	[98], %	[99], %
It's good for the family	28	71
It's rather good for the family	43	
It's rather bad for the family		26.9
It's bad for the family	27	
No answer	2	2.1

As for the motivation for the daily activities of the post-Soviet family, the term 'utilitarian' provides a more accurate description than 'traditional'. Let us return to the taxonomy of the characteristic values/conditions/resources (the four variations most frequently retained for each of the three):

Table 3.21 Normative basis of the family

	Terminal values (d)	*Conditions (e)*	*Resources/means (f)*
Trust	4	4	11
Family	3	1	9
Work	2	5	1
Property	8	2	5
Empathy	7	8	6
Moral	5	7	10
Freedom	6	9	4
Law	1	6	3
Equality	9	11	7
Tradition	10	10	8
Profit	11	3	2

The post-Soviets do not consider tradition a value, a condition for their activities or a resource. As a negative value (ranking last in the hierarchy of the responses to questions about values), profit, the cement of utilitarianism, plays an essential role as a resource (ranking second) and a condition (ranking third on average). Moreover, it is a particular form of utilitarianism, simple utilitarianism. Alexander Ahiezer differentiates two types of utilitarianism: simple and complex (Ahiezer, 1991, p. 124).[12] Both imply that the alpha and omega of everyday life lie in the ostentatious search for utility, profit, but in a completely different manner. Complex utilitarianism is mentioned only when there is a link in the individual's mind between maximizing utility and his own productive activity. Simple utilitarianism, therefore, is reduced to the search for profit (not necessarily its maximization) by any means, except productive activity. The revolution of rising expectations provides an illustration of the second type of utilitarianism (Oberschall, 1993, pp. 125–129). It occurs when people who are used to a low standard of living learn about the existence of a remarkably higher standard of living, through the media, for example. The separation between the new motivation and resources, including social, cultural and organizational resources, produces a sense of profound frustration, which lies at the heart of the revolution of rising expectations.

The Soviet model only generates simple utilitarianism as part of the compromise between the authority and ordinary people. The authority agrees that Soviets work less for ideological reasons than for purely material reasons. Therefore, neither the bureaucratic promotion system nor the economy of shortages encourages people to view productive work as a source of material well-being. A

---

[12] See also Oleinik A., *Institucional'naja ekonomika*, chapter 4, reading 7.

contradiction appears between a 'growing interest in money' and the fact that 'a majority of the Soviet people do not want to work hard for additional income' (Shlapentokh, 1995, p. 65). How can the desire to work hard be justified if one's access to rare resources depends solely on his position in the social hierarchy? In order to have access to resources, one must either be part of the *nomenclatura*, the Party-State elite, or in a good position in the illicit hierarchy of Soviet society. This illicit hierarchy is based on access to rare resources, *deficit*, and includes workers in the tertiary sector, particularly those in the commercial or transportation sectors (*vezuny*), employees whose duties require them to travel abroad, etc. Moreover, the search for additional revenue is limited by the officially and socially accepted ceiling for well-being: an apartment, a car, a vacation home (*kvartira – mashina – dacha*). Everything in excess of this sacred trio attracts the interest of the police. Admiration for the Western way of life, particularly obvious during the 1960s–1970s, accentuated the internal separation of simple utilitarianism. 'Average Soviet citizens are extremely absorbed with the West and its mode of life, which they try to imitate in many respects' (Shlapentokh, 1995, p. 141) without also imitating the Western attitude towards work.

Let us summarize these arguments in the following statement. The specific form of utilitarianism, simple utilitarianism, creates conditions favorable to the expansion of family structures. Therefore, there are two factors that encourage the addition of new 'satellites' to the family orbit: family members (through the institution of the marriage of interests, *brak po raschetu*[13]), friends and acquaintances. On the one hand, the family tries to expand the space for trust relationships by personalizing its social, economic and political contacts (cf. the phenomenon of the presidential 'family'). On the other hand, the institutional context transforms personalized relations into the principal means for access to rare resources: you need to have your 'own' responsible for controlling the distribution of rare resources. According to János Kornaï, there are three means for distributing rare resources: the auction (market), the queue and assignation (the last two are specific to the bureaucratic system) (Kornaï, 1990, pp. 440–455). Given the lack of other transparent and predefined criteria–all petitioners are equal *de jure*–the assignation procedure objectively tends to promote the personalization of the relations between the distributor and the petitioner. 'The bureaucratic system in fact became personalized' (Ledeneva, 1998, p. 83). And although the consumption 'ceiling' is no longer valid in Russia today, privileged access to rare resources still depends on good relations with the State civil servants, particularly as part of what Jacques Sapir calls 'predatory annuitant system'(Sapir, 1996, p. 322), based on the exploitation of natural resources and/or the search for a bureaucratic rent. For example, the extraction of natural fuels (oil, gas), the single sure source of cash revenue, is controlled completely by the State.

---

[13] 'The marriage of interest is regaining popularity. Qualification, a job, epaulettes become more and more important since they make shoes, a fur coat, an apartment, a washroom, and that marvelous thing, a car, accessible. The struggle for a room in Moscow causes a significant number of couples to be formed and then break up' (Trotsky, 1988, p. 183).

Vladimir Shlapentokh described the tendency to personalize socioeconomic relations as a 'privatization' of the public space.

> 'This process, which increases the role of various activities based on the family as well as of small business and the natural non-monetary forms of exchange is somewhat opposed to the process assumed by the advocates of modernization theory, which presupposes a weakening of the family and the personal relationships due to technological progress' (Shlapentokh, 1995, p. 14).

Privatization occurs when *useful* people who have access to specific rare resources are transformed into *yours*: acquaintances, 'friends of friends', actual friends, even lovers or family members. In post-Soviet society, 'who is who' is transformed into 'who knows who'. An individual is characterized by his acquaintances rather than his profession, qualifications, diplomas, etc. Paradoxically,

> 'friendship plays a central role in the lives of people in non-democratic countries... The importance of friends is directly proportional to the unavailability of goods or services, and is inversely proportional to the importance of money in obtaining hard-to-find items' (Shlapentokh, 1995, pp. 173–174).[14]

In other words, the norm of simple utilitarianism and bureaucratic regulation remain the only factors that integrate the 'solar systems' of post-Soviet families. The 'large' society exists only to the extent that the 'small' family societies draw closer and form coalitions that help them obtain access to rare resources. Therefore, it is a purely negative integration.

The privatization of post-Soviet society takes two forms. On a micro-social level, *blat* relations are referred to as 'the use of personal networks and informal contacts to obtain goods and services in short supply and to find a way around formal procedures' (Ledeneva, 1998, p. 1). On a macro social level, the personal relations between the economic and political authorities replace licit and formal contacts. Moreover, ordinary people always have a personalized perception of the socialist and communist ideology. What counts for ordinary Russians is not political and economic discourse as such. The personality of the individual speaking counts for more than what he says. As demonstrated by historical studies, the perception of Soviet policy of the 1920s–1950s, was completely determined by the perception of the politicians of the time: Lenin, Trotsky, Stalin, and *tutti quanti* of the Soviet political elite (Lebina, 1999, pp. 152–156). Also the strong support given to the current president of the Russian Federation, Vladimir Putin, who has not even formulated his socioeconomic program (we will return to this matter in the '*Conclusion*') fits in with the logic of the personalization of politics.

As for *blat* relations, it is difficult to find a Soviet household that has never used its relationships to acquire a rare resource. Moreover, this phenomenon has no

---

[14] Cf. 'A particular role must be attributed to relations of friendship in maintaining the internal coherence of the clique and in expanding the sphere of influence' (Arlacchi, 1986, p. 65).

cultural connotations: surveys conducted at the end of the 1980s and the start of the 1990s indicate that *blat* existed in all socialist countries:[15]

Table 3.22 Households' portfolios

Households' portfolio of six economies	% of families involved in, [1991]				
	Poland	Czecho-slovakia	Bulgaria	Russia	Russia [93]
1. Official economy	81	89	79	70	81
2. Household production	81	69	79	54	81
3. Help friends and relatives	31	47	48	54	64
4. Second economy	33	34	14	19	27
5. Connections (blat, bribes)	35	57	40	49	35
6. Foreign currency	17	29	18	3	2

Blat provides a perfect example of the merging of the domestic world and the world by projects within the post-Soviet family. It is impossible to develop a univocal interpretation of *blat* relations. The rhetoric of friendship relationships is confused here with the purely utilitarian justification. Those who are involved directly in *blat* relationships try to interpret them using markers from the domestic world, whereas those who impartially observe *blat* give it a utilitarian interpretation. *Misrecognition*, namely 'a contradiction between what one sees in other people as an observer and in oneself as a participant' (Ledeneva, 1998, p. 60), is a result of the impossibility of finding a compromise between the various manners for justifying actions. In the terms of theory of conventions, it is relativisation: the actor and the interpreter do not agree on the univocal justification for an act. Let us apply the theoretical approach developed by Laurent Thévenot (Thévenot, 1995, p. 15) to the study of *blat* (the interpretations of an impartial observer are represented in the cells in the matrix):

Table 3.23 Justifying *blat*

		Actor	
		World of projects	Domestic world
Interpreter	World of projects	Barter, exchange of services	*Blat*
	Domestic world	*Blat*	Friendship, gift

The difficulty of proposing a definition of *blat* acceptable to the post-Soviets who are engaged in it is inherent in any study of the separation between 'yours', who are organized in a *blat* network, and the others, the strangers. Either direct questions are misinterpreted or the interviewees refuse to reveal their true position as a result of possible criticism on the part of the interpreters. We already noted the

---

[15] Sources: Rose R. 'Between State and Market...', p. 28 ; Boeva I., Shironin V., 'Russians between State and market. The Generations Compared' // *Studies in Public Policy*, n°205, 1992, p. 8–18 ; Rose R., 'Getting by without Government: Everyday Life in a Stressful Society' // *Studies in Public Policy*, n°227, 1994, p. 10.

impact this problem has on the inmates' survey: 36.2 per cent of the interviewees (40.9 per cent in Kazakhstan; first place in the hierarchy of variants) refused to differentiate their people from the others while a large number of them (8.2 per cent in Russia, 9.8 per cent in Kazakhstan) prefer to use their knowledge to react to uncivil behavior on the part of fellow inmates. The Russians were also very reticent to choose variants containing the word 'yours'. For example, only 10 per cent of the interviewees (eighth place) chose the variant 'Norms accepted for yours' when answering the question 'What rules would you never violate?' [98]. The frequency of the variant 'Moral norms' (57 per cent, first place) is probably a result of the desire of the interviewees to create a good impression.

Therefore, only indirect questions remain. The VCIOM team referred to the answers to the question 'What days do you consider holidays?' as evidence of the priority given to everything that is considered family-oriented, domestic. Domestic holidays are considered more important that officials ones: New Year's Day – 75 per cent, personal birthday – 46 per cent, anniversary of a close relative – 43 per cent, March 8 (international women's day, an official holiday in the USSR) – 35 per cent, and so on (Levada, 1993, p. 57). The question concerning the social groups with which the Russians associate also serves to identify the structure of social relations. It focusses on the hierarchical character of social relations and their focus on the family (it should be noted that the third variant implies personal knowledge) (Mansurov, 1999, pp. 17–18):

Table 3.24 Different degrees of social closeness

Do you feel being close with…?	Often	Some-times	Never	Don't know
My family	89.2%	8.9%	0.7%	1.2%
My friends	83.9	13.4	0.9	1.7
Those who have my vision of the world	75.6	17.9	1.7	4.8
The people of my generation	71.8	23.5	1.5	3.2
The people with the same living standard	64.1	26.9	2.1	6.9
My workmates (my classmates)	59.2	27.2	5	8.6
The people of my profession	58.1	29.2	4.9	7.8
Those who live in my city, village	57.2	32.5	3.6	6.8
With those of my nationality	56.5	32.6	3.3	7.6
Russians	44.7	32.8	6.1	16.5
With those who live in poverty	41.6	36.3	9.6	12.5
With those who respect local traditions	40.5	37.3	6.9	15.3
With self-made men	37.1	37	11.1	14.9
With supporters of the same political party	34.8	34.6	12.8	17.9
With those who respect Russian traditions	32	41.3	7.8	18.9
With those who are not interested in politics	30.3	42.8	12.2	14.7

The organization of the upper economic and political layers in post-Soviet society generally reproduces the logic of the privatization of the external environment. Impersonal planning *de jure* transformed *de facto* into a network of personal relations between the managers of State companies and the civil servants of the departments responsible for planning. As in the case of ordinary Soviets, Soviet bosses had no criminal intent. Instead, the personalization of relations enables planners to determine the actual potential of companies more accurately, whereas the companies hope to attain the objectives of the plan. Privatization of the plan, which certain people refer to as 'plan bargaining', is based on the 'operation of personalized mechanisms without the administrative procedures for making decisions concerning the plan' (Shohin, 1989, p. 74).[16]

Moreover, managers tended to personalize their horizontal relations since this made it easier to find a component that was currently lacking yet needed to implement the plan. The currency of *blat, Ty – mne, ja – tebe* (*I scratch your back, you scratch mine*), governs relations between the Soviet managers and encourages them to develop their own network of acquaintances. 'The supplier and the purchaser trade roles from time to time: today I help you with steel, tomorrow you help me with bolts' (Kornaï, 1990, p. 102). In the same manner that the family and its network of acquaintances serve as a basic unit for analysis in studies of daily Soviet life, the company network performs the same function in studies of the Soviet economic model. 'Socialism created networks of reciprocal social relations and associative contacts within the industrial structure' (Stark, 1992, p. 84).

Unlike other vestiges of socialism, the principal of the personalization of economic relations continues to determine the post-Soviet economic space. The high probability of opportunistic behavior of the partners on the Russian market enhances the value of trust relationships established during the Soviet period. In terms of the economics of institutions, the respect for commitments made to 'yours' reduces the probability of opportunistic behavior on the part of the partner and the cost of transactions.

> 'By maintaining the former contacts, the company must continue to respect the ethical norms developed by the traditional bosses' (Dolgopjatova, 1994, p. 44).

According to a survey made by the authors of the article in 1993–1994, 83 per cent of Russian businessmen maintain relations with suppliers that were established in the Soviet period, and 70 per cent do the same with purchasers. They are very skeptical about the need to establish new contacts with suppliers and purchasers. 'In the *krug* (circle) the personal reputation of a manager guarantees the economic survival of the company' (Kharkhordine, 1994, p. 30),[17] whereas distrust reigns outside the network and there is no guarantee that a contract will be executed.

---

[16] The concept of 'plan bargaining' was first introduced in Kornaï, J. *Deficit*, pp. 79–80.

[17] The *krug* is the institution based on the principle *ty-mne, ja-tebe* that existed in the traditional peasant community in Russia until the start of the 20th century.

Does the public/private border exist?

The tendency to expand family structures and the sphere controlled by the totalitarian State threatens the separation of the private and public spheres, the first from below and the second from above. Borrowing a term used by Michael Walzer, both are also dangerous for the 'art of separating' daily spheres of activity (Walzer, 1992, p. 109). Although, as part of the negative compromise, the State makes no direct attack on the private sphere, as in the case of Peter the Great or Stalin,[18] its absence makes the protection of the private sphere problematic. The failure of legal means for protecting private space is particularly obvious in everyday life. The evaluation of our interviewees with respect to the State's actual protection of their private sphere contrasts sharply with the importance they assign that duty. On the one hand, they rank the inviolability of personal life, private property and private space among the six most important factors for their family (see Table 3.8 providing the answers to the question 'What is most important for your family today?' in the section entitled '*Role of the Soviet State*'). On the other hand, the right to protection of the private sphere is one of the rights the least protected by the State (see Table 3.25 below, providing the answers to the question 'Which rights does the State protect the least in the everyday life of your family?'[98]).

Table 3.25 The least protected human rights

Right to social security	45%
Right to personal inviolability	38
Right to equal protection by the Law	38
Right to freely choose the job	37
Right to work	34
Right to inviolability of private property	28
Right to education	27
Right to protection of private life	14
Right to freely choose the religion	4

The lack of legal support for the protection of the private space occasionally takes on very material forms. A foreign visitor to an ordinary building in Moscow today would probably be surprised by the abundance of armored doors. According to our calculations, 80 per cent–100 per cent of the apartments in each building are equipped with such doors. In fact, when a family moves to a new apartment, they usually start by installing armored doors, if that has not already been done. Moreover, the post-Soviet concept of lodging has always been closely connected with the problem of protecting private space. During the Soviet period, most

---

[18] For example, certain historians consider the reforms of Peter the Great as an effort at improvement through the intervention of the state in the private sphere (Ahiezer, 1991, p. 138).

apartments belonged to the State or to State companies (*vedomstvennoe jil'e*): the lessees signed a type of lease with the State representatives. Unlike the English leasehold system, Soviets could never buy their lodging, regardless of the term of the lease.[19] Even after the massive privatization of apartments in the 1990s, one-third of Russians continued to live in State apartments, according to the results of our 1998 study.

State assumption of control over the construction, assignment and maintenance of apartments had serious consequences on the differentiation of the private/public spheres. First, the permanent shortage of apartments incited Soviets to use their personal contacts to obtain apartments. Despite numerous promises made by Soviet authorities to provide each family with a separate apartment, including the last one made at the 27th Congress of the Communist Party in 1987 ('A separate apartment for each family in 2000'), post-Soviet apartments remain overcrowded. Our 1998 investigation indicated the following distribution of households, along with the number of family members and the type of apartment (one room, 2P, 3P, 4P, 5P; see Table 3.26). The average household size is 3.3 individuals whereas the average apartment has 2 1/2 rooms. There is a certain art to configuring the family so as to increase the chance of improving housing conditions: including grandparents who have certain privileges, including/excluding brothers and sisters, 'optimizing' the number of children, establishing good relationships with the civil servants responsible for managing apartments, etc. In this way, the public management of the housing sector is *de facto* personalized and 'privatized'.

Table 3.26 Size of the household compared with size of the flat

[98]	1	2	3	4	5	6
Size of the household (number of persons)	0.4%	12.7%	34%	37.6%	9%	2.9%
Size of the flat (number of rooms)	12%	34%	44%	9%	1%	0%

Furthermore, the most common types of Soviet apartments, the barracks (*barak, kazarma*), the workers' and student's residences (*obschejitie, obschaga*), the communal apartment (*kommunalka*), and the standard apartment equivalent to low-cost housing (*hruschevka*), are extremely poorly suited for protecting private space. Their internal organization provides for very little room for private space. Let us take a closer look.

Almost every industrial Russian city, including Moscow today, has kept a few examples of the buildings known as barracks. They come from the 'golden years' of the workers' barracks, namely the end of the 19th and start of the 20th centuries (up to the 1920s–1930s). Before the 1917 Revolution, more than 60 per cent of the workers were required to live in barracks. The typical worker's barrack is

---

[19] The lease reform of 1967 enabled lessees to purchase the apartment leased or to renew the lease for a period up to 50 years (Krasheninnikova, Jidkova, 1999, pp. 554–555).

organized in the same manner as the prison barrack: large dormitories, the lack of partitions, common washrooms and kitchen, etc. Natalia Lebina, a historian specializing in the everyday life of the 1920s–1930s, stresses the fact that 'private possessions [in the barracks] were very primitive, the lifestyle was bereft of all elements of intimacy' (Lebina, 1999, p. 160).

At the time of the 1917 Revolution, the residence, the apartment shared by several people, were viewed as the model for the socialist dwelling. The idea of a common everyday life corresponded to socialist and communist principles. Even the new elite of the Soviet State, the State and party civil servants, preferred to live in residences until the end of the 1920s. The intellectual elite had its own residences–residences for writers and residences for artists. For example, in 1918, Nikolaj Gumilev lived in the Mojka residence for artists (St. Petersburg), Mikhail Bulgakov spoke of the Moscow writers' residence in his famous novel 'The Master and Margarita', etc. Nevertheless, there is nothing purely historical about the analysis of life in the residence, even in modern Russia. The residence continues to play a key role in the socialization of Russians since most students spend several years of their university lives in student residences. Unlike a students' residence in France, which provides individual rooms or rooms for two at most, individual rooms are very rare in Russian residences, even at the best universities such as the Lomonossov State University in Moscow. Usually, the rooms are for 3–8 people. One report by a student in the 1930s provides a good impression of common life in the residence:

> 'Overcrowding in the residence... Room for several dozen people. I fall asleep last, when the final arrivals have calmed down. It's almost impossible to concentrate, reflect, read and write. It's very disappointing' (Lebina, 1999, p. 171).

Here is the lay-out for a typical room in a students' residence (toilets, sinks, showers and kitchen are on another floor; Figure 3.4).

Figure 3.4 Plan of a typical room in a students' residence

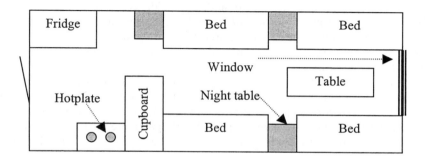

In the communal apartments, particularly during the 1930s–1960s, several families, occasionally up to a dozen, were required to organize their everyday lives together. They shared an entrance, a kitchen, a hallway with closets, washrooms, a telephone (see the plan for a communal apartment, Figure 3.5).

Figure 3.5 Plan of a communal apartment

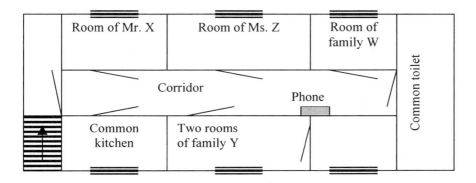

'The communal apartment is a strange collection of people who have come together against their will. Neighbors are not connected by common work, as in the residence, or by a common illness, as in the hospital, or by age, as in the residential school, or by a common crime, as in prison' (Lebina, 1999, p. 183).

The spirit of the communal apartments explains 'the lack of a clear concept of privacy in the Soviet mentality of the past' (Shlapentokh, 1998, p. 181).

The massive construction of apartments in the 1960s ended the period of the *kommunalka*, although certain inhabitants in many cities continue to live in communal apartments. Most Soviet families have been able to move into individual apartments, no matter how small and uncomfortable they may be. The progressive resolution of the housing problem kept another problem in the shadow, namely the means for protecting private space within the family. The concept of private life means that the individual can maintain his intimacy not only in his relations with others but also with those close to him, the members of his family. 'Individuals had the right to keep his or her personal life closed to other family members, even a spouse' (Shlapentokh, 1998, p. 182). The unwanted intervention of relatives in personal matters may be as violent as that of outsiders, as a result of the greater independence of family members and the fact that they are always present. The negative character of the compromise between the Soviet State and its subjects releases the State from its obligation to construct private space. 'You are given an apartment in exchange for your work for the State; it's up to you to manage the rest.'

The arrangement of space inside the standard apartment of the 1960s–1980s reflects this negative compromise. Economic considerations take precedence over all others, including the modernization of internal family life. The absence of hallways, the lack of a living room, and the fact that toilets are not separate from the washroom, are three distinctive signs of *hruschevka*, whereas, for example, 'the hallways permit types of privacy' (Giddens, 1984, p. 121) (see Figure 3.6: the floor plan for a standard 5–9 storey building, called *hruschevka*: two two-room apartments, one one-room apartment and one three-room apartment).

Figure 3.6 Plan of a standard apartment of the 1960s–1980s

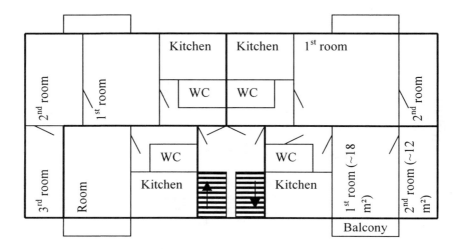

Moreover, the organization of social space at work provides a double attack on privacy from below and above. The Soviet man does not stand out from the work collective, which is constructed as an extension of the family orbital structure. 'The need to create his individual sphere, the zone of autonomy in which the individual acts autonomously' is not taken into consideration in the organization of the Soviet workplace (Morozov, 1991, t. 2, pp. 4, 12). The common practice involved, for example, making the family problems of a given member of the work collective public, even discussing them together. Adultery could be accepted as a topic of a collective meeting or a party discussion, occasionally at the request of the betrayed spouse.

The interviews we conducted with Russian businessmen in 1998–1999 leave no doubt that the transparency of the public/private border persists even in companies that were created after the dissolution of the USSR. In particular, we asked 'Do you think that intervening in the personal affairs of your employees is necessary for your company to function well?' Some of the interviewees focussed on the transparency of all information concerning the personal situations of their employees. This information becomes known, sometimes against the will of the person listening, as a result of the lack of a clear concept of private space. 'No, I don't intervene. But I am always aware of the [employees' personal situations].

You know, information gets through (*prosachivaetsja*)... It appears that even though the individual did not tell me, I'm aware of it. I remember one situation. A young girl, our employee, got pregnant and was hiding it because she thought we would leave her without maternity leave. You understand, you don't talk about it with everybody. So I learned this news a week later'.[20] 'Yes, here we're like sardines in a can. Our bank is small, relationships are informal. We don't need to ask directly, everything's in the air'.[21] The other portion of our interviewees mentioned the tendency to personalize professional relations, to bring them close to relations with friends or acquaintances. 'When the manager is aware of the personal problems of his subordinates, that's agreeable. This also applies in relations between the subordinate and the manager. If you have to get to know your manager better, you start by talking about personal matters – children, family...'[22] 'As for the [personal] problems of my subordinates, I'm aware of them in one way or another. Occasionally I take an interest in their family situation. Usually that makes them approve of their manager'.[23]

When summing up the Soviet model for organizing work, Yuri Levada constructed two types of ideals for the work collectivity, the kolkhoz and the *sharashka*. Within their framework,

> 'spheres as different in contemporary, developed societies as the State, the public and the private, work and leisure time, official conduct and unofficial conduct, interpenetrate here and can only be isolated through analysis' (Levada, 1993, p. 94).

The kolkhoz model focusses on the attack on the separation of the spheres of activity from below. It involves the 'privatization' and the expansion of the family model (cf. a slang term 'living in kolkhozian style' means 'living in a large family'). The *sharashka* reflects intervention in private space from above. It should be noted that the roots of the term *sharashka* go back to the penal world of the 1930s. This term means 'secret research institute where the State Security Committee organizes and supervises the work and the research done by scientists and engineers sentenced for "sabotage"' (Rossi, 1991, p. 453). In other words, in the case of the kolkhoz, the family takes over the public space whereas in the case of the *sharashka* intimacy is stolen and the private space, including the family, is reduced to nothing in the name of the State.

Constructing the enemy: then and now

The absenteeism of the State in any positive organization of its citizens' everyday life and the bipolar model of social space torn between 'yours' and others gives rise to a means for controlling violence specific to the Soviet model of society. The distrust of the State, as well as the State's refusal to help its citizens in everyday life, leaves them no choice but to turn away from the institutionalized violence and

---

[20] Interview No. 17*.
[21] Interview No. 19*.
[22] Interview No. 10*.
[23] Interview No. 12*.

substitute it for the search for a 'scapegoat'. If we refer to the development of means for controlling violence described by Girard, we easily find examples of the three steps: the search for a replacement victim, the search for a scapegoat, and the construction of a sacrificial victim.

Nevertheless, the crime rate recorded by the police is not very high from an international perspective. Even setting aside the problem of latent criminality, a curious foreigner visiting post-Soviet Russia would be negatively surprised by daily violence, which does not take on latent forms. Shoving in public transit, verbal insults, the hatred occasionally seen in the eyes of a chance passer-by, the refusal to provide information, the optional character of the forms of politeness such as 'Sir/Madam',[24] 'Excuse me', etc. Public discourse is often dominated by vulgarity and the recourse to the vulgar swearing of popular slang (*mat*). As a joke, it is often said that two languages are spoken in post-Soviet society: Russian and *mat*. Knowing how to use complex swear words is considered a sort of art. 'He swears artistically,' people say. A survey made of a representative sample by VCIOM in March 2000 demonstrates that almost one out of two Russian men, and one out of four Russian women use vulgar swearwords *daily*.[25] Only 30 per cent of post-Soviets say that they have never used *mat*. An analysis of the use of *mat* by age group, according to the results of the VCIOM survey made in 1989,[26] have convinced us that this is no recent phenomenon (see also Table 3.27).[27] Ordinary post-Soviet men aged 20–29 and 40–49 use vulgar swearwords most often. Moreover, three Russian men out of four and one Russian woman out of three have been involved in fights. Nine percent of Russians had fought in the month preceding the survey, namely February 2000. The ordinary Russian fights once a year on average.

Table 3.27 Spread of *mat*

Do you often speak mat?	1992	2000
Yes, often	13	12
Yes, sometimes	41	47
No, practically never	44	39
Don't know	2	2

The undeniable presence of violence in everyday life gives rise to a feeling of insecurity and a strong demand for order as the alternative for the failure to respect

---

[24] During the Soviet period, any unknown person was addressed as 'Citizen' (*grajdanin*) or 'Comrade' (*tovarisch*). Today, this expression has a pejorative meaning, without being replaced by 'Sir' (*gospodin*). In fact, no title is used when addressing someone.
[25] Golov A., 'Russkij byt v marte 2000 goda' // http://www.polit.ru, April 6, 2000. It should be noted that company managers are included in the three most 'vulgar' socioeconomic groups.
[26] 'One-third of Soviets recall the "verbal insults" they have received recently' (Levada, 1993, p. 116).
[27] 'Kak i zachem my materimsja' // http://www.polit.ru/documents/328336.html (the results of a VCIOM survey).

the rules, to *bespredel*. Post-Soviets define order in a negative manner. Let us take a look at the associations observed with the term 'order' in the two representative surveys conducted by VCIOM in 1994 and at the start of 2000:[28]

Table 3.28 Concept of order

What do you understand by the order?	1994	2000	2000/1994
Economic and political stability	37%	45%	+8%
Rule of the Law	31	35	+6
Absence of pillage of the country	21	33	+12
Stopping deterioration in the standard of living, stopping conflicts between the branches of political power	20	32	+12
Social protection of the poor	10	26	+16
Strict discipline	14	22	+8
Situation when everybody has an opportunity to protect his or her rights	14	17	+3
Turning to the army in order to fight against crime	12	13	+1
Limitation of rights and liberties	1	3	+2
A cover of the dictatorship	0	1	+1
Other	0	1	+1
Don't know	2	3	+1

Those interviewed prefer to define order by excluding crisis, pillaging, fights between powers rather than by referring to positive values (the Law, human rights). The dynamics of the past six years have merely accentuated the tendency to view order as the absence of *bespredel*. One other observation is necessary once we speak of the concept of order in the post-Soviet context. The desire for order takes precedence over the desire for means for satisfying it, namely over the desire for the institutional control of violence. When given two alternatives, order or about means for attaining order, an absolute majority of Russians choose the first:[29]

Table 3.29 Choosing between liberty and order

What is the most important for Russia from your point of view?	1998	1999	2000
Order, even if some democratic principles and human rights are not respected	70	74	72
Democracy, even if respect of democratic principles sometimes gives destroyers too much liberty	14	11	13
Don't know	16	15	15

---

[28] 'Strana, reformy, primety' // http://www.polit.ru, January 12, 2000.
[29] *Ibid.*

Therefore, Russians would give carte blanche to someone who promises to respect order using all means, both in the case of local order (in a company, a city or a region) or national order. The institutional control of violence is also complicated by the absence of the quasi institutional mechanisms we observed in prison. 'There, [outside prison]? What happens there? Exorbitant prices, *bespredel* everywhere...'[30] The fight against organized crime proclaimed as a means for maintaining order is often reduced to a fight against the illicit justice system which generally reproduces that of the penal world (we will discuss this matter in greater detail in sections '*Parallel market as a starting point*' and '*Market perspectives in Russia*'). Therefore, what means can post-Soviets use to avoid daily violence?

First, the separation between 'yours' and others enables people to find a substitute victim and target violence towards others, strangers. A person you jostle in the subway is obviously a stranger, someone you are seeing for the first and last time. Yet, you never jostle one of 'yours', you try to respect the rules of politeness with him. The popular expression, '*sorvat' svoju zlost' na kom-to*' (literally, 'to sublimate one's hatred on someone') implies that one can transpose his hatred in his relations with strangers. Usually, it should be noted, one who sublimates his hatred is not criticized for doing so. In fact, the post-Soviet context transforms hatred into a negative form of sociability. 'Its function is to disqualify a potential partner by transforming him into an adversary' (Levada, 1993, p. 110), a target of violence.

On a micro social level, strangers make the ideal substitute victims. During the iron curtain period, when *personal* contacts with strangers were closely regulated and uncommon, 'one saw [in the image of the stranger] what displeased you in yourself and what you wanted to get rid of' (Levada, 1993, p. 180).[31] The Soviet State took advantage of this 'natural' hatred for strangers by developing figures of the negative compromise with its citizens. It cultivated the fear of strangers, their aggressiveness, in order to replace the real sources of misfortune in everyday life with imaginary sources that were out of reach. 'There are forms of violence that turn the threat of close objects to more distant objects, specifically war' (Girard, 1972, p. 37).[32] The hierarchy of fears that Soviets experienced at the end of the 1980s reflects the results of the efforts to demonize strangers: 59 per cent of those interviewed feared the illness of someone close, 47 per cent – war, 42 per cent – natural disasters, 40 per cent – their own illness, etc. (for the breakdown of fears, see Table 3.30) (Levada, 1993, p. 266).[33] Moreover, even the end of the Cold War did not greatly reduce the fear of foreign aggression. At the end of 1998, 24 per cent of Russians still thought foreign aggression was highly likely

---

[30] Interview No. 31.
[31] 'Since the 16th century, Russians have viewed evil as originating in the West' (Ahiezer, 1991, p. 114).
[32] 'The danger of war becomes a capital argument for maintaining the *status quo*' (Timofeev, 1993, p. 133).
[33] Levada Yu., '*Chelovek sovetskij 10 let spustja: 1989–1999*' // http://www.polit.ru/documents/393366.html (results of the survey 'The Ordinary Soviet Man: Ten Years After').

(Mansurov, 1999, p. 11). Moreover, the dissolution of the USSR resulted in the construction of new enemies, those who were no longer 'yours': the people of the Baltic countries, certain central Asian countries and the Caucasus.

> 'Ours. As in games and street fights before. Ours! Whereas those [those who supported the independence of Lithuania] are the others. That's it... Our people are very particular. They know how to distinguish theirs from the others, not just based on skin color or membership in a class or religion. It goes without saying. They know how to distinguish others in keeping with a rating used to move up or down a staircase' (Dubov, 1999, pp. 280, 288).[34]

Table 3.30 Relative significance of fears

Fears	1989	1994	1999
An illness of the close relative	1	1	1
The world war	2	5	6
The death, respondent's own illness	3	4	3
Natural disasters	4	10	8
Old age	5		
The end of the world	6		
Arbitrary actions of the government's representatives	7	3	4
Sufferings, a pain	8		
A public humiliation	9	8	9
Crime	10	2	5
Poverty, unemployment		6	2

The other means for controlling violence, the search for a scapegoat victim, implies a search for enemies within the community. When it becomes difficult to make strangers responsible for all of the misfortunes of everyday life, a 'scapegoat', someone who looks like he is one of 'yours' must be designated. The 'task of intra-state pacification may also lead the State to define its own enemy within' (Schmitt, 1992, p. 86). Soviet history of the 1930s abounds with examples of this search for scapegoats. The list of internal enemies included 'those who were harmful' (*vrediteli*, 'harmful'), rich peasants (*kulaki*), supporters of Trotsky (*trockisty*), those with German names, etc. (Shalamov, 1998, p. 536)[35]. The Penal Code of the 1960s retained the article concerning responsibility for Acts detrimental to the national economy (Art. 69). In today's Russia there is no shortage of efforts to develop an internal enemy. The two Chechen wars of the 1990s (1994–1996 and 1999 to the present) serve as an example. The driving force of *internal* war in channeling violence only became clear during the second

---

[34] This is an account of the popular reaction to the events of Vilnius in January 1991.

[35] *Vrediteli* refers to 'those who are designated by the bureaucracy as scapegoats responsible for the failures of its own political economy' (Rossi, 1991, Vol. 1, p. 65). The criminalization of responsibility for alleged harm to the national economy is studied in detail in Solomon (1996).

campaign. The first campaign did not lie at the core of Russian public life, either positively or negatively.

> 'Let us compare the few hundred demonstrators gathered by *Memorial* or Egor Gaïdar against the Chechen war at the end of 1994/start of 1995 with the hundreds of thousands of people who took to the streets following the repressions in Vilnius in January 1991. *Yet, at the time, society was mobilized against a clearly identified enemy: Soviet power*' (Berelowitch, Wieviorka, 1996, p. 56).[36]

However, the second campaign made headlines from the start. Russians viewed it as the event of the year (1999) which, with 33 per cent of the votes, was far in advance of the NATO war in Yugoslavia (22 per cent), Parliamentary elections (20 per cent), the resignation of the Stepashin government (15 per cent), etc.[37] Official expiation involved punishing 'terrorists' who attack order and security *in everyday life* (a series of serious attacks, presumably by Chechens, served as a pretext for the second war). All in all, two words, hatred and fear, express the attitude of Russians with respect to Chechens. In March 2000, VCIOM surveyed a representative sample, using two questions: 'Do you hate Chechens?' and 'Are you afraid that Chechens will take vengeance on Russia and Russians?' Here are the answers:[38]

Table 3.31 Opinion about Chechens

Hatred and fear	28%
Hatred without fear	6%
Fear without hatred	42%
Neither hatred, nor fear	11%
Don't know	10%

Although a direct parallel does not appear pertinent, we propose to look at the problem of the death sentence from the point of view of looking for scapegoats responsible for *bespredel* in everyday life. The surveys conducted by VCIOM indicate that Russians strongly support capital punishment (Table 3.32).[39] The reasons given by those who oppose the abolition of capital punishment are very significant: 42 per cent view capital punishment as a good punishment for the crimes committed, 12 per cent are convinced that criminals (sic, criminals *in general*) bring capital punishment upon themselves.[40] Therefore, there is a need to designate scapegoats that personalize daily violence and *bespredel*, and provide exemplary punishment for them. Perhaps a society that controls daily violence perfectly is also more tolerant and humane with respect to criminals?

---

[36] Our emphasis. Memorial is a political movement against Stalinism.
[37] Results of a representative survey by VCIOM. Source: http://www.polit.ru, December 27, 1999.
[38] Sedov L., Golov A., 'Motiv mesti' // http://www.polit.ru, March 16, 2000.
[39] Levada Yu., '*Chelovek sovetskij 10 let spustja : 1989–1999*'.
[40] Source: http://www.romir.ru (results of a survey by ROMIR).

Table 3.32 Opinion about capital punishment

	1989	1994	1999
Capital punishment should be abolished	3	5	5
It should be abolished, but gradually	15	15	15
It should be maintained	33	37	36
It should be used more actively	35	25	23
Don't know	14	18	20

Double thinking

These two registers of daily behavior, relationships with 'yours' and those with others are the source of a mental construction that Alexander Hlopin refers to as double thinking (*dvoemyslie*). Double thinking refers to the

> 'respect manifested in public for ideals and norms that may not correspond to the personal convictions of individuals and may even contradict their actual behavior' (Hlopin, 1994, p. 51).

The personal convictions of post-Soviets are formed during their interactions with their own: only the lower layers of the family atmosphere are inhabitable. On the other hand, social life with its norms is virtually absent from the upper layers of the family atmosphere. It is the world of their own that causes social life to flourish in the Soviet institutional context. 'We're not just friends, but more than friends. We form a whole (*my – odno celoe*). *We form a world apart, with its rules, laws, joys, and pain*' (Dubov, 1999, p. 271).[41] The mentality formed within the 'small' society includes two sets of norms. The first governs relations with your own, the second, relations with others. Alena Ledeneva describes the make-up of the first set, the 'moral of the preferred circle of people' as follows: 'The obligation to help; Orientation towards an indefinite future' ('don't spit in the soup, you may need to eat it', *Ne pljui v kolodec – prigoditsja vody napit'sja*); Do not expect gratitude in return but be grateful yourself; Keep within limits (concerning what can be asked), and so on (Ledeneva, 1998, pp. 163–166).

In relations with others, Soviets are not required to respect these limits. They are free to do what they want, even if others criticize their behavior. Since the negative compromise with the State means that it lies in the world of the others, respect for the Law is optional. Moreover, this lack of respect never transforms into a flagrant refusal, a revolt against the imposed authority. Double thinking results from a double movement, on the one hand towards the negation of others, including the State, on the other, towards creation of the appearance of respect for them. The power of the State, as well as the negative dependence on the State, excludes revolt.

---

[41] Our stress.

'The Soviet individual is able to balance him or herself in the economic and political spheres by maintaining two different mental levels–pragmatic and ideological... Political obedience demands only public statements in the terms desired by the current leadership' (Shlapentokh, 1995, pp. 96–97).

Both parties are satisfied: the State receives apparent evidence of the effectiveness of its control and the individual purchases some leeway in everyday life and the right to maintain his personal belief in his own God. Does this double conscience represent an excessive price for freedom on the scale of the 'small' society?

The case of State civil servants and company managers deserves attention. On the one hand, as representatives of the State, they internalize its logic and values. On the other hand, in their everyday lives, they face the same dilemma as ordinary people. They too have their own 'private' morals, their 'own', their hatred of others, namely 'petitioners', the ordinary people. The contrary would be surprising: despite the material privileges of the members of the *nomenklatura*, they live in the same institutional context. The double thinking of the State civil servants becomes concrete, for example, in the opposition between tips as a norm of everyday life (a tribute imposed on others) and their legal prohibition (the principle of equal access to State services for all citizens) (Yakovlev, 1988, p. 32). As for company managers, we have already pointed out that their desire to attain the objectives set in the plan can only be fulfilled through the construction of networks of their 'own' and recourse to other illicit practices. The *tolkachi*, members of a Soviet corporate 'pressure group' provides an ideal example. Given the permanent shortages of raw materials, Soviet companies sought to develop informal contacts with their suppliers. The *tolkach* appeared following the specialization of certain corporate employees in illicit intermediation. Their primary duty was to interest those responsible for a supplier in supplying their firm rather than another. Small gifts and services: a bottle of Armenian brandy, a few tins of black caviar, a smoked salmon 'maintained the friendship'. Although each company had *tolkachi*, the USSR Penal Code of 1960 criminalized such activities (Yakovlev, 1988, p. 32).

Moreover, life in two registers and the internalization of the completely torn social space had serious consequences on the psychological health and internal balance of the Soviet individual. By studying the statistics on mental illnesses in the countryside, Lev Timofeev noted that such illnesses were mostly observed in young people, aged 15–16. Therefore, it is at that age that the conflict between the ideology and the official behavior taught at school and personal morals takes on the most extreme forms (Timofeev, 1993, pp. 64–65). It was not possible to live in the Soviet countryside without pillaging the kolkhozian raw materials (fodder, wheat, potatoes, etc.): the level of the official salary and the absence of a raw materials market left no other means for maintaining the peasant household. Yet, the worldview learned by Soviets at school violently blamed small pillagers of State property or kolkhoz (*nesyn*). A novel by Alexander Bek, 'A New Nomination' (*Novoe naznachenie*), provides another example of an inevitable mental illness in conditions of *stychka*, of violent conflict between personal convictions and the official rules.[42]

In medical terms, the transformation of the torn social space into double thinking increases the risk of schizophrenia. In particular, schizophrenia results in a decrease in the individual's capacity for empathy. He finds it difficult to put himself in another's place, particularly when the other is socially distant.

> 'Since schizophrenics have a little ability to understand, to react to the problems of others... their illness makes their social contacts and their perception of reality more problematic' (Eligulashvili, 1983, pp. 18, 23).[43]

The illness focusses on the separation between relations with your own and contacts with others. The importance of the family sphere takes on hyperbolic forms for schizophrenics.

> 'The family sphere is very important for schizophrenics, whereas the scope of friendships and particularly formal social relations are reduced' (Hlomov, 1985, p. 17).

Therefore, external social contradictions transform into internal conflicts. Occasionally, the only way to prevent the fragilization of the mental system involves 'closing one's eyes' to others, ignoring them. A hero of Venedikt Erofeev, a writer whose work provides a fresco of daily Soviet life in the 1970s–1980s, cried out in despair: 'Why is your skin so insensitive' (*Pochemy vy takie tolstokojie*)? (Erofeev, 1975).

The recent developments of the post-Soviet system have not changed the double thinking of Russians. The personal 'constitution' still differs from the public 'constitution' since the imposed character of the licit authority has not changed (we will return to this matter in the subsection entitled and '*Market perspectives in Russia*'). This enabled Wladimir Andreff to describe post-Soviet reality in terms of a 'double schizophrenia', the managers' schizophrenia and the public's schizophrenia. On the one hand, the behavior of those responsible for economic matters focusses on a contradictory objective: paternalistic policy (the company as a large family) and market policy (the official slogan of the free, competitive market) at the same time. On the other hand, ordinary people believe in a better market life, but their 'skepticism towards government policy probably points at people's reluctance to pay the bill for transforming the economy' (Andreff, 1995, pp. 18–19).

---

[42] Bek A., *Novoe naznachenie*, Kishinev : Kartja Moldavjaneske, 1988. It should be noted that the political career of Gavriil Popov, former mayor of Moscow, at that time professor at the Lomonossov University in Moscow, started with the publication in 1987 in *Nauka i Jizn'* of an article on this novel.

[43] The theory of set has greatly contributed to the understanding of schizophrenia. In its terms, the illness reflects the inability of the individual to control two contradictory sets: one is formed by the immediate social environment, the other by the more global institutional context (see Uznadze, 1966, p. 299).

On the congruence of norms

Looking at the post-Soviet model through the prism of the opposition of 'your own' and others helps to prevent the seduction by the magic of false pretences, occasionally observed in Western writings about Russia. As in the case of a linguistic 'false friend', one phenomenon of the post-Soviet reality, whose appearance brings to mind analogies with the 'large' societies, merely presents a false similarity. A recent comparative study by R. Inglehart clearly illustrates this danger. A series of structural indicators, including the predominance of safety factors over factors of shortages, the rejection of State authority, a high degree of individualization, the rejection of the West as a model, a decrease in the prestige of rationality, serve to position Russia as a post-modern country or a country on the path to post-modernization (Inglehart, 1995, pp. 441–443). A more in-depth analysis convinces us that, for example, in order to explain the concern for order, everyday violence and the feeling of *bespredel* must be considered rather than the characteristics of the risk society. Likewise, the rejection of the State and the emphasis placed on family are explained less by the driving force of the *personality* in post-Soviet society than by the absence of other means than a family shelter for ensuring the respect of individuality. Family values are experiencing a renaissance in post-modern societies, but they are closely linked to the context of the 'large' society.

However, the comparison of the two social structures, that of the post-Soviet society and that of the penal society, indicate their substantial congruence extends to the similarity of certain apparent forms. 'Here, it's the same world, but in miniature. Our world reflects everything that goes on in yours, but on a smaller scale'.[44] Let us take a closer look at the confidence expressed by both ordinary Russians and Russian inmates in various social institutions (see Table 3.33):

Table 3.33 Trust in different social institutions

	Russia [96]	Prisoners			
		Russia, N=1310	Kazakh., N=396	France, N=59	Canada, N=120
Family	71%	67.5	71.1	79.3	88.6
Friends	45	×	×	48.3	58.8
Church	24	20.2	14.5	17.2	29.8
Science	17	5	7.5	19	31.6
Workmates	8	×	×	8.6	11.4
Prisoners' leaders	×	18	14.2	×	×
Prisoners' community	×	14.1	12.3	×	6.1
People	7	5.4	3.8	×	×
Mass media	×	2.3	3.7	3.5	9.7
System of justice	×	1.1	2.1	17.2	7.9

---

[44] Letter from Interviewee No. 3a.

In two cases, the family ranks first, the Church second. Although we are not claming to have analyzed the role of religious conviction in the everyday life of post-Soviets, we would like to make a few observations. Most Russians (60.1 per cent) view themselves as believers, of whom 89.7 per cent are Orthodox (Mansurov, 1999, p. 22). These figures contrast strongly with VCIOM data on the number of Orthodox practitioners. For example, only 2 per cent of Russians fast for Lent, whereas 77 per cent continue to eat without restrictions.[45] Does this contradiction refer us back to the phenomenon of double thinking? 'There are believers like that. I believe in God, I respect the commandments, but if you touch me, I'll break your jaw, I'll rape you... It's nothing to do with Christianity'.[46]

Yet there is, hypothetically speaking, another, more subtle explanation. Is it not a form of fatalism that unites post-Soviets and inmates? Neither post-Soviets nor inmates are their own masters, real Subjects in everyday life. At least, several interviews and investigations point at this. 'What do you believe in? – In God and a little happiness (*na avos'*). Many go to church'.[47] The link between the belief in God and that in a little happiness in the discourse of our interviewee was not accidental. The individual allows things to pass *naturally*, without any conscious intervention. Confidence in one's sort appears to be the opposite side of the cost of distrust in others, in the imposed licit authority. 'I live for today, in keeping with God's will (*po boj'emy veleniju*). Evil unto the day is sufficient thereof. That's my motto. Today is no different from tomorrow'.[48] In other words, there is a 'dominant sense of the existence of *a natural course of events, the inevitable nature of events*' (Berelowitch, Wieviorka, 1996, p. 90).[49] Religion is merely one form of the belief in the natural course of events among others. Post-Soviets believe in fortune telling (57 per cent), astrology (33 per cent), UFOs (31 per cent), telepathy (28 per cent), magic (26 per cent) and many other things.[50] All that remains is for them to believe that people can transform themselves into Subjects solely through the framework of their family universes.

Therefore, it is the feeling of powerlessness that gives rise to this rudimentary form of fatalism. Since collective actions that are larger than your own are excluded from the directory of daily activities, the inmates *as well as* the post-Soviets are obliged to accept the *status quo*, as painful as it is. 'Usually, we don't change anything in the colonies. We accept things as they are (*kak postavleno, tak i jivut*). We put up with things calmly. Yes, there is always dissatisfaction, but that's kitchen dissatisfaction. When we're at home, we sit down and discuss politics. It's the same thing here. We sit down near a barrack and start debating. I don't like it...

---

[45] Kim N., Orlova Yu., 'Pravitel'stvo i reformy, maslennica i post' // http://www.polit.ru, March 14, 2000.
[46] Interview No. 13, was conducted with a believer.
[47] *Ibid.*
[48] Interview No. 16. Varlam Shalamov also speaks of fatalism as a central element in the prison decor: 'Any intervention in the natural course of events, desired by the Gods, is poorly viewed, contradicts the inmates' codes of behavior' (Shalamov, 1998 p. 42).
[49] Our stress.
[50] 'Strana, reformy, primety' // http://www.polit.ru, January 12, 2000 (VCIOM data); also Mansurov, 1999, p. 22.

We pick a topic for discussion. Some says "It shouldn't be like that." Someone else continues, "Yeah, OK, it was better before." A debate starts, but it's a kitchen debate. It never takes on an open format'.[51] Now, we are slipping towards today's Russian society. Dissatisfaction with the results of the reforms of the 1990s–only 8.6 per cent of Russians think that the reforms reflect their interests, whereas 48.1 per cent disagree (Mansurov, 1999, p. 16)–coexists in their minds with a strong sense that the course of change is *natural* (see the breakdown for the assessment of change [98]):

Table 3.34 Evaluation of socioeconomic changes

Changes go at a natural pace	34%
Changes go too slowly	24
Frankly speaking, there are no radical changes	22
Changes go too quickly	16

Let us continue with our overview of the similarities between the penal world and the post-Soviet world with a discussion of two phenomena. The first concerns the public sphere and the attitude towards work; the second concerns the private sphere and the model for relations between men and women. The forced labor system, the raison d'être of the Soviet penal system until the start of the 1990s, resulted in a particular attitude concerning work for the State. Since cheating with others is allowed, the obligation to work painfully for the State is transformed into finding all possible means for cheating at work. The term *tufta* refers to the range of illicit methods for cheating. The etymology of this term, which appeared for the first time at the Belomor-Baltic canal worksite, comes from the initials for the words *Tehnika Ucheta Fiktivnogo TrudA*, an 'accounting technique for fictional work' (Rossi, 1991, pp. 27, 415, 453).

The forced labor regime of the 1930s, particularly in the North (Vorkuta region) and the Extreme East of the USSR (Kolyma river basin), gave real meaning to the expressions 'working zealously kills', 'a large daily ration (*bol'shaja pajka*) kills',[52] etc. In other words, honest work for the State is always painful, even deadly. The context of the negative compromise with the State generalized *tufta* practices, transforming them into a common set. Although work for the State has not been deadly since the 1960s–1980s, it did not become reasonable. You have to remain zealous for your own work, namely household work, not 'for an uncle' (*rabotat' na chujogo djadju*), namely an *outsider*. By reproducing the same attitude, company managers filed falsified reports with the State regulatory organizations (*pripiski*). At the end of the 1980s, State regulatory organizations in

---

[51] Interview No. 25. It is a matter of the licit and illicit organization of everyday life. The expression 'kitchen debate' was very common during the Soviet period. The negative compromise with the State implied that all dissatisfaction could be expressed, but only with your own, *in the kitchen*.

[52] The large portion was reserved for those who worked zealously, cf. the title of the novel by Yulij Dubov, - *Bol'shaja pajka*.

the Ukraine accused 53 per cent of enterprises of doing this (Golvach, 1990. p. 19). The start of *perestroïka* was marked by a series of revelations (by Gdljan and Ivanov) concerning *pripiski* affecting cotton production in Uzbekistan. There, filing falsified reports was part of the republican policy concerning the central authority. Today, fiscal fraud has taken over in cheating against the State. It is difficult to conceive of the post-Soviet economic landscape without *double* accounting, with the first set of books for internal use and the second for tax inspectors.

The duality of the image of the relations between the sexes serves as additional proof of a 'barrier between "us" and "them" that crosses through all spheres of the social existence of the [post-Soviet] man' (Levada, 1993, p. 35). Social roles, and values remain torn between two poles, masculine and feminine. Study data indicates that men view women as others and women respond in kind. The breakdown of the responses to the question 'What do you appreciate most in men (women)?' reveals two distinctive portraits:[53]

Table 3.35 Relevant features for men and women compared

Relevant features (M – for men, W – for women)		For men	For women
Intelligence	M	58% (+29%)	29%
Nice look (*vnechnjaja privlecatel'nost'*)	W	8	40 (+32)
Honesty	M	53 (+23)	30
Ability to good housekeeping (*hozjajstvennost'*)	W	34	44 (+10)
Being hot-blooded	-	5	6
Stoicism	M	23 (+9)	14
Cheerfulness	W	9	16 (+7)
Sexuality	W	3	10 (+7)
A good temper	W	5	12 (+7)
Tenderness	W	24	31 (+7)
Independence	M	19 (+11)	8
Fidelity	W	27	33 (+5)
Don't know		4	3

The male image implies an intelligent, honest, independent individual whereas the female image is one of charm, an ability to keep house, fidelity and tenderness. Our study of the distribution of household chores in everyday life confirms that post-Soviets prefer to see the woman in charge of the housekeeping, as the real mistress of the house [98]:

---

[53] From 'Strana, reformy, primety' // http://www.polit.ru, January 12, 2000 (VCIOM data). For masculine and feminine values see also (Dubov, 1997, p. 78).

Table 3.36 Distribution of household chores

This task is done by...	Shopping (W)	Cooking (W)	Washing (W)	After-care (W)	Doing-it-yourself (M)
Wife	26%	34%	40	27	8
Usually by the wife	34	37	37	25	3
Usually together	29	22	16	38	12
Usually by the husband	6	2	2	3	31
Husband	1	0	0	1	40
No answer	3	4	5	5	5

Moreover, the divergence of social values and roles does not engender the mutual hostility that exists as part of relations between your own and others. However, a more subtle analysis of the responses to the question 'Who do you trust?' [99] reveals an obvious asymmetry. This concerns primarily men: four out of five prefer to trust men and distrust women:

Table 3.37 Trust in men and women compared

	Men	Women
Men have confidence rather in...	82%	18%
Women have confidence rather in...	55%[54]	45%

The distrust expressed by men with respect to women brings to mind the disregard for women as property, characteristic of the penal subculture. The inmates refuse to view the woman as a human being; she is a slave to their desires, a puppet, a prostitute. A content analysis of the novel '*Bol'shaja pajka*' illustrates this statement, which may appear exaggerated. In the following table, we have reproduced the few characteristics of all of the female characters in this novel, which was written by one of the business pioneers in post-Soviet Russia in the 1980s–1990s. Out of approximately 30 female characters, 27 are prostitutes, easy women or women who make their careers in bed! If a woman has a career, it is always thanks to a man. Only one female character is portrayed with respect – Penny MacFadden, *the wife of an American*.

---

[54] We have already noted greater flexibility on the part of female inmates with respect to masculine and feminine roles. As a hypothesis, it is the flexibility and versatility of the women which plays a stabilizing role in the post-Soviet world. This hypothesis deserves a special study.

Table 3.38 Characteristics of the female characters in a novel

Character	Brief characteristics
Lenka	Girlfriend of one of the principal characters, she makes her career in bed
Nina	Docile, but she is not successful in making the career
Vika	Girlfriend of one of the principal characters, she makes her career in bed and thanks to her husband
Lika	Wife of one of the principal characters, she makes her career in bed and commits the acts of conjugal infidelity
No names	Girls (about a dozen) from a top model agency, a masculine character sleeps with all of them
Marija	Girlfriend of one of the principal characters, she makes her career in bed
Nastija	Sister of Lika, prostitute who marries one of the principal characters
Tan'ka	Secretary of one of the principal characters, she is ready to satisfy all desires of her boss
Galja	Girl in a restaurant, she is chatted up by a masculine character
Anjuta	Wife of one of the principal characters, she is deserted
Eleonora L'vovna	She is rather good, but too bureaucratic
No names	Three secretaries put by three masculine characters in a bath of champagne
Pola	Secretary of one of the principal characters, his ex-girlfriend, she makes her career in bed
Penny	Wife of M. MacFadden, an American professor
Marusja	Russian prostitute in Swiss
Man'ka	Russian prostitute in Swiss
Tan'ja	She is afraid of everything
No name	Moscow's prostitute
Vera	Easy girl
Fira	Luxury prostitute for one of the principal characters
Lelja	Nurse, easy girl

We will summarize the study of the congruence between post-Soviet society and the penal society by focussing on the specific role that the penal subculture plays in the world outside prison. In the '*Introduction*', we noted the invasion of the Russian language by criminal slang. This concerns not only popular language but also the language of Russian literature. In his essays, 'Essays on the criminal world' Varlam Shalamov notes that 'literature has always portrayed criminals with compassion, occasionally obsequiousness' (Shalamov, 1998, p. 7). Great Russian and Soviet authors such as Dostoyevski, Gorky, Babel, Leonov, Esenin, Pogodin, and the songwriter Utesov have devoted one or more of their works to the penal and/or criminal world. The obsequiousness of popular culture with respect to the penal world is demonstrated by the popularity of *blatnye* (from the word *blat*) songs. During the Soviet period, these songs were the most in demand in restaurants and cabarets. Today, a portrait of Russian pop music would be incomplete without the numerous singers from the penal subculture.[55] How can we account for the scope and popularity of the *blat* subculture if we do not take into consideration the high degree of permeability between the two 'small' societies?

The etymology of the word *blat* that we used to describe personalized access to rare resources in the Soviet economy has its roots deep within the penal subculture. In the 19th century, the thieves of Odessa, the criminal capital in the Russian empire, called *blat* their palm (Rossi, 1991, p. 32). Everything that was touched by the palm of the thief became *blat*, a stolen object up to personal acquaintances: *we shake the hand* of the other party. In this way, *blat* means the extreme degree of closeness, of personalization that constitutes the raison d'être of the 'small' society, which reproduces *blat* relations naturally and is a *blat* society par excellence.

Is it any surprise that even the presidency, an impersonal and impartial institution elsewhere, is based on personalized relations, relations with 'someone's owns', namely *blat* relations in the post-Soviet societies?

> 'Constitutional arguments about the proper role of the presidency in a system of checks and balances played a very minor role. Instead, the presidency was designed to fit a particular candidate for the office' (Elster, 1996, p. 130).

It is *normal* in the context of the 'small' society for the newly elected president of the Russian Federation to first appoint those he knows *personally* for key government positions. This group, called the St. Petersburg group (cf. *zemljachestvo*) is replacing the Sverdlovsk group, which was powerful during the time of Yeltsin, not to mention the Dniepropetrovsk (which Leonid Brejnev came from) and numerous other powerful in-groups formed during the Soviet period. From the perspective of the 'small' society, the difference between these elite groups and street gangs does not count much. The torn, atomized society reproduces the criminal subculture at all levels: in prison, in the suburbs or large cities,[56] in the organization of power. For this reason, we do not agree with Alena Ledeneva's prognosis that 'blat is losing its central significance in the conditions of the post-Soviet world' (Ledeneva, 1998, p. 175). No, *blat* will remain as long as the post-Soviet society remains 'small'.

---

[55] Mikhail Krug, Evgenij Kemerovskij, the 'Lesopoval' group (its producer Mikhail Tanich was decorated in 1998 by the President of the Russian Federation for 'his contribution to Russian culture'). The Moscow's FM radio-station 'Chanson' broadcasting *blatnye* songs has an important share of the total radio-audience (8 per cent in July 2002, 6th rank of all FM radio-stations; see *Kommersant*, n°149, August 23, 2002, pp. 9, 11).

[56] We refer in particular to a study of the role played by the criminal subculture in the suburbs of Kazan', the capital of Tatarstan: Fathullin N., Zamorin A., 'Kazanskij fenomen: opyt sociologicheskogo issledovanija podrostkovoj prestupnosti', in *Problemy bor'by s organizovannoj prestupnost'ju i korrupciej*, Moskva: VNII MVD RF, 1993, pp. 59–62. As supported by the words of one of our interviewees, 'I learned less from my family than in the streets and I knew several things [about prison] well in advance'(Interview No. 26).

Chapter 4

Institutional Change: Two Cases Compared

The reforms of the 1990s in Russia were usually designed as an effort to modernize the Soviet model, to transform the 'small' society into a 'large' one. The vast movement of the economic, political and social reforms has not yet produced any advantageous results. A feeling of profound crisis has dominated public opinion over the past decade. At the end of 1998, when characterizing the economic situation in their country, 20.5 per cent of Russians described it as a 'catastrophe' and 63.7 per cent as a 'profound, long-term crisis'. As for the political situation, 27 per cent described it as an 'impasse', and 52.4 per cent as a 'profound long-term crisis' (Mansurov, 1999, p. 9). An analysis of the relative number of optimists indicates that the sense of despair is relatively stable (see Table 4.1 for the answers to the question 'What do you think the material situation of your family will be in five years?'[1]):

Table 4.1 Expectations about the material situation

	Mar. 95	Jan. 96	Jul. 96	Jan. 97	Mar. 98	Feb. 00
Much better than before	4	4	6	6	6	5
A little bit better than before	20	21	32	19	20	31
No changes	41	50	35	40	43	44
A little bit worse than before	18	13	16	18	17	13
Much worse than before	14	8	9	13	10	7

In order to explain the reform policy, we will verify our fifth initial hypothesis that the implementation of a new model will only succeed with the *ex ante* congruence of the formal norms used as the model and the informal norms existing in a 'receptor' society. The example of the market reforms (in fact, we will only speak of this aspect of the Russian reforms) contrasts with the second case studied, the reform of the penal system. Although the latter is more modest in scope – it is reduced to ensuring better control over violence and respecting the minimal rights of inmates – its relative success serves to highlight the faults of the overall reform policy. The principal lesson to be learned from the penal reform is that existing tendencies must be promoted and reconciled with the desired

---

[1] 'Material'noe polojenie rossijan' // http://www.polit.ru, March 2, 2000 (VCIOM data).

objectives of the changes. Otherwise, a vicious circle will result: the more we try to change an initial model, the more we tend to reproduce it.

Setting up the market: economic reform

Although market reform has been underway in Russia for more than 10 years, there is no sign of sustainable economic growth (see the breakdown of the principal economic indicators[2]). The progress of similar economic reforms in the other post-Soviet countries, particularly Poland and the Czech Republic, highlights the failure of the Russian market. For example, the annual rate of growth for 1990–1996 was 4.4 per cent in Slovenia, 3.3 per cent in Poland, and 0.9 per cent in the Czech Republic.[3]

Table 4.2 Basic macroeconomic indicators

	1992	1993	1994	1995	1996	1997	1998	1999
GNP	85.5	91.3	87.3	95.9	96.6	100.9	95.1	103.2
Industrial production	82	86	79	97	96	102	95	108
Agricultural production	91	96	88	92	95	101.5	77.7	109
Investments	60	88	76	90	82	95	93.3	104.5

The current crisis has a systemic and *institutional* character; namely, it is the result of the transition from one model for economic organization, the command economy, to another, the market economy, which sets it apart from short-term cyclical crises (called Kitchin, conjectural crises), medium-term ones (called Juglar, they include four phases: prosperity, crisis, depression, recovery) and long-term ones (called Kondtratiev[4]). Douglass North, winner of the Nobel Prize in economics, considers the sequence of temporal institutional changes even longer. He feels that they arise out of the new configuration of the authority which, in turn, depends on technological, conjectural and other changes (see Figure 4.1) (North, 1981, pp. 207–208).

---

[2] Source: http://www.gks.ru, '*Russia in Figures – 1999*' (in percentage for the previous year).
[3] *Britannica Book of the Year 1999*, p. 788 (World Bank data), http://www.gks.ru, '*Russia 2000*' (1998 and 1999). The positive effects of the devaluation of the ruble in August 1998 account for the 1999–2002 indicators. The effects are no longer in force: according to the official statistical data, economic growth stopped by the end of 2001. This negative tendency is up to now counterbalanced by a rise in oil prices on the international markets.
[4] Long-term cycles (of about 50 years) are related to the appearance of new technologies, a radical change in industrial equipment (Kondrat'ev N., Oparin D., *Bol'shie cikly kon'unktury*, Moskva: 1928). For a review of cycles in Soviet history, see Sapir J., *Les fluctuations économiques en URSS. 1941–1985*, Paris: Editions de l'E.H.E.S.S., 1989.

Figure 4.1 Sequence of institutional changes

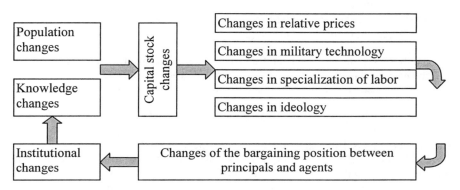

This analytic framework deserves attention since it enables us to consider an entire set of factors that contributed to the re-orientation of the post-Soviet State towards the market at the start of the 1990s. An economic crisis (a drop in oil prices), long-term stagnation in productivity and accumulation combined with a crisis of the central authority (centrifugal tendencies in the USSR) which resulted in a new configuration of State authority. It is the State, the licit authority, which took the initiative for institutional change in economic matters. When deprived of its *natural* character, the market becomes one alternative institution for the command economy among others. In fact, it is a coherent set of norms based on an organization of economic interactions other than bureaucratic control.

> 'Since the market is treated as an "institution"… the "norms" or "rules" that implies become visible' (Thévenot, 1995, p. 169).

Thus, how can we theorize about the flagrant refusal of post-Soviet Russians to respect market rules and 'play' a *full-fledged* market? The search for answers is all the more motivating since the market experience has never been foreign to Soviets, regardless of how paradoxical this statement may initially seem.

Parallel market as a starting point

The illegal economy, called the gray or black market, is both foreign and specific to the Soviet economic model. On the one hand, the illegal economy ensures the horizontal coordination of the economic activities that represent an alternative to the mediation and control of the State civil servants. On the other hand, the command economy can only function if the economic agents always enjoy recourse to illicit practices. 'Any product can be the object of the black market at one time or another as a result of the propagation of shortages' (Andreff, 1993, p. 212).[5] In other words, illicit practices were used in order to fulfill a plan when

---

[5] See also (Kornaï, 1990, p. 279).

resources were lacking. Then, the reciprocal, but *illicit* exchanges, between the planners and company managers, as part of 'plan bargaining', ensured that the planning procedure was more flexible and better adapted to reality. Moreover, the State representatives transformed the illicit bargaining practices into an effective means of control and pressure.

> 'Unofficial system – a result of bargaining – let the explicit system function well. Moreover, it transforms into a powerful tool of control. Agents, who act illegally, become hostages to the tolerance of their superiors' (Sapir, 1990, p. 71).

The interpenetration of the two sectors of the Soviet economy translates into a palette of colors, used to describe illicit practices, yellow, gray, brown, black, etc. The farther one is from the licit economy, the darker the colors. Moreover the range of colors reflects another problem, that of defining illicit activities. The adjectives 'informal', 'fictional', 'criminal', 'irregular', 'extralegal', 'unofficial' express the various qualities of the market that exists inside the command economy. The absence of legal support, the lack of respect for legal means, ensures that these adjectives belong to a common type. From this point of view, the notion of the extralegal, informal economy seems to provide the most general idea of the market specific to the Soviet socioeconomic mode (Olejnik, 1996a). Therefore, by informal market we mean any economic activity organized without reference to the Law and without the support of legal means. This does not mean that informal economic activities remain unorganized. '"Informal" activities, far from being open to anarchy, have developed their own rights and institutions' (Soto, 1994, p. 22). Personalized relations serve as the framework for the informal market, making the informal market and the 'small' society opposite sides of the same coin. The informal market appears when 'the economy is not completely differentiated from other systems of action' (Bagnasco, 1990, p. 159). Thus, is it possible to apply the theoretical indicators we developed to study the 'small' society, namely personalized relations, the non-differentiation of spheres, the duality of norms and the imperfect control of violence, to an analysis of the informal market?

Figure 4.2 Sectors of the informal market

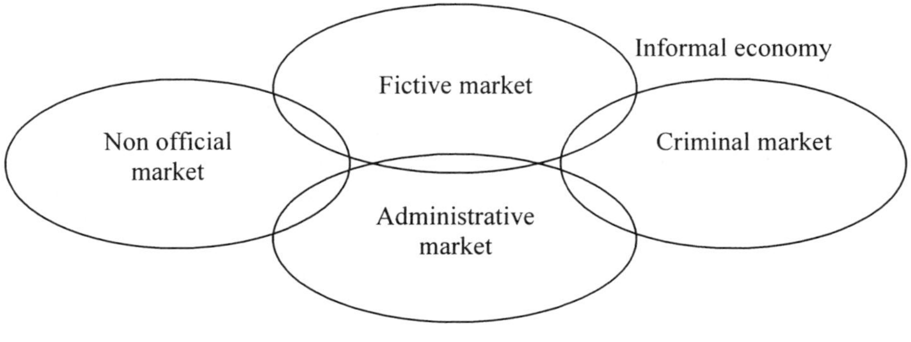

The informal market is broken down into the following sectors: an unofficial market, an administrative market, a fictional market, and a criminal market (Figure 4.2). The unofficial market includes the transactions that escape from State control and are not reflected in national accounting. Household production serves as a major source of the products and services circulating on the unofficial market. The following table illustrates the importance of the contribution made by households to total agricultural production (Jerebin, Romanov, 1998, p. 28):

Table 4.3 Share of household production

Agricultural product	1980	1990	1991	1992	1993	1994	1995
Potato	65.4	66.1	72.2	78	82.5	88.1	89.9
Vegetables	32.8	30.1	46.4	54.7	64.5	66.7	73.4
Meat	29.8	24.8	30.5	35.3	39.5	43.2	48.6
Milk	26.9	23.8	26	31.4	34.7	38.7	41.4
Wheat	0.4	0.3	0.4	0.5	0.6	0.7	0.9
Sugar beet	0	0	0.03	0.2	0.3	0.7	0.9

Household production was focussed not only on internal consumption but also on selling on agricultural markets (*kolhoznyj rynok*) where there were no price controls. The role of the State on these markets was limited to arranging the territory and ensuring a minimal sanitary control. Activities on the unofficial market are supported by the family structure. As a recent study demonstrated, 'The social capital of households is strongly associated with the amount of meat they sold' (O'Brien et al., 1996, p. 17). When a presidential decree on freedom of trade went into effect at the start of 1992, it allowed post-Soviets to sell anything on the flea markets. Although the almost wild flea markets reached a peak in 1993–1995, groups of elderly women selling cigarettes and other essential items have always been part of the landscape in small and large Russian cities (in Moscow, there is such a flea market near every subway station).

Unlike the unofficial market, which developed in its socioeconomic niche, the administrative market enjoyed a larger scope. The idea of the administrative market involves transforming things which are a pertinent part of the command economy into market goods, namely appropriating and 'privatizing them'.

> 'On the Soviet administrative market, one sold not only services and goods, but also everything the hierarchical society valued: social position, power and submission, laws and the rights to violate them' (Najshul', 1992, p. 70).

The administrative market arose out of the tendency to personalize 'public' relations which, in turn, created conditions favorable to the appropriation of goods and services. Hush money reflects the price to be paid for the good or service that is *de jure* public, but *de facto* privatized and intended exclusively for one's own group. On the administrative market, 'we sell the right to allocate goods, rather than the goods themselves' (Timofeev, 1993, p. 201). From this point of view, the post-Soviet context *naturally* produces sets for bribing.

Practices intended to cheat the State (called *tufta*) gave rise to the fictional market, namely the exchange of goods and services that do not really exist. Speculative transactions (*spekuljacija*) illustrate how the fictional market operates. According to a definition that has become classic, speculation is

> 'the purchase (or sale) of merchandise to be sold again (or purchased again) at a later date, and the reason for such an action is the anticipation of a change in the current price and not an advantage resulting from the use of the merchandise' (Kaldor, 1987, p. 49).

Soviet speculators (or *baryga* in prison slang) purchased items which were in short supply at state prices, taking advantage of their privileged access to their distribution in order to sell them later at free prices. The speculators convert their networks of acquaintances into profit for which the source, as a result, has nothing to do with the risk management characteristic of the activities of the arbitrageurs. In the same way that the State civil servants privatize public goods and services, Soviet speculators privatize access to rare resources.

Since the start of the market reforms, the basic transaction on the fictional market has changed form. In order to minimize taxes, company managers use fictional transactions, which serve to reduce or cover actual transactions. Although the Civil Code of the Russian Federation has declared fictional transactions void (Art. 170) and the Penal Code criminalizes some of them (Makarov, 1998), the motivation for committing fraud prevails over any possible legal proceedings. For example, an important portion of external trade is covered by fictional transactions. Let us look at one case, that of the payment of a deposit. A Russian firm pays a deposit to a foreign firm. Under their previous agreement, the contract will not be fulfilled, based on an 'abuse of trust on the part of the foreign firm'. In fact, the contract serves to cover the transfer of capital abroad: the foreign firm receives a commission and transfers the sum of the deposit to an account in a Western bank identified by the Russian firm.

One distinction between the criminal market and the other sectors of the informal economy is the criminal trusteeship that oversees it. Criminal trusteeship is ensured by the thieves-in-law whose influence is not limited to the penal society. Generally, the thieves-in-law fulfill four functions for those who take part in the informal market:

- To maintain the socioeconomic situation within acceptable limits, from the point of view of illicit norms;
- To exercise justice and settle differences between those involved in the informal market;
- To protect against unorganized crime; and
- To loan shark.

As in prison, the various sectors of the informal market have their illicit 'constitutions' governing daily activities. Although these constitutions are not written, their norms were known to everyone involved in the informal market. Take, for example, the commercial moral code of the 1960s: stealing is accepted, honesty is reserved for the Don Quixotes; man is a wolf for man (*Homo homini lupus*); one's conscience must be elastic; an innocent person is a thief who has not been caught; anyone who repents becomes a pariah, etc. (Dolgova, Djakov, 1989, p. 212). The duality of these norms is flagrant since any commercial employee was one of 'yours'. This should not be surprising: at the time, there was a lot of talk about the 'commercial Mafia', someone outside the network of acquaintances who existed in trade could never find a position in a more or less prestigious store, which automatically provided access to goods with limited availability. Although illicit norms were developed and applied spontaneously, the thieves-in-law occasionally had to intervene to maintain the illicit order. They ensured the absence of *bespredel*, namely they made sure the illicit norms were respected. 'The purpose [of the thief-in-law] is to disallow *bespredel*. If there were no thieves-in-law, it would be *bespredel* everywhere. You're talking about the business world? – In the business and the criminal worlds... If you go to the thieves-in-law, they can protect you against *bespredel*. In fact, that's all they can really do'.[6] Moreover, the concern for order only recently moved to the forefront of the activities of the thieves-in-law, towards the end of the 1980s.

The precedents of the role of the mediator in conflicts involving agents of the informal economy first appeared in the 1960s. Moreover, the thieves-in-law intervened not only in conflicts; they also occasionally served as purely commercial mediators (Dolgova, Djakov, 1989, pp. 171–172). Commercial mediation brings to mind the production and sale of trust by the Sicilian Mafia. When the parties to an illicit contract belong to diverse groups and there are no personal connections between them, the mediation of the thief-in-law, whose personal reputation is known to both, becomes inevitable. The question of the mediator's fees is always open. On the one hand, 'they [the thieves-in-law] do not ask for payment, they expect a service on the part of those requesting mediation, when needed' (Podlesskih, Tereshonok, 1995, p. 216). On the other hand, recourse to the patronage of the thieves-in-law is fairly costly. 'How do the merchants pay for the service? I'm not familiar with the current situation, since I've been in prison some time, but before there was a fixed percentage [of sales] that could not be increased or decreased. In one sense, there was a single percentage before'.[7] Police sources confirm the existence of the fixed percentage (cf. the *pizzo* of the Sicilian Mafia[8]). According to them, the sole price for the thieves-in-law was set at a meeting (*shodka*) held in Kislovodsk (Caucas) in 1979–10 per cent of net profits. Towards the end of the 1980s, this amount doubled (20–25 per cent of net profits) (Gurov, 1991, p. 124). The duality of this collection policy reflects the absence of a compromise between the world by projects and the domestic world: the informal tax is collected if relations shift to reciprocal exchanges while a chain of personal dependencies is created if domestic sets prevail over the logic of projects.

---

[6] Interview No. 25.
[7] Interview No. 4.
[8] The *pizzo* 'is set by the head of the family, based on the supposed or future income of the "taxpayer"' (Padovani, 1987, p. 62).

It should be noted that the reward also includes the price of certain other services rendered by the thieves-in-law and their lieutenants, particularly the price for protection against unorganized crime: small racketeers, thieves, bandits, crooks. 'Your friend, the merchant (*cooperator*), did he ask you something specific? – He offered to let me work with him. In what capacity? – I asked him the same question. He explained that I had to follow him everywhere, make sure I was with him. When I asked him for details, it appeared that he wanted me to be a body guard. He didn't say so directly, just let me reach that conclusion'.[9] Paradoxically, criminal protection reduces the crime rate. There is even some statistical evidence of a negative correlation between the crime rate and the scope of the informal market. On a regional level, the crime rate drops as informal transactions increase in importance and are better organized.[10] This paradox may explain the current reputation of St. Petersburg, which is known throughout Russia as the criminal capital and city of *bespredel*. A few of those interviewed stated that this city is one of the rare places where the thieves-in-law and their lieutenants are absent. '*Bespredel* comes from there. There are criminal groups that do not recognize the thieves-in-law. Particularly in Petersburg. I wasn't there, but I know it well. In the *Kresty* [a renowned prison in St. Petersburg], they don't recognize anyone. They're placed in special cells. It makes no difference to them–thief-in-law or not'.[11]

The volume of the funds controlled by the thieves-in-law was considerable: in addition to the illicit taxes paid by the informal businessmen, there were the voluntary contributions of the so-called proud criminals, who transmit the values of the prison sub-culture. They transfer a portion of their revenues from robbing subjects who are not protected by the thieves-in-law to the common funds (*obshak*). 'When I lived in Simferopol [Crimea], I knew the guy who controlled the city *obshak*. We stole something... So, I could choose to contribute or not. It was my decision. No one forced me to do it. No one was entitled to tell me, "You, you have to contribute". We had a four-man gang. Once we stole three, four thousand rubles. We sat down and decided that we would contribute two, three hundred rubles to the *obshak*. I knew Mulja, dead now, who controlled the *obshak* then. We went to his place: "Hi Mulja, here's our share. Here's our contribution to the common fund". With a tribute on the merchants, it's the same thing. The gangs that impose the tribute on the merchants must transfer their share to the *obshak*. They keep a portion for themselves; the rest goes to the *obshak*. Payments for protection, etc. Usually the thief-in-law controls it'.[12]

The funds collected by the thieves-in-law serve not only to help criminals who are arrested by the police but also to make loans to the agents of the informal

---

[9] Interview No. 24. This was a proposal made at the end of the 1980s. At the time, the small and medium merchants whose activities were legalized by the Act regarding the development of cooperation (1988) were called cooperators (*cooperatory*).
[10] Rossijsko-Evropejskij Centr Ekonomicheskoj Politiki, *Obzor ekonomiki Rossii. Osnovnye tendencii razvitija. IV kvartal 1997*, Moskva: 1998, p. 242.
[11] Interview No. 18. Interviewee No. 23 made similar observations.
[12] Interview No. 18. For reference purposes, the monthly salary of a Soviet engineer was approximately 120–130 rubles at the time.

market. On the criminal market, credit is often transformed into a means for controlling the borrower. At least, the logic of developing a long-term dependency prevails over that of maximizing interest. 'Did you collect interest? – I did not collect interest. It's a principle for me. A principle? So, what did your interest consist of? – Services. The borrower will do a service for me in the future. What can you ask him to do as a service? – To sign a document. A permit to build, sell...'[13] There is nothing to prevent the means for creating dependency from turning violent. The criminals occasionally try to artificially lead their clients into debt so they can then manipulate them, particularly if they don't really belong to one of their groups. 'Why do we go to the criminals? At the start, we didn't think about the possibility of problems. It was easier to get loans from them. "Finally, you've decided to talk with us. We're part of the same world," they told me. The first time I borrowed money from them, I quickly had a sense of their power and my powerlessness. We had an excavator – we extract sand and sell it. They [the criminals] placed a grenade under the excavator. As a result, we lost three days repairing it. They give you money and then immediately cut off all your sources of revenue. They do that so I can't pay the debt. Then they demand exorbitant interest and start to manipulate you'.[14] The logic of the 'small' society is more important for criminals than the market logic, an element of the 'large' society.

Therefore, there is a direct link between the penal and criminal worlds, on the one hand, and the post-Soviet economy on the other. The penal subculture is disseminated first in the criminal economy, then in the entire informal economy and finally in the post-Soviet economy. The State, disjointed and cut off from its subjects as the indirect means for transmitting the penal subculture, is completed by a direct means, transactions on the criminal market. The criminals are the organizers and the key players on this market. Moreover, the transformation of the thieves-in-law, who are 'crowned', as players on the criminal market, is a rather recent phenomenon, unlike their organizing function. In the past, they were prohibited from having interests in the illicit companies (the interest resulting from usury, for example) and they were merely intermediaries between the criminal market and the penal world. Our interviewees' responses to the question 'Do you think the thieves-in-law should do business?' reveal a negative attitude:[15]

---

[13] Interview No. 5. As this interviewee testified, certain State civil servants make up the clientele of the criminal 'bankers'.
[14] Interview No. 6.
[15] The large number of 'Don't know' responses is explained by the fact that the lower illicit categories are not allowed to judge the actions of the thieves-in-law.

Table 4.4 Attitude toward direct involvement of thieves-in-law in business

	Russia, N=1310	Kazakhstan, N=396
Yes	8.9	13.1
Yes, as mediators	6	6.6
Yes, as private protectors	5.3	5.6
No	30.2	26.5
Don't know	30.2	31.1
Under pressure of circumstances	5.6	8.8
No answer	13.9	8.3

The plurality of the sectors of the informal market gives rise to a great deal of divergence in its quantitative assessments. In fact, all we have are approximations of the turnover on that market. In the 1960s–1970s, illicit transactions accounted for 7.5–10 per cent of the Gross National Product, 15–20 per cent at the end of the 1980s, 23–25 per cent in 1996, 32–37 per cent in 1998.[16] As a comparison, at the end of the 1970s, sales on the informal market were evaluated at 20–25 per cent of the GNP in Italy, 11–20 per cent in Belgium, 10 per cent in Denmark and Germany, 8–10 per cent in the U.S., 7–8 per cent in Great Britain and 4 per cent in Switzerland (Dallago, 1990, pp. 21–23). A sectorial cross-section highlights the scope of illicit transactions in agriculture (the unofficial market) and commerce (the fictional and black markets) (Korjagina, 1991, pp. 40–41; Ispravnikov, Kulikov, 1997, p. 29):

Table 4.5 Scope of the informal market

Sector of economy	Rubles, billions, current prices		% of GNP
	1960 (USSR)	1990 (USSR)	1996 (Russia)
Total	5	90	23–25
Industry	0.3	10	11
Agriculture	0.6	23	48
Transport and communications	0.2	8	9
Construction	0.2	12	8
Trade		17	63
Medical services	0.5	6.2	
Communal services	1.6	6.7	

---

[16] Sources: Andreff W., *La crise des économies socialistes*, p. 215 (for the 1960s–1970s); Korjagina T., 'Analiz, ocenki, prognozy', in *Tenevaja ekonomika*, p. 40 (for the 1980s); Ispravnikov V., Kulikov V., *Tenevaja ekonomika v Rossii : inoj put' i tret'ja sila*, Moskva: Rossijskij ekonomicheskij jurnal, 1997, p. 29 (for 1996); Rossijsko-Evropejskij Centr Ekonomicheskoj Politiki, *Op. cit.*, p. 244 (for 1998).

Let us conclude our brief sketch of the post-Soviet informal market with a taxonomy of contracts on the legal, informal and criminal markets.[17]

Table 4.6 Taxonomy of contracts

Characteristics	Legal contract	Informal contract	Criminal contract
Trust	Impersonal	Personalized	Personalized
Probability of opportunistic behavior	It depends on the intensity of competition on the market	Low if the contract is made within a group of one's own people. High in other cases.	Close to zero if the contract is made within a group of one's own people. Close to 100% in other cases.
Sanctions available in the case of opportunistic behavior	Indemnification of the damaged party according to the Civil Code and the terms of the contract	Social sanctions (exclusion, boycott, etc.)	Physical violence
Procedure of conflict resolution	Referring a matter to the court, submitting a dispute to arbitration by a third party	Reaching an agreement without involving any third party	'Trial by battle'
Duration	Short, middle or long term	Short or middle term	Exclusively short term[18]
Mode of payment	Payment by check, banking order	Payment in cash, barter is also desirable	Payment in cash exclusively

In other words, the informal market fits in with the logic of the 'small' society. On the one hand, it relies on the support of personalized relations, the expansion of the private sphere and the discrimination of the partners between those who are 'theirs' and others.

> 'Instead of resulting in a purely market or competitive regulation of the informal economy, the lack of respect for the Laws results in the implementation of private codes and the development of neo-paternalistic relations' (Lautier, 1994, p. 107).

---

[17] Oleinik A., *Institucional'naja ekonomika*, Chapter 6, reading 12.
[18] As a result of the possibility of legal sanctions, the agents of the criminal market must change partners constantly and reconfigure their networks (see Turvani M., 'Illegal Markets and New Institutional Economics', in Ménard C. (ed.), *Transaction Costs Economics: Recent Developments*, Cheltenham: Edward Elgar Publishing Co., 1997).

208　　*Organized Crime, Prison and Post-Soviet Societies*

On the other hand, it leads to the intervention of the criminals, who reproduce the logic of the 'small' prison society. As a result, the experience of transactions on the informal market does not add much to the general experience of life in a 'small' society. The informal market is just one mechanism for reproducing the 'small' society among many others.

Two market reform policies

The parameters of the informal market as an element that makes up the 'small' society are similar to those of the local market that existed in medieval Europe and *preceded* the market economy. Karl Polanyi describes the local market in completely different terms than the so-called modern market, specific to a 'large' society. First, 'barter or individual trades do not lead to the creation of markets in societies where other principles of economic behavior prevail' (Polanyi, 1983, p. 93). The existence of an informal market is not equivalent to the existence of market rules. Also, can we propose a Marxist reading of the submission of the local market to the operating principles of a Soviet type socioeconomic system? Within the system, the market exists only in a transformed, estranged form (from the German word *Entfremdung*). According to Marx, the *direct* relation between work and value *changes its nature* in the capitalist system following the mediation of money, capital (Marx, 1975, pp. 323–323). In a similar manner, market relations can undergo a metamorphosis and change their nature once they are placed inside the 'small' society. They become a mere shadow of themselves in other institutional contexts.

　　Second, the 'small' society does not allow competition within the in-groups that serve as the social basis for the local markets.

> 'This type of commerce does not need competition and if it tended to disorganize it, there would be nothing contradictory in eliminating it' (Polanyi, 1983, p. 92).

Figure 4.3 Monetary form of value

$$\left. \begin{array}{l} X \text{ of good A} \\ Y \text{ of good B} \\ Z \text{ of good C} \\ \ldots \end{array} \right\} W \text{ of good ß}$$

The 'small' society reserves solidarity and mutual help for its own, violence for others, whereas competition as an intermediary form is excluded. In the words of Max Weber, strong solidarity does not transform into weak solidarity (Lindenberg, 1988, pp. 42–44). Third, the local market tends to substitute barter, or the exchange of goods for goods, payment in kind, or the exchange of goods for services, and *blat*, or the exchange of services for services, for monetary exchanges. These forms of exchange reinforce the closeness of the in-group, since they are *personalized* means of payment. As soon as they lose their personal character, adapted to the specifics of a concrete transaction, the costs of transactions become exorbitant. Let us illustrate this point with an argument borrowed from Karl Marx. According to Marx, there are three forms of value: simple, complex and monetary (Marx, 1988, pp. 57–74). The simple form involves isolated transactions of X amount of good A = Y amount of good B *or* Z of good C, etc. Complex form implies a chain: X of good A = Y of good B = Z of good C =… A monetary transaction involves the existence of a common denominator, a good β, which serves to measure the relative value of all other merchandises (see Figure 4.3).

The paradoxical situation of the presence of the market and the simultaneous absence of market rules provides a new point for looking at reform policies in post-Soviet Russia. Generally, there are two reform variations, genetic and teleological.

> 'In economics, the genetic approach involves focussing the analysis on the existing constraints of the interdependencies that form each economic system and highlighting the possible perspectives and modes of evolution, whether they are the most desirable or not' (Andreff, 1993, p. 12).

Therefore, in a genetic policy, we must take the informal market as it existed for a starting point. There is no *ex ante* predetermined point of arrival. On the contrary, the teleological policy focusses on a result set from the outset–the pure and perfect market as described in manuals of economics. By borrowing an expression used by Harold Demsetz, a North American economist, we could call the second variation of the reform policy 'the nirvana approach'. Numerous other definitions, changes that are induced *rather than* imposed, endogenous *rather than* exogenous, etc. are developed in keeping with the same idea of the opposition between the starting and ending points of the reforms.[19] Since the post-Soviet mutations provide ample illustration of both approaches, let us take a closer look at them.

Followers of the genetic approach propose to build a new building from the cubes inherited from the Soviet model. They speak about 'the process of complex reconfigurations of institutional elements rather than their immediate replacement' (Stark, 1992, p. 22). As we have already seen, the principal legacy of the Soviet model includes the elements of the 'small' society such as the informal market and in-groups. Thus, they must be considered as the principal resources of the market reforms, according to supporters of this approach. 'In place of transition we analyze transformations, in which the introduction of new elements most typically combines with adaptation, rearrangements, permutations, and reconfigurations of

---

[19] Pejovich S., 'The Market for Institutions Vs. the Strong Hand of the State: the Case of Eastern Europe', in Dallago B., Mittone L. (eds.), *Institutions, Markets and Competition. Centralization and Decentralization in the Transformation of Economic Systems*, Cheltenham: Edward Elgar, 1996, p. 115–117; Knaqck R., 'The Collapse of the Russian Economy: an Institutional Explanation', *Ibid.*, p. 261.

existing organizational forms'.[20] One of the arguments developed to support genetic reforms involves focussing on the tendencies produced by the Soviet institutional context. The destruction of institutions and organizations automatically implies the loss of a portion of the practical knowledge acquired during the course of daily activities. Filling in gaps in practical knowledge takes time and cognitive resources; moreover, it is never perfect with respect to non-discursive conscience (routines, habits, tendencies, etc.).[21] The destruction of routines forces the individual to pay attention to the processes that used to take place in the sphere of the extra-conscience; it reactivates sets. Radical changes are difficult for individuals; making them feel as if they are unable to control the organization of everyday life (Oleinik, 1998). As a result, gradual and moderate reforms are required. From this point of view, we often refer to the experience of the Czech Republic, which focussed on the legacy of the Soviet model.

> 'The [Czech] State recognized the properties of the networks of liabilities and takes part in meso-networks where the recombination of assets is negotiated' (Stark, 1996, p. 107).

Arguments close to these cause certain partisans of genetic reforms to take an extreme, even extremist position. They proclaim that no one should interfere in the natural course of matters. It is enough to legalize existing tendencies within the former system, without changing them. 'In order for economic relations to be free, written Law and the norms of customary Law must correspond' (Najshul', 1992, p. 75).[22] For example, Vitalij Najshul' proposed legalizing the illicit property rights on which the administrative market was based. According to Najshul', it was necessary to recognize the property rights of the bureaucrats so as to be able to purchase them back. Although such proposals were never explicitly implemented, other, less provocative ones were. Certain experts consider the Act concerning the development of cooperation (1988) to be the result of lobbying for the legalization of the unofficial, administrative and criminal markets. According to one estimate, 'up to 95 per cent of the former illicit production units (*ceh*) were already legalized [at the start of the 1990s] in one form or another' (Grib, 1993, p. 17; Gurov, 1995, p. 176).

---

[20] Stark D., 'Not by Design: the Myth of Designer Capitalism in Eastern Europe', in Hausner J., Jessop B., Nielsen K. (eds.), *Strategic Choice and Path Dependency in Post-Socialism. Institutional Dynamics in the Transformation Process*, Aldershot: Edward Elgar, 1995, p.69; see also Stark D., 'Recombinant Property in East European Capitalism' // *American Journal of Sociology*, Vol.101, n°4, 1996, p.994.

[21] Murrell P., 'Evolutionary and Radical Approaches to Economic Reforms' // *Economics of Planning*, Vol.25, n°1, 1992, p.84–85. The role of routine in the storage of the practical knowledge that is indispensable for company activities is developed in Nelson R., Winter S., 1982, *An Evolutionary Theory of Economic Change*, Cambridge: Belknap Press, 1982.

[22] We can also refer to the comments of the other liberal, Hernando De Soto: 'instead of claiming to subject reality to its plans, the State must transform the practices that have proven themselves into laws... We must find inspiration in extralegal norms' (Soto, 1994, pp.144, 207).

Yet, legalizing the elements of the 'small' society does not change their nature; at the most, their smallness becomes apparent and obvious. Simply legalizing the norm 'A member of your group is by force a friend' (or the more familiar form, 'Don't dump on someone you live with', to which we will return in the section entitled *'Market Perspectives in Russia'*) does not transform it into a 'large' society norm any more than legalizing the informal market civilizes it. Transforming the 'small' society into a 'large' one requires *interpreting* the norms of the 'small' society in a new institutional context.

> 'One principal condition for converting "small" worlds into a "large" society... involves surpassing the simple extrapolation' of norms (Ahiezer, 1991, pp. 71–72).

It is up to the State, a mediator between local worlds, to take charge of interpreting local norms. This refers to a State that is not absent but capable of getting out of the negative compromise with its subjects.

The inability of the post-Soviet State to change itself and the absence of collective Subjects other than in-groups in the post-Soviet institutional context leave no other option than an alternative reform policy, namely the teleological approach. There are several means of institutional importation. If the existing tendencies do not satisfy the reformers, they can look to the experiences of other countries, to a theoretical construction, or to an institution that existed in history to find a *model*. For example, the market reforms of the 1980s in Tunisia posed the question of controlling the quality of consumer goods. The Tunisian State decided to recreate the institution that existed up to the start of the 20th century, guilds presided over by *amins* (Kuran, 1989). At the time, the *amins* controlled the local markets and their personal reputations guaranteed the quality of the products sold on those markets. The impersonal character of today's market, as well as the arrival on local markets of imported products, has transformed the *amins* into a simple institutional atavism.

Recourse to a theoretical model is more common in institutional importation. Paradoxically, Karl Polanyi sees the expansion of the market in Great Britain in the 18th century as an illustration of this. According to Polanyi, the popularity of the works of A. Smith, I. Bentham and W. Townsend with members of Parliament accounts for the promulgation of the institutional frameworks of the market.

> 'There was nothing natural about laissez-faire, free markets would never have been developed if we had let matters alone' (Polanyi, 1983, p. 189; see also North, 1981, p. 156).

For a brief period from the Revolution of October 1917 until mid-1918, institutional changes in Russia reproduced another theoretical model, that of K. Marx and F. Engels. The revolutionaries tried to construct an entire society based on a 'unique production cooperative' that functioned in keeping with 'communist and proletarian supply and distribution' (Lenin, 1973, v. 37, p. 472).

Post-Soviet market reforms are characterized by two factors, the driving role of the technocrats and the importance of technical and financial aid from the

Western countries, which has enabled us to classify the institutional changes as an example of a double import: the experience of the Western countries and the neoclassic economic models developed in the framework of the mainstream economics. The population of the post-Soviet countries considers the power of the experts, technocrats, the best possible alternative (see Table 4.7). Support for the technocrats is support for purely teleological reforms since a

> 'technocrat [is] a policymaker who is motivated to pursue the objectives postulated by traditional *normative* economic analysis' (Mishler, Rose, 1995, pp. 12, 16).

Table 4.7 Popular support of different political regimes

	Monarchy	Military rule	Communism	Strong leader	Experts' rule
Bulgaria	20	15	25	45	66
Czech Republic	3	2	7	16	80
Slovakia	1	4	16	25	90
Hungary	5	2	18	18	83
Poland	7	11	18	36	60
Romania	17	18	12	31	56
Slovenia		8	12	41	63
Byelorussia	9	14	37	57	76
Ukraine	7	11	25	55	78

The dependence of the reformers on the technical and financial assistance of the Western countries reinforces the desire for institutional importation.

> 'Assistance is now conditional on the acceptance by the dominated state of an economic structure that complies with the views and options of the Western countries' (Badie, 1992, p. 60).

Bernard Badie's remark is illustrated by the endless negotiations between the Russian government and representatives of the International Monetary Fund concerning the parameters of the budgetary and monetary policy. Yet, can the teleological approach radically transform the nature of the market and deprive it of its local character?

Market expansion and increased atomization

One immediate result of the teleological reforms lies in the perception by the economic agents of the most apparent attributes of the market. Then the post-Soviets interpret them in keeping with tendencies that were the result of the Soviet experience.

> 'Individuals change their view of the world, if [and only if] a new experience does not allow for its interpretation within the former cognitive markers' (North, 1981, p. 50).

Douglass North and Arthur Denzau propose the following representation of the process for appropriating new rules (Figure 4.4) (Denzau, North, 1994).

Figure 4.4 Process for appropriating new rules

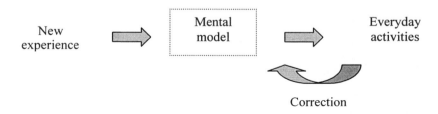

The sets produced by the informal market serve as cognitive markers during the appropriation of the *abstract* model of the ideal market. The market is validated by analogy, namely an analogy with the informal market. Thus, the principle of utilitarianism is translated by simple utilitarianism, the norm of freedom by negative freedom, subjectivation by atomization and ardent individualism, etc. In an unexpected and paradoxical manner, teleological market reforms reinforce the sets leading towards the 'privatization' of public space, giving it a market justification.

The implementation of the market in the post-Soviet context pushes the desire to 'privatize' to its extreme, with privatization taking place even within the in-groups! 'I was an officer and I did my military service abroad. "Volodja, I need this, buy it for me please," those close to me asked. And like an imbecile, I bought clothing, shoes, cars, and other things. When I was sentenced the first time, no one helped me. So, when I got back, I got even more calls. "We're going to eat out? Help me with this, help me with that..." I found a good job for my sister's husband... When I was sentenced the second time, no one helped either. Within three, four months, the firm [where the sister's husband worked] went bankrupt. Now they live off me...'[23] When studying the recent evolution of the *blat,* Alena Ledeneva made a similar observation. 'Acquaintance's "social" charge seems to have been overtaken by their "functional" (calculated) one' (Ledeneva, 1998, p. 200). Certain observers see this as a sign of positive changes, an emphasis on self reliance (*samostojatel'nost'*). Self reliance means that the individual must 'only rely on himself, not depend on the will of someone else or that will, incarnated in an institutional constraint' (Kharkhordine, 1994, p. 46).

This simplistic and, consequently, optimistic view of recent developments generated a great deal of criticism. First, it is a matter of *negative* freedom. It excludes any collective action, any common activity with others, any effort to change the institutional frameworks of everyday life together. Yet,

---

[23] Interview No. 39.

> 'the degree of freedom is a function of the individual's activity and his ability to use as many external bodies as possible since a better knowledge of their nature enables the individual to better fulfil his interests, to depend less on external constraints' (Il' enkov, 1991, p. 105).

This is positive freedom, the freedom to act individually and *in groups*, which ensures better control over the social and institutional frameworks of everyday life. Second, even negative freedom has its limitations in the post-Soviet context.

> 'Russian entrepreneurs want to be self-reliant only up to the point at which self-reliance ceases to be profitable, beyond that, they want all the State protection they can get' (Brym, 1996, p. 414).[24]

The inability of the citizens to get the State to serve their needs results in a negative dependence on the State that persists, despite efforts to acquire independence, which is still negative. Third, the imperative of self reliance ends in the complete de-socialization of the post-Soviets. Even the in-groups are progressively losing their importance as means for socialization. In fact, we are observing a

> 'fragmentation of the society: almost all social institutions and groups and networks which previously implemented social control over the conduct of Soviet individual ceased to restrain "the appetites" of the individual and leads to "moral deregulation" to use Durkheimian terms' (Shlapentokh, 1995, p. 270).

The solar system of the in-group collapses. 'You don't want to meet with other inmates after your release to help one another? – No, I don't. We make jokes here [about the situation outside]. There is no communication. People are closed there'.[25]

These tendencies towards de-socialization make money the only cement that solidifies social links. In the post-Soviet context, only the possession of significant financial resources ensures a respectable social position. Other efforts to organize everyday life socially become superficial. 'Have you thought about how to organize your life after you get out? – I have money. I don't need to think about finding the cash to buy a French croissant. I can buy one in France. So, what's the point of thinking? Think about what? I'll keep on living. I have money...'[26] This raises a new paradox. The weakening of social links in the 'small' society may provoke a tyranny of economic wealth without a stable and full-fledged market.

We usually speak about the dictatorship of the market, particularly the international market, when it becomes so powerful that it submits the other spheres of human activity to its logic.

---

[24] See also (Oleinik, 2002c) for an analysis of the willingness of Russian businessmen to accept a positive dependence vis-a-vis the State.
[25] Interview No. 1a.
[26] Interview No. 39.

'Capitalism is a market economy as long as it refuses any external control and, on the contrary, tries to act on society as a whole in keeping with its own interests' (Touraine, 1999, p. 21).

Once again, a false similarity could lead our analysis onto the wrong track. Market expansion is usually associated with modern society where the *existing* differentiation of the spheres undergoes a test of its solidity. The art of separating spheres requires permanent improvement.

'We must make a careful study of the manners in which economic wealth, once tyranny has been abolished, can itself take on tyrannical forms' (Walzer, 1992, p. 113).

The transformation of the production of public services into a purely commercial and lucrative activity, of users into clients, serves as an example of market expansion *within the contest of the modern society* (Wieviorka, Trihn, 1989, pp. 18, 52). However, the tyranny of economic wealth in the context of the 'small' society is less a result of the strength and autonomy of the market than the weakness of other socialization mechanisms. From this point of view, the current situation in Russia resembles the so-called 'wild' model of capitalism that existed in the United States in the second half of the 19th century. At that time, the weakness of non-market social links accounted, in particular, for the transformation of universities and philanthropic organizations into firms guided by the profit logic (Debouzy, 1992, pp. 209–216).

Regardless of whether a society is 'small' or 'large', market expansion hinders the stability of the socioeconomic system. On one hand, market expansion in a 'large' society increases uncertainty. In terms of game theory, the market can only result in a Nash equilibrium, the situation when no individual can unilaterally increase his gains. Now, many social situations involve a plurality of Nash equilibria or their absence. These involve problems of coordination (the existence of several Nash equilibria) and compatibility (the absence of a Nash equilibrium) (Schotter, 1981, pp. 22–24). However, according to the basic theorem of neo-classical theory (called the Walras – Arrow – Debreu theorem) there is always an equilibrium on the competitive market and it is unique and coincides with the Pareto optimum. The selection of one Nash equilibrium from among several is based on criteria other than purely market criteria.

'If pro-market policies do succeed in undermining non-market values, then it carries the implication that markets will begin to flounder as participants lose their sources of shared extraneous information' (Heap, 1995, p. 50).

Therefore, the birth of a risk society materializes the tendencies inherent in modern society.

On the other hand, the imperative of economic wealth slows the modernization process because it ruins the solid links, regardless of how local they may be, and prevents the development of public space. 'Between the market and private life there is a *no-man's-land* where we can still see the ruins of public life' (Touraine, 1992, p. 431). In other words, the market is a necessary but insufficient condition for modernization. A good modernization policy, a policy of building the 'large' society, serves 'to control the modernization process so that it does not destroy a good part of the reciprocal relations' (Kolm, 1984, p. 106). On the contrary, the Russian reforms may result in a mutation of the local market, which is as far from the classical market as from the market that actually exists in the Western countries.

Market perspectives in Russia

Scientific and political discussions about the nature of the quasi market institution which has appeared in post-Soviet Russia are not based on a univocal idea. A so-called Eastern European capitalism resulting from a recombination of networks of in-groups, a predatory rent-seeking system, a mobilized economy, a peripheral market economy close to the Latin American or Maghrebian model and a corporate capitalism–there is no shortage of alternative concepts.[27] Let us try to sketch out this new economic institution. Taking into consideration our interest in informal norms as a framework for daily activities, we must develop a 'constitution' of quasi-market interactions in the post-Soviet institutional context. The economy as a 'constitutional order' takes form as a 'series of rules or constraints, within which individuals and organizations of individuals interact with one another by attaining their individual objectives'(Buchanan, 1994, p. 90). The constitution for the post-Soviet market will probably include the following norms: simple utilitarianism, rationality of values, duality of norms, personalized trust, a search for protection and patronage.

Let us first compare the answers of Russian businessmen to the same questions we asked post-Soviets in general (see the section entitled '*A mistrustful society*'):

a) What is an ideal society based on in Russia?
b) What do you consider when making an important decision?
c) What can you use to resolve an important problem?

---

[27] Stark D., 'Recombinant Property in East European Capitalism'; Delorme R. (ed.), *A l'est, du nouveau*...; Hausner J., Jessop B., Nielsen K. (eds.), *Strategic Choice and Path-Dependency in Post-Socialism*...; Buzgalin A., *Perehodnaja ekonomika*, Moskva: Taurus, 1994.

Table 4.8 Russian businessmen's normative basis of everyday life

[01*]	(a) – Terminal values	(b) – Conditions	(c) – Resources (means)
Profit	8	1–2	2
Trust	5	5	4
Property	4	4	5
Family	2	1–2	9
Law	1	3	3
Moral	7	6	7
Freedom	6	9	6
Work	3	7	1
Empathy	9–10	8	8
Equality	11	11	10
Tradition	9–10	10	11

These hierarchies of values, conditions and resources are significantly different from those observed in ordinary Russians. Trust, the value and condition for ordinary Russians is transformed into a value, condition and resource in the minds of Russian businessmen; the Law undergoes a similar transformation; freedom is no longer considered a resource and becomes a value; work, which was a value, condition and resource for ordinary Russians, loses its status as value and condition. Let us attempt to interpret these changes by addressing the hypothetical constitution of the post-Soviet market.

Although profit maintains its negative value in the mind of businessmen, it ranks first in the hierarchy of resources and conditions. Do Russian businessmen make a link between maximizing profit and their own productive activity? Two factors raise doubts in this respect. First, unlike ordinary Russians, the businessmen do not consider work an important condition for maximizing utility (cf. a popular expression 'work will not feed you' – *Gorbom syt ne budesh'*). Second, work only moved to the top of the hierarchy of conditions relatively recently. The study we made in 1998, before the August crisis, indicated that ordinary Russians ranked work sixth in response to Question (a) and fourth in response to Question (c). Considering the fact that the progression of work is practically the only significant change with respect to the results of the studies of 1998 and 1999, we cannot determine if it is a long-term tendency or a short-term one caused by the crisis (Oleinik, 2001). In any case, the dissonance between the key role of profit in the everyday life of businessmen and the relatively negligible position of work confirms our hypothesis on the simple nature of utilitarianism in post-Soviet Russia.

> 'The State socialist economy generated a state of mind, a set of attitudes, preferences and expectations, such as apathy, unwillingness to take responsibility, lack of respect for formal rules, and "a grab and run" attitude toward economic gain, that are proving inimical to the growth of democratic capitalist and civil institutions' (Nielsen et al., 1995, p. 36).

Possibly the widespread belief in today's Russia that the greatest fortunes were made as a result of privileged access to strategic resources, with no connection with productive activity, is a result of this dissonance. The responses to the VCIOM question, 'What does continuing the reform policy mean to you?' illustrates this point:[28]

Table 4.9 Expectations about the results of the reforms

Economic revival of Russia	32%
Pillage of national heritage by "new Russians"	*27*
Absence of shortage	24
Breakdown of the economy, bankruptcy of national producers	*23*
Protection of private owners' rights	16
Democratic liberties	15
Economic dependency upon Western countries	13

During the study they made at the end of 1998, researchers at the Institute of Sociology asked interviewees to compare fortunate living conditions in Soviet and Russian society. It appears that, according to post-Soviets, neither society considered a determination to attain objectives and hard work (Mansurov, 1999, pp. 29–30):

Table 4.10 Conditions of success in Soviet and Russian societies compared

In 1988	*Conditions of success*	In 1998	1998/88
46.8%	In-born intelligence	45.7%	-6 ranks
43.6	A large number of helpful acquaintances	75.7%	+1
42.9	Good education	46	-3
40.6	Obstinacy in accomplishing goals	43.9	-5
40.2	Diligence	34	-7
39.1	Flexibility. ability to adapt to circumstances	60.8	+2
38.6	Good luck	50.8	+2
38.4	Close relatives at important hierarchical positions	72.7	+6
29.8	Political correctness	11.1	-10
25	Rich parents	72.4	+9

The second element in the post-Soviet economic constitution implies value-rational behavior, which is different from the norm of instrumental rationality (*zweckrational*) specific to the classic market model. The economic agent only freely chooses the means while the objectives are imposed on him from outside. Value-rational behavior (*wertrational*) is determined by a

---

[28] Kim N., Orlova Yu., 'Pravitel'stvo i reformy, maslennica i post' // http://www.polit.ru, March 14, 2000.

'conscious belief in the value for its own sake of some ethical, aesthetic, religious, or other form of behavior, independently of its prospects of success' (Weber, 1978, p. 25).

Many studies have confirmed the scope of value-rational behavior in the post-Soviet business environment. Up to 75 per cent of Russian managers correspond to an ethical type, compared to 3 per cent for the United States (Morozov, 1991, t. 1, pp. 82–85).[29] The idea of common economic activity focussed on maintaining personalized relations instead of on a result dominates the economic space in Russia today. The desire to maintain the company, regardless of the results of its economic activity, is very important for the economic agents whose careers started in the Soviet period. They view the company first as a *nexus of social ties*[30] and economic parameters rank second. The bankruptcy of the company, as well as the layoffs necessary to optimize personnel levels, is not acceptable for them. An expression, the company focussed on survival (*predprijatie orientirovannoe na vyjivanie*), was proposed to describe economic behavior that is guided by the imperative of maintaining the work collective.[31]

Figure 4.5 Elements of rational decision-making

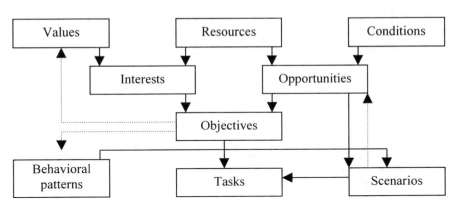

The data provided by our study provides additional evidence of the incomplete rationalization of economic activity. Instrument rationality implies a

---

[29] See also Radaev, V. 'Vneekonomicheskie motivy predprinimatel'skoj dejatel'notsi' // *Voprosy Ekonomiki*, No. 7, 1994, p. 97: 'Russian businessmen rank value-rational behavior first in importance and degree of attainment'.

[30] Cf. The concept of the company as a *nexus of contracts*, specific to the neo-institutional economics: Cheung S., 'The Contractual Nature of the Firm' // *Journal of Law and Economics*, Vol. XXVI, April 1983.

[31] Ikes B., Ritterman R., 'Ot predprijatija k firme: zametki po teorii predprijatija perehodnogo perioda' // *Voprosy Ekonomiki*, n°8, 1994, p. 31. According to data from 1994–1995, 60 per cent of Russian companies focus on survival and only 19 per cent focus on the maximization of profit (Dolgopjatova, 1995, p. 85).

complete differentiation of the elements that make up everyday life: values, resources, conditions, objectives, interests, behavioral patterns, etc. (Cymburskij, 1995, p. 19, see Figure 4.5). A comparison of the hierarchy of values with those for resources and conditions serves to measure the differentiation/lack of differentiation of these elements. Russian businessmen perceive trust (a resource) differently whereas all the other elements play a double, even triple, role.

Table 4.11 Hierarchy of values, conditions and resources

	Russia						Prisoners											
	Ordinary people [99], N=1351			Business men [01*], N=219			Russia, N=769			Kazakhstan, N=396			France, N=59			Canada, N=120		
	V.	C.	R.	V.	C.	R.	V.	C.	R.	V.	C.	R.	V.	C.	R.	V.	C.	R.
Trust	4	4	11	5	5	4	2	2	2	3	2	1	6	1	2	5	10	1
Family	3	1	9	2	1-2	9	4	1	8	4	1	9	2	2	3-4	2	5	2
Work	2	5	1	3	7	1	5	9	1	5	7	2	7	7	5-6	3	11	8
Property	8	2	5	4	4	5	10	10	6	10	10	8	11	11	11	10	7	10
Empathy	7	8	6	9-10	8	8	6	3	5	7	5	5	9	5	5-6	8-9	3	4
Moral	5	7	10	7	6	7	9	6	9	8	9	10	5	3	3-4	7	2	5-6
Freedom	6	9	4	6	9	6	1	5	4	1	4	4	1	4	7	1	1	3
Law	1	6	3	1	3	3	7	8	7	6	6	6	4	6	1	6	4	5-6
Equality	9	11	7	11	11	10	3	7	10	2	8	7	3	8-9	8	4	8-9	7
Tradition	10	10	8	9-10	10	11	8	11	11	9	11	11	8	10	9-10	8-9	8-9	11
Profit	11	3	2	8	1-2	2	11	4	3	11	3	3	10	8-9	9-10	11	6	9

We did not learn much from the direct analysis of the manner in which commercial partners discriminate between members of their own groups and others. At least, our interviewees refused to answer the direct question, 'What does "yours" mean to you?' 'Yours? The question isn't clear to me. I can't give a concrete answer'.[32] 'I don't know how to answer. I don't understand the question. What did the others answer? No, I don't know'.[33] But a subject related directly to the division between 'yours' and others appeared spontaneously during one of our first interviews. There is a very popular expression in social groups that are very different, namely the students at the Lomonossov University in Moscow and a work collective at an ordinary company, 'Don't dump on those you live with' (*Ne gad' tam, gde esh'*, direct translation – 'Don't shit on those you live with'). Some of our interviewees used it spontaneously and we decided to ask about the nature of this principle. 'A good, even marvelous rule... It's widespread in the banking

---

[32] Interview No. 4*.
[33] Interview No. 6*.

sphere'[34]. 'It's a very useful rule. It must always be respected'.[35] The structure of these rules implies an underlying discrimination between those with whom you live and those you meet without developing a lasting relationship. The attribute 'those with whom you live' determines the group with whom honest behavior is required, namely your group. However, in a fortuitous, *impersonal* relationship, the parties do not have to behave honestly. 'How do I view this rule? Positively. I have a limited number of friends and acquaintances and, naturally, I have no interest in ruining my relations with them'.[36] 'I view it positively. It's a good rule for work and for everyday life. If someone does not respect it, he will not be able to adapt to the environment. A man builds his network of acquaintances, his reputation. If he ignores this rule, sooner or later everyone will know about it and he will be excluded, if not punished'.[37] 'It's an essential rule. It's valid not only for work but also for everyday life. Everyone must maintain good relations with those around them. It's necessary for survival in a society'.[38] Moreover, certain passages concerning the role of violence in business imply that it is not excluded, in relations with *others*. 'Violence has no right to exist. But… We have to pay attention to the personality of our creditor and the amount of his debt'.[39] '*Because all our clients know one another*, we never resort to violence in our relations with them'.[40]

The duality of behavior in terms of the separation between members of your group and others is reflected in the specificity of trust relations in the business environment. For any market transaction, except for the simplest and most spontaneous, the partners must trust one another. 'A market economy is based on the existence of a set of shared values such that trust can exist' (Denzau, North, 1994, p. 20).[41] A simple model from game theory serves as an illustration. Let us suppose that a Seller will only sell his goods to one Buyer as long as the Buyer pays in advance. The Buyer either accepts this condition or does not, in which case the transaction does not take place. After receiving the advance payment, the Seller either fulfills his contractual obligations or disappears with the advance payment, namely 50 per cent of the contract price. In order to exchange money for a good or service, the Buyer must, therefore, trust the Seller (Kreps, 1990, p. 100):

---

[34] Interview No. 19*.
[35] Interview No. 17*.
[36] Interview No. 15*.
[37] Interview No. 18*.
[38] Interview No. 21*.
[39] Interview No. 16*.
[40] Interview No. 22*, our stress.
[41] 'Each system contains "impurities" which are not typical of the whole, but which are nevertheless necessary for the system to function' (Hodgson, 1988, p.167), this is the case of confidence on the market as a result of organic, non-contractual solidarity.

Table 4.12 Trust game revisited

		Seller	
		To fulfill the contract, [P]	To cheat, [1-P]
Buyer	To make an advance	10, 10	-5, 15
	Don't make an advance	0, 0	0, 0 N

The minimum level of trust, namely the value P, the probability that the Seller will fulfill his contractual obligations *in keeping with the Buyer's belief*, must be greater than or equal to 1/3 (~33.3 per cent) : $EU_{\text{make the payment}} > EU_{\text{do not make the payment}} \Rightarrow 10 \times P + (-5) \times (1-P) > 0 \Rightarrow 15P > 5 \Rightarrow P > 1/3$. Although the minimal level of trust varies in keeping with the contract price and the amount of the advance, without positive trust the deal will fall through. Moreover, with market transactions that are more sophisticated than purchase/sell, the level of trust greatly surpasses this minimal level. In this case, we speak of *extended* trust, as compared to minimal trust.

> 'Minimal trust [is] the ordering of the relationships required for basic market transactions. Extended [trust] sustains the cooperation seen in industrial supply chains and clusters' (Humphrey, Schmitz, 1998, p. 33).

An analysis of the structure of payments in Russian business highlights the desire of merchants to avoid advances (see the percentage of merchants who use a given form of payment) (Dolgopjatova, 1998, p. 89). It should be noted that granting credit symmetrically shifts the trust problem from the Seller to the Buyer. 'Before, we trusted more, which caused us to lose great amounts. We no longer give credit'.[42]

Table 4.13 Modes of payment

Modes of payment	By a banking order	In cash
An advance	31.4%	9.4%
Simple sale	25.6	35.7
On credit	58.6	58.6

The role of trust to cement transactions is perceived clearly even by the inmates. In response to our question, 'In your opinion, which principles support the market' they ranked trust first in the hierarchy of market principles:

---

[42] Interview No. 8*.

Table 4.14 Market principles perceived by inmates

	Russia, N=1310	Kazakhstan, N=396	France, N=59	Canada, N=120
Trust	31	32.3	57.4	73.7
Rationality	25.7	28.2	24.1	22.8
Empathy	23.7	30.9	27.8	14.8
Respect of the contract	20	18.2	66.7	47.5
I scratch your back, you scratch mine, *Ty – mne, ja – tebe*	14.2	12.4	×	×
Utility, profit	11.4	9.7	5.6	13.9
Freedom	9.2	13	25.9	40.6
Equality	9.2	12.7	33.3	38.6
If the adversary does not give in, he deserves to be destroyed	3.2	2	×	×
First come, first served	3.1	2.5	×	×
Trial by battle	1.6	1.7	5.6	6.9

The practical conscience of Russian businessmen is extremely hostile to trust. Only 25.8 per cent (sic!) of the businessmen interviewed [01*] selected the response 'We can trust people' (cf. 32.1 per cent of ordinary Russians and 14.6 per cent of Russians think this[43]). Moreover, as in the case of the inmates and the ordinary post-Soviets, the duality of norms transforms impersonal distrust into personalized trust, trust in your own group. 'What allows you to trust someone? – Personal knowledge. If I know someone personally for a relatively long time, I know if I can trust him or not'.[44] 'If I don't know him [a partner], I will not trust him. If we don't know one another, there will be no trust'.[45]

From the point of view of the separation between impersonal distrust and personalized trust, a high level of trust in commercial partners loses its paradoxical character. More than three-quarters of the businessmen (84.5 per cent [01*]) claim that they trust their commercial partners. They trust them because they know one another personally. Here are a few answers to the question, 'What are your principal criteria for choosing a partner?' 'Usually, we share a common friend, an acquaintance with our partners. There is a relational chain between us'.[46] 'The principal criterion is knowledge, personal knowledge. The other approach – the people I trust, who I trust a lot, recommend someone to me. But in this case, a

---

[43] The surveys conducted by the author as part of his coursework at the Moscow State Lomonossov University and the State University – the Higher School of Economics (Moscow) with several samples of students in law and economics indicate that their level of trust ranges from 5 per cent (a group of law students) to 35 per cent (20–25 per cent on average).
[44] Interview No. 4*.
[45] Interview No. 9*.
[46] Interview No. 21*.

relatively long observation period is required [to get closer to him]'.[47] 'I prefer to work only with those who are close to me and my friends. *They're mine.* You can't do business otherwise, particularly in the banking business'.[48] 'The capital principal involves trust. Without trust, we don't sign any contract. We abide by this principle in our relations with the Russian and Italian partners. This is most important for us. We even think that *trust is not enough, there must be friendship*'.[49]

The final remark highlights a tendency to transform friends and old acquaintances into commercial partners. Sixty-six percent [99*] of the businessmen interviewed responded that their friends and acquaintances often became their business partners. 'The special thing about Russia is that you don't do business with an organization, a bank, but with people. To be honest, it doesn't matter whether it is a large bank or a small one. If you know a friend there, one you trust and he gives you guarantees, then the contract will be fulfilled'.[50] 'Now, it's the common business that links us. On that basis, I maintain relations with old friends, I make new friends. It's all a part of our common business'.[51] It should be noted that the opposite, namely converting business partners into friends, only rarely occurs. Sixty-eight percent [99*] of the businessmen interviewed answered that their business partners did not become friends. This figure, which is radically opposed to the previous one, reflects the fragility of friendships that are based on common business interests. In this case as well, the absence of a compromise between the world by projects and the domestic world is observed. 'There are no friends in business. It's a principle. If you do business with a friend, it will end badly... when you need to share profits, there are no friends. Business and friendship are not compatible'.[52] 'Neither those [friends who become partners], or the others [partners who become friends] are true friends. If you have a friend you'll do everything to keep him. There's no easier way to lose a friend than to involve him in business'.[53]

In this way, we can acknowledge that the conflict between the internal limits of the 'small' society and the imperatives of the market world and the world by projects plays a driving role in the evolution of the business sector in Russia. This compromise, which is difficult to sustain in other institutional contexts, becomes unattainable on the 'small' market. A close reading of a novel already cited, 'Supplementary Ration' (*Bol'shaja pajka*) by Yulij Dubov, general manager of *LogoVAZ*, the firm that controls a large portion of the new car market in Russia, provides complementary arguments for this hypothesis. The story of a group of friends, researchers at a prestigious institute during the Soviet period, who gradually transform into businessmen, illustrates the conflict between the two logic

---

[47] Interview No. 15*.
[48] Interview No. 23*, our stress.
[49] Interview No. 4*, our stress.
[50] Interview No. 15*.
[51] Interview No. 18*.
[52] Interview No. 20*.
[53] Interview No. 21*.

systems. On the one hand, one cannot do business in Russia today without relying on your group.

> 'From now on, we will only hire members of our own group for management positions. From our institute! They don't know anything? No problem. They'll learn the trade. At least they won't rob us' (Dubov, 1999, p. 299).

On the other hand, the de-socialization resulting from the rules of the 'wild' market ruin even long-lasting friendships.

> 'Three good men get together. They have no money, but they invest their last cent into their common business. Their idea looked good, the first profits come in and they start to look at one another suspiciously. The profits increase – they stop trusting one another. The friends become every rich – nothing is left of their past relationship' (Ibid., p. 583).

The sets generated by the post-Soviet institutional context block the progress towards a civilized market. Quasi market transactions are reduced to the search for short-term profit in less sophisticated businesses. People need to develop trust on the market, but no one can trust on the post-Soviet market.

> 'In business, you can't trust anyone. Not your friend, not your brother, not your mother... This may shock you, but it's a common rule. An axiom, if you want. Any human activity based on trust is condemned' (Ibid., p. 155).

The *natural* reaction to three elements of the post-Soviet context, the imposed character of the licit authority, impersonal distrust and destruction of personalized trust, lies in the search for alternative guarantees for fulfilling contracts.

> 'In every transaction in which at least one party does not trust the other to comply with the rules, protection becomes desirable, even if it is a poor and costly substitute for trust' (Gambetta, 1993, p. 2).

In the commercial slang of contemporary Russia, the term *krysha* (the roof, literally, the protective umbrella, the piston, etc.) describes the *private* protection purchased from the State or organized crime. It should be noted that businessmen do not view State protection that is purchased more or less illicitly much differently than Mafia protection. The 'privatization' of services makes it possible to *sell* them to private firms and individuals. 'The roof? Ha, ha! This term can be understood in several ways. We only use the benefits of the official structures. Using criminals is just another headache. When it comes to the decisive moment, they may blackmail you'.[54] The words of an inmate provide a similar paradoxical image: 'Before, they [the merchants] paid the first one who came and said, "Hey, you're going to pay me for protection". Now, they think more about their security, they have their own body guards, their guards, or they go to the *RUOP* (a police department responsible for fighting against organized crime), other organizations

---

[54] Interview No. 16*.

like that. They are protected by them. The venality of these organizations is their fault. Their biggest fault. Corruption without limits'.[55]

The purchase of private protection has two sides, negative and positive. By purchasing protection, the company is trying to defend itself against extortion on the part of its 'protector', legal or otherwise. The imposed character of the State authority, as we have seen, transforms tax into a tribute in the minds of its subjects. 'The most serious problem is blackmail (*naezd*) by the Mafia *or* the income tax police'.[56] The businessmen face blackmail on both sides; the expression *naezd* highlights the unjust character of the demands by the Mafia *and* the State. Therefore, private protection serves as a guarantee against the otherwise inevitable unjustness of the protectors. Therefore, the currency of the Great [market] Transformation of the 18th–19th centuries, *laissez faire*, is given a more concrete connotation in post-Soviet Russia, *laissez faire without extortion*.

As for the positive side, private protection implies purchasing order in the broader sense: defense against the extortion of others, against petty delinquency, justice and the settlement of commercial differences. The local, *private*, 'small' order makes up for the failure of order on a macro social level. 'What did your support for your friends, businessmen, entail? – I took care of their petty concerns, contacts with the racketeers... How did you settle the problem with the racketeers? – We met (*zabili strelku*), we reached an agreement... You were alone? – Why alone? I arranged for the meeting myself. So how many aids did you have? – I didn't have aids, I have friends'.[57] 'We took care of everything, including solving family conflicts. God knows what can happen in relationships with neighbors... You're not happy with something, someone has offended you...'[58] The businessmen let their protectors solve their business conflicts instead of going to the courts and arbitrators. 'You can submit a conflict to the court. Then, you'll have to wait for justice for the rest of your life. With the Mafia (*bratva*) justice is quicker, but more expensive. If you were involved in a matter that was watched by the Mafia, it wouldn't take long to understand [the nature of the conflict]. Of course, you have to avoid violence. But what can you do if there is no other solution? Today, other options simply do not exist'.[59]

The recourse to violence should not be surprising: violence is accepted in relations with others, whether it is a matter of private protection purchased from the State or criminals. It is the principle of 'might makes right' that counts. 'The person with the more powerful protection is always right (*prav tot, u kogo kruche krysha*)' (Dubov, 1999, p. 699). 'When I faced a kalashnikov for the first time, I never even thought that there were gladiators like that. Now, it's a rule. *In this conflict with the parade of kalashnikovs, businessmen from another city, strangers* (ne svoi), *were involved*. The merchants from my city who had interests in Moscow, Petersburg, had some problems with the businessmen there. They had

---

[55] Interview No. 25.
[56] Interview No. 6*, our stress.
[57] Interview No. 22.
[58] Interview No. 5.
[59] Interview No. 5*.

their own protectors. We decided to meet. So, I arrived and I saw the guys with the kalashnikovs. Nevertheless, we tried to talk. However, now we don't talk anymore, we shoot'.[60] The State protectors organize parades with armed people less often, although it does happen as, for example, during a conflict between the State and the financial group *MOST*, which broke out at the end of the 1990s. But the State has other means than pure and brutal violence for exerting pressure. 'You have to avoid violence. But in some case, you don't have a choice. No, I'm not talking about the Mafia, criminals (the guys, *rebjata*). Anything can be organized another way. The person who displeases you will cease to exist in business. One day, the income tax police will arrive at his door, or the sanitary and epidemiological inspectors (*Sanepidemstancija*) will "accidentally" take an interest in his firm... Now, these guys (sic) will never let you go once they've caught you. They'll hook you up to a pump and start pumping out the money. Forever. So, it is possible to arrange things quietly, honestly, without weapons. But in the case of absolute need...'[61] Obviously, the State organizations' potential for violence greatly surpasses that of the criminal organizations. The State has an entire range of forms of violence, some apparent, others hidden. That is the only comparative advantage of recourse to the State as a private protector. Therefore, there is no protective umbrella more powerful (*kruche*) than that of the State.

Our survey of businessmen revealed that acquaintances in the State organizations serve to guarantee the security of business in the three sections of the Russian economy: legal, informal and criminal. Our interviewees ranked this variant at the top of the hierarchy of the elements characteristic to each of the three sectors (see table of responses to the question, 'In your opinion, which elements characterize the legal/informal/criminal sector of the Russian economy?' [99*]):

---

[60] Interview No. 4, our stress.
[61] Interview No. 12*.

Table 4.15 Comparative characteristics of the legal, informal and criminal economies

Features	Sector	Legal	Informal	Criminal
Payment in cash	Legal/Informal	2	2	8
Friends and acquaintances as commercial partners	Informal/Criminal	9	3	5
Payment of salary in cash	Informal/Criminal	12	1	4
Bank credits	Legal	5	7	9
Payments in foreign currencies	Informal/Criminal	11	4	3
Labor contracts	Legal	1	9	13
Private protection done by criminals	Criminal	13	6	1
Contribution to social security		10	10	10
Written contracts		6	8	11
Privileged contacts with bureaucrats	All three sectors	3	5	2
Payment of excises		8	13	6
Payment of taxes on profit	Legal	4	12	7
Payment of VAT		7	11	12

Violence is rejected only when the parties to a conflict are protected by the same private protector, whether licit or not. When there is no unique and absolute justice, violence flourishes at the borders between the various jurisdictions. For example, the protection of the thieves-in-law reduces the risk that violence will erupt one day between those they protect. 'If a thief-in-law protects a businessman and another thief protects the other businessman, and the thief-in-law with the most authority backs his own businessman, whether he is right or wrong, then we'll organize a meeting of thieves-in-law (*shodka*). The thief-in-law with the best reputation (*avtoritet*) will judge the situation. And we try to determine which party is right. The thief-in-law whose support was merely purchased will be uncrowned'.[62] Paradoxically, if the State cannot ensure its monopoly over licit justice, it should let the thieves-in-law act. This is one way in which to avoid the generalization of the principle 'might makes right' in the 'small' society.

The 'privatization' of public order reinforces the penetrability of the public/private border. Moreover, it takes all meaning from the notion of private property in the post-Soviet context. All in all, it is the protector who acquires possession of the assets that belong *de jure* to those he protects. At least, the right to possession (*ius possendi*) as the element that constitutes the right to property is transferred, voluntarily or otherwise, to the protector. This corresponds, moreover,

---

[62] Interview No. 25.

to the model of relations between a lord and a vassal.[63] The right to possession consists of the

> 'control over property possessed (*corpus possessionis*); and intention to exert exclusive control (*animus possidendi*). Control may be exercised by means of others, e.g. employees and agents' (Redmond, Shears, 1964, pp. 271–272).

Now, physical control is only the other side of the coin with respect to protection in a broad sense. 'Were you aware of monetary flows, business details? – No. So, you were only responsible... – I was responsible for everything. ...for solving conflicts? – I was responsible for everything'.[64] 'What do you mean by "your" store, "your" casino, "your" street? In fact, the store belongs to someone else? – In practice, it's my store. How can you say that? – It's my reputation (*avtoritet*) that provides protection... In conflicts, the one with the most famous reputation wins. We acquire a reputation as we get involved in more and more conflicts... We lose our reputation if we do nothing'.[65] The State as a private protector is no exception to this rule. It continues to intervene in the business of the *privatized* companies if they remain under its patronage. David Stark speaks in these words about the penetrability of the border between State property and private property in the Eastern European countries (Stark, 1996). The relations of the Russian State with the major oil companies, including *LUKOil*, serve as an example.

Therefore, we return to the direct link between the functions of supervising and maintaining order as observed in the penal environment. The thieves-in-law and their lieutenants do not supervise in order to punish, they supervise to maintain local order. It is difficult, even impossible to differentiate local order from surveillance. In summary, the post-Soviet market is based on two principles, locality and dependency. The context of the 'small' society brings the viability and autonomy of the market into question. The duality of norms specific to the 'small' society contradicts the imperative of generalized trust without which long-term market transactions are impossible. The search for a release from the impasse of distrust has caused post-Soviet businessmen to take shelter under private protection. The local market transforms into a market that depends on the State, organized crime, international economic powers... Unless Russian society transforms into a 'large' society, the market will not stop oscillating between two extremes, complete localness and just as complete dependency.

---

[63] The lord *owned* the land and could delegate the right to use it (*ius utendi*) and dispose of it (*ius abutendi*), along with the other rights, to the vassal. Socialist law treated a comparable judicial construction, the 'supervised management' (*operativnoe hozjajstvennoe upravlenie*) of State property. The Civil Code of 1994 maintained this construction (Art. 296¹) for the so-called unitary State companies.

[64] Interview No. 5. This refers to a garage that was protected by the interviewee at the time.

[65] Interview No. 23.

...orm

the market reforms, the penal reform, which also began at the start of the ,, is pursuing more limited objectives. It is not a matter of transforming prison society into a 'large' society, but of recognizing the minimal rights of the inmates and reducing the level of violence in the penal setting. On the one hand, the relative success of the penal reform, for which the dynamics of the infractions committed in detention serves as evidence, is a result of the moderate character of its objectives (Olejnik, 1999b). On the other hand, this reform is based on a logic that is completely different than the simple choice between the teleological and genetic approaches. Penal reformers were attempting to reconcile *existing* tendencies with *desirable* principles of organization. They interpreted the elements that make up prison society and institutionalized some of them.

> 'Pragmatic institutions can be subjected to a legitimacy test (by comparing the manifest aims with the needs of the community) and an efficiency test (by comparing the actual construction with the theoretically highest possible satisfaction of social needs)' (Wagener, 1992, p. 19).

Brief history of the Code for applying sentences

From 1895 to 1921 and from October 1956 to April 1957, the Russian (Soviet) penal system was under the jurisdiction of the Ministry of Justice. Outside this brief period, the supervisory organization was the Ministry of Internal Affairs (*MVD – Ministerstvo Vnutrennih Del*). Russian inmates were only returned to the supervision of the Ministry of Justice in 1998 (Kazakhstan prisoners, in 2001), although the civil servants of the penal administration continue to wear the uniform of the militia (green as opposed to the blue worn by Justice employees). The matter of the uniform would be unimportant as such if it were not linked to a much more serious problem, that of protecting the inmates' rights. From this point of view the supervision of the Ministry of Justice seems necessary and logical. Although the Soviet State recognized *de jure* the idea of inmates' rights,[66] the inmates only felt the first *real* changes at the start of the 1990s. 'Already from 1987 to 1990, the administration wanted to show that it respected human rights. For example, they could insult you or hit you before 1987. They could do what they wanted. I felt that. Well, in 1987… The changes were sudden, not gradual. Everything changed (*perestraivalsja*, from *perestroïka*). There and here too. The boss [the director], who considered you a wild animal the day before, started to

---

[66] A passage from 'Kolyma Tales' by V. Shalamov is pertinent 'On the barracks walls, we sometimes see the "Rights and obligations of the inmates" posted. Inmates have many obligations and few rights. The "right" to submit to a demand from a superior but not a collective demand… the "right" to write censored letters to your family… the "right" to medical aid…' (Shalamov V., 1998, t. 1, p. 141).

talk with you, quietly. They were ordered to stop being boors. And they started to learn that inmates are human beings first of all'.[67]

If a Russian inmate who has spent a lot of time in detention is asked to recall the most painful, hardest times, he will undoubtedly refer to the deprivations he experienced in the disciplinary quarters. The 'limited rations' regime was common until the 1990s. 'In the 1970s, I recall the pittance was only distributed to the inmates [in solitary] every other day. The first day, you were given breakfast and dinner, soup and the dish of the day. The second day, you were given *funt*, a cup of hot water and salt. The *funt* is a ration of bread? – Yes, 450 grams of bread. Usually, you're given 650 grams per day, but only 450 in the disciplinary quarter'.[68] Moreover, the administration often viewed punishment in solitary as an almost legal pretext for hitting an inmate guilty of an offence. 'When I arrived [in prison] in 1995, they used to hit us. Now the situation has changed. If they use physical force, it's more the exception than the rule'.[69] No letters, visits or packages were authorized for inmates in solitary. Under the Law, the prison director was responsible for determining the duration of the discipline. 'There were no limits set with respect to the time spent in solitary (*PKT*). In fact, it could last for the remainder of the sentence'.[70] 'Before, the boss didn't discuss things. He could confine you to solitary for four consecutive two-week periods. This was very difficult for an ordinary man to bear. It was like Buchenwald'.[71]

The Law of June 12, 1992 set a limit for disciplinary punishment for the first time. That Law resulted in a series of amendments to the Code for Applying Sentences (*Ispravitel'no-Trudovoj Kodeks*), implemented on June 1, 1971. In particular, the Law of June 12, 1992 explicitly listed the inmates' rights, including freedom of religious conviction, the right to personal safety, the right to information[72] about the inmate's rights and obligations, the right to correspondence, visits and telephone calls, the right to leave, the right to move about freely within the prison, the right to sign insurance contracts. The same Law also eliminated weight restrictions for parcels addressed to the inmates (before, the inmates could receive parcels weighing less than 3 kilos only during the second half of their total time in prison), abolished the removal of sleeping materials from the solitary cells, and provided for the public control of penal institutions. Then, the Law of February 18, 1993 ended the practice of deportation (*vysylka*) and exile (*ssylka*). The Law of July 6, 1993 ended the rule that separated those who were repeat offenders and those who committed serious crimes for the first time, bringing into question the existence of the 'white swans', the maximum security prisons created specifically to house repeat offenders.

---

[67] Interview No. 14.
[68] Interview No. 21.
[69] Interview No. 29.
[70] *Kommentarij k Ispravitel'no-Trudovomu Kodeksu RSFSR*, Moskva: Yuridicheskaja literatura, 1979, p.120.
[71] Interview No. 21.
[72] The free sale of the Penal Code and the Code for Applying Sentences was only authorized for a brief period of time after the death of Stalin (Rossi, 1991, p. 425).

The new Code for Applying Sentences (*Ugolovno-Ispolnitel'nyj Kodeks*), implemented on July 1, 1998, summarized these developments. It guarantees the inmates' rights, including the right to personal safety (Art. 13), the right to purchase items in the canteen, the right to visits, the right to receive parcels, the right to correspondence and telephone calls, and the right to walks, to watch TV, to read books and magazines (Art. 88–95).[73] The following table illustrates the progress made with respect to humanizing the treatment of inmates compared to the previous Soviet Code for Applying Sentences:[74]

Table 4.16 Treatment of inmates under Soviet and post-Soviet rule

The prisoner is allowed to (per year)	Code of 1998		Code of 1971					
	Minimal security penitentiary camp[75] — Ordinary conditions	Minimal security penitentiary camp[75] — Relaxed conditions	Minimal security penitentiary camp	Medium security penitentiary camp	Maximum security penitentiary camp	Special security penitentiary camp	Prison	Maximum security prison
Send letters	No limits		36	24		12		6
Receive parcels	6	12	2					
Have visits in visiting room	4	6	3	2	1	2		0
Have long-term visits from close relatives	4	6	2+1 (as a reward)		1+1 (as a reward)		0	
Receive food parcels	6	12	3	2	1		0	
			Only during the second half of the term					
Buy products in canteen (per month)	50%	100%	7+4	6+3	5+2	4+1	3+1	2
	Of the minimal salary fixed by the Law		In rubles, (+) : as a reward (cf. average salary was about 100–120 rubles)					

---

[73] *Ugolovno-Ispolnitel'nyj Kodeks Rossijskoj Federacii*, Moskva: Infra M, 1997, pp. 7, 46–58.

[74] *Ugolovno-Ispolnitel'nyj Kodeks Rossijskoj Federacii*; Rossi J., *Op. cit.*, p. 481.

[75] By developing the progressive system, the 1998 CAS provided not only for various detention systems but also various conditions within a given system (Tkatchevskij, 1997, pp. 86–99).

Inmates' rights: Law and reality

Generally, the inmates view the changes in the organization of their lives that resulted from the penal reform positively. We were involved in on-site work during the period that immediately preceded and followed the implementation of the new Code for Applying Sentences. This adds additional credibility to the judgments of those we interviewed: a majority has lived under at least two penal systems. In response to the question, 'Has your personal situation improved in recent years?', 34.7 per cent said 'yes' (Table 4.17). Recent developments encourage optimism on the part of the inmates, which translates into expectations of ongoing improvements in their immediate future. A majority of the interviewees, 51.1 per cent, responded 'yes' in response to the question 'Do you expect your life in prison to improve?' (Table 4.18). Perceptions are even more optimistic in Kazakhstan, as we already supposed, probably as a result of a sort of euphoria characteristic of the first stages of reform. Paradoxically, more optimists are found among Russian inmates than ordinary Russians. At least, the dynamics of the responses to the question asked at the end of each year by the VCIOM, 'What will the New Year be like for you?' implies this (Table 4.19).[76]

Table 4.17 Assessments of personal situation in prison

	Russia, 1998–2001, N=1120	Kazakhstan, N=396
Yes	34.7	50.8
No	56.3	38.6
No answer	8.9	10.6

Table 4.18 Prisoners' expectations about improvements in the future

	Russia, 1998–2001, N=1120	Kazakhstan, N=396
Yes	51.1	64.9
No	45	30.1
No answer	3.9	5

Table 4.19 Russians' expectations about improvements in the future

	1993	1994	1995	1996	1997	1998	1999	2000
Better than before	4	6	6	5	5	4	2	6
I hope that it would be better than before	35	42	36	33	28	31	27	49

In order to differentiate between the optimism generated by institutional reform from so-called natural optimism, characteristic of certain moods and certain

---

[76] 'Uhodjaschij god' // http://www.polit.ru, December 27, 1999. We have only reproduced the positive responses.

conditions, let us examine a new image of the administration in the inmates' minds. Although the responses to the question 'Are there positive changes in the prison guards' attitudes toward people like you?' are not univocal (Table 4.20), there is a positive correlation between them and the responses to the question on trust in the administration.[77] In other words, the inmates who trust the penal administration are more likely to expect improvements in their personal situations.

Table 4.20 Perception of the prison guards' attitudes towards inmates

	Russia, 1998–2001, N=1120	Kazakhstan, N=396
No changes	50.9	46.7
Yes, there are positive changes	20.4	37.4
No, there are negative changes	18	8.1
No answer	10.7	7.8

The interview results confirm that the most odious traits move into the background in the inmates' perception of the licit authority. 'People start to feel a little freer, a little more relaxed. Before, you could be hit for any infraction, now that's over. A man can let the guard, the head of the *otrjad* know he disagrees, if he thinks they are wrong'.[78] 'I wouldn't say that the administration's attitude [toward the inmates] is wrong. There's no more rough treatment, our relations are correct. If we compare the situation today to the past, well, relations are better, more humane. That can't be denied... We can solve problems together with the administration. Before, it was harsh, brutal. We see more justice now'.[79] The inmates are particularly appreciative when they are addressed correctly, which is the best proof that they are now being treated like men. 'Now, I can go to Andrei Yur'evich [a correctional officer] because attitudes have changed. Even towards me. I can talk with him quietly. He no longer considers me a wild beast. He tries to understand me. If there's a conflict in the cell, I go to the head of the *otrjad*. If he treats me correctly, I would never allow myself to get carried away. But if they were to start treating me like before, I would disobey again. I would act badly and look for any pretext to rebel'.[80]

---

[77] Russia, N=1120 *Are there positive changes in prison guards' attitude toward the people like you?*

Do you have confidence in the administration of this penitentiary?		No (100%)	Positive changes (100%)	Negative changes (100%)
	Yes	14.9%	49.3%	7.6%
	No	85.1%	50.7%	92.4%

[78] Interview No. 25. Cf. 'Why did they shoot? "For offending the guards". An insult, an obviously merciless answer, any "discourse" in the ranks could be considered offensive' (Shalamov, 1998, v.1, p.54).

[79] Interview No. 18.

[80] Interview No. 3a.

The key explanation for the gradual improvement in the image of the licit authority lies in its respect for the minimal rights of the inmates. The principles of civic duty, once unthinkable not only in prison but also Soviet society, are starting to influence the organization of life in prison. 'Beings are human when they are likely to have rights and obligations' (Boltanski, Thévenot, 1991, p. 233). The hierarchy of rights granted by the CAS[81] (responses to the question 'What rights are most important to you?', three variations at most were allowed) highlights the importance of 'non-economic' rights:

Table 4.21 Hierarchy of the most important prisoners' rights

Right to	Russia, N=1120	Kazakhstan, N=396	France, N=59	Canada, N=120
Correct treatment	68.8	77.4	75.9	54.8
Have visits	48.4	42	50	61.7
Receive parcels, send letters	35.1	23.6	46.6	20.9
Personal security	30.3	33.6	20.7	23.5
Watch TV	27	32.6	3.5	15.7
Buy products in canteen	18.7	10.5	13.8	15.7
Telephone communications	14.8	16.8	×	×
Have a walk	8.4	6.3	10.3	16.5
Work	×	×	×	48.7

The value of the right to correct treatment in the inmates' minds drew our attention in particular: more than 20 per cent (more than 35 per cent in Kazakhstan!) separate this right from the right ranked second. A comment by Jacques Rossi appears pertinent in this respect: 'At the end of the 1940s, I witnessed a brigade of inmates agree to work after having already worked 11½ hours for a simple reason. The site manager addressed them with the words, "I'm asking you *comrades*"' (Rossi, 1991, p. 409).[82] Internal regulations explicitly define correct treatment as follows: 'The penal administration must use formal language when speaking with inmates and address them as "Convict or citizen", followed by their family name'.[83] Now, the inmates do not reduce correct treatment to the simple fact of formal addresses. For them, it is more a matter of minimum tact, minimum respect for others. 'The head of your *otrjad* sometimes treats you

---

[81] A large number of inmates have read the CAS:

Did you read text of the Code?	Russia, N=769	Kazakhstan, N=396	Canada, N=120
Yes	54.5	36.1	55.8
No	40.7	59.9	37.5
No answer	4.8	4	6.7

[82] Cf. the usual response in the past to an inmate who called a member of the administration 'Comrade': 'wolf in the Briansk forest is your comrade'. The inmates had to precede every sentence with the phrase, 'Comrade, my superior...' (*Grajdanin nachal'nik*).
[83] *Pravila vnutrenego rasporjadka ispravitel'nyh uchrejdenij*, p. 6.

like a wild beast. You're not a man for him, you have no rights... I went to sleep on Sunday. He came and tore a curtain from my bed. I said, "Boss, why are you tearing off the curtain?" He started to shout, "Go screw yourself!" and so on. Then I went to his office and complained about his crudeness. "And how do you want to be treated?" he asked. I said that it would be better if he addressed me formally, we not friendly enough to use informal forms of address... So, they should not provoke us. Their rudeness is provocative. They're always provoking you. Sometimes their tone of voice is provocative. When you reply in the same tone, they start to refer to the Law. They put you in solitary for offending the administration'.[84] Correct treatment in a broad sense, therefore, requires tact and respect from a good distance in a world where there are no other means for protecting private space. Trust in the administration enjoys a positive and significant correlation (0.38 at p<0.05, N=874 in Russia) with its respect for the inmates' right to correct treatment, which proves our hypothesis concerning the direct link between tact and trust (see the subsection entitled, *Trust in the prison*'). Therefore, there is a causal chain that links tact to the optimistic attitude concerning personal prospects in prison through an intermediate link–trust in the administration.

The importance the inmates give to the rights guaranteed by the CAS does not coincide with the administration's hierarchy of priorities, at least not at present. The responses to a question concerning inmates' rights made the gap between the two viewpoints, from above and below, obvious (see Table 4.22, per cent of 'yes, I can value this right' responses). The right to correct treatment that is most valued by the inmates is also the least protected.

Table 4.22 Respect of the inmates' rights

Are the following rights respected in this penitentiary?	Russia, N=1120	Kazakh., N=396	France, N=59	Canada, N=120	Variation of rank (importance – respect)			
					Rus.	Kaz.	Fr.	Can.
Right to have a walk	56.2	51.8	83.1	88.3	+7	+7	+4	+2
Right to keep books and journals	52.9	56.6	×	×	×	×	×	×
Right to have visits	49.8	50.3	83.1	82.5	0	-1	0	-4
Right to receive parcels and to send letters	49.7	50.8	81.4	87.5	0	+3	-1.5	0
Right to watch TV	45.5	46.2	83.1	93.3	+1	0	+5	+5.5
Right to telephone communications	31.7	36.1	×	×	+2	+1	×	×
Right to personal security	35	31.1	76.3	66.7	-2	-3	-2.5	-3
Right to correct treatment	27.9	27.5	76.3	58.3	-6	-7	-5.5	-5
Right to buy products in canteen	25.6	29	81.4	89.2	-2	0	+0.5	+4.5

---

[84] Interview No. 35a.

What factors prevent the inmates from exercising their rights and could lead to a situation similar to that in Germany? 'In German history the recognition of inmate's rights in theory coincides with the ignorance of such rights in practice' (Feest, Weber, 1996, p. 253) As we will demonstrate, certain obstacles have a technical or objective character whereas others highlight the need for completely going beyond the model of imposed and hostile authority. The reform triggered this process, but it is far from complete.

Figure 4.6 Sequence for institutional change

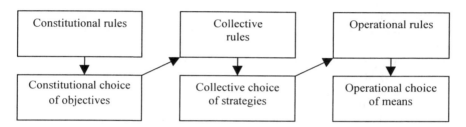

First, the centralized and bureaucratic form of management specific to the Soviet model is based on a series of administrative devices and the laws are only the tip of the iceberg in this case. Ministerial decrees, orders, standard regulations and regulations specific to each prison form a body of complex, heterogeneous rules. Even in a stable situation, the exorbitant number of elements in the bureaucratic machinery make it extremely difficult, even impossible for them to agree. Moving the system aggravates the situation by creating permanent gaps and blockages. The desirable sequence for institutional changes (see Figure 4.6) (Ostrom, 1990, p. 53) remains an unattainable ideal within any total institution.

The implementation of the new CAS (the change in constitutive rules) was not followed by immediate changes in the rules at lower levels of the penal system. For example, the internal regulations in effect were developed by the Ministry of Internal Affairs, the former ministry that oversaw prisons. As a result, the Regulations define the inmates' rights differently than the Code for Applying Sentences.

The fact that the constitutive and operational definitions of rights do not coincide facilitates the opportunistic and discretionary behavior of the penal administration–they transform into commentators on regulatory texts. 'I read one thing in the Code, whereas the assistant director refers to other documents. He sticks to the explanations provided by his superiors. He does not hold with the Code established by the State'.[85] 'The Law is enacted, whereas its application

---

[85] Interview No. 5.

remains obscure'.⁸⁶ Our interviewees provided numerous examples to illustrate the obscurity and contradictory character of the application of the CAS.

Inmates are allowed to purchase TV sets in order to exercise their right to watch it, but only *collectively*. Private use is prohibited according to the Code commentators. Yet, one single TV set is not sufficient for a hundred people, which gives rise to small conflicts concerning the program to be watched, etc. Next, no one understands why inmates are not allowed to own tape recorders. The internal regulations explicitly authorize only TV sets, according to the penal administration. 'I personally broke three tape recorders. They [the administration] came to take the tape recorders and I broke them so they couldn't remove them. I own these tape recorders legally. I have all the documents… How can they forbid me to use them?'⁸⁷ The right to watch television often contradicts the requirements of the internal regulations with respect to the use of time. The networks prefer to broadcast movies and interesting programs at the prime time when there is a large audience (from 8:00 p.m. to 11:00 p.m.), whereas the inmates are obliged to go to bed at 10:00 p.m. 'A man works all day and would like to watch TV in the evening. They broadcast movies then. You can only watch movies in the evening. A movie starts at 9:00 p.m. and finishes at 11:00 p.m. Well, at 10:00 p.m., I have to go to sleep… I miss the movie…'.⁸⁸

Our interviewees often mentioned economic problems as obstacles hindering the exercise of their rights. The economic crisis in the country left most inmates unemployed, even in the camps in Northern Russia which were organized in the 1930s–1940s for the sole purpose of logging in virgin forests. In the forestry colonies (that is the official term – *Upravlenie Lesnyh Ispravitel'nyh Uchrejdenij, ULIU*) we visited, only one in ten inmates works and earns his living.⁸⁹ Moreover, few jobs provide a relatively satisfactory income: as a general rule, the inmates earn 30–100 rubles. It appears that they form a unique socio-professional category whose income does not exceed the minimum salary guaranteed by Law, namely approximately 80 rubles.⁹⁰

During the Soviet period, the inmate in the forestry colonies could earn up to several hundred rubles per month. 'Under the communists, you would have 10,000–15,000 rubles when you got out'.⁹¹ In the past, an inmate needed only 5–7 rubles to buy the essentials (tea, cigarettes, preserves, pastries), but today, since the prices were freed, 400–500 rubles is not sufficient. 'Five rubles were enough. After a trip to the canteen, the night table was full. Today, people work – and don't earn

---

⁸⁶ Interview No. 29.
⁸⁷ Interview No. 38.
⁸⁸ Interview No. 35a.
⁸⁹ The unemployment rate in Russia was approximately 1 per cent en 1996, 12.5 per cent in 1997, 14 per cent in 1998, 13 per cent in 1999. Source: http://gks.ru, '*Russia in Figures – 1999*', '*Russia – 2000*'.
⁹⁰ In January 1999, the minimum for living was 885 rubles per month, per capita, the average income – 1,207 rubles (Ministerstvo truda i social'nogo razvitija RF, *Monitoring 'Dohody i uroven' jizni naselenija'*, I quarter 1999).
⁹¹ Interview No. 38. It should be noted that the average salary was 100–120 rubles and the price of a car, 5,000 rubles.

anything'.[92] Under these conditions, most inmates cannot buy the items they want from the canteen unless they are assisted by their families. Naturally, most of our interviewees, namely 55.8 per cent (65.9 per cent in Kazakhstan), think that the lack of work for inmates worsens their situation. 'Before, they let the inmates live. Everyone had work, everyone earned their living... Now that's been taken away from people. Penal society has started to differentiate. Some have everything and others have nothing'.[93] Possibly the explanation for the willingness of certain inmates to return to Soviet prison life lies in the worsening of economic conditions. Almost one inmate out of eight would have liked to serve his sentence during the Brezhnev period (during the 1970s, see the table of the responses to the question 'When would you have preferred to serve your sentence?').[94]

Table 4.23 Preferable time for serving the current sentence

	Russia, N=1120	Kazakhstan, N=396
Today	20.1	19.7
In 1991–1997	13.5	7.8
During Brezhnev's rule	11.7	14.6
In 1985–1990	3.5	3
Before 1917 revolution	1.3	0.8
During Stalin's rule	0.8	0.5
Anywhere and anytime except today's Russia (Kazakhstan)	41.6	48.5
No answer	7.5	5.1

In any event, the economic problems have a rather objective character and their solution does not depend on the will of the penal administration. However, references to objective difficulties do not clarify the nature of the final obstacle to the defense of the inmates' rights that we were able to discover. The new Code for Applying Sentences gave the inmates rights without establishing mechanisms for defending them. The administration's goodwill is the only guarantee. 'Here there is no mechanism for defending rights... Everything depends on the personality [of the penal administration staff]'.[95] 'Everything will be organized to please the superior (*nachal'nik*). The Code means nothing for him. He defines the rules himself'.[96] Moreover, if an inmate goes to anyone at all (the solicitor, the Ministry of Justice) to defend his rights, he will be treated even worse. That was a common

---

[92] Interview No. 24. Interviewees Nos. 21, 22, 37 and 38 confirm this.
[93] Interview No. 35. Cf. 'The poor individual cannot shop at the canteen or only shops a minimum amount' (Marchetti, 1997, p. 107).
[94] It should be noted that the current system is more popular with inmates than ordinary Russians. Only 5 per cent of ordinary Russians in 1998 and 13 per cent in 2000 supported the 'current system', compared to the other socioeconomic systems possible ('Strana, reformy, primety' // http://www.polit.ru, January 12, 2000 [VCIOM data]).
[95] Interview No. 11.
[96] Interview No. 16.

practice during the Soviet period. 'Complaining about the administration only made the situation worse. Complainants were pressured on two sides, by the administration and the *blatnye*. At the request of the administration, the *blatnye*, started to torture them, to humiliate them: "Shit for you". And so on. The *blatnye* isolated them [the complainants] socially'.[97] In another form, this remains a dominant tendency today. 'So I can defend my rights? Ha, ha! Well, people had to be changed, not the Code. Well, I'll explain. We depend on the administration; the administration maintains good relations with the Department (*Upravlenie*), the solicitor, the magistrates... For example, if I file a complaint [against the administration], it gets back to the administration. Nothing happens'.[98] The procedure for filing a complaint does not exclude the abuse of power: 'the inmates submit their requests, proposals and complaints in an envelope to the administration. The administration sends them to the recipients'.[99]

This discussion demonstrates that the penal reform does not promote the transformation of the penal world into a 'large' society. The lack of impersonal legal means for defending rights makes them personal. We encountered numerous penal civil servants who sincerely try to humanize the treatment of inmates. Yet, there are also others who consider the reform as a 'game involving human rights' (according to the expression used by the head of an *otrjad* in a colony in Northern Russia). 'They can address me formally, but no more... If they wanted to, they would trample you underfoot. I'm not exaggerating...'[100] In a torn society, there is no guarantee that the rights established by Law will be respected in everyday life and that they will structure daily relations among people. Therefore, the relative success of the penal reform cannot be explained either by the implementation of new, more democratic mechanisms for controlling the application of sentences or by opening up the prison to the outside. According to our hypothesis, it is a weaving together of two tendencies, one concerning humanization and the other

---

[97] Interview No. 18. Cf. 'Complaints against the administration often turn against the complainants. For example, the administration gives the names of the complainants to the *blatnye*' (Rossi, 1991, p. 112).

[98] Interview No. 5. Interviewee No. 38 also stated that the administration tries to maintain good relations with the regulatory groups, occasionally by means of bribes that result in the 'taxation' of the illicit production of the inmates (see the section entitled '*Characteristics of relations with the licit authority*').

[99] *Pravila vnutrennego rasporjadka ispravitel'nyh uchrejdenij*, p. 10. The inmates do not believe that the administration respects the confidentiality of their messages. Some of those interviewed asked us, as an illicit favor, to place the letters addressed to the solicitor in a mail box outside the colony. At the least, that would have reassured them that the complaints would be sent.

[100] Interview No. 13. Cf. the character in 'Kolyma Tales', the guard Fadeev, who addressed the inmates formally and kicked them at the same time (Shalamov, 1998, v. 1, p. 54). Some of our interviewees recall the so-called 'prophylactic' operations at the start of the 1990s, when the specialized police forces (*OMON – Otrjad Milicii Osobogo Naznachenija*) came into prisons and started to beat all of the inmates *for no reason* (Interviews Nos. 3a, 14, 18 [at Zitomir, the Ukraine; the Moscow prison, *Butyrka*], 38 [at Skarlahta, in the Arkhangelsk region]).

concerning the reproduction of the elements of the 'small' society that facilitate the control of violence.

Interaction of formal and informal norms

Unlike the market reforms, the penal reform was never exclusively teleological. It is based on a long tradition of relations between two branches of authority in prison, the licit and the illicit. The licit authority was never, even during the Stalinist period, able to ensure total control over the daily lives of inmates. It appears that this type of control cannot be achieved at all within a system based on imprisonment in groups. As a result, the licit authority sought a compromise with its clandestine counterpart. Moreover,

> 'rather than speaking of an informal and formal system, we should refer to controlled regulation and autonomous regulation... the real work is a compromise between two regulatory systems' (Reynaud, 1989, pp. 106, 108).

Let us take a closer look at the figures of this compromise.

Although the hypothesis that the administration initiated the appearance of thieves-in-law cannot be verified, numerous facts justify its support, direct or indirect, of their efforts to maintain order in the penal society. At the end of the 1940s, the administration appointed *blatnye* to head the brigades (*brigadir*), giving them a significant position in the licit penal hierarchy (Rossi, 1991, p. 38). During the 1960s–1970s, the directors of certain prisons that had no thieves-in-law found one to maintain order. 'Before, there were colonies with 10,000 men each. There was one thief-in-law, brought in specifically by the boss. The thief-in-law supervised the colony'.[101] It is only an impression that the administration plays no role in the so-called 'black' colonies (*chernye*) that are controlled by the thieves-in-law. On the contrary, the administration delegates part of its power to the thieves-in-law or their lieutenants in order to ensure order and the attainment of the plan objectives. The 'black' colonies provide an image of the amalgamation of the two branches of authority. 'Where is life easier for a "man"? – Maybe in a "black" colony. A man in a "black" colony lives peacefully, no one angers him, he has everything. *The administration and the licit authority give him more attention*, etc.'.[102] Here is an image of the compromise that is possible with respect to the organization of everyday life in the 'black' colony. 'There it was almost freedom... We had to go to sleep at 10:00 p.m., but how can you sleep at that time in the summer? In the "black" colony we stayed quietly in a local zone, we walked even. If you want to sleep, you go to sleep. The important thing is getting up on time in the morning'.[103]

---

[101] Interview No. 21. Researchers at a research institute under the jurisdiction of the Ministry of Internal Affairs justified the arrangements between the administration and the thieves-in-law concerning their participation in the organization of everyday life in the colonies (Podlesskih, Tereshonok, 1995, pp. 70–71, 88–89).

[102] Interview No. 24, our stress.

[103] Interview No. 39.

Recent developments have only transformed these tendencies into elements of a coherent and explicit policy. It is no accident that the first steps towards penal reform at the start of the 1990s coincided with the implementation of the illicit guards, the *smotrjashie*. They started to expand at precisely that time. 'Before, it was not done at the initiative of the administration [the illicit guards]. It came from our side. So now, everything goes through the administration. I understand now: the administration lets them live... it gives them a few privileges... and imposes its will implicitly. Within acceptable limits, of course. <u>Can one become an illicit guard without the support of the administration</u>? – No'.[104] The administration has two objectives. First, the tolerant attitude towards the illicit guards allowed the administration to maintain order, whether that is licit or illicit. 'If there is an illicit guard in the *otrjad*, the administration must support him. Because it makes him responsible for maintaining order. So there is no *bespredel*'.[105] Second, the administration supports the justice of the illicit guards because that makes relations in the prison more humane, less violent. In this way, the administration helps attain the objectives of the penal reform.

Changes in the relations between the two branches of power cannot be unilateral. The new attitude of the licit authority with respect to the *smotrjashie* casts doubt on one of the basic norms of the penal sub-culture (*ponjatia*), 'do not go to the administration'. In the section entitled '*Duality of norms*' we saw that this rule is progressively losing its influence of the behavior of the 'men'. There is a significant and negative correlation (-0.26 at p<0.05, N=857 in Russia) between trust in the administration and the fact of agreeing with the prohibition of contact with it. Moreover, the *blatnye* are also starting not to respect this prohibition. The illicit guards accept contact with the administration since it gives them complementary power resources. 'Today, each member of the administration can summon any *blatnoj*. He will come and agree to talk'.[106] These words from a member of the administration illustrate the fact that the opposition between the licit and illicit guards has shifted to the background, whereas the importance of cooperation is growing. 'The *blatnye* have changed a lot. There is no longer any opposition between them and the administration. If he [a *blatnoj*] doesn't please us, we'll do what we want with him. *They are responsible for order, particularly at night. It's a sort of division of work.* We require order from them, guarantees against the situation getting worse'.[107] The close ties of the illicit guards with the administration are particularly obvious in the gaols. The administration creates favorable conditions so that a good candidate from its point of view becomes the *smotrjashij* in a cell: it organizes his transfer from one cell to another, it can delay his transfer to the colony, etc. 'There [in the cells for young people] the administration appoints inmates to be illicit guards. It chooses them based on their

---

[104] Interview No. 16.
[105] Interview No. 2.
[106] Interview No. 18.
[107] Interview No. 40, our stress.

records and their sentence. Those with short sentences, one year or 18 months, are preferred'.[108]

In summary, only the administration benefits from delegating a part of its power to the illicit guards. It maintains order in the 'small' society, even permitting a more human order. 'The administration accepts that our life is based on the *ponjatija*. The *blatnye* can't do anything without the administration. I believe this deeply, based on 20 years' experience…'[109] Should we view the refusal to radically democratize the prison world, to transform it into a 'large' society as the exorbitant price to be paid for maintaining order? Order which does not coincide with an ideal type *versus* tests for reproducing the ideal type that casts doubt on the order and for which a positive result is not assured – is this a false dilemma? We will leave these questions without a response for now.

At the least, we must consider an analogy with a model for relations between the Italian state and the Mafia until the first half of the 1980s as soon as we look at how the penal reform is progressing in Russia. Despite their apparent rivalry, the Mafia and the Italian government found several spheres in which their interests coincided and complemented one another perfectly.

> 'In the traditional situation, the relationship between the Mafia head and the politician is a classical Patron – Client relationship' (Arlacchi, 1986, p. 58).

In particular, the compromise between the two branches of authority, licit and illicit, concerned maintaining order, electoral mobilization and collecting taxes. With respect to maintaining order, we have already indicated that the crime rate in the neighborhoods in Palermo, where police cars have never been seen, is not greater than that in the neighborhoods close to a police station. Regardless of the means used by the police and the Mafia to maintain order, the situation remains within acceptable limits for the population. The absence of collective actors other than the family and the networks of acquaintances in the 'small' society make electoral mobilization necessary. Therefore, the Mafia serves as an intermediary and ensures a link between the political sphere and the family, or private sphere (Arlacchi, 1986, pp. 54–56).[110] Finally, the public's distrust of the State and the normalcy of cheating the government hinder the government's fiscal interest. Delegating the right to collect income tax to the Mafia deprives income tax of its character as a tribute and taxation comes to be associated in the minds of the taxpayers with the illicit authority, which is less hostile and more present in their everyday life.

---

[108] Interview No. 32. Interviewee No. 34 confirmed this.
[109] Interview No. 18.
[110] As a result of the lack of autonomous mobilization, the head of the allied forces in WWII had to address the Mafia leaders for help in disembarking Allied forces in Sicily and for ensuring municipal management (Padovani, 1987, pp. 157–158; Rusakov, 1969, pp. 72–75).

'In Sicily, until 1984 tax collection was contracted through a private firm run by the Salvos, members of the Salemi family (for legal commission of up to 10 per cent of the taxes they collected)' (Gambetta, 1993, p. 160; see also Padovani, 1987, p. 175).

The licit authority which is unable to see that the 'large' society functions properly always tends to seek collusion with the illicit authority and join forces with it.

Market imperative: on the interference of the two reforms

Our analysis of the penal reform would be incomplete if we did not take into consideration the influences of the market imperative on the penal world. In fact, the expansion of the market rules is due to factors outside the penal world, principally market reforms in the post-Soviet society. In prison, even the circulation of money was always forbidden *de jure* and very limited *de facto*.[111] Putting prison society to the market test represents a natural testing of the stability of the 'small' society, of its resistance to external shocks. Our initial hypothesis is based on the inherent instability of this social construction. Every shock that destabilizes the 'small' society accentuates its dependency on the State or any other licit authority. When a relatively important change is imposed, the 'small' society stops reproducing. Its natural equilibrium is neither lasting nor viable. The market imperative 'privatizes' the penal society just as it does the post-Soviet society.

Despite the walls that separate the penal world from the outside world, the influence of the market challenge is clearly felt in the prison. Market initiatives are brought in by new arrivals. 'People arrive from outside completely different. It is harder and harder to speak with them. We call them margarine or new Russians... Not all of the new people are like that. At least half, though'.[112] The arrival of the first new inmates coincided with the start of market reform – at the end of the 1980s and start of the 1990s. 'Each man for himself. The goal was survival at any price. Before, it wasn't like that... When did this process start? – Maybe with perestroïka... In 1987? – No, later. At the start of the 1990s. I don't have contact with them... when someone needs their help, they will only help him if there's some profit in it for them'.[113] In other words, a particular interpretation of the market rules, what we refer to as the post-Soviet market, has been expanded. The search for short-term profit, resulting less from production than 'privatization', lies at the heart of this market. 'They have their own ideology. They ignore us. Their goals – to fill their bellies, to build up their muscles (*kachat'sja*), nothing more. The racketeers... they want to make their everyday life comfortable, that's all. They don't think of anything else'.[114] 'They have their own lives. Some

---

[111] With the remarkable exception of the so-called 'black' colonies where 'money circulates freely, almost as well as outside [the prison], people made commercial arrangements' (Interview No. 39).

[112] Interview No. 1a. According to another estimate, 60–70 per cent of inmates are 'margarines' (Interview No. 16).

[113] Interview No. 24.

[114] Interview No. 38.

understand, the others–not at all. They work out, they look for something to eat... they dream of racketeering, beating on everyone'.[115]

Despite the mutual ignorance among the inmates who transmit the penal subculture (*arestanty*) and the 'margarines', who transmit the values of the post-Soviet market, the penal city appears unable to resist the 'barbarian' invasion. Most of those interviewed (55.3 per cent, 56.6 per cent in Kazakhstan) agree with the statement that 'You can buy anything, it's only the price that counts'. 'Now, everything comes down to money whereas before there were ideas like honesty, the inmates' conscience, understand? Everyone is judged by his usefulness. Everything is sold today. Including politics, the common cause (*vorovskaja ideja*)'.[116] The hierarchy of the conditions for survival in prison highlights the essential importance of financial resources. In fact, money has replaced most other resources:

Table 4.24 Conditions for survival in the prison

	Russia, N=1310	Kazakh., N=396	France, N=59	Canada, N=120
Money	36.1	30	43.1	33.9
Intelligence	31.3	26	24.1	31.3
Knowledge of traditions, prisoners' subculture	25.6	38.4	27.6	28.7
Access to networks in the criminal and prisoners' milieus	23	17.8		
Access to networks in the milieu close to the administration	25.3	35.7	50	10.4
Patronage of the administration	11.4	15.4		
Physical force	12.8	5.7	10.3	6.1
Patronage of an influential inmate	5.1	4.6	×	×

'When you're rich or if your parents help you a lot, it's not important whether you're right or wrong... You can get around the Law, just like we can get around the prison law. We can get around it on any side'.[117] Moreover, the value of wealth depreciates that of the illicit categories. 'Money decides everything. No matter who I am, if I have money, I can do anything. Without money, your good points aren't worth much'.[118] The invasion of the quasi market logic forms a lasting and transposable set with the inmates. At least the majority of the interviewees view material prosperity as the first priority for their life after release (see Table 4.25 for the responses to the question 'What are your priorities for your life after your release from prison?').

---

[115] Interview No. 22.
[116] Interview No. 18.
[117] Interview No. 16. Cf. 'A man who is strong and rich can always buy justice, buy his innocence... the same rule applies here...' (Interview No. 2).
[118] Interview No. 16.

Table 4.25 Priorities after the release from prison

	Russia, N=902	Kazakhstan, N=396
Material wellbeing	38	37.3
Good reputation	25.8	29.8
Don't know	20.6	23
Wealth of opportunities	17.7	11
Citizen's duties	7.8	10.2
The same as before imprisonment	4.2	5.5

The responses to the question about the means that the inmates are prepared to use to attain their objectives confirm that the desire for wealth frees the individual but in a purely negative manner. Neither the support of family, nor legal of moral means compete with the principle of social withdrawal.

Table 4.26 Means to attain the objectives

	Russia, N=902	Kazakh., N=396	France, N=59
Those which are the most efficient	39.1	43.8	5.1
Recourse to acquaintances I had before imprisonment	23.6	26.5	45.8
Moral abiding behavior	23.5	20.5	13.6
Law abiding behavior	13	10.5	28.8
Recourse to acquaintances I found in the prison	5.8	4.1	×

The market challenge attacks two forms of socialization that serve as cement in the prison city, the illicit categories and the family. First, the merchants and other inmates who are punished for economic crimes (*baryga*), who were never respected in the prison world, are now starting to gain a certain undeniable notoriety. On the one hand, 'for me, a merchant is a *baryga*, I don't consider him human. We're forbidden to speak with the "roosters". For me, it's the same thing with the *baryga*'.[119] On the other hand, the merchant can use his resources to *buy* respect. 'Before, we pejoratively called him *baryga*, now he's become a merchant and lives worry-free. The attitude towards him has changed. They send him a heavy truck full of products. He bribes the administration to let the truck pass. And then–he becomes an illicit guard'.[120] In other words, the contrast between the material wealth of the merchants and the poverty of the ordinary inmates[121] means the latter are dependent on the former.

---

[119] Interview No. 41.
[120] Interview No. 22. Cf. 'We didn't take him seriously before. Now no. Before he was a *baryga*, now he's a businessman' (Interview No. 13).
[121] 'The poor one is in a way the ideal type of inmate, existing socially only as an inmate' (Marchetti, 1997, p.115).

Institutional Change: Two Cases Compared 247

The dependency takes form through the purchase and sale of positions in the illicit prison hierarchy, which even includes illicit guards and thieves-in-law. 'There are thieves-in-law who have never been in prison. They can fulfil the functions of thieves-in-law, but I can't respect those types'.[122] It should be noted that the first precedents of the 'crowning' of those who had contributed materially to the common fund (*obshak*) date back to the second half of the 1980s. The meeting of thieves-in-law (*shodka*) that took place in Krasnodar on November 24, 1983 first accepted the idea of rapprochement between the thieves-in-law and the merchants, who were clandestine at that time (*cehoviki*) (Gurov, 1995, p. 151). The purely market value of these titles results in their social devaluation. 'Before, when the thieves-in-law had nothing (the prohibition concerning material possession was discussed in the section entitled '*The illicit guard: the figure of the smotrjashij*'), everyone asked for their advice. We knew that the thief-in-law would take nothing, that he gave everything to the common cause. Now it's just the opposite. He has everything the others want and don't have... Yes, the guy who pays most is often right'.[123] In order to respond to the market challenge, the thieves-in-law try to become richer. They are far from finding a compromise between the logic of the short-term search for profit and the values of the penal sub-culture. It is more an expansion of the logic of the post-Soviet market from the top in the penal city.

> 'Interest is in this way their true motivation, specific to their ego, which makes them who they are while desiring satisfaction' (Boltanski, Thévenot, 1991, p. 246).

'The thieves-in-law are losing their reputation. They could be criticized, "Listen, your belly is full, you've got millions...Do you think about the ordinary guys?"'.[124]

Second, the scope of the mercantile interests is starting to be felt within the family of inmates, the sacred structure of the 'small' society. The number of inmates who choose solitary life, particularly among the new arrivals, is increasing. 'What's the point? He works, he earns money, whereas I don't work. Why would he feed me? He's more likely to push me away'.[125] Moreover, marriages of interest are not excluded. The poor inmates try to form families with the more fortunate. It should be noted that these 'marriages of interest' are extremely unstable as a result of the opportunistic behavior of the family members. 'For example, I arrive at the *otrjad*. There are always those who don't get help from their families. Yet they want everything right away. That kind of person approaches me and offers me friendship. "Of course", I say, "No problem". After my family visits, he takes everything and leaves me. Then it was explained to me'.[126]

We would like to propose a model based on the 'barbarian' invasion in the 'old' penal city. It works from the bottom, with the arrival of the 'margarines' as well as from the top, with the commercialization of the services provided by the

---

[122] Interview No. 41.
[123] Interview No. 25.
[124] Interview No. 18.
[125] Interview No. 36.
[126] Interview No. 20.

thieves-in-law. When an inmate who transmits quasi market values meets with one who transmits traditional values, the former wins and the latter loses. The experience of the marriage of interest recounted above illustrates this. Let us suppose the m is the number of 'merchants' in N, the total prison population of the penal city. Then, m/N is the probability that one inmate opts for a mercantile strategy in his daily interactions and $1-m/N$ is the probability that the inmate will behave in keeping with the traditional values of the penal sub-culture. We can then represent the stochastic interaction between two inmates using the following matrix:

Table 4.27 A model of market invasion in the penal city

		2nd inmate	
		Mercenary strategy (m/N)	Traditional strategy (1-m/N)
1st inmate	Mercenary strategy	0, 0 N_1	2, -1
	Traditional strategy	-1, 2	3, 3 N_2 P

In order for the first inmate to choose to respect the penal sub-culture, the following is necessary:

EU $_{mercenary}$ > EU $_{traditional}$ ⇒ 2×(1-m/N) > (-1)×(m/N)+3(1-m/N) ⇒ 2m/N>1 ⇒ m>N/2.

Figure 4.7 Mercantilist versus traditional behavior

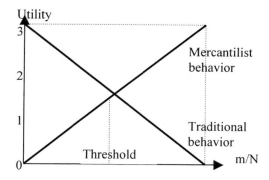

In other words, if the population of 'margarines' makes up more than half of the total prison population, all of the inmates should behave in a mercenary manner (for a graphic representation see Figure 4.7 (Boyer, Orléan, 1992, pp. 168–169)). Considering that, according to the inmates' estimates, the percentage of those who remained faithful to the value of the prison sub-culture does not exceed 50 per cent (in Kazakhstan this percentage is higher, see Table 4.24), it does not seem too likely to us that the 'small' society will be reproduced. 'The atmosphere in the colonies is not good. It's not our atmosphere'.[127]

We can summarize the analysis of the interference of two reforms by affirming that the ability of the 'small' society to remain balanced in the face of external shocks is fragile. The mercenary challenge attacks the principles by which the 'small' society functions. It destroys the strong sense of solidarity without also helping to transform it into a weak solidarity. In this way, the challenge casts doubt on the order on which the 'small' society is founded.

> 'If each being is dominated by his own interests, these interests are immeasurable and lead to a chaotic order that nothing can be said about' (Boltanski, Thévenot, 1991, p. 417).

These tendencies are observed in the post-Soviet society as well as in the Russian penal society. They require a radical change in the nature of both societies. Either the 'small' society must gradually be transformed into a 'large' society, or the internal mechanisms must stop ensuring a more or less stable order, regardless of its local and 'unmodern' character, and the situation will shift towards total de-socialization. De-socialization makes individuals even more powerless and dependent. 'The administration has now attained its goal. Everyone lives for himself. The administration has fulfilled all its dreams. The wolves are starting to eat one another'.[128] De-socialization results in a total absence of subjects. In the two cases considered, it is only possible to avoid the total dependence of individuals on the licit authority by stepping outside the limits of the 'small' society.

Comparing two cases

The destructive influence of the mercantile challenge is linked to the failure of the market reforms. This contrasts with the modest yet progressive dynamics of the penal reform. We proposed to explain this divergence by means of the radically different approaches specific to these reforms: teleological and genetic. The post-Soviet changes highlight the following dilemma. Either we continue with the genetic reforms, which serve to maintain order but exclude the replication of a given model with a large reputation or we refer to a model with a great reputation with no assurance that order will be maintained and the socioeconomic system will not break down. Let us now try to develop theories about the advantages and disadvantages of these two alternatives within the post-Soviet context.

---

[127] Interview No. 38.
[128] Interview No. 24.

Measuring the gap between formal and informal institutions

The dilemma formulated in this way implies a choice between the bad and the less bad. Can a compromise exist between two extreme affirmations? From this point of view, another formulation appears more pertinent to us. As the objectives of the reforms increasingly contradict the sets produced within a given institutional context, they increasingly cast doubt on the order and result in socioeconomic disequilibrium. Therefore, is it worth reducing the choice of the objectives for the teleological reforms to a search for a model with a large reputation that contradicts the sets less and possibly even coincides with them? The abundance of institutional models to be used, both theoretical and practical (American, French, Japanese, German, etc.) serves as an additional argument in support of this hypothesis.

The question of the degree of congruence/divergence between reality and the model, which replaces the initial dilemma, results in a practical and positive response that has nothing to do with the normative reasoning. There are at least four methods–the sociology of law method, the method of S. Cornell and J. Kalt, the method of G. Hofstede and the method that we can propose based on our own approach. First, the sociology of law is interested in the conditions that promote the legal graft that involves implementing in a judicial system an element from another system in which it demonstrated its usefulness and workability. From this point of view, 'the graft will only succeed if the donor system and the receptor system belong to the same class of equivalency' (Arnaud, 1993, p. 273). The fact that two judicial systems belong to the same class of equivalency, their congruence to use our terminology, results in relations of reflexivity, symmetry and transitivity between their elements. In other words, x is an element from the donor system, y – an element from the receptor system, R – a relationship between the elements. Thus, the relationship of reflexivity supposes that xRx and yRy, namely the two systems are coherent. The relationship of symmetry implies that xRy and yRx: the norm that is introduced in the institutional context plays the same role as the norm which it replaces. The relation of transitivity means that xRy and yRz lead to xRz, namely that we can implement any other norm that is congruent with the first two.

Second, S. Cornell and J. Kalt developed an approach that serves to evaluate the perspectives for the transfer of political institutions from one institutional context to another. The focus on political institutions accounts for the choice of four criteria (Cornell, Kalt, 1995, pp. 405–406). The first criterion concerns the structure of the authority. In order for the transfer to attain its objectives, the division of responsibilities in the receptor system and the donor system must be based on congruent principles. For example, neither illicit justice *nor* licit justice in the Russian prison is based on the principle of the complete differentiation of responsibilities (there is no figure comparable with that of the judge who applies sentences in France). The second criterion consists in the comparability of the scope of the authority: are there norms that establish rights that are, on the one hand, inviolable and, on the other hand, transferable to those in power. The American Bill of Rights and the European Convention for the Protection of Human Rights and Fundamental Freedoms serve as examples of the normative protection of inviolable rights (Coleman, 1990, p. 341). In a similar manner, the penal subculture and the new Code for Applying Sentences guarantee the basic rights of inmates, including the rights to justice and personal security. The third criterion concerns the location of the authority. The authority can be based on family structures, one's group, social categories, civil society, etc. In Russian prisons, recent developments indicate that the administration and the illicit guards are trying to play the role of an impartial mediator in conflicts between inmates. The fourth criterion concerns the sources of authority: traditional, charismatic, expert, etc. The authority of the illicit guards *as well as* the authority of the administration require a certain expert knowledge. The representatives of the two branches of power have a common tendency to become commentators on incomplete texts that are contradictory and, as a result, enshrined (the *ponjatija* and the CAS).

Third, based on his studies of multinational firms, G. Hofstede proposed a series of criteria that serve to measure the degree of congruence between economic institutions and management practices (Hofstede, 1980; Hofstede, 1991). This series includes the following indicators:

- The distance with respect to power – the maximum level of the socially acceptable unequal distribution of power;
- The scope of collectivist/individualist cultures – does the individual identify first with a social group, including his own group, or does he try to focus on his own individuality?
- The degree of differentiation between the so-called virile and feminine values: as the social roles of men and women become increasingly interchangeable, there is less differentiation;[129]
- The attitude with respect to risk: the economic sciences establish three types: aversion to risk, taste for risk and neutrality towards risk;
- The orientation towards short-, medium- and long-term objectives in daily activities.

Fourth, we can measure the degree of convergence using a two-by-two comparison of the norms on which the donor and recipient systems function. For this purpose, we first need to develop an ideal type for each institutional system.[130] For example, in order to measure the degree of convergence between the post-Soviet market and the *full-fledged* market, we propose to compare their constitutions, as summarized in the previous analysis (see Table 4.28).

---

[129] As a hypothesis, we suppose that, in Russia, social roles are more interchangeable from the point of women than that of men.

[130] Oleinik A., *Institucional'naja ekonomika*, Chapter 4, reading 7; Chapter 7, reading 14.

Table 4.28 Market constitutions compared

Constitution of full-fledged market	Constitution of post-Soviet market
Complex utilitarianism	Simple utilitarianism
Instrumentally rational action	Value-rational action
Impersonalized trust	Personalized trust
Empathy	Personalized empathy: "I scratch your back, you scratch mine"
Freedom in a positive sense	Freedom in a negative sense
Law abiding behavior	Double thinking

Then, we must find a scale for the distance that separates each pair of norms. For example, we will compare the level of trust observed empirically in the receptor society (32.1 per cent), considering either the critical threshold of confidence calculated according to a model (33.3 per cent), or the level of trust observed empirically in the donor society (>60 per cent). The difference between impersonal empathy and personalized empathy also has a quantitative dimension. We have already noted the existence of a close link between the principle 'I scratch your back, you scratch mine' and barter transactions. Now, for N goods, there are $½ N \times (N-1)$ barter transactions and $(N-1)$ monetary transactions (Eggertsson, 1990, p. 234). The portion of barter transactions in total sales provides, therefore, an idea of the scope of personalized empathy. All other norms are subject to quantitative evaluations.

Finally, we can imagine a negative convergence between two systems when an institutional graft provokes negative effects in the receptor society that are similar to those that took place in the donor society. For example, the interference of market reforms and penal reforms causes the weakening of the penal sub-culture and the de-socialization of the prison environment. Normative deregulation, anomie, results, in turn, in feelings of solitude, indifference, fear, fatigue. 'The feeling of solitude can be a good indicator of anomie' (Reynaud, 1989, p. 267). The inmates ranked solitude and fatigue third and fourth in the hierarchy of their usual feelings (see Table 2.3). Generally, this corresponds to the portrayal of the usual feelings of the post-Soviet man:[131]

Table 4.29 Usual feelings of the post-Soviet man

	1992	1993	1994	1995	1996	1997	1998	1999	2000
Fatigue, indifference	55%	52	40	41	43	42	45	38	39
Spite	30	39	10	28	29	27	35	25	20
Hope	17	15	16	21	20	17	13	27	31
Fear	26	22	22	19	17	16	24	19	16

---

[131] 'Uhodjaschij god' // http://www.polit.ru/documents/390969.html (VCIOM data); Kim N., 'Nadejda, ustalost', starost'' // *Ekonomicheskie i social'nye problemy. Monitoring obschestvennogo mnenija*, n°1 (39), 1999.

A vicious circle

However, if we do not find a good model to reproduce or if the political will needed to continue with *revised* teleological reforms is lacking, the model of the unbalanced society, torn between two poles, the State and the individual, could well be reproduced ad infinitum. As variable as the apparent forms are, the basis of the Russian/Soviet/post-Soviet model does not change, since there have been no radical changes in the model of the licit authority. When speaking of Russia's lengthy history, all we observe are minor fluctuations between the imposed authority and the disjoint authority.[132] Behind the appearance of faster and faster changes, lies the 'small' society which has not been transformed into a 'large' society over a long period of time. Words such as democratization, free competition, open-mindedness should not deceive us with respect to the nature of the post-Soviet society, despite the magic they evoke in the Western context. In Russia, these words require a hermeneutic interpretation within the borders of the 'small' society. We will only provide a few examples of these borders on a long-term basis.

Throughout Russian history, the traditional peasant community (*obshina*, *mir*) changed form several times without modifying its nature. The hostility and wariness with respect to the outside world and a strong internal solidarity (the mutual help system, *krug*) have played a key role in its social organization. The term *mir*, which in Russian means both the world and the local community, reflects the self-sufficiency of this local, almost familial universe. The *obshina* serves Russians as the basis for organizing their everyday life, well before the abolition of serfs in the second half of the 19th century. The reticence of the peasants to leave the community and start an independent economic and social life, despite the policy to encourage the dissolution of the *obshina* at the end of the 19th century (the reforms of N. Bunge and S. Witte) demonstrates the primordial influence of the *mir* in the rural setting before the October 1917 revolution. Yet, even the 1917 revolution did not change its nature. The collectivization of the 1920s–1930s gave rise to a new form of *obshina*, the *kolkhoz*.

> 'The socio-cultural organization of the *kolkhoz* reproduces the operating principles of the traditional community' (Ahiezer, 1991, p. 145).

Moreover, forced industrialization and urbanization facilitated the transfer of the traditional community to the urban setting. 'Corporate sub-culture is inherited from the traditional communities' (Ahiezer, 1991, p. 265).[133] Furthermore, we find

---

[132] The licit authority in Russia has never moved close to the model of conjoint authority. However, the various periods in the Russian/Soviet/post-Soviet history correspond to either the model of imposed authority (occasionally in its extreme form–the Totalitarian State) or the model of disjoint authority (the Brezhnev period highlighted certain elements of this model).

[133] We saw in the section entitled '*Does the public/private border exist?*' that the *kolkhoz* is one of two ideal types for the post-Soviet work collectivity.

traces of the *obshina* in the political institutions. We are referring in particular to the Soviets as the ideal materialization of *local* and *personalized* democracy (*sobornost'*) and to the parliament as the mechanism for proclaiming *local* needs (Ahiezer, 1991, p. 283).

Certain economists consider the model of so-called mobilized economy as an illustration of long-term continuity. It is the result of an effort to construct the 'large' economy using a corporate model, namely the model of the 'small' economy. The State tries to control and manage the activities of key corporations directly, without market mediation. The first economic 'mobilization' corresponds to the formation of large industries in Russia. It became obvious during WWI, with the creation of military-industrial committees (*VPK, Voenno-Promyshlennye Komitety*). Yet,

> 'the continuity of the economic institutions inherited from the czarist mobilization (1914–1918), the *VPK*, that of their administrators is at the heart of the implementation of the economic mobilization in Soviet Russia' (Sapir, 1989, p. 24).

These long-term tendencies also account for the important place still occupied by the military-industrial complex (*VPK, Voenno-Promyshlennyj Kompleks*) in the post-Soviet economy. Also, the economic mobilization initiated by the second war in Chechnya is part of this tendency.[134]

In terms of the economy of institutions, it is a matter of *path-dependency*.

> 'Path-dependency suggests that the institutional legacies of the past limit the range of current possibilities and/or options in institutional innovation' (Nielsen et al., 1995, p. 6).[135]

The concept of path dependency may account for the total absence of changes and also support a radically pessimistic vision. Douglass North uses these words to speak about an impasse in which the Latin American countries that had followed a path drawn by the Spanish, bearers of a mercantile version of Civil Law, found themselves. Unlike the North American countries colonized at the same time by the British, who transmitted Common Law, the South American countries are condemned to reproduce the paths of mercantilism (North, 1989, pp. 1327–1329). Another economist and politician, Hernando de Soto, is included in the list of those who accuse the mercantilist habitus. He focuses on the omnipresence of the desire to acquire wealth by means of the redistribution that arises out of mercantilist law. According to De Soto, in order to get rid of the mercantilist habitus, people must legalize the informal economy as a means for insurrection against the dominant

---

[134] Olejnik A. 'L'économie russe 2000: un retour vers la mobilisation?' // *Diagonales Est – Ouest*, n°63, January-February 2000, pp. 33–34.

[135] Cf. 'A path dependent sequence of economic changes is one of which important influence upon the eventual outcome can be exerted by temporally remote events, including happenings dominated by chance rather than systematic forces' (David P., 'CLIO and the Economics of QWERTY // *American Economic Review*, 1985, Vol.75, n°2, p. 332).

mercantilism (Soto, 1994, pp. 171–177). We have seen that the informal market can product a mercantilist attitude as well as the legal frameworks. In other words, reducing path-dependency to a habitus is the same as an apocalyptic visions of the post-Soviet mutations.

However, interpreting path-dependency through the concept of set leaves room for an historical maneuver while avoiding superficial optimism. Changes *appropriated* from the institutional context, namely the teleological changes that satisfy the requirements described in the previous sub-section, can gradually modify post-Soviet sets which are much more flexible than that of the habitus. We are of the opinion that *teleological* changes that are intended to ensure congruence with existing tendencies are both desirable and possible. The reforms that start from local and personalized trust finish with generalizable trust. In the words of Anthony Giddens, the reforms must replace social integration with system integration. Social integration means 'reciprocity between actors in contexts of co-presence', whereas system integration–'reciprocity between actors or collectivities across extended time-space' (Giddens, 1984, p. 28).

At present, only the mechanisms of social integration function in Russia. In this institutional context, everyday life provokes a contradictory feeling. The warmth of relations with those in your own group contrast strongly with the hostility and violence characteristic of relations with others. The separation between those in your group and others makes concern omnipresent.

> 'Feeling concerned means a concrete feeling of discomfort in being together: not in the reduced inter-subjective world, but in the mass of others… What is at stake in concern is the impossibility of negotiating interpersonal relationships with juxtaposed beings' (Roché, 1993, pp. 14, 16).

Therefore, local 'paradise' is opposed to general 'hell'.

Considering the fact that 'domestic devices are poorly equipped for action at a distance', we must question the paths for generalizing local trust. Game theory studies the technical, qualitative aspect of generalization. In order for the trust norm to become generalized, w must be greater than 2/3, where $w = \max \{T\text{-}R/R\text{-}S, T\text{-}R/T\text{-}K\}$ (Axelrod, 1990, p. 173).[136] Yet, each variable has an institutional and normative interpretation. For example, T, the gain of the player who abuses the trust of his partner, varies in keeping with the institutional context. The Law can increase the value of T even if the partners belong to the same group or it can reduce the attraction of abusing trust in relations between those in your group and others. The Soviet Penal Code (Art. 189, 190) considers the refusal to testify against a relative a crime, which was intended to increase the value of T in relations with those in the same group. The case of young Pavlik Morozov, who testified against his father, a wealthy peasant, at the start of collectivization and was then killed by his family, became sacred during the Soviet period.[137] It was

---

[136] This can be drawn from the Prisoner's Dilemma. For an explanation of the variables see the sub-section entitled '*Trust in the prison*' (Table 2.23).

[137] In keeping with the Law of July 20, 1934, relatives of a military person who was exiled abroad were punished by 5–10 years of confinement because they did not want to warn the

only in 1993 that Article 316 of the new Penal Code released Russians from the obligation to testify against their families. Therefore, it is still the State that establishes the legal devices that serve to either generalize the local paradise or transform the everyday life of 'small' societies into hell. All in all, we arrive at the same observation as that made by Karl Polanyi with respect to market evolution.

> 'Trade with neighbors, based on reciprocity, and trade at a distance, based on competition, were strictly separated. Interior trade was created in Western Europe by State intervention' (Polanyi, 1983, p. 96).

To sum up, we have a 'small' society that is breaking down and a 'large' society that is the target of the reforms. All we have to do is find a chain of benchmarks that ensure a sequence of congruent changes and the State will need to trigger them. These are the most difficult tasks and their analysis largely surpasses the framework of this work. We will simply allow ourselves to state that the refusal to take such a path would be equivalent to maintaining the vicious circle specific to the Russian/Soviet/post-Soviet historical development.

---

authorities about his intentions (Rossi, 1991, p. 233). A similar approach guided the preparation of Article 58^{12} of the 1926 Penal Code, concerning responsibility for so-called counter-revolutionary crimes.

Conclusion

About the Concept of the Mafia in the Post-Soviet Context

A dominant set structures the post-Soviet institutional context: the reproduction of the 'small' society model and the incomplete transformation of that society into a 'large' society. The apparent changes in socioeconomic forms is not accompanied by a change in the foundations of everyday life, its constitution. Nevertheless, the persistence of the 'small' society serves as a guarantee against total collapse following a given exogenous shock, including the shocks produced by the reforms of the 1990s. If everyday life continues within acceptable limits, it is a result of the stability of the rules, as 'unmodern' as they are. Let us explore this affirmation in greater depth.

Trust only exists within the 'small' society in its local and personalized form, which makes it impossible to construct a true collective subject. The scope of the actions of the Subject is always limited to the in-group, which serves as the basis for all everyday activities. In order to cross over the Rubicon of personalized trust, Subjects need to be supported by legal means that obliged the individual to fulfill obligations taken on voluntarily with respect to others, as foreign and distant as they may be. Now, the imposed and purely restrictive character of the licit authority prevents people from crossing over this river that cuts off the road to the 'large' city. Moreover, the State tries to exclude any effort to construct a collective Subject, creating a void between the everyday life of the local groups and the power. A society torn between two poles, an hourglass society, materializes the Russian/Soviet/post-Soviet model for State/citizen interactions.

Figure 5.1 An hourglass society

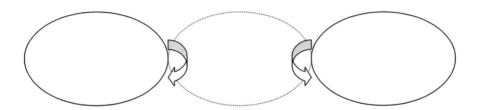

Returning to the analytical schema provided in the '*Introduction*', we can now provide more details about it. Two poles of the 'hour-glass society' lead to an almost autonomous and independent existence (Figure 5.1). The failure to complete the construction of the 'large' society implies that each element in the social construction represents a miniature universe, a *small society*. The absence of a justice system that is recognized by all of the actors translates into the coexistence of justice systems in each 'small' society. The absence of country-wide social and political representatives gives rise to mechanisms for social representative that are limited to the local groups. The inability to control violence in a modern manner, namely an institutional manner, accounts for the recurrence of violent behavior even within the groups, etc. In fact, this type of description brings to mind an autarchic economic model that is condemned to produce all of the components needed for economic and social functioning, without recourse to the outside world, to an international system of the division of labor. All in all, these components are produced, but at the price of higher costs, a more restricted nomenclature and without resort to the international market (an analogy of the 'large' society).

Moreover, the negative compromise made by individuals with the State, which could be described as 'If the state allows us to organize our everyday lives as we will, we will not question its character', does not correspond to a static situation. The negative compromise has its own dynamic, which translates into either the desire of the State to extend its control over everyday life or the desire of individuals to get rid of the State, to live without external constraints (*samostojatel'no*).[1] Generally, the history of the country in question is reduced to a perpetual oscillation of centripetal forces to centrifugal forces, from authoritarianism to localisms, and *vice versa*. Alexander Ahiezer, historian and philosopher, summarized Russia history up to the 1990s as two cycles that start with the explosion of local values and norms and ends with the rise of authoritarianism (Ahiezer, 1991) (Table 5.1). It seems that the current period is an extension of these cycles.

---

[1]This explains, moreover, the fluctuations in the authority model: from the imposed, even total authority to the disjoint authority, and vice versa.

Table 5.1 Two cycles in the history of Russia

Models of social relations	Phases of the first cycle (from antiquity till 1917)	Phases of the second cycle (from 1917 till 1991)
Early local ideal	Russia of Kiev	1917 – first half 1918
Early authoritarian ideal	From rule of Ivan Kalita till Great Troubles (*smuta*)	Military communism
Early ideal of compromise	From Great Troubles till rule of Alexeï Mikhailovich	New economic politics (NEP)
Extreme authoritarianism	From rule of Alexeï Mikhailovich till rule of Anna Ioannovna	Rule of Josef Stalin
Late ideal of compromise	1762 (liberation of noblesse, *dvorjanstvo*) – 1825 (December's movement)	'Thaw' (rule of Nikita Khrushchev)
Late authoritarian ideal	Rule of Nicholas I	Rule of Leonid Brezhnev
Late local ideal	Reforms of the second half of XIX century	Perestroïka (rule of Mikhail Gorbachev)

The perpetual oscillation shows that the State in this country is lacking its own logic that is often called in the Western countries the civic imperative supposing the focus on *general* interest (in terms used here, the conjoint authority of the State).

'The civic city becomes sovereign with the convergence of human wills when the citizens renounce their individuality and give up their particular interest to search for the common' (Boltanski, Thévenot, 1991, pp. 137–138).

On the contrary, the State itself reproduces the logic of the 'small' society.

'This State is not a set of institutions, but the *personification of the nation, the people*, so that the leader, identified with the State, is also directly identified with the people and the nation' (Touraine, 1988, p. 205).[2]

Therefore, everything depends on the specific interests of the local group in power: fiscal interests, interests in a geopolitical game, etc. In the 'small' society, the State always focusses on maximizing the revenue of the group in power, no matter how populist its slogans may be. Such objectives have nothing to do with maximizing the well-being of its constituents taken overall. This State is close to the ideal type that Douglass North calls the 'exploitive' State (North, 1981, pp. 22–24).[3] Its interests may coincide momentarily with the reinforcement of control, as well as with the liberalization of everyday life. The only decisive factor lies in the

---

[2] Our stress.

[3] The structure of the exploitive State was explored in more details in Oleinik A., *Institucional'naja ekonomika*, Chapter 11, reading 22.

socioeconomic and political conjecture at a given time. It is long-term cycles, Kondrat'ev cycles, that determine the oscillation between the authoritarian State (imposed) and the weak State (disjoint), whose functions are reduced to guarding a night table.[4]

The idea of the State as a group of people from your group among others, differentiated from others only by the importance of the resources at their disposal, gives us a new outlook for interpreting the associations of the State with the Mafia in the public mind. At a first glance, the response to the question, 'What do you mean by "Mafia"?' asked by the VCIOM at the start of the 1990s, may be surprising. More than two-thirds of respondents referred to the State (Table 5.2)![5]

Table 5.2 Associations with the word 'Mafia'

Actors of shadow economy	43%
Bureaucrats in ministries and public administration	36
Party-State apparatus	34
Criminals	25

Figure 5.2 'Privatization' of the civil society

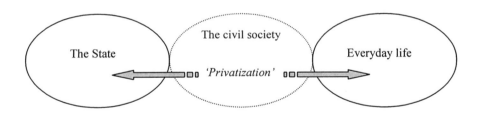

The association of the State with the Mafia loses its paradoxical character as soon as we focus on the congruence of the social organization of local groups in Russia and the Italian Mafia. In other words, in the minds of ordinary post-Soviets, the State is viewed as an in-group that appropriates and 'privatizes' the public space. The form this group takes, the nomenklatura, the presidential family or people from the State Security Committee (*FSB*), is not important. We have seen that this tendency to privatization accompanies the natural evolution of any in-

---

[4] This ideal is often interpreted by Russian liberals as a local ideal. See, for example, the ideas of Vitalij Najshul', one of the spokespeople for the Russian liberals, concerning the renaissance of pre-imperial Russia (Russia of cities) and the local market (Najshul' V., 'Rubej epoh. Rassujdenija ekonomista v kanun grjaduschej smeny politicheskogo rejima' // http://www.polit.ru, March 10, 2000).
[5] Levada Yu., *Op. cit.*, p.41. See also the table of the inmates' associations with the State (Note n°7 at p. 160).

group, since it is an amalgamation of the traditional world and the world of projects. As a result, the privatization of the public space by in-groups, regardless of their form, State controlled or not, places the institutions of the civil society in a state of coma. Tendencies to privatization can be used to develop theories about the extreme instability and the permanent breakdown of the institutions of civil society in post-Soviet countries (Figure 5.2).

The in-group privatizes the resources that are available to its members. The resources available to the members of the group that appropriates the State greatly exceed those available to all of the other groups. In Russia, a country that is rich in natural resources, these are added to the traditional revenues of the exploitive State: taxes and bribes. The State controlled by an in-group never considers taxes as a perfect substitute for bribes, because they exclude any control on the part of strangers, namely members of other groups. The State bypasses the Law in the same way that ordinary people do in order to attain their private objectives. In this way, the level of corruption serves as an indicator of the actual scope of the society. The greater the corruption, the smaller the society, regardless of its place in the geopolitical game. In keeping with this criterion, the post-Soviet countries are not as far along the road from the 'small' society to the 'large' society as many others. The table below (reflecting the rate of corruption of State civil servants) illustrates the backward position of the former USSR on this road (Kaufman, 1998, p. 523: the World Bank data):

Table 5.3 Level of corruption

Countries of the former USSR	65%
Countries of Maghreb	50
Countries of Eastern Europe	40
Countries of Latin America	39
Countries of the Middle East	36
Countries of the OECD	12

The perception of the State as an in-group, as a Mafia, explains the extraordinary duality in the attitude of post-Soviets to their State. On the one hand, they do not trust the State institutions and do not know how they function. If, in the 'large' society, distrust in a State institution does not exclude trust towards others (as a result of the 'fragmentation' of trust, see the section entitled '*Norm of trust*'), in Russia we have observed a lack of trust in all State institutions. Now,

> 'democracy does not require individuals to trust in all institutions, but it does suppose that they trust certain social institutions that promote their interests' (Rose, 1994a, p. 5).

This condition is not satisfied in the 'small' society.

On the other hand, the State respects the same rules as those on which ordinary Russians organize their daily lives. It is a sort of double, a monstrous double. 'The monstrous double replaces everything that everyone wants to absorb and destroy, incarnate and expel' (Girard, 1972, p. 230). The post-Soviets detest the State because it reproduces, for its own purposes, the logic of the in-group and considers its own citizens as others, strangers. Yet, at the same time, the post-Soviets do not manage to get rid of *such* a State because it incarnates their own lifestyle, it incarnates them. The imposed/disjoint State is only the opposite of the omnipresence of the 'small' society. In short, *such* a State becomes a perfect monstrous double of the 'small' society.

In this way, we can use this outlook to make a few observations concerning the phenomenon of the current president of the Russian Federation, Vladimir Putin. The phenomenon involves the support Russians give him, although his policy has resulted in no positive change to date. He was elected president without presenting any economic, political or social platform. Despite this, more than two-thirds of Russians (69 per cent in April 2000, 71 per cent in May 2000, 75 per cent in February 2001[6]) *personally* trust the President. It is not as if he has a charismatic personality since only 3 per cent of Russians admire V. Putin. The dominant attitude towards him can be phrased as: 'I can't say anything bad about him' (see table of answers to the question 'How do you describe your attitude towards V. Putin?'). Fifty-one percent of Russians do not criticize his proximity to the 'family' of the former president, Boris Yeltsin. How can you criticize someone for doing something you do in your everyday life? Faced with the paradox of the trust in the president, whose merits are not obvious, we must view it as an example of the oscillation between incarnation and expulsion. 'He's like us' (32 per cent of Russians feel *sympathy* for the president, cf. the Latin word *sympatia*, which means 'to feel the same emotions'). Moreover, the duality of the feeling will appear as of the first occasions and trust in the president in the post-Soviet context can very quickly transform into hatred, as in the case of the previous president.

---

[6] 'Otnoshenie k Vladimiru Putinu' // http://www.polit.ru; 'Putin: nadejdy i ojidanija' // http://www.polit.ru/documents/407923.html (the results of studies made by the VCIOM). It is interesting to note that public opinion uses the following argument to explain the trust in the president: 'He always does what he says' ('*u nego slova ne rashodjatsja s delom*'). Although the anticipation of the undeniable correspondence between appearance and actual actions is found at the heart of trust as a norm for daily behavior (see the section entitled '*Level of trust as a sociological indicator*'), it is not enough to support institutionalized trust, the key element of democratic institutions. Paradoxically, the Soviets of the 1930s would explain their admiration of Stalin in the same manner, 'He always does what he says' (see Lebina, 1999, p. 157).

Conclusion

Table 5.4 Attitudes towards V. Putin

Feeling	Mar. 2000	May 2000	Sept. 2000	Nov. 2000	Jan. 2001	Mar. 2001
I cannot say anything bad about him	34	35	33	36	41	34
Sympathy	29	28	25	31	29	32
Watchfulness	14	18	13	11	12	13
Indifference	11	8	12	11	10	10
I cannot say anything good about him	5	3	9	4	4	4
Antipathy	2	1	1	1	1	1
Admiration	3	3	3	4	2	3
Don't know	4	4	2	1	3	3

Figure 5.3 Market mediation between the State and the 'small' society

Although the President's socioeconomic program has not been proclaimed and submitted to a public debate, his actions lead people to believe that he sees the problem of the torn society in terms of a torn and regionalized imperial Russia. We can expect that his policy will shift either towards a pure and hard authoritarian model, which will fit in with the logic of the long-lasting cycles of Russian history, or towards a search to mediate between the State and the 'small' society. Taking into consideration the rules that the exploitive State respects, and the significant degree of its dependency on the international financial market (Russia has become the largest borrower from the international financial organizations), the search for mediating institutions may be reduced to reproducing the model of Chile of the 1970s–1980s, or certain elements of the Chinese model from the 1980s–1990s. In these countries, the market replaced the civil society as a mechanism for social and political integration (Figure 5.3). It should be noted that this is a local market on one side and an international market on the other. The formation of the *national* market as part of the 'small' society is excluded, as we have demonstrated. In other words, the current situation does not allow for much hope of an end to the oscillation between authoritarianism and localism, between the imposed authority and the disjoint authority.

* * *

Returning to the question asked in the *Introduction* with respect to whether or not the character of the term Mafia was appropriate in the post-Soviet context, we can summarize our analysis as follows. There is no doubt that organized crime is part of the landscape in Russia today. Moreover, its organization is based on unique principles, regardless of the region or sector of activity. The norms that arise out of the penal setting (*ponjatija*) and the judges responsible for their application (thieves-in-law and their lieutenants) serve as a framework for everything that is extra-legal and criminal in Russia. Nevertheless, the organization of Russian criminals is very different from that of the Mafia. For example, there is no organization in the Russian criminal world equivalent to the *Coupole*, the provincial and inter-provincial commissions (the regular meetings of the thieves-in-law, *shodki*, are occasional and less formal in character). The basic units or organized crime, *brigades*, are completely free of the patriarchal and domestic ambience specific to the Sicilian Mafia family, *coscà*, and so on. Therefore, if we limited ourselves to a structural and organization analysis, we would have to note that the Mafia is absent from the post-Soviet world. It would be no more than a pleasant short-cut facilitating political discourse.

However, as soon as we look at the sociological study of organized crime, we quickly recognize the congruence, the strange similarity of these two 'small' societies, Sicilian and post-Soviet. It is the context of the 'small' society that produces the Mafia mind-frame, the mind-frame of discriminating against others, those who do not belong to the Mafia-like in-group.

'The Mafia expresses an idea rather than a definitely organized institution... Mafia is a mental habit, a state of mind' (Schiavo, 1962, p. 21).

The Mafia mind-frame is found everywhere that the 'small' society has not been completely transformed into the large society. It is a 'trademark' of the 'small' society. Organized crime incarnates and refines the idea specific to the organization of everyday life in post-Soviet society in general. For this reason, it becomes the other monstrous double of the ordinary post-Soviet man, as perfect as the State. There is nothing surprising about the duplication of monstrous doubles following the reproduction of the same social model in various spheres of activity. The absence of boundaries between otherwise autonomous worlds facilitates this.

The post-Soviets feel hatred for the criminals, hatred that coincides *naturally* with the desire to behave like them, to resemble them. Despite this, the words *krutoj* (noun, adjective), *kruto* (adverb) usually used to describe successful criminals moved into the daily discourse of the 1990s and, moreover, have no pejorative connotation anymore. On the contrary, the adjective *krutoj* is usually attributed to a strong, rich, violent person who knows how to subject others, strangers to his will. If you question an ordinary post-Soviet adolescent girl about the male figure of her dreams, she will probably evoke the image of the criminal, whether he is explicitly referred to as such or not. As a hypothesis, we would like to presume that the tendency to expulsion prevails when appropriate or 'privatization' is judged by the impossible monstrous double whereas the tendency to incarnation prevails when it is possible to make the monstrous double one of yours or become one yourself.

The focus on norms as the cement in the Mafia construction provides a new point of view for criminological and police investigations. This process is part of the evolution of penal legislation, for example, in Italy. In particular, Article 416^1 of the Penal Code of the Italian Republic implies the responsibility for belonging to a Mafia-type association defined as subjugation to certain norms: the law of silence (*omertà*), the rejection of any contact with the agents of State justice, etc. From this point of view, it is the common normative space that links the various elements of criminal activity, that produces the phenomenon of *organized* crime. When it is difficult, even impossible to collect all of the information about a crime, the investigators may take an interest in studying the social type of those presumed guilty. If the elements of the criminal sub-culture determine their behavior in daily situations (this is discovered through structured interviews and a questionnaire designed specifically for this purpose), this will provide a complementary reason for continuing the investigation.[7]

* * *

The simultaneous presence of two monstrous doubles of the 'small' society, the imposed State and organized crime, leads to their rivalry, because their major function is to ensure that *order is based on rules that the public understands*, to maintain the balance of the 'small' society. Therefore, there is only one protection market, on which the State and organized crime try to sell substitute services. Since the State and organized crime are the principal actors on this market, it moves away from the competitive balance.[8] We will describe it instead in terms of an oligopolistic market, characterized by the radical instability and the lack of congruence between the equilibrium and Pareto optimum.[9] 'They [the thieves-in-law] protect you against *bespredel*, but you must pay them for their services. It's the same thing if you go under the protective umbrella (*krysha*) of the State organizations – *RUOP*, etc. Moreover, their rates are higher. <u>Perhaps because their</u>

---

[7] We tried to apply this approach to an investigation into the nature of capital transferred from Russia abroad: was it criminal, informal or legal capital? We developed a methodology that serves to highlight the information concerning the behavior of the party transferring the funds in a series of daily situations: behavior on the road, the role of family members in the business, the image of the ideal secretary, etc. (for an overview of this methodology, see Oleinik A. et al., 2000). Moreover, we are continuing to improve it as part of an ongoing project subsidized by the *Institut des Hautes Etudes de la Sécurité Intérieure* (IHESI, Paris).

[8] Cf. the conclusions of Peter Reuter concerning the competitive character of the illegal protection markets in the United States: Reuter P., *Disorganized Crime. The Economics of the Visible Hand*, Cambridge: the MIT Press, 1983.

[9] The so-called Cournaut equilibrium is determined by the terms for respective activities of rivals.

protection is more efficient? – Efficiency is the same in both cases. When I was free, I had eight guards certified by the State who had permits to bear arms, but I also contacted the thieves-in-law. There were cases like that. In general, the protection is not efficient. They [the State and the thieves-in-law] find it easier to reach agreements among themselves than with me. The guards and the illegal protectors quickly find a common language. "You don't touch this and we won't touch that"'.[10] As indicated with the associations with the word 'Mafia', described above, the State and organized crime represent the same thing, *Quisti è la stressa cosa – Cosa nostra*, in the minds of ordinary post-Soviets.

Economic stagnation causes the two protectors to compete for resources that become increasingly rare. If, at the start of the 1990s, the State could afford to allow organized crime to control numerous banks, the first decade of the 21st century will be marked by a merciless battle by the State against its main rival. Unfortunately, without a profound change in the nature of the Russia/Soviet/post-Soviet State, this battle will be no more than guerrilla warfare between two Mafias that are simultaneously distant and close to the population. In the best scenario, the order of the 'small' society will be maintained. The situation will be maintained as it is maintained today, at the price of refusing to progress further along the path towards a 'large' society. In the worst scenario, the fight against organized crime will lead to the deterioration of the former order, which will not be accompanied by the emergence of a new order. Therefore, it is up to the State to start this game of chess and win it, not through errors on the part of its adversary, but through a novel strategy. Playing e2-e4 as usual, namely continuing to reproduce the model of the 'small' society, will not only lead to failure in this game but will also cast doubt over the prospects of the country as such.

---

[10] Interview No. 25.

Postscript

Hostages of Authority

More than two years have passed since this book was completed. This distance allows a consideration of the empirical validity of some of the predictions made, within the framework of the study of the post-Soviet world as a small society. From this point of view, the terrorist crisis of October 2002 in Moscow appears especially revealing. It raises doubts about the appearance of stability and prosperity produced by the Russian mass-media, the majority of which is now (and particularly since the crisis) under close state control. Common sense suggests that a person's behavior in critical situations tells us much more about their real intentions than any proclamation or public speech. The crisis undoubtedly represents one such critical situation rendering the priorities of the licit authority more explicit.

About 700 theatre-goers, attending the performance of the patriotic musical 'North-East' (*Nord-Ost*, whose libretto was based on the novel 'Two captains' about WWII) in Melnikova Street, Moscow, were taken hostage on October, 23 by a group composed of a few dozen Chechen separatists. The hostages were held for three days; for the whole of this period the state's representatives declined any idea of negotiation with the terrorists. The only requirement put forward by the terrorists consisted in ending the war in Chechnya, started just before the presidential elections in 1999. Perhaps at this stage one should seek an explanation of the refusal of the state's representatives to listen the Chechen separatists, even when they had chosen an extremely violent form of guerilla warfare. As was argued in Chapter 3, in the section entitled '*Constructing the enemy: then and now*', the Chechen war has played a key role in the 'stabilization' of post-Soviet society. Consequently ending this war appears to be virtually impossible for the president, who won the elections thanks to 'channeling' the violence of Russian society towards a victim who could be sacrificed. The crisis ended with an attack in which all the terrorists and more than 120 hostages (according to the official data) were killed. Poisonous gas was used during the storming of the theatre and the majority of victims suffered not from the terrorists, but from this gas and the lack of medical assistance (in the city center!). It should be emphasized that these figures are far from being totally accurate: a few dozen hostages disappeared following the storm and the state's representatives not only refused to search for them, but they did not count them in the total number of victims. These victims included, the attack caused the death of almost a quarter of the total number of hostages.

Despite these facts, victorious reports about the release of the majority of hostages were greeted by the mass media with great enthusiasm and a sigh of relief: the threat to the reputation of the country seemed to have passed. The

Russian authorities had undergone a trial similar to that which befell the United States in September 2001. Official comment particularly emphasized the international dimension of the hostage-taking in Melnikova Street: it was seen as a kind of confirmation of the full participation of Russia in the processes of decision-making and problem-solving that face the international community. It does not matter that for the moment it is only problem solving – the days of enjoying the fruits of rapprochement with the West can not be too far off... It is difficult to say how much the storming of the building where the hostages were kept will contribute to a victory over international terrorism. It is more significant to put this situation in the context of Russian domestic policies. And it concerns not so much Russia's past – playing the Chechen card during the presidential elections of 1999, as its future. In this sense, the dramatic liberation of the hostages and the refusal to negotiate – though it may have seemed very attractive as a short-term prospect, creates significant problems for the authorities in the future. Will not this much-heralded victory over terrorists finally be seen as Pyrrhic?

First of all, the methods by which it was achieved, cause doubts. More than a hundred hostages were lost during the storm (the 'dosed' and fragmentary character of the official information does not allow us to cite with confidence the figures of 67, 90 or 120 victims, which were announced much later after the end of the operation). This might lead us to doubt the president's proclamation of the day before the storm, that the priority was the defense of their life and health. After its end, the presidential aide Sergey Yastrzhembsky admitted that such 'small' numbers of losses were a happy surprise to the organizers of the operation – the number of people saved could well have been less. As Sergey Kovalev, a well-known Russian defender of human rights, justly emphasizes, 'the main priority was not the life of hostages'. We are faced with the double thinking of the state's representatives (see the section entitles '*Double thinking*' in Chapter 3): they made an announcement of the purposes of the operation that would be admissible to the public, while in practice their aim was completely different – to find a way to get out of the crisis with minimal losses for the international reputation of the president and his high rating, for the present the only confirmation of Russian domestic stability. This double thinking is very familiar to Russians, for they had to resort to it in order to shoulder the burden of life in a system based on lies....

The low value put on the life of the hostages by the representatives of the state confirms our key thesis about the imposed character of authority in post-Soviet Russia (and not only in Russia – in this sense it does not differ very much from other post-Soviet countries). The interests of citizens and the interests of the representatives of authority coincide only casually, and there are no mechanisms allowing citizens to inform the authorities of their interests or to seek protection for them. Likewise it is impossible to consider formal voting procedures as a guarantee of democracy: a series of scandals connected with elections (in Krasnojarsk, Nijnij Novgorod, Elista and so on) deprive us of excessive optimism in this regard.

The imposed character of authority explains why, after all that has happened, the rating of the president has not been damaged and why voters will vote for him at next elections. Let us remember the 'Stockholm syndrome' of the solidarity between hostages and those who keep them contrary to their will. The hopeless character of the situation requires identifying with the imposed authority in order to survive. The real problem is that the hostages are not only those who were detained in Melnikova street, but – taking into account the imposed character of authority – all Russian citizens.

Surveys conducted one month after the terrorist crisis reveal that the rating of the president has risen by several percentage points. As was argued in the book's conclusion, the number of Russians who approve the actions of their president varied in 2000–2001 from 69 to 75 per cent. On the eve of the terrorist attack, in September–October 2002, his approval rating was about 77 per cent. In November 2002, 83 per cent of Russians, according to VCIOM's representative survey, approve the actions of the president.[1] This is the largest percentage since his election. It seems that the 'Stockholm syndrome' can indeed explain the paradox of people's fear of an authority able to sacrifice the lives of citizens and their simultaneous dependence on it. Any of Russia's citizens could become hostages – whether saved or sacrificed to the 'supreme interests of the state'. The chosen method of solving this crisis does not exclude the recurrence of such a situation. The authorities and the mass media tried to represent the hostage-takers as 'gangsters'. In fact, the level of organization involved and the symbolic character of the chosen place of detention – a theatre where a patriotic musical was running, confirm the strategic thought and conscientious planning of those who chose this road of terror. As the history of prison revolts teaches, a hostage-taking is often a reflection of the perpetrators' inability to communicate their opinion on vital questions by other means. After the crisis, the president reinforced his decision on the inadmissibility of any negotiations with the Chechen separatists and their supporters. Rallies by relatives of the hostages demanding an end to the war in Chechnya were banned by the authorities, who stated that 'now is not the time for discussion'. And this was despite the confidence of the majority of Muscovites interviewed by the ROMIR at the time of the crisis in the need to negotiate – as a minimum – with the aggressors. The image of a strong politician able to impose his will upon others appears to be more precious to the president than the lives of October's and – regrettable as it is – tomorrow's hostages. For tomorrow there is every possibility that more Russians will become victims of 'blind' terrorist actions. If, even in a situation of genuine threat to life the authorities reject any constructive negotiation, then forms of terror that obviously exclude dialogue (the installation of explosives, for example) become more probable in the future.

It is for this reason that – regrettable as it is – all Russians remain hostages: both of those who decided to struggle for the independence of Chechnya and of the representatives of the Russian state, for whom the majority of Russians will vote at the future elections… This is the real price to pay for living in a small society.

Moscow, November 28, 2002

---

[1] *Kommersant*, November 28, 2002, n. 216, p. 1.

Appendix

List of Inmates Interviewed

#	Name, age, illicit category[1]	Additional information	Place of interview	Date of interview
1a	Andrei, 35–40 y.o., B	An illicit guard of the subdivision. Second term of imprisonment. 15-year term for racketeering (1989-), Born in Yaroslav.	Camp in Yaroslav	Autumn 1997
1b	Alexei, 20–15 y.o., B	Six-year term for racketeering (1994-). Born in Yaroslav, helpmate of (1a).		
2	M	Born in Nijni Novgorod.	Prison in Vladimir	Autumn 1996
3a	Viktor Mantulin, 30+ y.o., I	Eighteen-year term for a murder in prison and an escape attempt (1984-). He started serving the sentence at a facility for young people.	Prison in Vladimir	Autumn 1996
3b	Andrei, 30+ y.o.	Correctional officer.		
4	Valeri Zabalkanski, 35–40 y.o., B	An illicit guard of the subdivision (previously an illicit guard of a city in Moscow region). His first sentence was in a facility for young people.	Camp in Plavsk, Tula region	Winter 1999
5	25–30 y.o.	Former leader of a gang of racketeers in a Moscow suburb. Second term.	Camp in Plavsk, Tula region	Winter 1999
6	35+ y.o., I	Swindler. Born in Crimea. First term.	Camp in Tula	Winter 1999

---

[1] B – for a *Blatnoj*, M – for a 'real man', S – for a 'scapegoat', I – for an independent inmate.

7	'Mironych', 50+ y.o., M	'Real man' who respects traditional values of the subculture ('*arestant*'). Term (1995–2005). He has been in prison several times.	Camp in Yasnaja Poljana, Tula region	Winter 1999
8	20–25 y.o., I	Racketeer. Born in a small village. First term.	Camp in Tula	Winter 1999
9	German, 27 y.o., S	Swindler. Born in Tula. First term (1994–2000). He holds an official position as *zavhoz*.	Camp in Tula	Winter 1999
10	30 y.o., S	Swindler. Born in Moldova. First term (1997-). He holds an official position as *zavhoz*.	Camp in Tula	Winter 1999
11	40+ y.o., S	Former officer of the traffic police. First term. He holds an official position as *zavhoz*.	Camp in Tula	Winter 1999
12	50+ y.o., M	'*Arestant*'. He has been in prison several times.	Camp in Tula	Winter 1999
13	Vladimir, 50+ y.o., M	He has been in prison several times since the 1970s. Term (1993–2003) for a murder in prison. Born in Tula. Believer.	Camp in Plavsk, Tula region	Winter 1999
14	40+ y.o., M	He has been in prison several times since the 1980s.	Camp in Plavsk, Tula region	Winter 1999
15	25 y.o., I	Customs officer. Born in Moscow. First term (1998–2004) for bribery.	Camp in Plavsk, Tula region	Winter 1999
16	Vladimir, 40+ y.o., M	He has been in prison several times since the 1970s. Sentenced for the murder of his brother.	Camp in Plavsk, Tula region	Winter 1999
17	50 y.o, M	Born in Kostroma. He has been in prison several times since the 1950s, including a facility for young people.	Camp in Arkhangelsk region	Spring 1999
18	50 y.o., M	Pickpocket (1997–1999). Born in Crimea, Ukrainian. He has been in prison 7 times (since 1967, 20 years in all).	Camp in Tula	Winter 1999
19	20+ y.o., M	Born in Tula. First term (1997–2004) for an economic crime.	Camp in Tula	Winter 1999

20	Sergei, <18 y.o., M	First term (1998–2001) for holding illegal drugs.	Camp for young people, Tula region	Winter 1999
21	Nikolai Suhanov, 51 y.o., M	'*Arestant*'. Born in Leningrad. He has been in prison several times since the 1970s.	Camp in Arkhangelsk region	Spring 1999
22	Nikolai, 50+ y.o., M	Born in Leningrad. He has been in prison several times since 1968. Term (1997–2006) for robbery.	Camp in Arkhangelsk region	Spring 1999
23	30+ y.o., B	An illicit guard of the subdivision. Racketeer in Tver. He is currently in the maximum security quarter.	Camp in Arkhangelsk region	Spring 1999
24	Yuri, 42 y.o., B	An illicit guard of the subdivision before being put in the maximum security quarter for two years. Born in Novgorod. He has been in prison several times since 1972 (prison for young people). Term (1991–1999) for a murder.	Camp in Arkhangelsk region	Spring 1999
25	30+ y.o., B	Swindler (1995–2001). Born in Baku (Azerbaijan), he was a businessman in Moscow. Childhood in a hostel.	Camp in Yasnaja Poljana, Tula region	Winter 1999
26	Roman, 35+ y.o., I	Born in Tula. He has been in prison several times. Term (1997–2000).	Camp in Tula	Winter 1999
27a	20+ y.o., B	Born in Novomoskovsk (Tula region). Term (1994–2009).	Camp in Tula	Winter 1999
27b	Nikolai, 30+ y.o., B	An illicit guard of the subdivision.		
28	40+ y.o., M	Born in Novgorod. Second term (1980-).	Camp in Arkhangelsk region	Spring 1999

29	35+ y.o., M	Born in Moscow. First term (1994-).	Camp in Tula	Winter 1999
30	Shatohin, <18 y.o., B/S	Term (1996–2000) for robbery. Born in Shekino (Tula region). He is '*bugor*', this position in prisons for young people represents a strange mix of official duties and illicit powers.	Camp for young people, Tula region	Winter 1999
31	Valeri, 18 y.o.	Term (1998-). He was in conflict with '*bugry*'.	Camp for young people, Tula region	Winter 1999
32	20 y.o., M	Born in Moscow. Term (1997–2000). He was interviewed just after his arrival in the camp. He demonstrated a willingness to be transferred to a camp for adults.	Camp for young people, Tula region	Winter 1999
33 a,b,c	Sergei, Nikolai, Il'ja, <18 y.o.	All these young men are trying to respect the traditional values of the subculture. One of them holds an official position (leader of a team composed of 5 inmates).	Camp for young people, Tula region	Winter 1999
34	Sergei, <18 y.o.	Term (1996–2001).	Camp for young people, Tula region	Winter 1999
35a	25+ y.o., B	An illicit guard of the subdivision. He discussed the results of our survey.	Camp in Arkhangelsk region	Spring 1999
35b	35+ y.o., B	Another participant in the discussion.		
36	41 y.o., M	Born in Arkhangelsk. He has been in prison several times since 1976. Term (1997–2011). 'Especially dangerous inmate'.	Camp in Arkhangelsk region	Spring 1999
37	40+, S	He holds an official position as *zavhoz*. Born in Arkhangelsk. He has been in prison 4 times since 1977. Term (1994–2005).	Camp in Arkhangelsk region	Spring 1999

38	Sergei, 37 y.o., B	Born in Orel. He has been in prison several times since 1979.	Camp in Arkhangelsk region	Spring 1999
39	35+ y.o., M	Businessman. Born in Moscow. He has been in prison 3 times since 1985.	Camp in Tula	Winter 1999
40	Vladimir Kucher, 40+ y.o.	Correctional officer.	Camp in Arkhangelsk region	Spring 1999
41	Sergei Burov, 30+ y.o., B	An illicit guard responsible for games. Term for theft. Unrecorded interview.	Camp in Arkhangelsk region	Spring 1999

Topics of the Interviews with the Inmates

Everyday life in prison:
    Trust and mistrust. What do you understand by trust?
    Family in inmates' milieu.
    Compatriots.
    Material well-being, its dynamics since the fall of the Soviet Union.
    Work in the prison.
    Moonlighting in prison. Black market.
    Prisoners' society vs. post-Soviet society: ways to compare.

Illicit authority in prison:
    Everyday conflicts and their resolution.
    Illicit guards and their functions.
    Trust in illicit guards.
    History of illicit guards.
    Informal justice: norms of the subculture (*ponjatija*) and their changes.
    System of sanctions.
    Violence in prison: its forms and their evolution.
    Common funds (*obshak*) and their management.
    Illicit guards in Russian business.
    Newcomer's first days in prison.

Legal authority in prison:
    Prisoners' relationships with the administration.
    Trust in the administration.
    Legitimized violence.
    Comparing everyday life in different prisons (minimum, medium and maximum security).
    Solitary confinement vs. imprisonment in groups.
    'Black' and 'red' prisons.
    Prisoners' rights and their protection.

Categories in prisoners' milieu:
    Illicit categorization and the duality of rules.
    Homosexuality in prison.
    The role that money plays in prison.

Is it possible to remain a Subject in prison?
    The absence of a public/private border.
    Autonomy vs. dependence in relation with the administration.
    Perspectives of reintegration after release.
    Business experience.

Questionnaire Distributed in the Prisons*

Which one of the following statements is closer to your convictions:
    In general, people can be trusted
    You should take care when dealing with people

Do you trust the people around you today (other inmates):
    Yes   No   I don't know

Do you count among your current friends:
Friends of childhood	Classmates	Other inmates
Workmates	People whom I knew previously in the prison	
I don't have friends		

Have you observed changes for the better in your current situation as compared to two-three years before?
    Yes   No   Doesn't concern me

Do you expect changes for the better in your current situation?
    Yes   No

How would you describe your most common situation (please, indicate two-three choices)?
Solitude	Hope	Anxiousness
Irritation	Patience	I'm lost
Decisiveness to change life for the better	Tiredness	

Whose help can you count on in difficult situations?
Anybody, myself	Family members	Other inmates
Friends	Government	Administration
Gang leaders		

Who did you help recently?
Anybody, myself	Family members	Other inmates
Friends	Government	Administration
Gang leaders		

Last month did you receive
Letters:	Yes	No
Parcels:	Yes	No
Telephone calls:	Yes	No
Visits:	Yes	No

What are the qualities you most appreciate in your friends, acquaintances (please, indicate four qualities at maximum)?
Intelligence	Physical force	Strength of will
Common sense	Respect of others' opinion	Sense of justice
Responsibility	Decency	Openness, sociability
Kindness	Candidness	

---

* Version distributed in Canadian prisons (questions were adapted to a North-American respondent).

Will you take part in actions of mass protest, if there are any?
    Yes, in any case   It will depend on requirements
    No   It will depend on personalities of other protesters
    I don't know

Which type of conflict resolution is the most common in this penitentiary?
    Might makes right
    The opponent who doesn't capitulate must be wiped out
    The winner is never judged
    Poor peace is better than a good war
    True solutions are usually found not in discussions, but thanks to the intelligence and force of some guys
    First come, first served
    Dialog and efforts to find a compromise

Whose intervention is usually welcome in the conflicts in your milieu?
    Administration   Gang leaders
    Legal bodies   There shouldn't be any third party

If an inmate started intimidating you, what you would do?
    I will use my relationships and acquaintances
    I will ask a gang leader for help
    I will be patient
    I will ask the administration for help
    I will try to solve the problem   I will fight for my safety
    I will ask the representatives of a legal body for help
    I will join my efforts with those of other intimidated people

Lack of respect for which type of norms is the most dangerous?
    Norms enforced by the administration   Law
    Norms enforced by the gang leaders
    Informal norms of our milieu
    Norms in which I've been educated

What are the qualities you can most appreciate in a gang leader? (please, indicate four qualities at maximum)
    Intelligence   Physical force   Strength of will
    Common sense   Respect of others' opinion   Sense of justice
    Responsibility   Decency   Openness, sociability
    Kindness   Candidness
    Control over financial resources
    Rejecting all contacts with the administration

Do you trust the administration of your correctional facility?
    Yes   No

Do you agree with the statement that everything can be bought, the only question is the price?
    Yes   No

Do you think the level of violence in the inmates' milieu has diminished during last two-three years?
    Yes   No   No changes
    Don't know

What are the conditions for survival in this prison (please, indicate a maximum of two variants)?
    Money
    Acquaintances in the milieu close to the administration
    Physical force
    Acquaintances in the criminal milieu
    Intelligence
    Knowledge of criminal traditions and informal norms
    Possibility of finding a protector
    Closeness to the administration

Are you ready to continue a relationship with an unpleasant but useful person?
    Yes   No

How often you can remember the following situations during last 6 months?
    Conflicts between inmates without use of physical force
    Conflicts between inmates where physical force has been used
    Conflicts between inmates where fire arms have been used
    Homosexual contacts under compulsion, rape
    Unsanctioned use of violence by the correctional officers
    Threats of vengeance addressed to the administration

Do you remember in this prison collective actions on the part of inmates in any of following forms?
    No, I don't remember
    Repairs to the prison's facilities
    Common fund
    Organization of cultural or sportive events
    Submitting collective demands
    Common discussion of inmates' problems

In which case could you trust the administration more?
    If there were more trustful personalities
    If the administration always respected the Law
    If the administration took our interests into consideration
    Never

Can you recognize the authority of a personally unpleasant individual whose behavior corresponds to the widespread perceptions of the authority in the inmates' milieu?
    Yes   No

Do you trust the gang leaders?
    Yes   No

Whose opinion is the most important to you?
    The guys I know well personally
    Family members   Gang leaders
    Administration   Public opinion

Do you have a 'family' here?
    Yes   No

Have you ever changed your 'family' since your transfer to this prison?
    Yes   No

Who are the members of your 'family' here?
    The people I trust
    The people with the same life style
    The people from the region I come from
    Those who were sentenced for the same type of crime

How many members are there in your 'family'?
    Two   Three   Four and more
    It's variable

Can you ask for some help and protection, if necessary:
    Administration   Legal bodies   My lawyer
    Gang leaders   Other inmates   No, I can't

Do you trust the people who work closely with the administration?
    Yes   No

During which period would you like to serve your present term of imprisonment, if you could chose:
    Today   Second half of the 19th century
    Sixties   Cold War
    Anywhere and anytime, but not in this country

Generally speaking, during which period of time would you prefer to live (please, indicate maximum two choices)
    Second half of the 19th century
    World War II   President Kennedy's term
    President Reagan's term   Civil War

Have you observed some changes in the treatment of the inmates by the staff during last two-three years?
    Yes, for the better   Yes, for the worst
    No changes

Did you read the text of the Federal Prisons Act?
    Yes   No

Which rights are the most important for you as an inmate (please, indicate a maximum of three choices)
    Correct treatment   Personal safety and security
    Visits   Communications (letters, parcels)
    Telephone calls   Walks
    Canteen   Watching TV
    Keeping books

Do you think the following rights are protected here? (Yes-No)
    Correct treatment   Personal safety and security
    Visits   Communications (letters, parcels)
    Telephone calls   Walks
    Canteen   Watching TV
    Keeping books

Do you agree that the impossibility of providing all the inmates with jobs has a negative influence on their well-being?
    Yes   No

Do you agree with the following rules? (Yes-No)
    Don't ransack your close associates
    Don't do the things that can be harmful to all of us
    Don't eye the others
    Don't denounce the others
    Don't ask the administration for help in conflicts with other inmates
    Don't have knifes with you, respect the others' right to inviolability
    Fight for your safety
    Don't ask too many personal questions
    Don't lose too much in games
    Don't take food in the canteen
    Don't have any contacts with the victims of homosexual assaults
    Don't try to solve conflicts while using drugs
    Deny any bad rumors about you, otherwise they will be considered as true

What do you think about homosexual relations between inmates?
    I completely reject them
    They are normal, if they are based on voluntary agreement
    They are a kind of punishment
    I don't know

Which institutions do you trust?

Other inmates	Family	American people
Business	Science	Mass media
Church	Science	Political parties
Parliament	Government	Attorney
Courts	Police	Army
Gang leaders	Trade unions	

Which kind of associations come to mind when speaking about Law? (please, indicate a maximum of four variants)

Instrument in private use	Forced restriction
Legal interdiction	Civil obligation
Voluntary obligation	Common goods
Justice	

    Rule corresponding to the interest of the majority

Do you trust the government?
    Yes   No

Which kind of associations come to mind when speaking about the government? (please, indicate a maximum of four variants)

Security	Corruption	Mafia
Violence	Human rights	Justice
Prison	Stable rules of the game	

Do you think you are responsible for (Yes-No)

Your own actions	The actions of your close relatives
The actions of your ancestors	The actions of the people around me
The children's actions	The gang leaders' actions
The government's actions	The events occurring in the prison
The actions of the people of your milieu	

Are there any people you could consider as yours?
    Close relatives
    The people with the same life style
    The people from the region I come from
    Those who were sentenced for the same type of crime
    Those introduced by a well-known person
    Those who are doing the same thing I do
    I don't class people in such a way

What are the basic principles for a better society in this country?

Profit	Trust	Property
Family	Respect of others' opinions	
Law	Tradition	Morals
Labor	Equality	Freedom

Do you think that in this country
    All the Laws could be and must be respected
    Some Laws should be respected, while others – not
    In this country good laws don't exist

Do you think you might adapt to life after release?

Yes, certainly	I'm not sure
No, I can't	I don't know

Would you agree that life in prison is easier than life outside of it?

Yes	No

How are you going to earn your living after release?
    I will look for a job
    I will try to start my own business
    I will work for anybody who pays me well
    Any way of earning a living is respectable
    I don't know yet

On which principles should market transactions be based?
    You scratch my back and I'll scratch yours
    First come, first served
    Freedom
    Trust
    Search for profit in any situation
    Might is always right
    The opponent who doesn't capitulate must be wiped out
    The winner is never judged
    Respect for the partner's interests
    Equality
    Rationality
    Empathy

To what do you pay attention while solving a complex problem?

Profit	Trust	Property
Family	Respect of others' opinions	
Law	Tradition	Morals
Labor	Equality	Freedom

What can you make use of as a mean to achieve your goals?
    Profit   Trust   Property
    Family   Respect of others' opinions
    Law   Tradition   Morals
    Labor   Equality   Freedom

What do you think about making marriage contracts between spouses?
    It harms the trust between spouses
    It allows those who can earn the money to better protect their interests
    It allows people to refer to the Law while having financial problems within the family
    Other

Do you think it is worthwhile to do business with close relatives?
    Yes, it creates an atmosphere of trust
    No, conflicts between close relatives will inevitably arise over profit sharing
    No, discipline will be distorted
    Other

How should the blood market be organized?
    The donors should be paid
    The donors act on the basis of civic convictions, no payment is allowed
    The donors should not be paid, but the most active of them should receive some material rewards
    Other

Age

Sex

Education

What are your musical preferences?
    Jazz   Rock   Country
    Blues   Classical music   Pop music
    Techno   Rap

Marital status

Do you have children?

Your profession before sentencing

Type of crime

Is this the first time you have been sentenced?

How long have you been in prison for the current sentence?

How much time do you have left in your sentence?

During the last 6 months, have you had an incident report that resulted in disciplinary segregation, disciplinary transfer?

List of Businessmen Interviewed

#	Sex	Age	Sphere of commercial activities	Size of business
1*	M	30	Wholesale and retail trade of Italian souvenirs.	Small
2*	M	40–45	Air conditioning systems: production and installation.	Big
3*	M	50	Industrial control systems.	Big
4*	F	45–50	Retail trade of Italian kitchens.	Middle
5*	M	40–45	Retail trade of knitted wear and leatherwear.	Small
6*	M	35–40	Retail trade of Italian kitchens.	Middle
7*	M	50	Wholesale and retail trade of Italian and Chinese ceramics.	Middle
8*	M	30	Wholesale and retail trade of Italian furniture.	Middle
9*	M	45	Wholesale and retail trade of Italian furniture.	Middle
10*	M	35	Software production.	Middle
11*	M	35–40	Wholesale and retail trade of Italian furniture.	Middle
12*	M	40	Wholesale and retail trade of Italian furniture.	Middle
13*	M	35–37	Retail trade of leatherwear and jeans.	Small
14*	M	50	Air conditioning systems: production and installation.	Big
15*	M	30–35	Senior manager of a bank.	Middle
16*	M	50	CEO of a bank.	Middle
17*	M	45–50	Senior manager of a bank.	Big
18*	M	30–35	Senior manager of a bank.	Big
19*	M	30	Head of a department at a bank.	Big
20*	M	40–45	Chief executive officer of a bank.	Middle
21*	M	45–50	Senior manager of a bank.	Big
22*	M	35–40	Vice-president of a bank.	Middle
23*	M	35–40	Head of a department at a bank.	Big

Topics of the Interviews with the Businessmen

How are your parents?
Do your parents help you?
Do you remember any situations in which you could not give help to relatives who had got into difficulties? If you could not help, what were your reasons?
What kind of help do you usually give them?
How would you act if relatives ask you for help at a time when all your money is tied up?
Do you bring relatives into your business?
For what purpose?
What are your terms in such a case?
Which cases of hiring a relative seem advantageous (or useful) for you, and when don't they seem advantageous?
What is your opinion about having to deal with relatives? Is it easier or more difficult? Can you explain why that is so?
Do your business relations with relatives differ from those with other people?
How would you act if some problems arise in business relations with relatives?
Do you think it is necessary, for the sake of your business, to intervene in your employees' domestic problems?
What occurs more often in your life: your friends become your business partners, or, on the contrary, your business partners become your friends?
For a long time I have been wondering, why do advertisements for personal secretaries always want 'girls aged 20–25'?
It is known that now there is a great demand for the various erotic services. What is usually bought, in your opinion, a service or a woman?
Please, tell me about your most memorable undertaking, or deal in recent years.
How could you estimate the ratio of successful and abortive deals, proceeding, of course, from your own experience?
What ratio seems to you acceptable for Russian conditions?
Please, tell me about the foundation of your bank.
How was everything going on? Had you a business plan? (To what extent was the foundation accomplished according to the business plan, for what purpose did you need it?) To what extent was this business plan fulfilled? Why did this happened?
What factors favored (or hindered) your undertaking?
Which criteria of success (or failure) were realized in such a case?
Did you have a preliminary discussion about an undertaking (or deal) with the future partner (that is to say, 'sounding out' the situation)?
What agreements did you have to change?
Did the undertaking turn out to be simpler (or more complex), than expected?
How and where did you get information about the possibility of this undertaking?
What source of information do you consider reliable and why?
How did you check on the information?
What was the difference between the information in this and other cases?
What are your main criteria for evaluating information?
Where did you learn about the interests of your partners and consumers?

Do you investigate the interests of your consumers?
What is the main criterion for choosing a potential partner?
Is trust the criterion for choosing your potential partner?
What is your ground rule for trusting a person?
By the way, relying on your own life experience, which of the two statements seems valid to you: 1) People can be trusted; 2) People ought to be dealt with carefully.
What do you generally mean by 'trust'?
How did you arrange the agreement?
What do you mean by *force majeure* circumstances?
How are rules of the game are changing under *force majeure* circumstances in your business?
In your opinion, what are the main ways to transfer funds abroad which are used in Russia?
In your opinion, what is the most original way of transferring funds abroad?
While the fund are being transferred abroad how are the activities of real contractors brought under control?
What is the most real threat for the contractor in these operations?
Who is interested in such kind of operations?
Probably, you have a constant circle of personal contacts. Please, tell me how it developed?
Who is included in this circle, and does it coincide with your business contacts?
What human qualities are appreciated among the businessmen you communicate with?
Which of these qualities have been difficult for you? In other words, what did you have to change in yourselves, in your own habits, or nature?
In your opinion, what entertainment expenses are reasonable?
What company-owned car do you use now? Why did you choose this model?
When you have extra money, what do you spend it on?
Could you point out one or more rules which you most often use in business?
Do you consider it possible to exert some mental or physical force on your business partners (or to use threats against them) in case of their nonfeasance? If it is possible, in what cases?
What do you think of the role of law in Russia? Are laws significant for business?
Do you think that a successful entrepreneur ought to observe the rules of Law without exception? Could you admit that such a requirement is applicable only sometimes, or it is right only for particular events, or it is absolutely untrue?
In this case, what do you think of following statement: 'Don't shit where you eat'
How risky is it not to follow laws?
Can you see any clear trend in the growth of violence (or in its decrease)?
Probably, you have a stable circle of partners, to whom you could apply for credit. What would you prefer, nevertheless, if you had to choose between your traditional partner and someone who offers you more advantageous credit conditions?
Have you or your acquaintances had any experience with applying to court or arbitration? How do you evaluate this experience?
How important is the business plan for conducting credit negotiations?

Otherwise, what is important?
Are your partners usually worried about the formal aspects of deals and in what cases? Which is better – to make a credit deal in writing and notarize or to have a spoken agreement?
Suppose you have given someone credit. Do you see a possibility that you may be deceived?
Are you willing to resign yourselves to the loss of money?
Otherwise, what do you rely on in case some problems arise ('*krysha*', readiness to take a risk, negotiations)? Would you take any measures against a deceitful partner?
How much will solving problems cost? How does the cost depend on the solution chosen?
What is the usual way for getting a job in your company?
Please, name your most essential requirements for a secretary applying for a job?
Has your bank any experience with long-term cooperation with foreign banks?
Do you have partners abroad?
Are all your foreign partner-companies located in the same region?
Tell me how you made your first contact abroad.
Do your contacts in Russia and abroad help you to expand your operations abroad?
What can you say on the basis of your experience: is there a great difference between levels of confidence in the foreign and in the Russian bank business? How do you account for this?
What do foreign partners primarily pay attention to, when deciding to take or not to take an offer from the Russian businessman?
How would you explain your regional specialization?
How are the deals concluded (formally or informally)?
How do you evaluate the efficiency of currency control?
Do you intend to establish an affiliate abroad?
How high is your reputation (in monetary terms)? Was it difficult to create it?
What do you do, if the fulfillment of a contract with the foreign partner is impossible under the circumstances?

Bibliography

Abramkin Valerij and Chijov Yuri (1992), *Kak vyzit' v sovetskoj tjur'me. V pomosch' uzniku*, Vostok, Krasnojarsk.
Ahiezer Aleksandr S. (1991), *Rossija: kritika istoricheskogo opyta*, Filosofskoe obshestvo SSSR, Moskva. – 3 vol.
Andreff Wladimir (1992), 'Convergence or Congruence Between Eastern and Western Economic Systems', in Dallago B., Brezinski H., Andreff W. (eds.), *Convergence and System Change. The Convergence Hypothesis in the Light of Transition in Eastern Europe*, Dartmouth, Aldershot.
Andreff Wladimir (1993), *La crise des économies socialistes: la rupture d'un système*, Presses Universitaires de Grenoble, Grenoble.
Andreff Wladimir (1995), 'Corporate Governance of Privatized Enterprises in Transforming Economies: A Theoretical Approach', in *Conference papers*, European Association For Evolutionary Political Economy, Krakow.
Anisimkov V. (1993), *Turemnaja obshina: 'vehi' istorii*, Moskva.
Aoki Masahito (1990), 'Toward an Economic Model of the Japanese Firm', *Journal of Economic Literature*, Vol. XXVIII, March.
Aoki Masahito (1991), *Economie Japonaise. Information, Motivations et Marchandage*, Economica, Paris.
Arellando R. (1994), 'Les méthodes de commercialisation', in Arellando R., Gasse Y., Verna G. (eds.), *Les entreprises informelles dans le monde*, Presses Universitaires de l'Université Laval, Sainte-Foi.
Arlacchi Pino (1986), *Mafia et compagnies. L'éthique mafiosa et l'esprit du capitalisme*, Presses Universitaires de Grenoble, Grenoble.
Arlacchi Pino (1996), *Buscetta. La mafia par l'un des siens*, Ed. du Félin, Paris.
Arnaud André-Jean (1993), 'Greffe juridique', in Arnaud André-Jean (ed.), *Dictionnaire encyclopédique de théorie et de sociologie du droit*, Librairie Générale de Droit et de Jurisprudence (LGDJ), Paris – 2e édition.
Arnaud-Duc N. (1993), 'Loi', in Arnaud André-Jean (ed.), *Dictionnaire encyclopédique de théorie et de sociologie du droit*, Librairie Générale de Droit et de Jurisprudence (LGDJ), Paris – 2e édition.
Axelrod Robert (1990), *The Evolution of Co-operation*, Penguin Books, London.
Azariadis Costas, Guesnerie Roger (1986), 'Sunspots and Cycles', *Review of Economic Studies*, Vol. 58, October, pp. 725–737.
Badie Bertrand (1992), *L'état importé. Essai sur l'occidentalisation de l'ordre politique*, Fayard, Paris.
Bagnasco Arnaldo (1990), 'The Informal Economy', in Martinelli Alberto, Smelser Neil J. (eds.), *Economy and Society. Overviews in Economic Sociology*, SAGE Publications, London.
Banfield Edward C. (1958), *The Moral Basis of a Backward Society*, The Free Press, Chicago.
Batishev V. (1994), *Postojannaja prestupnaja gruppa*, Izdatel'stvo Voronejskogo universiteta, Voronej.
Bayart J.-F. (1994), 'L'invention paradoxale de la modernité économique', in Bayart J.-F. (ed.), *La réinvention du capitalisme*, Ed. Karthala, Paris.

Bek Aleksandr (1988), *Novoe naznachenie*, Kartja Moldavjaneske, Kishinev.
Berelowitch Alexis, Wieviorka Michel (1996), *Les Russes d'en bas. Enquête sur la Russie post-communiste*, Ed. du Seuil, Paris – Col. L'épreuve des faits.
Berger H., Noorderhaven N., Nooteboom B. (1995), 'Determinants of Supplier Dependence: An Empirical Study', in Groenewengen J., Pitelis C., Sjöstrand S.-E. (eds.), *On Economic Institutions. Theory and Applications*, Edward Elgar, Aldershot.
Bettelheim Bruno (1991), *Le poids d'une vie. Essais-souvenirs*, Robert Laffont, Paris.
Boettke P. J. (1995), 'Credibility, Commitment and Soviet Economic Reform', in Lazear E. (ed.), *Economic Transition in Eastern Europe and Russia: Realities of Reform*, Hoover Institution Press, Stanford.
Boeva Irina, Shironin Viacheslav (1992), 'Russians Between State and Market. The Generations Compared', *Studies in Public Policy*, n°205.
Boltanski Luc, Thévenot Laurent (1991), *De la justification. Les économies de la grandeur*, Gallimard, Paris.
Boltanski Luc, Chiapello Eve (1999), *Le nouvel esprit du capitalisme*, Gallimard, Paris.
Bonafé-Schmitt Jean-Pierre (1993), 'Justice alternative', in Arnaud André-Jean (ed.), *Dictionnaire encyclopédique de théorie et de sociologie du droit*, Librairie Générale de Droit et de Jurisprudence (LGDJ), Paris – 2e édition.
Bourdieu Pierre (1980a), *Questions de la sociologie*, Ed. de Minuit, Paris.
Bourdieu Pierre (1980b), *Le sens pratique*, Ed. de Minuit, Paris.
Bourdieu Pierre, Passeron Jean-Claude (1970), *La reproduction. Eléments pour une théorie du système d'enseignement*, Ed. de Minuit, Paris.
Boyer Robert, Orléan André (1992), 'How Do Conventions Evolve?', *Evolutionary Economics*, Vol. 2, n°3, pp.165–177.
Brigham John (1997), 'The Other Countries of American Law', *Droit et Société*, Vol. 36/37, pp. 363–378.
Brown M. (1998), 'Can Culture Be Copyrighted?', *Current Anthropology*, April, Vol. 39, n°2.
Brym R. (1996), 'The Ethics of Self-Reliance and the Spirit of Capitalism in Russia', *International Sociology*, December, Vol. 4, n°4, pp. 409–426.
Buchanan James M. (1994), *The Economics and Ethics of Constitutional Order*, The University of Michigan Press, Ann Arbor.
Buzgalin Aleksander (1994), *Perehodnaja ekonomika*, Taurus, Moskva.
Caillé A. (1994), 'Présentation', *Revue du MAUSS*, second semestre, n°4.
Cesoni Maria Luisa (1995), *Développement du Mezzogionro et criminalités. La consolidation économique des réseaux camoristes*, thèse de doctorat: sociologie, l'Ecole des Hautes Etudes en Sciences Sociales, Paris.
Chauvenet Antoinette, Orlic Françoise, Benguigui Gorges (1994), *Le monde des surveillants de prison*, Presses Universitaires de France, Paris.
Cheung S. (1983), 'The Contractual Nature of the Firm', *Journal of Law and Economics*, Vol. XXVI, April.
Code de Procédure Pénale (1995), Litec, Paris – 8ème édition mise au jour au 31 août 1995.
Coleman James S. (1990), *Foundations of Social Theory*, The Belknap Press of Harvard University Press, Cambridge, London.
Coase Ronald (1988), *The Firm, the Market and the Law*, The University of Chicago Press, Chicago.
Cornell S., Kalt J. (1995), 'Where Does Economic Development Really Come From? Constitutional Rule Among the Contemporary Sioux and Apache', *Economic Inquiry*, Vol. XXXIII, July.
Cotta Alain (1984), *Le corporatisme*, Presses Universitaires de France, Paris – Coll. Que sais-je?

Crawford S., Ostrom Elinor (1995), 'A Grammar of Institutions', *American Political Science Review*, Vol. 89, n°3, September.
Cusson Maurice (1981), *Délinquants pourquoi?*, Arman Colin, Paris.
Cymburskij Vitalij (1995), 'Chelovek politicheskij mejdu ratio i otvetami na stimuly. K ichisleniu kognitivnyh tipov prinjatija reshenij', *POLIS – Politicheskie Issledovanija*, t.29, n°5.
Dallago Bruno (1990), *The 'Underground' Economy and the 'Black' Labour Market*, Dartmouth, Aldershot.
Dasgupta Partha (2000), 'Economic progress and the idea of social capital', in: Dasgupta Partha, Serageldin Ismail (eds.), *Social Capital. A Multifaceted Perspective*, The World Bank, Washington, D.C.
David Paul A. (1985), 'CLIO and the Economics of QWERTY', *American Economic Review*, Vol. 75, n° 2.
Debouzy Marianne (1992), *Le capitalisme 'sauvage' aux Etats-Unis. 1860–1900*, Ed. du Seuil, Paris.
Denzau Arthur T., North Douglass C. (1994), 'Shared Mental Models: Ideologies and Institutions', *Kyklos*, Vol. 47, n° 1, pp. 3–31.
Diligenskij German G. (1996), 'Rossijskie arhetipy i sovremennost', *Vestnik Fonda 'Rossijskij obshestvenno-politicheskij centr'*, Dekabr', n°2, pp. 45–52.
Dolgopjatova Tatjana, Evseeva I. (1994), 'Ekonomicheskoe povedenie promyshlennyh predpijatij v perehodnoj ekonomike', *Voprosy Ekonomiki*, Avgust, n°8.
Dolgopjatova Tatjana (1995), *Rossijskie predprijatija v perehodnoj ekonomike: ekonomicheskie problemy i povedenie*, Delo, Moskva.
Dolgopjatova Tatjana (ed.) (1998), *Neformal'nyj sekror v rossijskoj ekonomike: formy sushestvovanija, rol' i masshtaby*, Institut Strategičeskogo Analiza i Razvitija Predprinimatel'stva, Moskva.
Douglas Mary (1986), *How Institutions Think*, Syracuse University Press, Syracuse, New York.
Douglass Dorothy W. (1972), *Transitional Economic Systems: The Polish-Czech Example*, Monthly Review Press, New York, London – 2nd edition.
Dolgova A., Djakov S. (eds.) (1989), *Organizovannaja prestupnost'*, Yuridicheskaja literatura, Moskva.
Dubet François (1994), *Sociologie de l'expérience*, Ed. du Seuil, Paris.
Dubov I. (ed.) (1997), *Mental'nost' rossijan. Specifika soznanija bol'shih grupp naselanija Rossii*, Psihologicheskij institut RAO / Imidj kontakt, Moskva.
Dubov Ylij (1999), *Bol'shaja pajka*, Vagrius, Moskva.
Duncker Karl (1964), 'The Solution of Practical Problems', in Mandler J., Mandler G. (eds.), *Thinking: From Association to Gestalt*, John Wiley & Sons, New York.
Durand Yves (1987), *La vie quotidienne des prisonniers de guerre dans les stalags, les oflags et les kommandos 1939–1945*, Hachette, Paris.
Easterlin R. (1974), 'Does economic growth improve the human lot? Some empirical evidence', in: David P., Reder W. (eds.), *Nation's households in economic growth. Essays in honor of Moses Abramowitz*, Academic Press, New York.
Eggertsson Thráinn (1990), *Economic Behavior and Institutions*, Cambridge University Press, Cambridge.
Ekonomika perehodnogo perioda, Institut Ekonomiki Perehodnogo Perioda, Moskva.
Eligulashvili E. (1983), *Rol' obshenija v processe vzaimodejstvija lichnosti s real'nost'u*, thèse de doctorat: psychologie, Institut psihologii im. Uznadze, Tbilissi.
Elster John (1988), 'Economic Order and Social Norms', *Journal of Institutional and Theoretical Economics*, Vol. 144, n°2.

Elster John, (1996), 'Introduction', in Elster John (ed.), *The Roundtable Talks and the Breakdown of Communism*, The University of Chicago Press, Chicago.
Ensminger Jean (1992), *Making a Market. The Institutional Transformation of an African Society*, Cambridge University Press, Cambridge.
Erikson Erik H. (1959), 'Identity and the Life Cycle', *Psychological Issues*, 1959, Vol. 1, n°1, monograph 1.
Erofeev Venedikt (1975), *Moscou – Pétouchki*, A. Michel, Paris – Traduit du Russe par A. Sabatier et A. Pingaud.
Etzioni Amitai (1988), *The Moral Dimension. Toward a New Economics*, The Free Press, New York, London.
Fadat M. (1996), 'Faire lire "Surveiller et punir"', *Sociétés et représentations*, Novembre, n°3, numéro spécial 'Michel Foucault "Surveiller et punir": la prison vingt ans après'.
Fathullin N., Zamorin A. (1993), Kazanskij fenomen: opyt sociologicheskogo osmyslenija podrostkovoj problemy, in *'Problemy bor'by s organizovannoj prestupnost'u i korrupciej'*, sbornik nauchnyh trudov, Vsesouznyj nauchno-issledovatel'skij institut MVD RF, Moskva.
Feest Johannes, Weber Hartmut-Michael (1996), 'Germany: Ups and Downs to Imprisonment – Strategic or Unplanned Outcomes?', in Weiss R., South N. (eds.), *Comparing Prisons Systems: Toward a Comparative and International Penology*, Gordon and Breach Publishers, pp. 233–261.
Foucault Michel (1995), *Discipline and Punish: The Birth of the Prison*, Vintage Books – 2nd edition. Translator Alan Sheridan.
Furukawa T., Sarason I., Sarason B. (1998), 'Social Support and Adjustment to a Novel Social Environment', *International Journal of Social Psychiatry*, Vol. 44, n°1, pp. 56–70.
Gambetta Diego (1988), 'Fragments of an Economic Theory of the Mafia', *Archives européennes de sociologie*, Vol. XXIX, n°1, pp. 127–145.
Gambetta Diego (1993), *The Sicilian Mafia. The Business of Private Protection*, Harvard University Press, Cambridge.
Garfinkel Harold (1967), *Studies in Ethnomethodology*, Prentice Hall, Englewood Cliffs.
Gasadamont M. (1996), 'M. Foucault et le champ carcéral', *Sociétés et représentations*, Novembre, n°3, numéro spécial 'Michel Foucault "Surveiller et punir": la prison vingt ans après'.
Gatrell Peter (1995), 'Economic Culture, Economic Policy and Economic Growth in Russia 1861–1914', *Cahiers du Monde Russe*, Janvier – Juin, Vol. XXXVI, n°1–2.
Geertz Clifford (1996), *Ici et Là-bas. L'anthropologue comme acteur*, Ed. Métaillé, Paris.
Giddens Anthony (1984), *The Constitution of Society. Outline of the Theory of Structuration*, Polity Press, Cambridge.
Giddens Anthony (1996), *In Defence of Sociology. Essays, Interpretations and Rejoinders*, Polity Press, Cambridge.
Girard René (1972), *La violence et le sacré*, Bernard Grasset, Paris.
Goffman Erving (1968), *Asiles. Etudes sur la condition sociale des maladies mentaux et autres reclus*, Ed. de Minuit, Paris.
Golovach V. (1990), 'Organizovannaja ekonomicheskaja prestupnost'' i mery bor'by s nej', in *Problemy bor'by s prestuplenijami v sfere ekonomiki*, sbornik nauchnyh trudov, Kievskaja vyshaja shkola milicii MVD SSSR im. Dzerjinskogo, Kiev.
Gorjainov K. (1993), 'Latentnaja prestupnost'' v Rossii: rezultaty issledovanija i mery bor'by', in *Latentnaja prestupnost'': poznanie, politika, strategija*, sbornik materialov mejdunarodnogo seminara, Vsesouznyj nauchno-issledovatel'skij institut MVD RF, Moskva.

Granovetter Mark (1985), Economic Action and Social Structure: The Problem of Embeddedness, *American Journal of Sociology*, November, Vol. 91, n°3, pp. 481–510.
Grib V. (1993), 'Protivodejstvie organizovannoj prestupnosti: ob'edinenie usilij i centralizacija rukovodstva', in *Problemy bor'by s organizovannoj prestupnost'u i korrupciej*, sbornik nauchnyh trudov, Vsesouznyj nauchno-issledovatel'skij institut MVD RF, Moskva.
Groenewengen J. (1995), 'Introduction', in Groenewengen J., Pitelis C., Sjöstrand S.-E. (eds.), *On Economic Institutions. Theory and Applications*, Edward Elgar, Aldershot.
Gurov A. (1995), *Krasnaja Mafija*, Samocvet, Moskva.
Gurov A. (1991), 'Organizovannaja prestupnost'' i tenevaja ekonomika', in *Tenevaja ekonomika*, Ekonomika, Moskva.
Haerpfer Christian, Rose Richard (1993), 'Adapting to Transition in the Eastern Europe. New Democracies Barometer – II', *Studies in Public Policy*, n°212.
Hahn Jeffrey W. (1997), 'Russian Political Culture in a Time of Troubles. Yaroslavl 1990–96', *Studies in Public Policy*, n°295.
Heap S.H. (1995), 'Rational Action and Institutional Change', in Groenewengen J., Pitelis C., Sjöstrand S.-E. (eds.), *On Economic Institutions. Theory and Applications*, Edward Elgar, Aldershot.
Hermann-Pillath C. (1994), 'China's Transition to the Market: A Paradox of Transformation and its Institutional Solution', in Wagener Hans-Jürgen (ed.), *The Political Economy of Transformation*, Physica-Verlag, Heidelberg.
Hirschman Albert (1970), *Exit, Voice, and Loyalty*, Harvard University Press, Cambridge.
Hirschi Travis (1969), *Causes of Delinquency*, University of California Press, Berkeley.
Hlomov D. (1985), *Osobennosti vosprijatija mejlichnostyh vzaimodejstvij bol'nymi shizofreniej*, thèse de doctorat: psychologie, fakul'tet psihologii MGU, Moskva.
Hlopin Aleksandr D. (1994), 'Fenomen 'dvoemyslija': Zapad i Rossija (osobennosti rolevogo povedenija', *Obshestvennye nauki i sovremennost'*, Mart, n°3.
Hodgson Geoffrey M. (1988), *Economics and Institutions. A Manifesto for a Modern Institutional Economics*, Polity Press, Cambridge.
Hofstede G. (1980), *Culture's consequences: international differences in work-related values*, Beverly Hills.
Hofstede G. (1991), *Cultures and Organizations*, Cambridge University Press, Cambridge.
Hoggart Richard (1970), *La culture du pauvre. Etude sur la style de vie des classes populaires en Angleterre*, Ed. de Minuit, Paris.
Humphrey John, Schmitz Hubert (1998), 'Trust and Inter-Firm Relations in Developing and Transition Economies', *The Journal of Development Studies*, Vol. 34, n°4, April, pp. 32–61.
Ikes B., Ritterman R. (1994), 'Ot predprijatija k firme: zametki po teorii predprijatija perehodnogo perioda', *Voprosy Ekonomiki*, n°8.
Il'enkov Eval'd (1991), *Filosofija i kul'tura*, Izdatel'stvo politicheskoj literatury, Moskva.
Inglehart R. (1990), *Culture Shift in Advanced Industrial Society*, Princeton University Press, Princeton.
Inglehart R. (1995), 'Modification des valeurs, développement économique et évolution politique', *Revue Internationale des Sciences Sociales*, Vol. 145, Septembre, pp. 433–460.
Ispravnikov V., Kulikov V. (1997), *Tenevaja ekonomika v Rossii: inoj put' i tret'ja sila*, Rossijskij ekonomicheskij jurnal, Moskva.
James Philip S. (1989), *Introduction to English Law*, Butterworths, London – 12th edition.
Jerebin V., Romanov A. (1998), *Ekonomika domashnih hozjajstv*, Finansy/UNITY, Moskva.

Jotsen M. (1993), 'Latentnaja prestupnost' i zakonodatel'stvo: nacional'nyj i mejdunarodnyj opyt', in *Latentnaja prestupnost': poznanie, politika, strategija*, sbornik materialov mejdunarodnogo seminara, Vsesouznyj nauchno-issledovatel'skij institut MVD RF, Moskva.

Kaldor N. (1987), *Economie et instabilité*, Economica, Paris.

Kaufman Daniel (1998), 'Corruption in transition economies', in Newman Peter (ed.), *The New Palgrave Dictionary of Economics and the Law*, Macmillan, London – 3 volumes.

Keynes John M. (1993), *Izbrannye proizvedenija*, Ekonomika, Moskva.

Kim N. (1999), 'Nadejda, ustalost', starost', *Ekonomicheskie i social'nye problemy. Monitoring obshestvennogo mnenija*, n°1 (39).

Kharhordine Oleg (1994), 'L'éthique corporatiste, l'éthique de samostojatel'nost' et l'esprit du capitalisme: réflexions sur la création du marché en Russie post-soviétique', *Revue d'études comparatives Est – Ouest*, Vol. 25, n°2, Juin.

Knaqck R. (1996), 'The Collapse of the Russian Economy: an Institutional Explanation', in Dallago Bruno, Mittone L. (eds.), *Institutions, Markets and Competition. Centralization and Decentralization in the Transformation of Economic Systems*, Edward Elgar, Cheltenham.

Koffka K. (1935), *Principles of Gestalt Psychology*, Routledge & Kegan Paul, London.

Kolesnikov V. (1994), *Ekonomicheskaja prestupnost' i rynochnye reformy. Politiko-ekonomicheskie aspekty*, Izdatel'stvo Sankt-Peterburgskogo universiteta ekonomiki i finansov, Sankt-Peterburg.

Kolm Serge-Christophe (1984), *La bonne économie. La Réciprocité générale*, Presses Universitaires de France, Paris.

Kommentarij k Ispravitel'no-trudovomu kodeksu RSFSR (1979), Yridicheskaja literatura, Moskva.

Kondrat'ev Nikolai, Oparin Dmitrij (1928), *Bol'shie cikly kon'unktury*, Moskva.

Kornaï János (1992), *The Socialist System. The Political Economy of Communism*, Princeton University Press, Princeton.

Kornaï János (1990), *Deficit*, Nauka, Moskva.

Korjagina Tat'jana (1991), 'Analiz, ocenki, prognozy', in *Tenevaja economika*, Ekonomika, Moskva.

Krasheninnikova N., Jidkova O. (eds.) (1999), *Istorija gosudarstva i prava zarubejnyh stran*, Norma, Moskva – 2 vol.

Kreps David (1990), 'Corporate culture and economic theory', in Alt J., Shepsle K. (eds.), *Perspectives on Positive Political Economy*, Cambridge University Press, Cambridge.

Kriminal'naja situacija v Rossii i ee izmenenija (1996), Kriminologicheskaja associacija, Moskva.

Krugman Paul R. (1996), *The Self-Organizing Economy*, Blackwell, Cambridge.

Kulikov V. (1994), *Osonvy kriminalisticheskoj teorii organizovannoj prestupnoj dejatel'nosti*, Ul'janovskij filial MGU, Ul'janovsk.

Kuran Timur (1989), 'The Craft Guilds of Tunis and their Amins: A Study of Institutional Atrophy', in Nabli M., Nugent J. (eds.), *The New Institutional Economics and Development. Theory and Applications to Tunisia*, North-Holland, Amsterdam.

Lafaye C., Thévenot Laurent (1993), Une justification écologique? Conflits dans l'aménagement de la nature, *Revue Française de Sociologie*, Vol. XXXIV, n°4, mars.

Langlois Richard (1986), 'Rationality, Institutions, and Explanation', in Langlois Richard (ed.), *Economics as a Process. Essays in the New Institutional Economics*, Cambridge University Press, Cambridge.

Lautier Bruno (1994), *L'économie informelle dans le Tiers monde*, La Découverte, Paris – Col. Repères.
Laville Frédéric (1998), 'Modélisation de la rationalité limitée: de quel outils dispose-t-on?', *Revue Economique*, Vol. 49, n°2, mars.
Leader Sheldon (1993), 'Common Law', in Arnaud André-Jean (ed.), *Dictionnaire encyclopédique de théorie et de sociologie du droit*, Librairie Générale de Droit et de Jurisprudence (LGDJ), Paris – 2e édition.
Ledeneva Alena V. (1998), *Russia's Economy of Favours. Blat, Networking and Informal Exchange*, Cambridge University Press, Cambridge – Col. Cambridge Russian, Soviet and Post-Soviet Studies, n° 102.
Lenin Vladimir (1971–1975), *Polnoe sobranie sochinenij*, Politizdat, Moskva.
Lebina Natal'ja B. (1999), *Povsednevnaja jizn' sovetskogo goroda. 1920–1930 gody*, Neva – Letnij Sad, Sankt-Peterburg.
Levada Youri (1993), *Entre passé et l'avenir. L'homme soviétique ordinaire. Enquête*, Presses de la Fondation Nationale des Sciences Politiques, Paris.
Le Roy Etienne (1993), 'Conciliation', in Arnaud André-Jean (ed.), *Dictionnaire encyclopédique de théorie et de sociologie du droit*, Librairie Générale de Droit et de Jurisprudence (LGDJ), Paris – 2e édition.
Lindenberg S. (1988), 'Contractual Relations and Weak Solidarity: The Behavioral Basis of Restraints of Gain Maximization', *Journal of Institutional and Theoretical Economics*, Vol. 144, n°1.
Livet Pierre, Thévenot Laurent (1994), 'Les catégories de l'action collective', in Orléan André (ed.), *Analyse économique des conventions*, Presse Universitaires de France, Paris – Col. Economie. – pp. 139–168.
Lochak Danièle (1993), 'Institution', in Arnaud André-Jean (ed.), *Dictionnaire encyclopédique de théorie et de sociologie du droit*, Librairie Générale de Droit et de Jurisprudence (LGDJ), Paris – 2e édition.
Lodge David (1985), *Small world. An academic romance*, Penguin Books, London.
Łos M. (1987), 'The Dynamics of the Second Economy in Poland', in Łos M. (ed.), *The Second Economy in Marxist States*, Macmillan, London.
Makarov Dmitrij (1998), 'Ekonomicheskie i pravovye aspekty tenevoj ekonomiki v Rossii', *Voprosy ekonomiki*, n°3.
Manaï Dominique (1993), 'Equité', in Arnaud André-Jean (ed.), *Dictionnaire encyclopédique de théorie et de sociologie du droit*, Librairie Générale de Droit et de Jurisprudence (LGDJ), Paris – 2e édition.
Mansurov V. (ed.) (1999), *Sovremennoe rossijskoe obshestvo: perehodnyj period*, rezul'taty sociologicheskogo oprosa naselenija Rossii, provedennogo v dekabre 1998 goda, Institut sociologii RAN, Moskva.
Marchetti Anne-Marie (1997), *Pauvretés en prison*, Erès, Ramonville Saint-Agne.
Marie Jean-Bernard (1993), 'Droits de l'homme', in Arnaud André-Jean (ed.), *Dictionnaire encyclopédique de théorie et de sociologie du droit*, Librairie Générale de Droit et de Jurisprudence (LGDJ), Paris – 2e édition.
Marquart James W. (1986), 'Prison Guards and the Use of Physical Coercion as a Mechanism of Prisoner Control', *Criminology*, Vol. 24, n°2, pp. 347–366.
Marx Karl (1975), *Early Writings*, Penguin Books, London.
Marx Karl (1988), *Kapital*, Izdatel'stvo politicheskoj literatury, Moskva – 3 vol.
Matza David (1990), *Delinquency and Drift*, Transaction Publishers, New Brunswick – 2nd edition.
Mauger G. (1996), 'Un nouveau militantisme', *Sociétés et représentations*, n°3, Novembre, numéro spécial 'Michel Foucault "Surveiller et punir": la prison vingt ans après'.

Merton Robert (1938), 'Social Structure and Anomie', *American Sociological Review*, October, Vol.3, n°5, pp. 672–682.

Milgrom Paul, North Douglass, Weingast Barry (1990), 'The Role of Institutions in the Revival of Trade: the Law Merchant, Private Judges, and the Champagne Fairs', *Economics and Politics*, Vol. 2, n°1, March, pp. 1–23.

Mishler William, Rose Richard (1995), 'What are the Alternatives to Democracy in Post-Communist Societies?', *Studies in Public Policy*, n°248.

Monroe Kristen R. (1994), 'A Fat Lady in a Corset: Altruism and Social Theory', *American Journal of Political Science*, Vol. 38, n°4, November.

Moore Mick (1999), 'Truth, Trust and Market Transactions: What Do We Know?', *The Journal of Development Studies*, Vol. 36, n°1, October, pp. 74–88.

Morozov Yuri (1991–1992), *Puti Rossii. Modernizacija neevropejskih kul'tur*, Moskva – 4 vol.

Murrell P. (1992), 'Evolutionary and Radical Approaches to Economic Reforms', *Economics of Planning*, 1992, Vol. 25, n°1, pp. 79–95.

Najshul' Vitalij (1992), 'Liberalizm i ekonomicheskie reformy', *Mirovaja ekonomika i mejdunarodnye otnoshenija*, n°8.

Nelson R., Winter S. (1982), *An Evolutionary Theory of Economic Change*, Belknap Press, Cambridge.

Nielsen K., Jessop B., Hausner J. (1995), 'Institutional Change in Post-Socialism', in Nielsen K., Jessop B., Hausner J. (eds.), *Strategic Choice and Path-Dependency in Post-Socialism. Institutional Dynamics in the Transformation Process*, Edward Elgar, Aldershot.

North Douglass (1989), 'Institutions and Economic Growth: An Historical Introduction', *World Development*, Vol. 17, n°9, special issue 'The Role of Institutions in Economic Development'.

North Douglass (1981), *Structure and Change in Economic History*, Norton, New York.

Oberschall Anthony (1993), *Social Movements: Ideologies, Interests and Identities*, Transaction Publishers, New Brunswick.

O'Brien David, Patsiorkovski Valeri, Dershem Larry, Lylova Oksana (1996), 'Social capital and adaptation to social change in Russian villages', *Studies in Public Policy*, n°263.

Observatoire international des prisons (1996), *Le guide du prisonnier*, Les Editions de l'Atelier / Editions Ouvrières, Paris.

Obzor ekonomiki Rossii. Osnovnye tendencii razvitija. 1997 god, IV kvartal (1998), Rossijsko-evropejskij centr ekonomicheskoj politiki, Moskva.

Offe Claus (1994), 'Capitalism by Democratic Design?', in Wagener Hans-Jürgen (ed.), *The Political Economy of Transformation*, Physica-Verlag, Heidelberg.

Offe Claus (1995), 'Designing Institutions for East European Transitions', in Nielsen K., Jessop B., Hausner J. (eds.), *Strategic Choice and Path-Dependency in Post-Socialism. Institutional Dynamics in the Transformation Process*, Edward Elgar, Aldershot.

Oleynik Anton N. (1996a), 'Evolution de l'économie informelle en ex-URSS: quelques éléments de réflexion', in Cusinato Augusto (ed.), *Economia Informale e Istituzioni. Processi di reciproco adattamento*, l'Harmattan Italia, Milano.

Oleinik Anton N. (1996b), 'Est' li perspektiva u social'nyh dvijenij v Rossii: primer shahterskogo dvijenija 1991–1995', *POLIS – Politicheskie issledovanija*, n°3.

Oleinik Anton N. (1998), 'K analizu effektivnosti social'noj politiki', *POLIS – Politicheskie Issledovanija*, n°5, pp. 139–144.

Oleinik Anton N. (1997–1998), 'Izderjki i perspektivy rossijskih reform', *MEiMO - Mirovaja ekonomika i mejdunarodnye otnoshenija*, n°12, 1997; n°1, 1998.

Oleinik Anton N. (1999a), 'Rossijskaja ekonomicheskaja nauka: istorija znachima', *Voprosy ekonomiki*, n°1.
Olejnik Anton N. (1999b), 'Le changement institutionnel: une analyse sociologique de la réforme pénitentiaire en Russie', *Revue d'études comparatives Est – Ouest*, Vol.30, n°1, pp. 165–188.
Oleinik Anton N. (2000a), *Institucional'naja ekonomika*, Infra M, Moskva.
Oleinik Anton N. (2000b), *Institucional'nye aspekty social'no-ekonomicheskih transformacij*, TEIS, Moskva.
Oleinik Anton N. (2001), 'Changes in the Organization of Everyday Life in the Wake of Financial Crisis', in Segbers Klaus (ed.), *Explaining Post-Soviet Patchworks*, vol. 2, 'Pathways from the past to the global', Ashgate, Aldershot, pp. 362–384.
Oleinik Anton N. (2002a), 'La réforme administrative, élément clé de la réforme pénitentiaire dans les Républiques post-Soviétiques', *Revue française d'administration publique*, numéro spécial 'Administration et politiques pénitentiaires', n°99, pp. 513–522.
Oleinik Anton N. (2002b), 'V zakluchenii v bashne iz... (k voprosy ob institucional'noj organizacii nauki)', *Voprosy ekonomiki*, n°9, pp. 117–126.
Oleinik Anton N. (2002c), 'Deficit Prava (k kritike politicheskoj ekonomii chastnoj zashity), *Voprosy ekonomiki*, n°4, pp. 23–45.
Oleinik Anton N., Gvozdeva Evgenia, Kashturov Aleksandr, Patrushev Sergej (2000), 'Mejdisciplinarnyj podhod k analizu vyvoza kapitala iz Rossii', *Voprosy ekonomiki*, n°2.
Organizovannaja prestupnost' – 2. Problemy, disskussii, predlojenija. Kruglyj stol Kriminologicheskoj associacii (1993), Kriminologicheskaja associacija, Moskva.
Orléan André (1994), 'Sur le rôle respectif de la confiance et de l'intérêt dans la constitution de l'ordre marchand', *Revue du MAUSS*, second semestre, n°4.
Orrù M. (1993), 'Institutional Cooperation in Japanese and German Capitalism', in Sjöstrand S.-E. (ed.), *Institutional Change. Theory and Empirical Findings*, M. E. Sharpe, Armonk.
Ostrom Elinor (1990), *Governing the Commons. The Evaluation of Institutions for Collective Action*, Cambridge University Press, Cambridge.
Ostrom Elinor (1998), 'A Behavioral Approach to the Rational Choice Theory of Collective Action. Presidential Address, American Political Science Association, 1997', *American Political Science Review*, Vol. 92, n°1, March, pp. 1–22.
Oswald (1997), 'Happiness and Economic Performance', *Economic Journal*, Vol. 107, pp. 1815–1830.
Ovchinskij Vladimir, Ovchinskij S. (1993), *Bor'ba s mafiej v Rossii. Posobie v voprosah i otvetah dlja sotrudnikov organov vnutrennih del*, Ministerstvo Vnutrennih Del RF, Moskva.
Padovani Marcelle (1987), *Les dernières années de la mafia*, Gallimard, Paris.
Pejovich S. (1995), 'Privatizing the Process of Institutional Change in Eastern Europe', in *Conference papers*, European Association For Evolutionary Political Economy, Krakow.
Pejovich S. (1996), 'The Market for Institutions Vs. the Strong Hand of the State: the Case of Eastern Europe', in Dallago Bruno, Mittone L. (eds.), *Institutions, Markets and Competition. Centralization and Decentralization in the Transformation of Economic Systems*, Edward Elgar, Cheltenham.
Pelevin Viktor (1997), *Chapaev i Pustota*, Vagrius, Moskva.
Peneff Jean (1992), *L'hôpital en urgence. Etude par observation participante*, Ed. Métailié, Paris.
Peralva Angelina (1996), *La violence au collège: une étude de cas*, document de travail du CADIS, Paris, juillet.

Perrot M. (1997), 'Préface', in Marchetti A.-M., *Pauvrétés en prison*, Erès, Ramonville Saint-Agne.
Perrow C. (1993), 'Small Firm Networks', in Sjöstrand S.-E. (ed.), *Institutional Change. Theory and Empirical Findings*, M. E. Sharpe, Armonk.
Petit Jacques-Guy, Gastan Nicole, Faugeron Claude, Pierre Michel, Zysberg André (1991), *Histoire des galères, bagnes et prisons. Introduction à l'histoire pénale de la France*, Bibliothèque historique Privat, Toulouse.
Piette Albert (1996), *Ethnographie de l'action. L'observation des détails*, Ed. Métailé, Paris.
Platek Monika (1990), 'Prison Subculture in Poland', *International Journal of the Sociology of Law*, Vol. 18, n°4, November.
Podlesskih G., Tereshenok A. (1995), *Vory v zakone: brosok k vlasti*, Hudojestvennaja literatura, Moskva.
Polanyi Karl (1983), *La Grande Transformation. Aux origines politiques et économiques de notre temps*, Gallimard, Paris.
Pravila vnutrennego rasporjadka ispravitel'nyh uchrejdenij, oficial'nyj tekst (1997), Moskva.
Putnam Robert D. (1993), 'The Prosperous Community. Social Capital and Public Life', *The American Prospect*, n°13, Spring, pp. 35–42.
Putnam Robert D. with Leonardi Robert, Nanetti Rafaella (1993), *Making Democracy Work. Civic Traditions in Modern Italy*, Princeton University Press, Princeton.
Radaev Vadim V. (1994), 'Vneekonomicheskie motivy predprinimatel'skoj dejatel'nosti', *Voprosy Ekonomiki*, n°7.
Redmond P., Shears P. (1964), *General Principles of English Law*, Pitman Publishing, London.
Reuter Peter (1983), *Disorganized Crime. The Economics of the Visible Hand*, The MIT Press, Cambridge.
Reynaud Jean-Daniel (1989), *Les règles du jeu. L'action collective et la régulation sociale*, Armand Colin, Paris.
Rocca J.-L. (1994), 'La "mise au travail" capitaliste des Chinois', in Bayart J.-F. (ed.), *La réinvention du capitalisme*, Ed. Karthala, Paris.
Roché Sebastian (1993), *Le sentiment d'insécurité*, Presses Universitaires de France, Paris – Coll. Sociologie d'aujourd'hui.
Rosanvallon Pierre (1988), *La question syndicale. Histoire et avenir d'une forme sociale*, Calmann-Lévy, Paris.
Rose Richard (1991), 'Between State and Market. Key Indicators of Transition in Eastern Europe', *Studies in Public Policy*, n°196.
Rose Richard (1994a), 'Distrust as an Obstacle to Civil Society', *Studies in Public Policy*, n°226.
Rose Richard (1994b), 'Getting By Without Government: Everyday Life in a Stressful Society', *Studies in Public Policy*, n°227.
Rose Richard (1995), 'La liberté, valeur fondamentale', *Revue Internationale des Sciences Sociales*, Vol. 145, Septembre, pp. 519–536.
Rose Richard, Mishler William (1994), 'Mass Reaction to Regime Change in Eastern Europe: Polarization or Leaders and Laggards?', *British Journal of Political Science*, Vol. 24.
Rose Richard, Mishler William, Haerpfer Christian (1997), 'Getting Real: Social Capital in Post-Communist Societies', *Studies in Public Policy*, n°278.
Rosen S. (1988), 'Promotions, Elections and Other Contests', *Journal of Institutional and Theoretical Economics*, Vol. 144, n°1.
Rossi Jacques (1991), *Spavochnik po GULAGu*, Prosvet, Moskva – 2 vol.

Rossijsko-evropejskij centr ekonomicheskoj politiki (1998), *Obzor ekonomiki Rossii. Osnovnye tendencii razvitija. IV kvartal 1997*, RECER, Moskva.
Rostang Corinne (1994), *Prisons de femmes. Les échanges et les marges de manœuvre dans une institution contraignante*, Thèse de doctorat: Sociologie, l'Ecole des Hautes Etudes en Sciences Sociales, Paris.
Rousselet Kathy (1994), 'Russie: libéralisation économique et bricolage culturel', in Bayart J.-F. (ed.), *La réinvention du capitalisme*, Ed. Karthala, Paris.
Rusakov N. P. (1969), *Iz istorii sicilijskoj mafii*, Nauka, Moskva.
Rusche Georg, Kirchheimer Otto (1994), *Peine et structure sociale. Histoire et 'Théorie critique' de régime pénal*, Ed. du Cerf, Paris.
Sapir Jacques (1989), *Les fluctuations économiques en URSS. 1941–1985*, Editions de l'Ecole des Hautes Etudes en Sciences Sociales, Paris.
Sapir Jacques (1990), *L'économie mobilisée*, Ed. La Découverte, Paris.
Sapir Jacques (1996), 'Désintégration économique, transition et politiques publiques en Russie', in Delorme R. (ed.), *A l'est, du nouveau. Changement institutionnel et transformations économiques*, l'Harmattan, Paris.
Saylor William G. (1984), *Surveying Prison Environments*, working paper, Office of Research and Evaluation, Federal Bureau of Prisons, Washington D.C.
Saylor William G. (1989), 'Quality Control for Prison Managers. The Key Indicators / Strategic Support System', *Federal Prisons Journal*, Fall, pp. 39–42.
Schiavo Giovanni (1962), *The Truth about the Mafia and Organized Crime in America*, The Vigo Press, New York.
Schlicht E. (1988), 'A Comment on S. Rosen "Promotions, Elections and Other Contests"', *Journal of Institutional and Theoretical Economics*, Vol. 144, n°1.
Schmitt Karl (1992), *La notion de politique. Théorie du partisan*, Flammarion, Paris.
Schober Michael, Conrad Frederic (1997), 'Does Conversational Interviewing Reduce Survey Measurement Error?', *Public Opinion Quarterly*, Vol. 61, n°4, Winter, pp. 576–602.
Schotter Andrew (1981), *The Economic Theory of Social Institutions*, Cambridge University Press, Cambridge.
Schutz Alfred (1987), *Le chercheur et le quotidien. Phénoménologie des sciences sociales*, Méridiens Klincksieck, Paris.
Sen Amartya (1987), *On Ethics & Economics*, Blackwell, Oxford.
Seyler Monique (1990), *L'isolement en prison. L'un et le multiple*, Centre de Recherches Sociologiques sur le Droit et le Institutions Pénales, Paris.
Sjöstrand S.-E. (1993), 'On Institutional Thought in the Social and Economic Sciences', in Sjöstrand S.-E. (ed.), *Institutional Change. Theory and Empirical Findings*, M. E. Sharpe, Armonk.
Shalamov Varlam (1998), *Sobranie sochinenij v 4-h tomah*, Hudojestvennaja literatura / Vagrius, Moskva.
Shlapentokh Vladimir (1989), *Public and Private Life of the Soviet People. Changing Values in Post-Stalin Russia*, Oxford University Press, Oxford.
Shlapentokh Vladimir (1995), 'Russian Patience: A Reasonable Behavior and a Social Strategy', *Archives Européennes de Sociologie*, Vol. XXXVI, n°2, pp. 247–280.
Shohin Aleksandr (1989), *Social'nye problemy perestrojki*, Ekonomika, Moskva.
Skoblikov Petr (2001), *Imuschestvennye spory i kriminal v sovremennoj Rossii*, Delo, Moskva.
Smeilser Neil J. (1998), 'The Rational and the Ambivalent in the Social Sciences', *American Sociological Review*, Vol. 63, n°1, February, pp. 1–16.
Solomon Peter H., Jr. (1996), *Soviet Criminal Justice under Stalin*, Cambridge University Press, Cambridge – Cambridge Russian, Soviet and Post-Soviet Studies.

Soto Hernando, de (1994), *L'autre sentier. La révolution informelle dans le tiers monde*, La Découverte, Paris.
Stark David (1992), 'Path Dependence and Privatization Strategies in East Central Europe', *East European Politics and Societies*, Vol. 6, n°1, Winter.
Stark David (1995), 'Not by Design: the Myth of Designer Capitalism in Eastern Europe', in Nielsen K., Jessop B., Hausner J. (eds.), *Strategic Choice and Path-Dependency in Post-Socialism. Institutional Dynamics in the Transformation Process*, Edward Elgar, Aldershot.
Stark David (1996), 'Recombinant Property in East European Capitalism', *American Journal of Sociology*, Vol. 101, n°4, pp. 993–1027.
Stark David, Bruszt L. (1996), 'Restructurer les réseaux dans le post-socialisme: la propriété inter-entreprises en Hongrie et en République tchèque', in Delorme R. (ed.), *A l'est, du nouveau. Changement institutionnel et transformations économiques*, l'Harmattan, Paris.
Stephenson K., Hayden F. (1995), 'Comparison of the Corporate Decision Networks of Nebraska and the United States', *Journal of Economic Issues*, Vol. XXIX, n°3, September.
Stiglitz J. (1987), 'Principal and Agent', in Eatwell J., Milgate M. and Newman P. (eds.), *The New Palgrave: A Dictionary of Economics*, Macmillan, London.
Sykes Gresham M. (1958), *The Society of Captives. A Study of a Maximum Security Prison*, Princeton University Press, Princeton.
Thévenot Laurent (1989), 'Equilibre et rationalité dans un univers complexe', *Revue économique*, Vol. 40, n°2, mars.
Thévenot Laurent (1995), 'Rationalité ou normes sociales: une opposition dépassée?', in Gérard-Varet Louis-André, Passeron Jean-Claude (eds.), *Le modèle et l'enquête. Les usages du principe de rationalité dans les sciences sociales*, Ed. de l'Ecole des Hautes Etudes en Sciences Sociales, Paris, pp. 149–192.
Thomas-Slayter Barbara (1994), 'Structural Change, Power Politics, and Community Organizations in Africa: Challenging the Patterns, Puzzles and Paradoxes', *World Development*, Vol. 22, n°10.
Timofeev Lev (1993), *Chernyj rynok kak politicheskaja sistema*, VIMO, Vil'nus-Moskva.
Tkachevskij Y. (1997), *Progressivnaja sistema ispolnenija ugolovnyh nakazanij*, uchebnoe posobie, Zercalo, Moskva.
Tocqueville Alexis de, Beaumont Gustave de (1984), 'Système pénitentiaire aux Etats-Unis et son application en France', in Tocqueville Alexis de, *Œuvres complètes. Ecrits sur le système pénitentiaire en France et à l'étranger*, Gallimard, Paris – Tome 4, Volume 1.
Touraine Alain (1965), *Sociologie de l'action*, Ed. du Seuil, Paris.
Touraine Alain, Dubet François, Wieviorka Michel, Strzelecki Jan (1982), *Solidarité*, Fayard, Paris.
Touraine Alain, Wieviorka Michel, Dubet François (1984), *Le mouvement ouvrier*, Fayard, Paris.
Touraine Alain (1988), *La parole et le sang. Politique et société en Amérique Latine*, Ed. Odil Jacob, Paris.
Touraine Alain (1992), *Critique de la modernité*, Fayard, Paris.
Touraine Alain (1993), *Production de la société*, Ed. du Seuil, Paris – 2e éd.
Touraine Alain (1994), *Qu'est-ce que la démocratie?*, Fayard, Paris.
Touraine Alain (1999), *Comment sortir du libéralisme*, Fayard, Paris.
Tremblay Pierre (1991), *Possible Prisons*, unpublished manuscript, McGill University, department of sociology, Montreal, September.
Trockij Lev, *Chto takoe SSSR?*, Slovo, Paris.

Bibliography

Troper Michel, Lochak Danièle, Jori Mario (1993), 'Norme', in Arnaud André-Jean (ed.), *Dictionnaire encyclopédique de théorie et de sociologie du droit*, Librairie Générale de Droit et de Jurisprudence (LGDJ), Paris – 2e édition.

Turvani Margherita (1997), 'Illegal Markets and New Institutional Economics', in Ménard Claude (ed.), *Transaction Costs Economics: Recent Developments*, Edward Elgar Publishing Co., Cheltenham.

Ugolovno-ispolnitel'nyj kodeks Rossijskoj Federacii, oficial'nyj tekst (1997), Infra M, Moskva.

Useem Bert, Reising Michael (1999), 'Collective Actions in Prisons: Protests, Disturbances and Riots', *Criminology*, Vol. 37, n°4, November, pp. 735–760.

Uznadze D. (1966), *Psihologicheskie issledovanija*, Nauka, Moskva.

Vacheret Marion, Dozois Jean, Lemire Guy (1998), 'Le système correctionnel canadien et la nouvelle pénologie: la notion de risque', *Déviance et Société*, Vol. 22, n°1, pp. 37–50.

Van Den Bergh G. C. J. J. (1993), 'Réception', in Arnaud André-Jean (ed.), *Dictionnaire encyclopédique de théorie et de sociologie du droit*, Librairie Générale de Droit et de Jurisprudence (LGDJ), Paris – 2e édition.

Wacquant Loïc (1998), 'Crime et châtiment en Amérique de Nixon à Clinton', *Archives de politique criminelle*, n°20, pp. 123–138.

Wacquant Loïc (2001), 'Deadly symbiosis. When ghetto and prison meet and mesh', *Punishment and Society*, Vol. 3, n°1, pp. 95–133.

Wagener H.-J. (1992), 'Pragmatic and Organic Change in Socio-economic Institutions', in Dallago B., Brezinski H., Andreff W. (eds.), *Convergence and System Change. The Convergence Hypothesis in the Light of Transition in Eastern Europe*, Dartmouth, Aldershot.

Walzer Michael (1992), 'La justice dans les institutions', *Esprit*, Vol. 180, n°3-4.

Weber Max (1964), *The Theory of Social and Economic Organization*, The Free Press, New York.

Weber Max (1965), *Essais sur la théorie de la science*, Librairie Plon, Paris – Coll. Recherches en Sciences humaines, n°19.

Weber Max (1968), *Economy and Society. An Outline of Interpretative Sociology*, University of California Press, Berkeley, Vol. 1.

Weyrauch Walter O. (1971), 'The "Basic Law" or "Constitution" of a Small Group', *Journal of Social Issues*, Vol. 27, n°2, pp. 49–63.

Wieviorka Michel, Trihn Sylviane (1989), *Le modèle EDF: Essai de sociologie des organisations*, La Découverte, Paris.

Wieviorka Michel, Bataille Philippe, Clément Karine, Cousin Olivier, Khosrovkhavar Fahrad, Labat Sandrine, Macé Eric, Rebughini Paola, Tietze Nikola (1999), *Violence en France*, Ed. du Seuil, Paris – Coll. Epreuve des faits.

Wiles P. (1987), 'The Second Economy, Its Definitional Problems', in Alessandrini S., Dallago Bruno (eds.), *The Unofficial Economy. Consequences and Perspectives in Different Economic Systems*, Gower, Aldershot.

Yakovlev A. (1988), *Sociologija ekonomicheskoj prestupnosi*, Nauka, Moskva.

Zakon o federal'nom budgete 2002 goda, utverjdennyj Gosudarstvennoj Dumoj 14.12.2001 (www.minfin.ru)

Index

Analogy (validation by) 39, 213
Acquaintances 15, 21, 59, 61, 82, 167-175, 181, 196, 202-203, 213, 218, 221-224, 227-228, 243, 246
Apartment
    Communal 177-179
    Standard 177-179
Assize court 136-137
Authority
    Conjoint 24-25, 143-144, 253fn, 259
    Disjoint 24-25, 143-144, 205, 253, 253fn, 258fn, 260, 262, 264
    Imposed 24-27, 33-34, 45, 51, 85, 89, 94, 143-144, 151, 155, 163, 187-191, 225-226, 237, 253, 253fn, 257, 258fn, 260, 262-265, 268
    Total *or* Totalitarian 4, 14, 17, 17fn, 27-29, 34, 45-48, 72, 90, 98, 104, 109-110, 115-119, 124-126, 138, 141-144, 151, 156, 163, 176, 237, 253fn, 258fn

Barrack 28, 47-50, 52-53, 59, 65, 74, 110, 117, 126, 177-178, 191, 230fn
Barter 106fn, 173, 207-209, 252-253
Baryga 64-66, 202, 246
Belomor-Baltic canal 85, 96, 192
Blackmail *see also* Racketeering 225
Blat xiii-xiv, 172-173, 196, 208, 213
    Blatnaya culture 70, 195
    'Blatnye' 65, 69-70, 73-75, 79-80, 94-98, 111, 121-122, 137, 240-243
Budget
    Family, of 169
    Government, of 49, 138, 147, 161-162

Camorra 3, 152
Canada 43, 51, 56fn, 57, 58fn, 62, 77, 84, 94, 99, 108, 118-119, 127, 132-133, 136, 139, 141-149, 157, 160, 160fn, 190, 220, 223, 235, 235fn, 245
Cell 48-49, 53, 53fn, 59-74, 77, 87, 104-105, 123, 126, 204, 231, 234, 242
Chechnya 93fn, 185-186, 254, 267-269
China 39, 51, 139, 151
Church xv, 34, 124, 190-191
City *see also* Convention
    Domestic 13-16, 21, 68, 70, 128, 155, 168, 173-174, 204
    Projects, by 13, 21, 71, 129, 168, 173, 203-204, 224
Code
    Applying Sentences, for *or* CAS 41fn, 49, 49fn, 52, 111, 230-239, 232fn, 251
    Civil 37, 202, 207, 229fn
    Penal 63, 71, 81, 100, 117, 134-135, 146, 163, 185, 188, 202, 231fn, 255-256, 256fn, 265
Collective action 32fn, 34, 61, 109, 118-119, 191, 213
Collective protests 116-118, 117fn
Common cause, *see also* Obshak 66, 106, 111-112, 125, 153, 245, 247
Common sense 136, 140, 267
Concentration camp 4, 46-47, 59, 123, 126
Conflict resolution 78, 131, 131fn, 154, 207
Congruence
    Institutional 22-25, 23fn, 27, 29, 34-40, 44, 86-88, 190-197, 250-251, 255, 260, 264-265
    Mathematics, in 23
Constitution of market 216-218, 251-252
Convention *see also* City 13, 16, 70, 173
Corruption 2, 160fn, 226, 261-262
Cosa Nostra *see also* Common cause 1fn, 15, 24, 106fn, 266
Crime
    Latent 162, 182

Organized 1-5, 1fn, 184, 225, 229, 264-266
Crisis of August 1998 44, 159, 198fn, 217

Dedovschina 28-29, 104
Democracy xv, 27, 143-144, 183, 254, 261, 268
Denunciation 55, 66-67, 109-110, 121
Development (socioeconomic) xii-xiii, 1, 19, 34-37, 152, 189, 213, 256
Disjuncture 23-24
Double thinking 187-191, 252, 268
Duality (of norms) 12, 16-20, 25, 25fn, 73, 77-83, 82fn, 92-95, 111, 128fn, 153-154, 163, 193, 200, 203, 216, 221, 223, 229, 261-262

Empathy 108, 149, 165, 170, 189, 217, 220, 223, 252
England xv, 13
Enemy xiii, 1, 16-20, 82, 181, 185-186
Equilibrium 78, 90-91, 90fn, 107, 148-149, 215, 244, 265, 265fn

Family
  In post-Soviet society 80, 108, 131fn, 137, 165-181, 187, 189-191, 196fn, 197, 201, 217, 220, 226, 230fn, 243, 246, 255, 260, 262, 265fn
  In prison 56, 72, 124-131, 126fn, 149, 247, 251
  In Sicily 153-154, 203fn, 243-244, 264
Freedom xv, 45, 108, 115, 117-119, 122, 136, 149, 165, 169-170, 188, 201, 213-214, 217, 220, 223, 231, 241, 251
Friends xiii, 14, 19-21, 54, 58, 63, 82, 107, 127-128, 135-136, 153-154, 167-174, 172fn, 181, 187-190, 195-196, 204, 211, 221, 223-228, 236, 247

Game
  Card 64-66, 74, 80, 88, 98, 100-101
  Theory 89, 106, 112, 215, 221, 254

Gaol *see also* SIZO 43, 48-50, 52, 53fn, 56, 63, 71, 74, 97, 103-104, 109, 111, 114, 117fn, 126, 243
Germany 39, 145, 164, 206, 237
Gestalt 23, 28, 39
Ghetto 3fn, 17, 122

Habitus 27-31, 30fn, 254
Holland xv
Homosexuality xiv, 60, 63, 67, 83-84, 95, 97-98, 100

Ideal type 11, 12fn, 13fn, 13-14, 17, 20, 42, 45, 50, 83, 88, 115-116, 135, 138, 144, 243, 251, 246fh, 253fn, 259
Importation (institutional) 37-40, 211-212
Indian Reorganization Act 36
Initiation rite 68-69, 68fn
Insecurity 87, 182
Italy xv, 2, 3fn, 37, 39, 51, 151-155, 165, 206, 265

Judge 72fn, 77, 109, 130, 133-137, 147, 250, 264
Justice
  Illicit 2, 73, 77, 79, 130-138, 184, 202, 206, 226, 242, 250, 258
  Official 44, 49, 125, 132, 134-138, 145-147, 152, 161-162, 190, 226, 228, 230, 234, 239, 246fn, 250, 258, 265

Kazakhstan 43, 50-51, 56fn, 57, 58fn, 62, 77, 79-80, 83-84, 94-95, 94fn, 99, 102-103, 108, 114, 118-119, 126fn, 127-133, 136-137, 139, 141-149, 157, 160, 160fn, 174, 190, 206, 220, 223, 230, 233-235, 235fn, 239, 245-246, 249
Key Indicators / Strategic Support System (KI/SSS) 140
Kitchen debate 192, 192fn
Kolkhoz 126, 181-182, 188, 253, 253fn
Krysha *see also* Private protection 225-226, 265

Index

Latin America 12-14, 37, 216, 254, 261
Law
  Civil 254
  Common 36-37, 136-138, 254
  Good continuation, of 29, 39

Mafia
  Italy, in 1-5, 14-15, 20-21, 31, 70, 138, 152-155, 152fn, 203, 243, 243fn, 264-266
  Russia, in *or* Red Mafia xiii-xv, 1-5, 160fn, 203, 225-227, 257-261, 264-266
Man (in prison) 64-66, 67, 71, 78, 80, 82, 84, 96, 115, 120, 122, 130, 238
Market
  Black 158, 199-200, 206
  Extralegal 200
Mat xv-xvi, 182-183
Mexico xiv-xv
Modernization xiii-xiv, 10-18, 21-22, 26, 36, 51, 155, 172, 180, 190, 215-216
Moscow 41, 44, 53fn, 60, 60fn, 69-70, 104, 107, 114, 117fn, 125, 125fn, 141, 171fn, 176-178, 189fn, 195, 196fn, 201, 223fn, 226, 240fn, 267

Network 15, 15fn, 20-21, 153, 167-169, 172-175, 188, 202-203, 207fn, 210, 214-216, 221, 238, 243, 245
Norms
  Declared vs. Applied 131, 168
  Formal *see also* Law, Code 9, 11, 24, 34-36, 37-40, 45, 104, 122, 197, 217, 241
  Informal 11, 22-24, 34-37, 39-40, 45, 79-80, 98-100, 98fn, 134, 197, 216, 241

Obshak *see also* Common cause 110-112, 119, 204, 247
Obshina 253-254
Opportunism 14, 27, 90
Order xiii, xv, 14-15, 31fn, 37, 46-48, 71-78, 81, 101-103, 137, 182-184, 186, 190, 203, 216, 226, 229, 241-243, 249-250, 265-267

Participant observation 40

Path-dependency 254
Penal subculture 8-10, 20, 22, 24, 26, 31, 34, 44, 68, 71-73, 77, 83-84, 86, 89, 92, 96, 98, 101, 103-104, 109, 120-121, 129, 134, 155, 194-196, 205
Personalized relationships 14-15, 20-21, 51, 56, 59-60, 68, 95, 109, 130, 152-153, 166, 168, 171, 196, 200, 207, 219
Physical force 64, 90fn, 100-101, 103-104, 120, 153, 231, 245
Plan bargaining 175, 175fn, 200
President (of the Russian Federation) 93fn, 171-172, 196fn, 196, 260-263, 262fn, 267-269
Principal 24-27, 25fn, 144, 163, 199
Principal-Agent model 25-27, 40, 162-163
Prison
  Administration of 8, 41-43, 48-50, 53, 63, 65-68, 71-72, 74-77, 80, 82, 85-96, 94fn, 98-104, 109-110, 112-118, 121-122, 124, 127, 132, 138, 142-144, 147-148, 155, 160, 230-243, 234fn, 235fn, 240fn, 241fn, 245-246, 249-251
  History of 45-48, 64, 110, 117, 230-237, 269
  Missions of 45-46, 62, 87
  Types of 41, 45, 49-50, 85-86, 111, 115, 138, 140, 143-146
Prisoners' Dilemma 107, 141-142, 255fn
Private protection *see also* Krysha 225-229
Private sphere *or* Privacy xi, xiii-xiv, 9, 12-14, 26, 47-48, 51-55, 63-64, 83, 87, 96, 99, 105-106, 109, 124-126, 130, 153, 156, 161, 176-181, 176fn, 192, 207, 216, 229, 236, 243
Privatization 172, 174-177, 181, 213, 225, 228, 244, 260-261, 265
Poland 12, 33, 39, 173, 198, 212
Police 3fn, 9fn, 35, 60, 63, 73, 92, 118, 155, 162, 171, 182, 203-204, 225-227, 240fn, 243, 265
Ponjatia 78, 80, 98fn, 122, 135, 242-243, 251, 264
Power xiii-xvi, 8, 24, 33-34, 30fn, 38, 40, 71, 83, 89-90, 93, 96, 104, 109, 133, 143-144, 146, 152, 162-164, 183, 186-187, 196, 201,

205, 212, 230, 240-243, 250-251, 257, 259

Racketeering *see also* Blackmail 245
Ration 4fn, 120-121, 127, 192, 224, 231
Rationality xiv-xv, 7, 25, 30fn, 31, 31fn, 190, 216, 218-219, 223
Reforms
    Market 36, 38-39, 158, 160, 197-198, 202, 208-209, 211-213, 230, 240-244, 249, 252
    Penitentiary *or* Penal 26, 43, 144-146, 197, 230, 233, 240-242, 244, 249, 252
    Peter the Great, of 37, 176fn
Residence 127, 177-179
Revolution 47, 49, 64, 71, 110, 139, 170, 177-178, 211, 239, 253
Rights
    Human xiv, 160fn, 161, 176, 183, 230, 240, 250, 268
    Prisoners, of 145, 230-240
    Property 152, 210
Roosters (in prison) 65, 67, 76, 78, 80, 82, 84, 88, 98, 246
Routine 30, 30fn, 40, 120, 122-124, 210, 210fn

Sacrificial victim 16, 85, 88, 100, 154, 182
Scapegoat (in prison) 66, 88, 121
Scapegoat victim 16, 182, 185-186, 185fn
Schizophrenia 189, 189fn
Set
    In everyday life 32-34, 192, 201, 203, 210, 213, 225, 245, 250, 255, 257
    Theory of 29-31, 189fn, 255
SIZO *see also* Gaol 49, 52, 61, 97, 103, 109
Slang 4, 4fn, 50, 54, 61, 83, 94, 96, 102, 111, 115, 121, 126-127, 144, 181-182, 195, 202, 225
Smotrjashij
    Functions of 56, 71, 74-78, 99, 101, 103, 133, 242
    Procedure of nominating 74-75
Social support 56-58, 108
Society
    Civil 5, 156, 251, 260-261, 263-263

    Large xiii-xvi, 9-10, 12-16, 18, 26, 31fn, 46, 50-51, 83, 87, 105, 131, 138, 153-154, 172, 190, 198, 205, 208, 211, 215-216, 230, 240, 243-244, 249, 253-254, 256-258, 261, 264, 266
    Post-Soviet xv, 4, 10-11, 43, 87, 89, 152, 166, 172, 174, 182, 190, 195-196, 218, 244-245, 249, 253, 264, 267-268
    Small xi-xiv, 10-12, 11fn, 12fn, 14-16, 18, 20, 26, 43, 51, 59, 65, 68, 71, 83, 86, 92, 95, 99, 101-102, 105-106, 109-110, 124, 126, 130, 135, 137-138, 151-155, 168, 172, 187-188, 196-197, 200, 205, 207-211, 214-215, 224, 228-229, 241, 243-244, 247-249, 253-254, 256-267, 269
    Soviet 4, 12, 14, 22, 24, 26-28, 31, 33, 43-45, 70, 85-86, 96, 111, 125, 152, 155-156, 161-162, 166, 171-172, 174, 181, 190, 195-197, 208, 218, 235, 244-245, 253
Sociology
    Action, of 18, 32
    Critical 3, 27-28, 86
Solidarity 12, 17, 31fn, 61-65, 116, 140, 143, 208, 221fn, 249, 253, 268
Solitude 48, 56-57, 122, 156, 252
Speculation 66, 202
Stranger xvi, 16, 18-19, 41, 69, 94, 126, 130, 155, 173, 184-185, 226, 261-262, 264
Subject
    Collective 32-34, 62, 116, 119, 211, 257
    Individual 31fn, 32-34, 83, 96, 116, 130
Suits (in prison) 65, 75-76, 82, 84, 92, 100

Tax evasion 158
Thief-in-Law 71-75, 73fn, 77fn, 78, 133, 202-206, 205fn, 228-229, 241, 241fn, 247-248, 264-266
Total institution 17, 17fn, 27-28, 45-46, 72, 98, 104, 109-110, 115-119, 124-126, 138, 141, 143-144, 156, 237
Totalitarian State 4, 47, 156, 176, 253fn

Tradition xv, 39, 68, 108, 110, 116, 129, 149, 165-170, 174, 217, 220, 241, 245
Transaction costs 15, 35-36, 40, 175, 209
Trace 28-30
Trust xv, 105-108, 105fn, 112-113
    Impersonal 32fn, 55, 108, 110-116, 141-142, 144, 149, 155, 163-170, 194, 203, 207, 217, 220-225, 223fn, 229, 252, 255, 257, 261, 261fn
    Institutional 94-95, 112-116, 132-133, 141-144, 147-148, 159-161, 181, 190, 234, 236, 242, 261
    Personalized 18, 42, 75, 78, 106-108, 110, 112, 127-128, 141-144, 155, 166-168, 171, 175, 202, 207, 216, 223-225, 252, 255, 257, 262, 262fn

United States 1fn, 2, 3fn, 36, 39, 50-51, 67, 89, 139, 215, 219, 265fn, 267
University 11fn, 42, 44, 141, 142fn, 143, 167, 178, 189fn, 220, 223fn
Utilitarianism 170-172, 213, 216-217, 252

Vilnius 185fn, 186
Violence
    Control of 12, 15-16, 19-20, 51, 85-88, 85fn, 93, 96-101, 120, 130, 153-154, 160fn, 162, 181-186, 197, 200, 208, 226-228, 258, 267
    Symbolic 86, 89
    Types of Physical 64, 83, 87, 87fn, 96-97, 100-102, 105, 131-132, 140, 207, 221
    Verbal 87, 89, 140, 181

White swan 94, 231

Zavhoz 53, 66, 72, 76-77, 87-88